Theatre in Spain 1490–1700

Theatre in Spain
1490–1700

MELVEENA McKENDRICK

FELLOW OF GIRTON COLLEGE, LECTURER IN SPANISH,
UNIVERSITY OF CAMBRIDGE

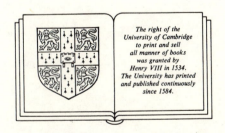

The right of the
University of Cambridge
to print and sell
all manner of books
was granted by
Henry VIII in 1534.
The University has printed
and published continuously
since 1584.

CAMBRIDGE UNIVERSITY PRESS

CAMBRIDGE

NEW YORK   PORT CHESTER

MELBOURNE   SYDNEY

Published by the Press Syndicate of the University of Cambridge
The Pitt Building, Trumpington Street, Cambridge CB2 1RP
40 West 20th Street, New York, NY 10011, USA
10 Stamford Road, Oakleigh, Melbourne 3166, Australia

First published 1989

Printed in Great Britain by the University Press, Cambridge

British Library cataloguing in publication data
McKendrick, Melveena.
Theatre in Spain 1490–1700.
1. Spain. Theatre, 1490–1700.
I. Title.
792'.0946

Library of Congress cataloguing in publication data
McKendrick, Melveena.
Theatre in Spain, 1490–1700/Melveena McKendrick.
p.   cm.
Bibliography.
Includes index.
ISBN 0 521 35592 3.
1. Spanish drama – Classical period, 1500–1700 – History and
criticism. 2. Theater – Spain – History. I. Title.
PQ6105.M24   1989.
862'.309 – dc20   89–31433   CIP.

ISBN 0 521 35592 3

For Olivia and Cornelia

Contents

Plates

Preface

I have set myself within the limited space of this book a formidable task: to give an account of the rise and reign of Spain's extraordinary national theatre in the sixteenth and seventeenth centuries in all its aspects – the commercial theatre, the court drama and the Corpus *autos*, the organization of theatrical life, the theatres themselves and their public, the literary and moral controversies, and the plays as literary texts. As far as I am aware, no other existing work examines the theatre from this multiple perspective. Difficult decisions obviously had to be made and some account of my procedure is therefore necessary.

I have devoted more space than is usual in literary histories of the Golden-Age theatre to the experimental drama of the sixteenth century before Lope de Vega arrived on the scene, not only because it contains much of great interest in its own right but because it seemed to me that a true understanding of the phenomenon of the *comedia nueva* depends on an awareness of what had gone before, of the slow and very varied processes by which a flourishing commercial theatre evolved from the court mimes and from the *tableaux vivants* and enacted dialogues of religious celebration. In my discussion of the early drama my aim has been constantly to bear in mind this evolutionary process. One great and influential work enters only peripherally into the discussion. *La Celestina* (1492), Fernando de Rojas's enormously successful novel in dialogue form, portrays a courtly lover, Calisto, who engages the services of a witch and bawd, Celestina, to further his love for Melibea and in the process brings the world of idealized romance into deadly collision with the realities of lust, greed and deception. The work was influenced by Latin comedy and in its turn influenced Spain's early dramatists. Its racy depiction of life's seamy underbelly, its low-life humour and characters, its sophisticated dialogue and its depiction of the destructive power of passion are clearly detectable in the works of Spanish dramatists for decades after and occasionally direct references to it surface even in plays written over a hundred years later. *La Celestina*, however, was not conceived or written as a dramatic action and is certainly much too long to be performed as it stands, so while it is mentioned on a number of occasions it is not presented as part of the development of the idea of the play.

Where the seventeenth-century theatre is concerned, limitations of space made selection of plays inevitable. Obviously in a drama as huge as the Spanish *comedia* such selection runs even greater risks than usual of creating a distorted picture of the whole. Nonetheless, since this book does not set out to be a comprehensive manual, I have chosen to include what I consider to be a reasonably representative selection of plays so that I could linger over a few and thereby try to give a better idea of what the drama at its best and most interesting could be. I make no apology for exercising the author's privilege of choosing some personal favourites, nor for making what in some cases may appear to be predictable choices – the best-known works of literature after all, like the best-known beauty spots, generally speaking owe their popularity and renown to their own attractions. If any seventeenth-century dramatists seem in this respect to have been given short shrift, it was to allow room at various stages for general discussion of the nature and significance of the *comedia* as a genre, which I regarded as essential to the purpose of this book. Since the playwrights of this time, unlike those of the sixteenth century, were writing to a general pattern, such discussion is relevant to all the dramatists of the period and to some extent subsumes detailed and possibly repetitive discussion of individuals. My focus has been the growth and the success of the theatre as a national institution rather than the individual playwrights themselves, although I have tried to do justice both to those principally responsible for innovation and change and to distinctive individual achievement. While my aim has been to make the overall pattern I trace as coherent and interlocking as possible, I am aware that many readers will not read this book from cover to cover and I have therefore attempted to make each chapter relatively self-contained.

I have chosen for the most part not to give dates for seventeenth-century plays since the dates of composition of so many of them are either conjectural or unknown, and dates of publication, often years later, would not in the present context be particularly helpful. Information about dating may be obtained from studies mentioned in chapter notes and in the bibliography. The bibliography itself does not and could not pretend to be comprehensive, and for the most part collects together the references and suggestions for further reading given in the notes to the chapters. For the sake of readers without Spanish, the suggestions have a slight bias towards criticism in English and titles of plays are translated into English in brackets, normally when first discussed.

My thanks are due to those who have helped in the preparation of this book: to the University of Cambridge for two travel grants to allow me to study in Spain; to the University and to Girton College for study leave in 1986; to Jonathan Brown, J. H. Elliott, N. D. Shergold and J. E. Varey for kindly giving or lending me photographs for the illustrations; to Sarah Stanton, Victoria L. Cooper and Margaret Jull Costa of Cambridge University Press for their help at the editing stage; and to Rosangela Nigro and Jean Smith for word-processing the typescript. As always my warmest thanks go to Neil McKendrick for his unfailing interest, encouragement and advice.

Girton College
Cambridge
3 May 1988

Abbreviations

Introduction

For much of the period covered by this book, Spain – originally a collection of kingdoms and still a country of entrenched regionalism – enjoyed a pre-eminent position in Europe and indeed the world. In the second half of the fifteenth century the Catholic Monarchs, Ferdinand and Isabella (1474–1516), had united the kingdoms of Castile and Aragon (including Catalonia and Aragon's possessions in Italy), and later annexed Navarre. They brought internal stability to Castile, and centralized political and administrative power in the Crown. The country assumed its full role in the arena of European politics and diplomacy and Isabella's enthusiasm for the new learning of the Renaissance infused the country with renewed cultural activity. Religious uniformity and orthodoxy were imposed by the establishment of a Spanish Inquisition in 1478 to stamp out heresy, and then, in 1492, by the conquest of Granada, the last vestige of Islamic Spain, and by the expulsion of those Jews unwilling to accept conversion. In that same momentous year, Columbus discovered a New World and placed it at the feet of his sponsor, Spain.

In 1516 Ferdinand and Isabella's young Flemish grandson inherited Spain. Three years later he succeeded his other grandfather, Maximilian I, as Holy Roman Emperor as well and became head of an empire that included Spain, the Indies, the Franche-Comté, Roussillon, the Low Countries, Germany and half of Italy – the greatest empire since Rome. The accession of Charles V (1516–56) initiated the period of Spanish history and culture known as the Golden Age. And indeed in literature and the arts Spain during this time produced a glittering constellation of figures of world stature: the painters Velázquez, El Greco and Murillo; the sculptor Berruguete; the poets and writers Garcilaso de la Vega, St John of the Cross, St Teresa of Ávila, Cervantes, Góngora, Quevedo; and the dramatists Lope de Vega, Tirso de Molina and Calderón de la Barca, to name only the most famous. Charles's huge and varied legacies, however, brought with them severe burdens. The extent of Spain's possessions excited the envy and animosity of the two other major European powers, England and France, and involved Spain for two centuries in a series of wars that drained her of resources, human and financial. The colonization of the New World attracted away from Spain manpower it could ill spare, and the influx of American bullion created an inflationary spiral with which Spain's unstable economy was quite unable to cope. Most burdensome of all in an age of religious upheaval was Spain's inherited, self-appointed role as defender of the faith. The ecclesiastical reforms undertaken by Cardinal Cisneros for Isabella had anticipated the attacks on the Church by sixteenth-century reformers and in some measure insulated Spain against them. For a time Erasmus was even the main influence behind Charles V's religious policy. However, in the early 1530s identification with the views of Luther made Erasmus suspect in Spain; persecution of Spanish Protestant groups was systematically undertaken and Spain's liberal intellectuals were forced to choose exile or repression. The existence of a machinery of repression – the Inquisition – meant that at home orthodoxy was fairly swiftly achieved. The violent burgeoning of the Protestant Reformation, however, brought Spain right into the heart of the struggle in Europe. Charles ruled Germany and the Netherlands, the very countries where local princes seized the opportunity of the religious schism to make a bid for independence, and Spain soon found itself in charge of the Catholic conscience of Europe. It became the spokesman for Catholicism at the Council of Trent and the spearhead of the Counter-Reformation. Meanwhile, as political ambition and religious dissent tore Europe apart, Christianity itself was under threat from the Ottoman Turks. In spite of two and a half decades of war with a France frustrated in its own imperial ambitions in Italy and on the Spanish border, and wary of encirclement by Spain, Spain took charge of the offensive against Islam as well.

The defeat of Charles's Spanish and Flemish troops by the German princes and the Council of Trent's failure to produce a solution to the schism drove him in 1556 to abdicate the thrones of Spain, Italy and the Netherlands in favour of his son, Philip II: the German empire he passed to his brother Ferdinand. In the event, losing the Holy Roman Empire added to the strains on the Spanish Crown rather than diminishing them. With Germany gone, the Netherlands, where the battle with Protestantism would be fought, could only be defended from the sea, an uneasy situation that depended on the co-operation or subjugation of France and England. Spanish power in Italy ensured the continuing hostility of France, while as far as England was concerned Philip's reign (1556–98) was the period in which Spain and England danced their elaborate galliard of flirtation and deadly rivalry. Philip's ambition was always to win England for Catholicism and Spain, and to this end he married Mary Tudor, wooed Elizabeth I, and finally planned to invade England. From there he intended to subdue the Netherlands, where revolt after revolt had been put down by Philip's troops in a series of campaigns noted for their brutality. In 1588, however, these dreams came to a disastrous end with the defeat by the English, with the help of the weather, of the so-called Invincible Armada. It was the first really crushing blow dealt Spain since the first flowering of her imperial ambitions.

At home, too, Philip's sense of religious mission dictated his policies. Determined to avoid contagion with a Europe riddled with heterodoxy, Spain turned in on itself and closed its doors on the outside world. The publication and import of books were rigidly controlled and Spaniards were prohibited from studying in foreign universities other than Bologna. New developments in learning and the empirical sciences were denied Spain. Secular and religious life, the interests of State and Church, became virtually inseparable, and the Inquisition imposed a religious orthodoxy seen as essential to the well-being of the nation. Spaniards themselves, it must be emphasized, shared their monarch's sense of religious and imperial destiny; the Inquisition was not a tyranny forced upon a terrorized people against their will but an instrument of government which reflected their convictions and prejudices and operated with their implicit consent.

Spain's withdrawal into itself after the accession of Philip II was reflected in the behaviour of the monarch himself. Unlike Charles, who had spent many years away from Spain fighting his wars, Philip, after a few early excursions, never set foot outside Spain again. He made Madrid his capital in 1561, and from there and from his palace-monastery, the Escorial, Europe's first bureaucratic king manipulated the reigns of his unwieldy, far-flung empire. His reign had its moments of euphoria – the spectacular sea victory over the Turks at Lepanto in 1571 and the annexation of Portugal in 1580 amongst them – but the defeat of the Armada and the growing economic problems created by Spain's inability to adapt itself to the emerging capitalist world sowed the seeds of a pessimism that fostered in Spanish intellectuals a psychology of decline which anticipated by half a century any real, irreversible decline in political and military terms. To make matters worse, when Philip died in 1598 he bequeathed to Spain not only an empty treasury but a weak and inexperienced son.

The century that began with the accession of Philip III was a century of poignant contrasts. For this period of unsurpassed literary brilliance and splendour at court was also the age when the cancer of Spain's growing ills rose to the surface and proceeded to devour the visible as well as the hidden body of Spain. The deterioration was symbolized in the persons of the monarchs themselves. Philip III (1598–1621) and his son Philip IV (1621–65) were but shadows of their predecessors and recognized the fact by handing over the reins of government to their favourites, the Duke of Lerma and the Count-Duke of Olivares respectively. At court the mood of gravity and austerity imposed by Philip II yielded to one of frivolity and extravagance that percolated down to other levels of society, particularly in the capital. In the reign of Philip IV, the morals of the capital and the court, which was the most lavish and ceremonious in Europe, never failed to elicit the disapproval of shocked foreigners. The decline in standards was both a reflection of and a reaction to a grave national malaise. The delegation of government to two grandees marked the political supremacy of the landed aristocracy and under Lerma administrative and bureaucratic corruption reached heights unknown since Isabella initiated her policy of appointment by merit. The ravages of war, famine, pestilence and poverty emptied towns and countryside, agriculture foundered and looms fell silent. At the beginning of the century the currency was devalued and thereafter financial crisis followed financial crisis. Peace had been concluded with France, the Netherlands and England in the early years of the century, but war broke out again in Italy in 1615 and when hostilities subsequently erupted between Protestants and Catholics in Germany, Spain was dragged into the Thirty Years War. At home, Catalonia, driven to desperate measures by Madrid's unconstitutional centralizing policies, rose in armed revolt, in 1640 even Aragon tried to secede from the Crown, while in 1658 Portugal regained her independence. Meanwhile, upon the battlefield of Europe the formerly glorious Spanish infantry left their flags and their reputation in tatters – at the battles of Rocroi (1643), Lens (1648) and the Dunes (1658). The Spanish people, for their part, from the late sixteenth century on combated their growing sense of insecurity by despising the material world that was increasingly denied them and embracing vaguer but less painful prizes – religion, honour, purity of blood and nobility. The society of seventeenth-century Spain was a society obsessed with appearances and display, with reputation, self-image and rank.

The reign of the last Spanish Hapsburg, Charles II (1665–1700), in spite of a certain degree of economic recovery, was a sad, confused one. Physically malformed and mentally subnormal, Charles survived for thirty-five years as nominal head of an Empire that was ruled by scheming regents and their favourites. Throughout his reign an enfeebled Spain fought to defend her possessions in the Netherlands, Sicily and Catalonia against France, but in spite of help from other countries – England, Sweden, the Austrian Empire, Holland – the Franche-Comté and the great frontier towns of Flanders were lost. After thirty years of war, peace came at last in 1697, but even then not for long. As Charles's pathetic body and mind weakened, France and the Austrian Empire intrigued in favour of their claims to the Spanish throne. Before dying, Charles decided in favour of Philip of Anjou, who succeeded to the throne in 1700 as Philip V, first of the Spanish Bourbons. Austria, however, refused to accept the decision and almost before the new king had replaced the old, the War of the Spanish Succession had erupted. Spain, the first nation to have an empire on which the sun literally never set, for the first time, but not the last, had become Europe's pawn.

1

The birth of the drama

The beginnings

In Spain, as in the rest of Europe, it was the sixteenth century that saw the emergence of the theatre as we would still recognize it today – the theatre understood as performances by professional players before a public audience in a secular setting. In spite of their distinctive characteristics these national theatres, which sprang up in response to complex social and cultural circumstances, shared for the most part a common heritage and common origins. The sung tropes (interpolated phrases) which from the ninth century on formed part of church worship evolved into dramatic enactments performed in church – at first in Latin, later on often in the vernacular – as part of the celebration of Christmas and Easter. Naturally the medieval churches were not the only places where performances containing the seeds of theatre occurred. Troubadours and jongleurs entertained palaces and public squares with songs and tales with great potential for dramaticized delivery; mummers still carried on the long tradition of the Roman mime; and in the later Middle Ages, with the growth of the guilds, the processions and pageants which marked the great feast days of the Church calendar became elaborate and colourful spectacles, with floats, scenery, painted figures and, eventually, *tableaux vivants*. Elements of these found their way into the theatre of the sixteenth century and, with the Renaissance, classical influences also came into play, affecting the development of the drama to different degrees and in various ways in different countries. But for all the gaps in our understanding of the way in which the liturgical drama in Europe evolved, the mystery and morality plays represent the single most important influence on the early development of drama as a genre. The public theatre grew out of the ritual of religious worship as this ritual gradually overflowed the confines of churches and cathedrals into the streets and market places.[1]

The problem where Spain is concerned is that it does not quite fit into this scheme of things as historians of the early European drama now see it. It is known that the liturgical drama in Latin was as strong in Catalonia as anywhere else in Europe and probably dates back as far.[2] Reconquered by Charlemagne from the Moslems within a hundred years of the invasion of the Peninsula in 711, Catalonia was incorporated into the Carolingian Empire as the Spanish March and the flavour of life there remained essentially French rather than Iberian until the twelfth century. The Catalan monastery of Ripoll was in close contact with the French monasteries associated with the birth of the liturgical drama and in all probability played a part in its development. In the centre of the Peninsula, however, there is no real evidence of the existence of any native medieval liturgical drama.

The traditional view of scholars in the face of this inconvenient lacuna was that if the church drama had flourished so long and so vigorously in the eastern Peninsula under the influence of the Catalan monasteries, it was inconceivable that it had not also flourished in Castile: the evidence, like so much other medieval material in Spain, had simply been a casualty of Castile's long and turbulent history of warfare with the infidel. However, in the early 1950s the peg on which the critics traditionally hung their conviction that medieval Castile must have had a religious drama of some sort – the twelfth-century fragment of the *Auto de los reyes magos* (*The Magi*), found in Toledo – was revealed to be probably the work of a Gascon.[3] Then in 1958 R. B. Donovan faced the facts more squarely and came to the conclusion that if there is no evidence of liturgical plays in Latin in Castile, in all probability there had not been any.[4] He did envisage the likelihood of a later flowering, under French influence, of religious plays in the vernacular in Castile which, being informal, even oral, and impromptu compositions, would almost certainly have been lost. H. López Morales subsequently rejected even this crumb of comfort, asserting that the Peninsula's historical past had militated for too long against the emergence of an indigenous religious drama and that in Castile the drama's only early precedents were effectively the mummers, jugglers and performing poets.[5] Even so, belief in the existence of a religious drama, albeit in the vernacular and albeit primitive, dies hard.[6] Alfonso X does make a reference, however vague, in his thirteenth-century legal treatise, the *Siete Partidas*, to Christmas and Easter performances and other 'unseemly' religious plays[7] and for many it makes no sense to believe that on religious occasions of great popular appeal such as Christmas, Epiphany and Easter, celebratory enactments in some way akin to the often elaborate performances put on in eastern Spain and the rest of Europe just did not form any part of the festivities in Castile before the late fifteenth century – by which time Christmas and Easter plays were, we know, being performed in churches and private halls and chapels.

Recently, work done in the mid-1970s by two archivists on the accounts books of the chapter of Toledo cathedral has turned up new information.[8] Carmen Torroja Menéndez and María Rivas Palá discovered that elaborate processions were taking place in Toledo not only at Christmas and in Holy Week but at Corpus Christi as well, as early as 1418. Hitherto the earliest known Corpus procession outside Aragon was that of 1454 in Seville. Throughout the first half of the century there are references in the Toledo accounts to processions with *tableaux vivants* and then, in 1445, there crop up for the first time references to 'juegos' (games, entertainments or plays) which included shepherd-characters who were paid for their services. In the years that follow references to 'juegos' become a constant. From the mid-1450s, the person in charge of the Toledo celebrations for seven or so years was Alfonso Martínez, Archpriest of Talavera and prebendary of the cathedral, who was not only a man of letters with a marked interest in dialogue and popular speech,[9] but had lived for ten years in Valencia and for a time in Barcelona. The possibility that the 'juegos' at this point became more sophisticated and more literary in character is therefore clearly fairly strong. From this time on they certainly became more elaborate, acquired more characters and took up a larger part of the budget allocated to the festivities for Corpus Christi, which themselves began to dominate the celebrations in the Church calendar. In the records for 1476 and 1481 it becomes clear that the plays concerned formed part of the processions themselves and in the 1490s wheeled *carros* (carts) were being used for the performances, sometimes more than one per play, for different scenes. These carts were hitherto thought not to have appeared until the second quarter of the sixteenth century. Between 1493 and 1510 an average of seven *autos* (one-act plays on religious and moral themes) a year were performed in Toledo for Corpus Christi, involving thirty-three different *autos*. Up to 1500 the organization of the festivities was the responsibility of a cathedral officer, who engaged actors (mainly ecclesiastics), bought props and provided texts by writing them himself, commissioning them or adapting existing material. In 1500 charge of the celebrations was handed over to laymen, sometimes to groups such as guilds who provided their own actors and scenery, sometimes to individuals from elsewhere.

As a result of these discoveries the medieval drama debate has taken on new life and the dates of the birth of Castile's Corpus Christi festivities, to become so important in the sixteenth and seventeenth centuries, have been pushed back almost half a century. But we must still be cautious in claiming too much for them. We still do not know when dialogue first transformed the *tableaux vivants* into plays and whether there was an intermediate mime stage. The 674-line *Auto de la Pasión* which Torroja Menéndez discovered written in a discarded accounts book is late, probably 1486–97, and its text in any case consists of a series of stilted, declamatory addresses rather than dialogue proper. There is no evidence that the pieces performed were not still fairly rudimentary in literary terms, and in terms of production, certainly, they were a mixture of the relatively sophisticated and the downright amateur: in 1500 *La Ascensión* used machinery of some sort for the play's dramatic climax but the mountain was a table covered in a green cloth. There was an element of satire in some plays from 1501 on but as yet no sign of the comic rustic or the symbolic figures of later years – scenes, stories and characters are all biblical. So when Torroja Menéndez and Rivas Palá take their discoveries as firm evidence of a rich, flourishing, fifteenth-century religious drama which was the fruit of a long, well-established tradition of such drama in Castile, they overstate their case. The detailed accounts they give if anything argue the reverse. For while these certainly suggest a tradition of public religious celebration going back beyond the fifteenth century even for Corpus Christi, they seem at the same time to show that a real dramatic element only entered these celebrations when the fifteenth century was already well underway and that this dramatic element remained fairly elementary until the century's second half. They do not, of course, provide any evidence for a liturgical drama as such. The use of duplicate, even multiple characters as well as carts – in 1505 there were three Saint Johns for the same *auto* – must have made for stiff, largely static performances – a sort of *tableau vivant* with words added – that was still some distance away from either real dialogue or real action. It is unlikely, furthermore, that things were much more highly developed elsewhere in Castile. What scraps of evidence of dramatic activity there are have always been associated with Toledo and the fact that in 1500 Antonio de Sernisal from Guadalajara produced the Corpus plays there cannot be taken as evidence of a flourishing dramatic tradition in other cities as well: he might well have acquired his dramatic experience in the east of Spain. Torroja Menéndez and Rivas Palá themselves concede that the fact that the *Auto de la Pasión* draws heavily on a contemporary *poem* indicates, perhaps, the lack of suitable dramatic models.[10] Their important discoveries are likely to be far more significant for the study of the development of Corpus festivities in Castile and hence for the history of the *auto sacramental* (the one-act play about the Holy Sacrament performed on Corpus Christi Day) than they are for our understanding of the birth of the theatre. They do not alter the fact that at the start of the 1490s any tradition of drama in Castile was still rudimentary and quite unlike the rich cycles of morality and mystery plays of the rest of Europe.

So effectively the history of the Spanish theatre begins at the close of the medieval period. There had been a flourishing dialogue literature in Spain in the Middle Ages and critics have been fond of fishing in it for precedents for the drama. A handful of transitional fifteenth-century compositions – no longer narrative but not yet drama – have in particular been singled out as heralding the new genre: Gómez Manrique's *Representación del Nacimiento de Nuestro Señor* (*Representation of the Birth of Our Lord*), written between 1467 and 1481, which must count as the earliest surviving descendant in Castile of the *Officium pastorum*; the anonymous tract for the time, *Coplas de Mingo Revulgo* (*Mingo Revulgo's Stanzas*);[11] Fray Íñigo de Mendoza's *Vita Christi* (c. 1480); and Francisco de Madrid's *Égloga* (*Eclogue*), a piece of political propaganda in support of King Ferdinand written around 1495. There is no evidence that the last three of these were written with perform-ance in mind and since performance – impersonation – must be the *sine qua non* of drama it is misleading to think of them as in any real sense dramatic works. Manrique's work is a rather different case, for it *was* performed, at the convent where Manrique's sister was a nun, and although it is a succes-sion of scenes illustrating the work's theme rather than a connected action, it does have an essentially dramatic identity. It is very reminiscent of the *tableaux parlants*, as one might call them, of the Corpus celebrations. These *tableaux parlants*, together with the antics of the mummers and the consti-tutional dramatic ritual of the day, constitute the only true dramatic prece-dents for the theatre that was about to emerge. Even so an equestrian leap of the imagination would be needed to transform religious *tableaux* and dia-logue texts, even dialogue intended for reading aloud, into drama and the stimulus to that leap in the event came in the form of practical necessity: the need felt by a court poet to find new ways of amusing his lord and lady.

Juan del Encina 1468?–1529

Encina, always dubbed the 'Father of the Spanish drama', emerges from recent research with his reputation as initiator intact, and his first attempts at the genre bear out the idea of an existing though very rudimentary tradition of religious play.[12] His earliest pieces were indeed written to celebrate religious festivities, albeit within the confines of the ducal court where he served the Duke of Alba as poet, composer and playwright, but they are so simple as virtually to rule out the possibility of a well-developed tradition of such plays – even the twelfth-century *Auto de los reyes magos* is dramatically more sophisticated. Like most of Spain's earliest playwrights he displays a dramatic primitivism quite out of keeping with the sophistication of other aspects of his work.

Encina was a shoemaker's son whose restless ambition and creative energies took him from his law studies in his home town of Salamanca first to the palace of the Duke of Alba at Alba de Tormes, where he functioned as master of ducal entertainments, then in 1500 to Rome, where he became a favourite of cardinals and popes, and later back to Spain to various ecclesiastical posts. His fourteen (one more is disputed) dramatic pieces were written for the entertainment of private audiences in ducal or ecclesiastical circles, and Encina himself performed in them. Called *églogas* after Virgil in the manner of the Italian eclogues that abounded in the Renaissance, they are essentially verse dialogues, mainly between shepherds or other rustic characters, written in a mixture of standard Spanish (for the courtly or educated characters) and *sayagués*, a local Salamancan dialect which Encina developed into a literary patois for use by comic rustics. Not the first writer to use *sayagués* – it is found in both the *Coplas de Mingo Revulgo* and the *Vita Christi* – he exploited to the full its comic appeal for aristocratic audiences and passed it on to his successors as the standard stage dialect. His thematic range is not wide. Of the eight eclogues thought to be his earliest and written in pairs, presumably to provide a more substantial entertainment for each occasion, four are religious pieces concerned with Christmas, Lent and Easter, two are rustic dialogues bearing on contemporary issues, and two introduce the themes of love and courtly life. The remaining eclogues, particularly those written during Encina's extended exposure to the humanist atmosphere of Renaissance Rome, mark a striking secularization of Encina's interests with the emphasis now firmly on love, although his two best comic pieces also fall into this period.

While Encina's most ambitious and memorable work belongs to the second group of plays, the earlier pieces are of considerable interest in that they show how laboriously drama moved away from dependence on the real world of ritual, enacted beliefs and contemporary events into a self-contained world of its own, a world of the imagination. In them the presence of the ducal household is assumed and we are the spectators not just of a dramatized dialogue but of a spectacle that includes audience as well as actors. This intimate relationship between watchers and watched becomes explicit when two shepherds vie for the favours of their master and mistress, the Duke and Duchess themselves (*Égloga representada en la noche de Navidad* – *Eclogue performed on Christmas Night*), when a shepherd laments the Duke's imminent departure for the wars in France (*Égloga representada en la noche postrera de Carnaval* – *Eclogue performed on the Last Night of Shrovetide*) and when the shepherds and shepherdesses through the transforming power of love embrace a courtly life whose location becomes the ducal court itself (*Égloga representada por los mismos pastores Gil, Pascuala, Mingo y Menga* – *Eclogue performed by the same shepherds Gil, Pascuala, Mingo and Menga*). Even more destructive of the dramatic illusion is Encina's own intervention: Juan, Beneyto and Mingo are Encina's own mouthpieces as they discuss their status and reputation as poets, the quality and composition of their work and offer the fruits of their literary labours to their all-powerful patron. The worlds of the plays, the playwright and the audience mingle and merge in the same way that past, present and future become one continuous time span in the religious pieces – most notably in the *Égloga representada en la misma noche de Navidad* – (*Eclogue performed on the same Christmas Night*), where the shepherds Juan, Mateo, Lucas and Marco, after some conversation as contemporary shepherds, are transmuted into the four evangelists discussing the birth of Christ and then into the biblical shepherds as they leave to find the Christ child. This instability in the dimensions of drama is rooted in the medieval conception of art as the handmaiden of religious belief and of drama as inseparable from ritual, but Encina exploits it to flatter and find favour with his illustrious patron.

Encina's sources of inspiration in these early works were traditional – the biblical and apocryphal stories, the Lenten Battle, Virgil (whose *Eclogues* Encina translated), the medieval *pastourelles*, possibly Latin tropes, real life. Structurally simple with fixed scenes[13] and finishing invariably in song, they rely for their effects on the naturalness, pace and humour of their dialogue, although the *Égloga representada en requesta de unos amores* (*Eclogue performed in the Pursuit of a Love Affair*) and its sequel show the rudiments of a real plot and a fairly wide range of emotions. The greatest significance of these two pieces, however, lies in their introduction into the Spanish drama of a theme which will become central to its concerns – the power of love.

Two intermediary works bridge the gap between the eight eclogues of Encina's first period and his Roman plays. The eclogue nicknamed 'de las grandes lluvias' ('About the Great Floods') enacts the appearance of the angels to the shepherds, but its primary interest lies in the rich detail of country life that emerges from the shepherds' discussion of the recent floods. The piece dubbed *El triunfo del amor* (*The Triumph of Love*), written to celebrate the marriage of the Infante don Juan in 1497, betrays Encina's growing interest in the theme of the irresistible power of a love that blinds reason and inhibits free action. Its four distinct scenes reveal it as something of a landmark in Encina's craft, indicating a move towards a more structured plot.

Encina's exposure to the hedonistic atmosphere and cultural ferment of Rome had a profound effect on his work. Not only does he experiment with Italian metres, but his shepherds lose their honest Spanish names and find new ones of allegorical significance or classical provenance. Figures like Venus and Mercury find their way into the cast and Ovid, the *Aeneid*, Italian pastoral comedy, Sannazaro's *Arcadia* and Antonio Tebaldeo's eclogues join the sources of inspiration so far offered by Spain itself. Encina's art becomes more ambitious and more experimental, sloughing off the simple innocence of devotional enactment and rustic humour, and embracing the preoccupations of literary humanism in an unconstrained way that takes him to the edge of the sacrilegious and occasionally beyond. His interest in love's power becomes paramount, having now found a firm ideological underpinning for it in Italian humanism, and the greater part of his work henceforth is devoted to an allegorical working out of these ideas.

In the *Égloga en la cual se introducen tres pastores* (*Eclogue Involving Three Shepherds*) the suffering lover actually does what he always threatens to do in courtly love poetry – he dies, but by his own hand. Historically the piece is interesting in that it contains the first dramatic expression in Spain of the feminist debate, as Fileno inveighs against women and Cardonio leaps to their defence. It is not quite as solemn as it sounds, however, and it is difficult now to decide with what degree of seriousness such plays were intended to be acted and received. Love's ravages are seen to be very real yet at the same time the audience is invited to laugh at them. In the *Égloga de Cristino y Febea*, a skilfully constructed piece with seven scenes and balanced pairings of characters, love dares to pit its strength against religion itself. Cristino retreats from passion into the life of a hermit only to be reclaimed for love by the devil figure, the nymph Febea. The ending has a flippancy belied by Cristino's very real sadness and remorse and the eclogue effectively depicts an unresolved tension between the claims of love and Christian conscience – an issue already becoming a central one in the battles between the Church and its critics and of intense interest, we can be sure, to the ecclesiastics in Encina's audience. The play has recently been seen as an allegory of the struggle in Encina's own life between worldly ambition and a priestly vocation,[14] which perhaps accounts for its powerful intensity as drama. It is certainly the most impressive of his plays.

The problem of intention and reception is presented particularly forcibly by Encina's longest and most ambitious piece, the *Égloga de Plácida y Victoriano*. Here the same tension between love and conscience surfaces, not directly in the plot but indirectly in the way in which the psychology of love feeds off the experience and language of religion. The play was performed on Twelfth Night 1513 at the Roman court of the Valencian cardinal Jaime Serra, before an audience described by an eyewitness as being predominantly Spanish and containing more Spanish prostitutes than Italian ones – so the tension was clearly not an imaginary one. The audience is addressed directly in a prologue to the play – the first proper dramatic prologue in the Spanish drama – which introduces the characters and summarizes the plot, in recognition presumably of its unaccustomed length and complexity.

The play has thirteen scenes divided by a song into what are effectively two acts and its time span extends over several days. Despite the similar circumstances of performance, therefore, Encina's art had come a long way from his first simple devotional offerings at the court of the Duke of Alba. Religion, however, is never far away: a lovers' tiff drives Plácida to suicide and the discovery of her body inspires the grief-stricken Victoriano to a series of prayers and laments that are effectively a parody of the Office for the Dead, since the god to which he prays is Cupid; Venus materializes to prevent him from killing himself and then invokes Mercury to restore Plácida to life to reward Victoriano for his resolute love. Suicide, liturgical parody, resurrection: little wonder that the play was not received well even by the Cardinal's hedonistic guests and that it subsequently appeared on the Inquisition's Valladolid Index of 1559. Unpalatable, too, to ecclesiastical and inquisitorial tastes must have been the essentially superfluous scene which interrupts the sequence of events to talk of broken maidenheads, priestly involvement in pregnancies, transactions in newborn babies and witchcraft. This may just have been a tasteless attempt at raunchy humour on the model of *La Celestina* (1492), to which the play owes a great deal, but more probably it was a somewhat hamfisted effort to follow Rojas's deeper purpose and undermine the assumptions and the ethos of the world of love. Certainly the play elsewhere carries within itself its own subversion: the sixth scene is a dialogue between two shepherds which denounces the behaviour of town and palace dwellers and their lover's antics. It is a moment when the outside world breaks through love's sealed bubble and establishes an objective perspective on the goings-on inside the play. It serves, too, of course, as a device to relieve tension – one that will become a standard technique of the later drama where acts were divided in performance by humorous sketches – and again marks Encina's growing sense of what constitutes drama.

It has been argued that the transformation of real shepherd into biblical shepherd, of shepherd into author and back, in Encina's eclogues reveals him to be a true dramatist, indicating a dramatist's preoccupation with change, identity and impersonation.[15] In fact, metamorphosis is inherent in the pastoral mode and the conflation of contemporary present and biblical past owes its authority to the belief that revealed truth knows no chronological barriers. Even Encina's own appearances and self-references are the natural outcome of his presence on stage as one of the actors. Spontaneous and unselfconscious as these features might be, however, the result is indeed the sort of dynamism essential to drama. What was new in Spain with Encina was the ability of performed dialogue to reach out beyond enactment, instruction and humorous relief to the world of ideas and imagination, without losing theatrical impact. The movement towards a more or less self-contained dramatic world was a natural outcome of this. Encina's instinct for the dramatic, it has to be said, was by no means infallible. Victoriano's multiform expression of grief in *Plácida y Victoriano* is extremely long and virtually impossible, one would think, to perform with any conviction. Here ideology weighs performance into the ground. Even when he does not quite bring it off, however, Encina does not lose sight of the fact that some form of conflict is essential to drama. The way in which the role of conflict develops in the course of his work can be seen in the *Auto del repelón (The Hair-Pulling Skit)*, effectively Spain's first farce, where the much more static rustic dialogue of the earlier Salamancan eclogues is transformed into a clash between two shepherds and some students with a great deal of coarse banter, slapstick and a drubbing at the end. If Encina did indeed bring the skit back from Rome with him between 1507 and 1509 as is thought to have been the case, then he brought back a developed sense of the dramatic which, although still crude, was a significant step in the direction of theatre.

Encina had the satisfaction of being a success in his own day. Seven editions of his works were published between 1496 and 1516; his plays were performed in private and in public in Spain, and in Italy; he was known, admired and his importance was acknowledged. The same was not true of his younger contemporary and rival, Lucas Fernández.

Lucas Fernández (1474–1542)

Fernández also wrote for the ducal court of Alba and was in addition hired by the chapter of the cathedral at Salamanca, where he became Professor of Music at the University, to write and present plays for religious celebrations. Those of his works that have come down to us, the *Farsas y Églogas* published in 1514, comprise one song drama and six plays, of which three are profane, two are a mixture of the profane and the religious, as contemporary shepherds become transmogrified into biblical shepherds, and one is full-blown religious drama. Fernández's is a more limited, less sophisticated talent than Encina's but in some ways more powerful and incisive.[16] His depiction of rural life is natural and sharply observed and his vivid use of *sayagués* is rightly regarded as the most consistent and accurate in the Spanish drama. His quick-witted, quick-tongued shepherds have an earthy, even crude, forcefulness that is extremely funny. Nonetheless, the sense of a dialogue and an action (albeit skeletal) at the service of an idea is as paramount in his plays as it is in Encina's. They are clearly intended for the listening eye: the plot is there to hang ideas and instruction on rather than as a dramatic action in its own right, and songs are used to clinch the play's message. The Christmas plays are a reaffirmation and celebration of Christian belief appropriate to their purpose and their conception, and they address themselves to an audience whose presence is strongly felt, for all that it is never mentioned. The secular plays and the song drama are bound to a different ideological framework – the nature and effects of human love again. The assumptions of Fernández's characters are those of Encina's – love is a devastating experience that subverts the lover's health and peace of mind – but here the atmosphere is less intense and suicidal. The *Diálogo para cantar (Dialogue for Singing)* carries every sign of having been written for young Prince Juan, who in 1496 was awaiting the arrival of his betrothed Margaret of Austria, and takes love appropriately solemnly. His *Comedia (Play)*, however, where we see young love in conflict with the older generation for the first time in a drama which will become intensely preoccupied with this theme, handles passion with a vigour and an optimistic earthiness that subverts the assumptions of courtly love; while both the *Farsa o quasi comedia de la doncella (Farce or Almost-Play about a Damsel)* and the *Farsa de Prabos (Farce about Prabos)* give the strong impression that love is being exploited at least in part for parodic purposes and humorous effect. These three plays end optimistically, two in marriage, while poor Prabos, after a thrashing from the courtier who is his rival (these early plays are larded with class assumptions, which is hardly surprising given their destination), is persuaded to concede defeat grace-fully. The view of love as enduring torment is rejected.

For all this difference of emphasis, Fernández's debt to Encina was in all probability considerable. The *Farsa de la doncella* would seem to be based on Encina's *Égloga representada en requesta de unos amores*, while Prabos actually cites not only one of Fernández's characters from a different play, but some of Encina's characters as well, as examples of those who have suffered for love. The authorization of one fiction with another is of course an intertextual joke and this moment when a character in a play reaches outside himself to refer to characters in other fictions and by another playwright, effectively marks the beginning of the Spanish drama as a literary activity with a self-aware, corporate identity.

Fernández's dramatic structures are for the most part rudimentary, with little action, fixed scenes, much conversation, some element of conflict (though the *Comedia* with its confrontation between the generations opens up wider vistas) and with the role of song and dance again emphasizing the intimate relationship of early drama to spectacle and lyric. Its specifically ritual and liturgical associations are brought out in what is undoubtedly Fernández's most ambitious and most accomplished play, the *Auto de la Pasión (Auto of the Passion)*. His Christmas piece *Égloga o Farsa del Nacimiento de Nuestro Redentor Jesucristo (Eclogue or Farce of the Birth of Our Redeemer Jesus Christ)* had already given some indication of the lyric power of his pen, and now in this play, written for presentation in Salamanca cathedral just before Easter 1503, that power is unleashed.[17] Gone are the rustic shepherds and their banter. Instead St Peter bewails his denial of Christ, St Dionysius asks for an explanation of the eclipse he has just witnessed and Peter then rehearses the lesson of the Redemption, describing the events of Holy Week in words calculated to move the congregation to tears. St Matthew describes Christ's agony and there follows a counterpoint of grief between the three Marys and the saints. Explicit stage directions order the appearance of an 'Ecce Homo' 'to move the people to devotion' and the characters kneel and chant. The punishing dialogue continues, retelling details of trial and crucifixion, and at the crucial emotional climax a cross is revealed, at the sight of which all kneel and worship. The play ends as the players approach the sepulchre, kneel, and are joined by the organ – and presumably the congregation – in a long hymn of lamentation.

There is nothing in the Spanish religious drama comparable in sheer power to this before Calderón in the seventeenth century. Neither is there anything in the early drama that can compete with it for theatricality –

occasion and playwright join together to produce the earliest Spanish drama known to us to exploit to the full the combined effects of language and stage spectacle. It directs itself at the minds and hearts of its audience, it draws them into its world as ritual always sets out to do, but it also exploits the separateness of spectacle and it does so in the presence of a public audience.

By now the highly fluid nature of the early drama will be self-evident. Although responding to the dual stimulus of private patronage and religious celebration, the division between devout and profane drama is not at all clear. We know little, for example, about the circumstances of the public performances of Encina's plays. In the case of Fernández, not only were semi-religious pieces performed at the ducal court but secular plays were written for religious festivals – for example the *Comedia* was presented as part of the Corpus Christi celebrations in Salamanca in 1501. Almost certainly when plays were performed first in private they were then put on again in public, and at this stage religious and secular themes alike were grist to the mill of the Church calendar and its festivities. This lack of clear definition extends to the works themselves. It is obvious from the fact that the playwrights used dramatic terminology so vaguely that they had little clear idea of dramatic genre or even what it was that they were trying to produce. The terms *égloga, farsa, representación, auto, comedia* are deployed without firm differentiation. Fernández's indecision is even reflected in the alternatives he offers – *Farsa o quasi comedia de la doncella, Égloga o Farsa del nacimiento*, and his use of 'quasi comedia' is no guarantee that for him *comedia* (comedy or play) itself meant very much, for his *Comedia* is structurally as simple as any of his plays. Several fifteenth-century Spanish writers had commented briefly on genre division along classical lines and were familiar to some extent both with the comedies of Terence and Plautus and with Italian humanistic comedy: but like writers elsewhere they regarded comedy and tragedy as terms applicable to literature at large, using them for such compositions as poetic narratives, addresses and laments. Only with the appearance in Italy in 1498 of a Latin translation of Aristotle's *Poetics* was dramatic theory as such born in Europe and its influence had scarcely had time to make itself felt in the years of which we are speaking. The early drama in Spain probably had no real sense of itself as literature and even when the new theories began to spread it is highly unlikely that Spain's first dramatic practitioners saw themselves as engaged upon the same activities as those described by Aristotle. Hence their lack of concern with labels at a time when already there was sufficient genre awareness in Spain to produce a change in the descriptive label given the novel in dialogue form *La Celestina*, from *comedia* (1492 edition) to *tragicomedia* (1502 edition).[18] In spite of the fact that the term *tragicomedia* had been coined by Plautus, the question of the legitimacy of mixed drama was, of course, a vexed question which was to bubble vigorously away in Italy and elsewhere for a century or more. Encina, however, saw nothing incongruous about it even fifteen years after the appearance of Aristotle's *Poetics* in Latin (although it has been suggested that the adverse reception given to *Plácida y Victoriano* in Cardinal Arborea's palace in Rome in 1513 was due to his mingling of comic with tragic)[19] and this attitude was to prove prophetic: the Spanish theatre's respect later on for rules that constricted its activities was scant, to say the least.

It is fairly certain that Lucas Fernández at some time visited the glittering Portuguese court in Lisbon – all three wives of Manuel I were wholly or partly Spanish, as was the wife of his successor John III, and the Portuguese court was accordingly bilingual. Queen María actually mentioned Fernández in her will so he must have made a good impression. The extent of his acquaintanceship with the Portuguese dramatist Gil Vicente, however, is far from clear, though efforts have been made to show that they were close friends who worked together and that Vicente's *Auto pastoril castellano* (*Pastoral Auto in Castilian*) was directly inspired by Fernández's *Comedia*. While no documentary evidence of friendship or collaboration exists, it seems inevitable that they would have met and discussed their shared interest in drama and poetry.

Gil Vicente (1465?–1536?)

The relevance of this here is two-fold. First, Vicente, although Portuguese, wrote eleven of his forty-four plays in Castilian and eighteen in a mixture of both languages. Second, he is justly regarded as the most gifted playwright in the Peninsula before Lope de Vega. His life is a mystery. If he is not the royal goldsmith Gil Vicente who made a monstrance for the monastery of Os Jerónimos at Belem in Lisbon out of gold brought back by Vasco da Gama from his second voyage to India, then we know almost nothing about him. His career as a playwright started a few years later than those of Encina and Fernández. On the night of 7 June 1502, on the day after the birth of Prince John, Vicente recited before the royal family a charming dramatic monologue with a single character – a cowherd – who wanders in, admires the Queen and her baby, and then calls on some shepherds to present gifts of eggs, milk, cheese and honey. This earliest surviving text of the Portuguese theatre – the *Auto de la Visitación* (*Auto of the Visitation*) – is in Castilian, with a nod towards *sayagués*. When asked to adapt it for performance at Christmas, Vicente produced instead a custom-written nativity play for the occasion – the *Auto pastoril castellano* – and at a stroke created for himself the post of court dramatist. The traces of *sayagués* in his first piece suggest that the work of Encina and Fernández was already known at the Portuguese court, either directly or indirectly, but a comparison of the *Auto pastoril castellano* with the Salamancans' equivalent pieces shows quite a different talent at work. The mixture of amusement, dancing, singing and instruction, the attempt at basic character differentiation, the talk of marriages, dowries and family trees are similar; but Vicente's version is richer and more varied, with extra threads woven into the fabric, such as the temperamental suitability of the shepherd chosen for receiving the Angel's message. Most distinctive, however, is the beauty of the poetry, which gives the *auto* an overall delicacy quite different from the vigour of Encina's rustic plays and the lively crudeness of Fernández's. Gil Vicente was a lyrical poet of the first order who used song not just to finish his pieces off but as an integral part of action and characterization.

With the encouragement of his royal patrons Vicente became a prolific deviser of stage entertainments. Like a Renaissance painter he worked to order, writing what his royal patron and the court calendar demanded. His only models, apart from the Salamancan playwrights, were on the one hand the liturgy and on the other the elaborate masque-like entertainments that formed a major part of public festivities and celebrations in the late fifteenth century; the cavalcade-like shape of many of his pieces clearly derives from these. With the exception of one play, there are no divisions in the action; his works are for the most part free, fast-moving and loosely knit, even sprawling, and some end with an abruptness that suggests they were written at short notice for very precisely designated slots in the royal diary. They range from the short lively sketch to the much longer and more leisurely 'play' clearly meant to be at least in part recited, rather than performed. There are devotional pieces, satirical farces, allegorical moralities that owe little to the European morality play as such, and romantic comedies. Depending on their subject matter – and in some of the pieces the religious and secular mingle – their tone ranges from the devout to the sharply satirical, from the energetic to the languid. They reveal, nonetheless, a consistent and distinctive voice, that of one who sees the world with a clear, uncompromising eye for hypocrisy and sham. Indeed his later works reveal a pronounced Erasmian concern with social abuse and ecclesiastical corruption and his outspokenness led to many of his works being subsequently mutilated, and a number of them banned, by the Inquisition.[20]

It has been justly said of Gil Vicente that he had a 'genius for organising scattered elements into new compounds'.[21] The use of the pastoral convention to create a world separate from but parallel to the real world; the use of song; the idea of temporal fluidity; the handling of his more complicated plots – all these owe much to Encina. Fernández had shown him that the rigours of the weather and the idea of the levelling power of love could make useful dramatic material, while from another Spanish playwright, his younger contemporary Torres Naharro (of whom more later), he almost certainly learnt the value of the dramatic prologue. But neither Encina nor Fernández can compare with him in versatility, in originality of vision nor, Fernández's *Auto de la Pasión* apart, in dramatic and poetic power. A handful of his works far excel anything else either of the other two wrote and all his pieces give tantalizing glimpses of the dramatist he could have been had he not been writing virtually *ex nihilo* and almost entirely subject to the whims of his patrons. His farces, for example, are remarkably advanced in their technical skill and comic sophistication; while he had an exceptionally good ear not only for different accents and speech mannerisms but for the way speech responds to the development of situation and the interaction of personalities, a technique of dialogue he could well have observed in action in Rojas's *Celestina*. Since no Portuguese theatre worthy of the name emerged in the sixteenth century, Vicente has to be viewed historically in the context of the Spanish theatre, although geographical and cultural circumstances make any direct contribution to the development of the Spanish stage unlikely. It is the Castilian pieces, therefore, which concern us here.

Almost immediately after his Christmas success in 1502 Vicente wrote the *Auto de los Reyes Magos* (*Auto of the Three Kings*) for Epiphany. This piece, with a shepherd who finds it difficult to understand why God made shepherdesses so attractive if he intended them to be ignored, a dilatory friar and a knight who incompetently got left behind by the three kings, is a good example of how Vicente often incorporated interesting elements without having the time to develop them. His career as court entertainer was now underway. During the first eighteen years he wrote in all nineteen plays, almost all religious. In 1513 he produced one of his most remarkable works, the *Auto de la Sibila Casandra* (*Auto of the Sybil Cassandra*), performed before Queen Leonor in the monastery of Xóbregas on Christmas morning.[22] This *auto* marks an enormous advance in complexity, richness and artistic control and represents a landmark in the history of religious drama in the Peninsula. Starting off as rustic farce as the spirited shepherdess Casandra haughtily refuses to marry her prosperous suitor Salomón in spite of the cajolings and threats of three aunts and three uncles, its significance quickly deepens as it emerges that Casandra is in fact a sybil who, having foreseen the birth of Christ, arrogantly thinks that she is to be the chosen mother of God. Her aunts, also sybils, and her uncles, in fact Old Testament prophets, are suitably outraged because they know that the mother of God will be a paragon of humility. The sybil-aunts' moving visions of the birth and crucifixion of the Saviour of the world and of the Day of Judgement that makes his sacrifice necessary darken the *auto*'s mood, but terror and gloom are then resolved into a climax of tenderness and light as two curtains open to reveal the nativity scene surrounded by angels, and Casandra, humbled now by what she has heard, joins the others in adoring the Christ child, and singing and dancing round the manger. On the allegorical level, therefore, Casandra represents the benighted pagan world before the advent of Christ; by rejecting marriage with Salomón (King Solomon was a familiar medieval Christ-figure) she is rejecting spiritual marriage with the Good Shepherd himself and his Church.

The idea of the sybil who becomes convinced she is to become the mother of God is not original; Vicente appears to have taken the basic story from an early fifteenth-century chivalric romance *Guerino il Meschino*, by Andrea de' Magnabotti di Barberino (1370–1431), which was published in translation in Spain in 1512. It is his treatment of the theme which is so masterly. The structural and tonal control of the movement from comedy through evocations of doom and destruction to tender scene of adoration is effortless, the fusion of realism and symbolism is achieved with consummate naturalness, the lyricism is exquisite. Even more impressive is the way in which a complex network of traditional motifs and associations is brought to life in terms of human psychology. The confrontations between Casandra and Salomón and Casandra and the aunts and uncles are beautifully modulated and often very funny, while the characterization of Casandra herself has a psychological richness and an enigmatic open-endedness unique in the early drama.[23]

The *auto* bears eloquent testimony to Vicente's gift for binding a wide range of effects into a unique and entirely convincing whole. It is also a perfect example of drama's kinship to rite and spectacle – indeed the visual impact is one of its greatest charms, for symmetry of character is reflected in a symmetry of movement, as first Casandra then Salomón walk on scene and then first aunts then uncles dance into view, the whole ending with the discovery of the *tableau vivant* towards which all the characters together dance. Drama resolves itself into ritual, confrontation into celebration; the worlds of pagan, Old Testament, New Testament and contemporary characters have themselves been compressed into a timeless truth in a way that will become typical later on in the *auto sacramental*.

The *Auto de la Sibila Casandra*, with its combination of musical, visual and doctrinal effects, must surely be the most inspired of all nativity plays. It certainly belongs to a different order of achievement from those of Encina and Fernández and Vicente's earlier efforts. Vicente's one other nativity play in Castilian, the *Auto de los cuatro tiempos* (*Auto of the Four Seasons*), provisionally ascribed now to 1514, is even more ambitious theologically, if not nearly so complex dramatically. Performed on Christmas morning in the chapel of San Miguel in the palace of Alcaçova in Lisbon, it has a strong interweaving of liturgical elements. After the announcement by angels of the birth of Jesus and virtuoso descriptions of themselves by the four seasons personified as shepherds, first Jupiter then King David admit the superiority of Divine Grace personified in the Christ child. An apparently simple piece, it is in fact beautifully orchestrated with the stage gradually filling and the focus then moving to the manger, where the *auto* ends with all singing the *Te Deum*. The sense of two worlds, pre-Christian and Christian, meeting and of the earlier then dissolving is as powerful here as in the *Auto de la Sibila Casandra*.

Both these late nativity plays make use of symbol and allegory to get across their doctrinal message. Vicente had in fact introduced an allegorical character, Faith, into the Portuguese *Auto da Fé* as early as 1510, but it was with his trio of allegorical moralities, the *Autos de las Barcas* (*Autos of the Boats* 1517–19) that religious drama in Spain took a really significant step towards the *auto sacramental*. The last of the trilogy, the *Auto de la Barca de la Gloria* (*The Boat of Glory*), performed on Good Friday 1519 before King Manuel, is the only one in Castilian and the least impressive. As becomes its theme (entry to Paradise) and its august cast (which includes a pope, a cardinal, an archbishop, an emperor and a king), it is rather more staid than its companion pieces (Hell and Purgatory, with a predominantly lowly cast) and is somewhat repetitive with less character differentiation.[24] But Vicente again puts effects of symmetry and crescendo to good use and maintains the tension extremely skilfully as each soul expresses repentance and appeals for mercy, using fragments of lessons from the Office for the Dead. Right to the end, the angels about to row the Styx to Paradise ignore the appeal of the souls threatened by the Devil with damnation. Salvation, in fact, comes almost as an afterthought, as if Vicente at that point lost interest.

Somewhere around 1520 there occurred a reaction against the ascetic in Vicente's career which parallels that in Encina's. From this point on there is a noticeable emphasis on Erasmian concerns such as prayer, social abuses, judicial corruption, and on Renaissance preoccupations such as love and nature. There is no falling off in experimentation, however; indeed the new themes were probably in part a way of expanding his theatrical range. Of the four Castilian plays that belong to this second phase, one is a palace diversion without a plot. The other three are inspired by the European vogue for the chivalric romance, initiated by the publication in 1508 of the Spanish *Amadís de Gaula*. The *Tragicomedia de Don Duardos* (1522?) was effectively the first attempt in the Peninsula to dramatize a specific piece of narrative fiction (the romance called *Primaleón*, second in the *Palmerín* cycle) and might even have been intended to be read, since dramatic performances at court had been suspended on the death of King Manuel in December 1521. However, the problems posed for drama by a highly stylized and idealized love that is at once immediate and unchanging, languid and intense, were first faced by Vicente in his *Comedia del viudo* (*The Widower*, 1521?), a sort of rehearsal for *Don Duardos*. Here the theme of young love shares the action with that of the bereaved widower-father. The first part of the play, about the widower's grief over the death of his wife and his neighbour's grief over the survival of his, is a playlet in its own right only tenuously linked to the arrival on scene of Prince Rosvel of Hungary, disguised as a labourer to gain access to the widower's daughters. Vicente's plot space is not capacious enough for what he wants to pack into it and major connections in the love plot are given as explanatory stage directions which must have been read out by a 'link voice'. The play's identity as court entertainment is revealed by its sudden and complete rupture of the illusion of theatre: since Rosvel cannot choose between the girls, an appeal is eventually made to John III, still a prince at the time, in the audience, to decide which should have him. The double wooing is meant humorously, and there is more than a hint of malicious fun, in the earlier scenes with the father. The whole piece indeed smacks powerfully of parody.

In *Don Duardos* Vicente focuses more seriously and singlemindedly on the love theme. Don Duardos, Prince of England, falls in love with Flérida, daughter of the Emperor of Constantinople and in order to win her affections masquerades as her gardener's son. Don Duardos will not reveal his identity, insisting that he must be loved for himself, and the psychological conflict that follows lies at the very core of the play's philosophy. The play ends very movingly with Flérida leaving her beloved family and home and setting off into the unknown with a man whose identity is still a mystery. Only when the boat is under sail does Duardos tell her that England is their destination and that he is a prince. Duardos's stand is a risky and courageous one and introduces into the fantasy world of chivalric romance the painful choices of the real world. So although the play's tone, as becomes its love-sick hero, is inevitably sentimental, it has a real dramatic core. However, here again we find drama in search of dramatic form. The structure is essentially narrative and linear, little regard is paid to the passage of time (day becomes night becomes dawn in the space of a few lines), the action as in *El viudo* is at one point telescoped into a kind of stage direction and at the end one of Flérida's ladies-in-waiting assumes the role of narrator. There is scarcely a plot to speak of and little action; our attention is focused on what the main characters are feeling.

The play, along with *La Sibila Casandra*, represents Vicente's highest achievement in Castilian. For the beauty of its poetry, its emotional and psychological power, its Renaissance emphasis on individual human values and its masterly use of the garden which is not only the play's main setting but its central metaphor,[25] give it a magic all of its own. But it is obviously not drama in the conventional sense and appropriately enough its identity as court festivity, its kinship with masque and mumming, is strikingly revealed in the course of the play itself. The introductory scenes in which the Emperor's court watch first the combat between Don Duardos and Primaleón and then exit to see the fight between the rough knight Camilote (the wild man figure beloved of mummers) and the man who dares challenge the beauty of the loathly maiden Camilote loves, are not just performances within performances; because the real court is watching the fictional court watching other characters, the play actually mirrors its real-life context, sending back at the royal Portuguese audience an imperial reflection of itself.[26]

Vicente's other full-blown attempt at drama that draws explicitly on other literary works, is equally elaborate but has even less of a plot than *Don Duardos* and is structurally weaker. The *Tragicomedia de Amadís de Gaula* (1533?), which tells the story of the knight Amadís's love for Princess Oriana, is in fact inferior in every way to *Don Duardos* and it is difficult to believe it could have postdated it. The lovers' anguish when they fall victim to misunderstandings makes a certain impact, but the play has none of the lyrical beauty of *Don Duardos*, is not nearly as inventive and has none of its profundity. Oriana has been seen as a character of some complexity,[27] and indeed we do witness in her an initial struggle between love and pride which prefigures many such struggles later on in the Spanish drama, but her situation is nothing like as poignant or suggestive as Flérida's. *Amadís* deals in the same emotional currency as *Don Duardos* – love as a form of death, the despair of rejection – but it does not succeed as the other play does in engaging our interest in the lover's fate. The only satisfactory way to read *Amadís* is, perhaps, as a parody of the chivalric romance of that name or as a burlesque or satire of the entire genre. Certainly there are humorous touches; Amadís, for example, has to be taught how to beg when he becomes a hermit for love, he holds his broom like a sword, and Oriana's heartfelt reference at one point to the physical distance that separates her from Amadís is followed by a discussion of the accuracy of city clocks. Such anti-heroic subversion would have delighted a sophisticated audience immersed in the vogue for love in the context of the chivalresque.[28] There is in the play, however, a marked uncertainty of tone which reflects the general unease in the romantic plays as to how to deal in drama with non-dramatic themes. The only truly effective way of dramatizing courtly or romantic love is arguably, as Rojas's *Celestina* and Lope de Vega's plays show, to confront it with a world external to itself. Vicente goes some way to achieving this in *Don Duardos* but the play is still locked through its literary source into a world of sensibilities that are self-nourishing and self-fulfilling.

In *La Sibila Casandra* Vicente had shown that artistic control of a high order was by no means beyond him; his attempt to harness the chivalric romance to the purposes of theatre was an ambitious one bound to fail because both the internalized world of courtly love and the free-ranging adventures of knights errant are, if unmodified, inimical to the procedures of drama. If Vicente was indeed inspired to write his handful of romantic plays by Torres Naharro's *Propalladia*, published in Naples in 1517 and in Seville in 1520, as has been claimed,[29] then he learnt little from Torres Naharro's own theatrical practices. The fact that he chose not to suggests that he perceived himself as a deviser of court entertainments rather than as a dramatist in the classical sense. Only this can explain why he never allowed his inspiration or experimentation to be constrained by any idea of what drama should or should not be. He initiated many important dramatic developments – the use of narrative material, psychological penetration, the use of double identities, a rich vein of satire and irony, more sophisticated use of language and metaphor, the functional use of lyrics – but his inventiveness was simply too fertile and wide-ranging for the technical possibilities available. It would take a playwright of less literary and poetic genius but greater dramatic sense to begin to effect the change to drama proper.

Bartolomé de Torres Naharro (1485?–c. 1520)

Such a man was Bartolomé de Torres Naharro.[30] Since Torres Naharro lived in Rome as a member of a Cardinal's household and then in Naples in the service of the Fabrizio Colonna family and did most of his writing in Italy, his immediate impact on Spain was not as great as Encina's, but in the long run his influence was arguably more crucial. Lope de Vega may not have read Encina at all, but he almost certainly as a youth read Torres Naharro's plays which were republished in Madrid in 1573. Some of these plays, which were first published in Naples under the title *Propalladia*, come far closer to the modern concept of drama than anything else written for performance in this early period, having plots which although still rudimentary are real stage actions instead of narrational dialogue spiced with comings and goings. Not only was Torres Naharro a practising playwright of considerable skill and range, however; he was a dramatic theorist as well, Spain's first. His *Prohemio*, or preface, to the *Propalladia* is one of the earliest important statements on dramatic theory in Renaissance Europe and its very existence is a clear indication that drama, in Italy at least, was in the process of becoming a self-conscious art form. Torres Naharro's survey of classical views on comedy is impatient and cursory and largely derived from Terence by way of both early and Renaissance commentators.[31] He then moves on to give his own opinions. Comedy, he claims, is quite simply 'an ingenious confection of notable and finally happy events, disputed by characters', indicating a clear concern with performance and a stress on inventiveness that is significant in the light of the stress laid later on in the Spanish drama on ingenuity. He accepts Horace's division into five acts (subsequent Spanish dramatists, further removed from classical influence, would not be so acquiescent in this respect), which he called *jornadas*,[32] a term he bequeathed to the Spanish drama of the seventeenth century. His view on the size of the cast is judiciously explicit – 'it is my view that there ought not to be so few as to render the entertainment dull nor so many as to create confusion' – and he recommends decorum in plot, actions and speech.[33] Most importantly, he makes a distinction, which he broadly followed in his own plays, between *comedias a noticia* (plays of observation) and *comedias a fantasía* (plays of invention). The former deal in the picturesque realism of low life, the latter are self-confessed fictions that proclaim the value and validity of the imagination in drama while giving the impression of realism. For these Torres Naharro drew inspiration from various sources including traditional tales, the *Celestina* and the comedies of Plautus and Terence, which were currently in favour in Italy both in Latin and in Italian translation. Torres

Naharro's readiness to take only what he wanted from established practice
and for the rest go firmly his own way prefigures Lope de Vega's attitude,
and three quarters of a century apart though they were, Lope's ability to
produce a drama that drew on contemporary customs and aspirations for
inspiration but at the same time freely tapped the resources of the imagination is very reminiscent of Torres Naharro's earlier recipe for success.

The *Prohemio* is a mixture of prescription and description, for Torres's
recommendations were largely based on what he had found to be successful
with his audiences. These audiences were much more varied and socially
mixed than one might expect. Sometimes the plays were primarily aimed at
specific groups – educated young Spaniards living in Rome (*Diálogo del
nacimiento, Dialogue of the Nativity*, 1505–7), members of the Portuguese
embassy in the Vatican (*Comedia Trophea, The Triumph*, 1514?). But generally speaking they addressed audiences made up of aristocrats and
prelates, visitors, courtesans, retainers and servants – a polyglot mixture of
high and low, all of whom Torres was concerned to please.[34] A number of
his plays use several languages. Like Encina, Fernández and Vicente he
was intimately involved in the production of his works, organizing the
performances, acting, singing, even dancing in them, and was therefore in
an ideal position to gauge their success.

The greater dramatic sophistication of his work is due to his proximity
from the start of his career to those developments in Italian drama which
stemmed from the revival of interest in the classics. Unlike his fellow
Spaniards, Torres Naharro perceived himself as a dramatist working
within the tradition of drama established by the ancients and not just as a
court entertainer. As a result, he is more concerned than they to attempt to
separate the world of dramatic illusion from the audience's own world,
even in those works which still have their roots in the spectacle of the
medieval mummers. He does this by prefacing each play with an *introito*,
normally spoken in *sayagués* by a comic rustic from the Encina stable but
here squeezed out of the main action onto the side lines. Its purpose is
partly to 'soften up' the audience as the buffoon forgetfully and often
bawdily prattles on about this or that. But its main function is to set the
scene (in the absence presumably of much in the way of stage lighting and
scenery), to introduce the characters and to outline the plot – a neater
solution than Vicente's interpolated narrative to the problem of conveying
adequate information without overburdening the dialogue, but still fairly
primitive. This creation of a distinct, alternative reality aimed at an
audience but separate from it, is what gives Torres Naharro's plays the
flavour of drama as we have come to know it.

Between 1505 and 1520–3 he wrote one Christmas dialogue and eight plays, of which two are low-life comedies of manners modelled on the work of Machiavelli and Aretino (*Comedia Soldadesca, Soldiers*, and *Comedia Tinellaria, Below Stairs*)[35] while the remainder fit, some more, some less, comfortably, into his other category of plays of invention. They all have five acts, though the strain of conforming to this classical prescription frequently shows in very uneven act divisions (in *Tinellaria* the shortest act has 173 lines, the longest 514). The pace is vigorous with a great deal of comic relief and local colour – servants' chit-chat to add interest even in the love plots, for example. The tone is slightly mocking even when apparently serious matters are afoot, with a marked irreverence towards the sacred cows of literature (love) and society (masters and mistresses, the Church). The general level of rudery and innuendo is quite astonishing compared with the Spanish drama of later years, but these plays, of course, were written for private rather than public consumption in a vastly different cultural milieu. The language is supple and natural but on the whole plain and business-like, verse rather than poetry, though the two plays thought to be his last, *Comedia Calamita* and *Comedia Aquilana*, appear more ambitious in this respect. The metres used, interestingly enough given the growing interest in Italian metres in Spain, are Spanish. The settings are predominantly urban, as distinct from the mainly rustic or court settings of the other early dramatists – characteristically, outdoor places (street or garden) surrounded with doors and windows.

In terms of artistic achievement the plays vary. Of the two low-life comedies, *Soldadesca* (1510?)[36] is an extended cavalcade depicting the hurly-burly of a recruiting operation, with virtually no plot but much swearing and bawdiness, which depends for its effect on the robustness of its dialogue and its hectic air of the world coming and going. The much longer *Tinellaria* (1516?), which deals with life below stairs in the polyglot kitchen of a Cardinal's household, is a more carefully constructed and polished version of the same, with the servants' mealtime in Act III, when they are joined by two visiting grooms, giving the plot some shape. With little in the way of action to rely on for maintaining interest, the play is a *tour de force*. Sexual banter, discussions, nationalistic jibes, grumbles and gossip, petty thievery, altercations between members of the household, criticism of the Cardinal its master – all combine to produce a dialogue of tremendous pace and vigour which ends climactically with what sounds like drunken mayhem. The play's *introito*, spoken this time by the playwright himself without rustic disguise, is so carefully explanatory that it suggests that Torres Naharro was acutely conscious of breaking new ground with his novel subject matter and polyglot dialogue, which he justifies on grounds of realism (previously he had limited himself to Spanish, Italian and Latin).

The *comedias a fantasía* vary somewhat in kind and considerably in achievement. The plot in each case unfolds as one continuous action but there is a marked increase in complexity and control between the earlier and the later plays. Two of them have little in the way of plot. *Comedia Trophea* (1514?) is a diplomatic celebration of the military and maritime achievements of King Manuel in Portugal and of the birth of his son, performed before members of the Portuguese embassy in the Vatican. It is therefore the least self-contained dramatically of his plays. It is almost, indeed, a secular nativity, with foreign potentates arriving to kiss the King's feet and shepherds bringing gifts, and its combination of quarrelsome shepherds and allegory is not a particularly happy one. The considerably shorter *Comedia Jacinta* (1514–15?), too, is more palace entertainment than drama. With its vaguely allegorical storyline it is essentially a vehicle for set pieces on masters and false friends (a note of personal grievance seems to seep through here), on Rome (which is heavily criticized), on the world in general and above all on women, of whom it is a glorification. It was written either as a wedding play in honour of Vittoria Colonna or to celebrate the visit to Rome in the winter of 1514–15 of Isabella d'Este, Duchess of Mantua.

Fortunately Naharro's duties were not normally so specific and the four other *comedias a fantasía*, early and late, are romantic intrigues with a considerable debt to classical comedy. It is these plays above all which set a precedent for Lope de Vega's *comedia nueva* over half a century later (see chapters 2, 3 and 4). The conflict between love and social awareness, the threat of disaster that shadows the lovers' antics, the emphasis on freedom in the choice of marriage partners, the mixture of serious and comic, the tone of tolerance and humanity – all are strikingly reminiscent of Lope's own theatre.

Comedia Seraphina (1508–9), Torres Naharro's first full-length play, is simple enough. The plot is a working out of a situation that already exists at the start of the play, with no additional complications emerging in the course of it. It does have a comic sub-plot and it deals with a love tangle of the sort beloved of later public audiences. There is, however, a certain flippancy about it that will not be typical of the *comedia nueva*: when the unprincipled Floristán who has already contracted a clandestine marriage with Seraphina officially marries Orphea, he reacts to Seraphina's understandable distress by offering to kill Orphea, on the grounds that if he killed himself both women would take their own lives. The action, which eventually reaches a less drastic conclusion, is spare and speedy and, for all its simplicity, dramatically effective.

Of all Torres Naharro's plays it is his next love intrigue, *Comedia Himenea* (1516?), normally regarded as his best work, which is always recalled in the context of Spain's national theatre, because here he introduced into the Spanish drama the theme for which it was to become most famous – that of honour–vengeance.[37] As a prefiguration of the honour plot of later years it is, in fact, fairly sketchy. Himeneo courts Phebea and her brother threatens to kill him if he finds them together, but when he does surprise them Himeneo's offer of marriage immediately resolves tension into celebration. It is better to see the play as the forerunner of the many Golden-Age comedies that use honour as a complicating device in a love intrigue, rather than of those grave or tragic plays where honour saturates the very air and becomes a means of exploring serious moral and social dilemmas. An equally important but commonly ignored ingredient of *Himenea* is the introduction into the Spanish drama, in the character of Phebea's brother, of the authority figure so crucial to domestic love intrigues. Rivals in love are always a valuable source of plot complications and turbulent emotions but fathers or brothers (in the comedies) and husbands (in serious plays), representing as they do the full weight of social as well as masculine authority, can add a dimension that is at once wider and more threatening. In a drama like that of seventeenth-century Spain which portrays a society which revolves round reputation, a figure who threatens young love or individual well-being in the name of society was clearly doubly potent. When this figure is a brother, interesting ironies arise. Phebea's is the first of many stage brothers who express the view 'I take pleasure in wooing but not by God in my own house'.[38] A third feature of the play later adopted by Lope de Vega, albeit adapted probably from common sources like Terence and Plautus, was that of the servant lovers whose relationship comically parallels that of their master and mistress.

There is evidence in *Himenea* of a move towards complexity in Torres Naharro's love intrigues, for Himeneo with his two servants, one loyal, the other a toady, is clearly modelled on Calisto and his servants in Rojas's *Celestina*. But the action itself is still slight. *Comedia Calamita* (*c.* 1519)[39] is longer by 1,114 lines and altogether more sophisticated, with a well-worked-out action, lively amorous scenes, some very humorous incidents and language which itself is more ambitious and verges at times on the rhetorical. The use of language for comic effect is expanded, with the language of courtly love as well as rustic speech becoming the butt of laughter, a possible influence of Encina as well as Rojas. The plot itself shows signs of greater complication. Essentially it deals with Floribundo's attempts to woo Calamita, who lives with her rustic brother Torcazo and his wife Lubina, and his father's attempts to stop him marrying beneath himself; but there are interesting embroideries. Floribundo's servant manipulates the simple rustics both for amusement and to promote his own ends; the father's servant is also a stirrer; Calamita turns out to be of noble birth after all, making marriage possible; while Lubina's affair with the student Escolar adds much comic spice, especially when the latter, to further the affair, dresses up as a woman only to be sexually assaulted by Torcazo. Overt bawdiness apart, the play could be the recipe for a hundred Golden-Age plays.

His last and longest play, *Comedia Aquilana* (1520? 1523?), mines to the full the rich vein of comedy evident in the earlier plays – which explains, perhaps, its apparent popularity in its own day. Indeed, parody is never far below the surface of this love plot and the general note of comedy and rustic chit-chat is dominant enough to endanger Torres's own separation of his plays into the observed and the invented. The plot is based on the traditional story of the ailing man whose doctors fail to cure him until, when his beloved passes and sends his pulse racing, the cause is discovered. Fortunately Aquilano turns out to be a prince after all and can marry the king's daughter, so the spectre of dishonour that troubles Feliciana melts away without ever materializing. Act I has an amusing and original scene in which the comic servant grotesquely misreads a letter from Feliciana, whose handwriting is pronounced appalling; variations on the theme of love letters conveyed by servants are a staple ingredient of love comedies later on. There is a nice comic twist when the doctor at first announces that it is his own wife whom Aquilano loves and the king bids him be 'generous' for the sake of the young man's life. The suggestion of spoof grows stronger when Feliciana, calling for a knife when she thinks her love for Aquilano has been discovered by her father, is brought a gardening hoe too heavy to lift. There is throughout a subversive irony reminiscent of Gil Vicente's *Amadís de Gaula* and it is more than likely that Vicente knew the Torres Naharro play.

Together, Encina, Fernández, Vicente and Torres Naharro constitute the first generation of playwrights writing in Spanish and they were in their different ways a remarkably gifted quartet. The exact nature of any interaction between them is impossible to establish.[40] Torres Naharro possibly knew Encina's and Fernández's work in Spain before he turned up in Rome in 1503 and subsequently he and Encina almost certainly met in the Spanish expatriate community there. Torres Naharro's *sayagués*-speaking rustics owe a lot to Encina but at the same time Encina's *introito* to *Plácida y Victoriano* would seem to be based on Torres Naharro's introits. Several of Vicente's plays postdate the publication of the *Propalladia* in the Peninsula (Seville, 1520) and a number of apparent Vicente debts to it have been identified.[41] However, all these influences are essentially minor ones. Torres Naharro, whatever his early allegiance to the Salamancans, must be seen as a phenomenon apart. As a dramatic craftsman he was years in advance; even his earliest play employs the techniques of prefiguration and recapitulation which make an extended action possible and his simplest plot is highly organized. There are practical reasons why none of Torres's stagecraft rubbed off on his Spanish contemporaries. In Encina's case the chronology was wrong, for Torres Naharro's most ambitious plays postdate Encina's last; in Vicente's, the psychological remoteness of Portugal from Rome and the more specific and necessarily decorous requirements of a royal court made imitation less likely. But the crucial factor was that Torres Naharro was the only one of them who sensed what drama was really about. All wrote more or less to order for private patrons on designated occasions, yet Torres Naharro alone fully realized that drama was not just life or literature played out before an audience but a distinct art form which in order to evoke certain responses in its audience had to observe certain principles of construction and technique. The greater sophistication of the cultural context in which he wrote was undoubtedly largely responsible for this. In addition, of course, there is a marked difference of tone. Torres Naharro was essentially a secular dramatist writing in a hedonistic, even amoral atmosphere, where satire, iconoclasm and frankness were not merely tolerated but applauded; whereas his contemporaries were working for the most part in a much more constrained environment and in close association with the festivities of the Church. Anything which smacks of subversion in their works represents a daring departure from traditional attitudes and conventional morality, whereas Torres Naharro could afford to ignore such constraints. Encina's own change of gear on his arrival in Rome is a vivid illustration of the difference between the two cultural environments.

As far as is known, Torres Naharro's plays were never performed in Spain but they were widely read. Successive editions were published in Spain before 1557, when the plays were banned by the Inquisition: Torres Naharro is the only dramatist ever to earn the distinction of having his entire works proscribed. Between the 1520s and 1550s this popularity inspired a plethora of comedies in Torres Naharro's Italianate manner by a string of Spanish writers of uneven talent,[42] but it is unlikely that many of these plays were performed either. Indeed it is doubtful whether they were even intended primarily for performance. Like the imitators, in verse and prose, of Encina's elevated pastoral style and Rojas's *Celestina*,[43] Torres Naharro's followers were essentially Spanish humanists flexing their literary muscles. No doubt their plays were read aloud and occasionally performed at literary gatherings, in schools and universities, or in ecclesiastical circles, depending on the nature of the plays; but there is no evidence that they were performed in public by travelling theatre companies, as has on occasion been claimed. We do know, however, that they reached the reading public. In 1555 the *cortes* at Valladolid petitioned the King for the introduction of compulsory publishing licences for all books, verse and comedies, particularly love comedies, because of the harm they were doing to the idle young. The accumulative influence of this rich store of printed plays on the later drama, many of whose earliest exponents must have grown up reading them, cannot, therefore, be discounted.

There can be no doubt that until the mid-1550s performed drama in Spain was dominated by the Church and its activities. Private or royal patronage of the sort that produced Encina and Vicente did not continue and performances of festival plays were rare. Even in the case of the two we know something about, one in 1527, the other in 1548 and both in Valladolid, the earlier one, which celebrated the birth of the future Philip II, was a dramatization of the story of John the Baptist.[44] Once the Church started systematically commissioning works for its feast days – as it did of Lucas Fernández early on – then drama effectively moved out of the private sphere into the public arena. With the growth of guild involvement these festivities grew in number and importance; they therefore not only absorbed much of the dramatic talent available but they satisfied the very appetite for theatrical entertainment which they helped encourage. Charles V was not interested in drama and spent most of his reign outside Spain, so that there was no example of secular patronage at the top: indeed not until the seventeenth century, with the reign of Philip III, did a court theatre proper develop in Spain. The growing conservatism of Spain, too, probably helped consolidate the Church's dominance over dramatic activity. Even the dramatist regarded as Torres Naharro's foremost disciple, Bartolomé Palau (1525?–1570?), who adopted his five-act formula wholesale, wrote for the most part on sacred themes. Micael de Carvajal's *Tragedia llamada Josefina* (*Tragedy called Joseph*) (pub. 1535)[45] is another example, and a distinguished one at that, of a play written on a biblical theme in five acts with classical elements inspired by Renaissance humanism, such as a chorus. This smooth inter-weaving of religious and secular strands was to become one of the distinctive features of the Spanish drama and from the late sixteenth century on religious themes would form a significant proportion of the playgoers' diet even in the commercial theatre.

Josefina was certainly put on in a square in Palencia but it is not known how many other of these full-length humanistic religious plays, if any, were ever performed in public. It is not really necessary to see them as a response to market demand. This was an age of religious fervour and upheaval, and Spanish humanists naturally applied the exciting new literary formulae to religious subject matter, if only for the consumption of like-minded people. It is doubtful in any case whether the public at large would have appreciated these plays as they appreciated the one-act pieces in the native tradition established by Encina and Fernández, which soon came to constitute the meat and drink of church festivities. Of the many (named and anonymous) who supplied this diet three playwrights stand out. Fernán López de Yanguas, who, as far as is known, wrote two Encina-type eclogues and two allegorical farces, produced in his *Farsa sacramental* (1520?) the oldest known example of what was eventually to become the *auto sacramental*. Sebastián de Horozco (1510?–1580) wrote five plays of which one, *Representación de la parábola de Sant Mateo* (*The Parable of Saint Matthew*), was performed in Toledo in 1548 on the feast of Corpus Christi; another, *Representación de la historia evangélica del capítulo nono de San Juan* (*The Evangelical Story of Chapter Nine of St John*), has an opening scene which is almost a dramatization of the episode with the blind beggar in the picaresque work *Lazarillo de Tormes*. But it is the more prolific Diego Sánchez de Badajoz, the priest from Badajoz who was principal heir to the Salamancans,[46] who best illustrates the relatively wide range of material and tone which this increasingly flourishing, Church-based drama embraced.

Diego Sánchez de Badajoz (died c. 1549–52)

Badajoz's twenty-seven *farsas*, which were published in Seville in 1554 by his nephew under the title *Recopilación en metro*,[47] include nativity and *officium pastorum* pieces, allegorical farces, plays dramatizing the lives of the saints, prefigurations of the Eucharist, biblical material and the Dance of Death, as well as plays in honour of various guilds with eucharistic symbolism.[48] Their characters are taken now from the Bible, now from real life (soldiers, shepherds, blind men, friars, gentlemen, negresses, and so on), while others are allegorical (Justice, the Church, Understanding, etc.).

Badajoz's was neither a very poetic nor a particularly subtle talent but he was indubitably a religious dramatist of considerable skill and power. Eschewing the pagan and erotic elements of the later Encina, he placed the latter's general technique, his use of *sayagués*, his comic situations and characters entirely at the service of his faith. His work has a satirical edge and a robust energy that Encina's lacks and his humour is altogether redder meat than either Encina's or Fernández's, but the aim is always didactic and the overall tone moralizing. His contribution to the development of religious drama in Spain was outstanding. His exploitation of the idea of prefiguration, his dramatization of theological problems and above all his use of allegory, were more sophisticated than anything that had gone before.[49] He seems not to have seen the peculiar appropriateness of allegory to the presentation of the Eucharist and therefore did not produce a play specifically designed to illustrate the significance of Corpus Christi, but his ability to handle allegory to communicate abstruse ideas was impressive enough to persuade B. W. Wardropper that he would have rivalled Calderón himself had he been writing later in the development of allegorical drama.[50]

Two of Badajoz's works will suffice to convey the flavour of the popular religious drama of the day at its best. The *Farsa de Salomón* starts off in the usual way with a shepherd bewailing the shortage of bread and condemning the mercenary nature of the times. He then introduces Solomon with an 'if you don't believe me ask Solomon'-type remark. The episode of the baby and the two mothers ensues, during which Solomon, interestingly, refers to himself both in the past and the present tense: he is, as a dramatic character; he was, as a historical character. After this incident, a friar explains its allegorical significance: the baby is Christ, the two mothers are Synagogue and Church, Jews and Christians, body and soul. The friar, until now the voice of theology, suddenly becomes the parodied rascal of tradition. He takes advantage of his words about the penance of the body to talk the shepherd into beating himself and then at his suggestion they go off to trick a rich prostitute out of her ill-gotten gains. Meanwhile the prostitute has hired a young servant-lover and dresses him as a girl, 'with titties', to deflect gossip. The friar, when he sees her, fancies the 'girl' and proposes to enjoy her quickly before making off with the money. He ends up being beaten until contrite by prostitute and lover, with the shepherd egging them on. The play ends with a song. The farce shows how extraordinarily fluid such pieces were, with their protean characters, their suspended chronology and their mixture of theology, social criticism and titillation. It is noteworthy that the bawdiness here is part of the action and not just reported in the dialogue as it is in Encina and Fernández.

In the long nativity play *Farsa militar* (*Military Farce, c.* 1547) allegory is not merely explained but comes to life on stage. Since allegory might itself mislead the simple, a comic shepherd first reminds the audience that the Devil is in fact invisible although they will be seeing him played 'in brute form' in front of them. The Devil, the World, and the Flesh then set out to harvest souls. A friar preaches against Flesh, effectively woman, where-upon Flesh tries to seduce him by revealing her breasts and legs. The friar resists both this temptation and the financial blandishments of World, determining to give the money he is offered to three beggars. While he looks for them, however, World removes the money from its hiding place. The beggars suspect one another and start quarrelling, the Devil stirs things up by hitting the Blind Man, who thinks his attacker is the Lame Man. Contrite at the havoc he has caused, the friar starts to discipline himself, but the Devil sows seeds of doubt in his ear and only the appearance of his Guardian Angel saves him from despair. The Devil, having failed in invisible form (represented onstage by the wild beast) now tries again in human form by putting on World's cape. He so flatters the friar's gifts as a preacher that, his ambition aroused, he decides to go to Rome and seek his fortune. The Angel turns his back on him while the Devil jumps for joy and hooks him with a grappling iron – a visual representation of his fall from grace. The scene now becomes the open road. World and Flesh beguile the friar until he is completely won over – conveyed by the covering of his eyes, ears and nose, the binding of his feet and the removal of his cloak, begging purse, breviary and flail. They daub him with mud and spit on him, and the Devil prepares to cut off his head. The friar comes to his senses just in time and the Devil's band is routed. He assumes his habit again and the Angel helps him wash away the mud. The play moves into humour and revelation as the shepherd reappears and tries to tell a deaf man that Christ is born. They all move off to pay homage to the Christ child and the play ends with a gay dance promising festivities to come that night.

The theme is of course the redemptive power of contrition and penance, made possible by Christ's sacrifice – hence its relevance to the Nativity. The narrative above unequivocally reveals that here we have theological abstractions being dramatized in a visually potent way that plays unashamedly on the emotions and fears of the audience. The play is neither psychologically nor allegorically watertight; but no-one could question the play's power as drama or its effectiveness as instruction, and it gives an excellent insight into why popular religious drama in Spain was so enormously successful. Not all religious drama, it has to be said, was of this quality. A codex of anonymous sixteenth-century *autos, farsas y coloquios* in the Biblioteca Nacional in Madrid contains ninety-six pieces which are for the most part static discussion with little movement or conflict.[51]

The fact that Sánchez de Badajoz appended to the play an alternative scene for the shepherds and the deaf man which announces not the birth of Christ but the Emperor Charles V's victory over the German Protestants at the Battle of Mühlberg (1547), can leave little doubt that he was writing with performance in mind, and difficult as the ideas behind his plays and others like them are, there is no reason to suppose that his audience was limited to the more highly educated clergy any more than were those of the much more sophisticated and elaborate *autos sacramentales* later on. What these earlier religious performances lacked in spectacle and artistry they could make up for in energy, humour and variety. They have to be seen as part of the general festivities held at Christmas, Easter and Corpus Christi and on patron saints' days, when the atmosphere was one of relaxation and enjoyment as well as religious observation. And these popular festive pieces were by no means all religious. Like most playwrights during this period (and indeed later) Badajoz in addition to his religious *farsas* wrote various brief secular works – skits, dialogues and dances – whose only *raison d'être* can be that they were intended to form part of the celebrations, acting as hors d'œuvres or finales to the more serious plays. The city of Badajoz itself seems to have been particularly renowned in the middle of the sixteenth century for its dramatic activities, especially its Corpus performances which were evidently becoming gradually more spectacular.[52] Unusually, Sánchez occasionally gave stage directions for his plays which indicate that he was using the elevated stage and the *carros* (stages on wheels) long familiar in Corpus Christi processions. The way in which he refers to the latter indicate that their use for religious drama was normal practice.

It will be evident that the development of the Spanish drama in the first half of the sixteenth century is difficult to plot after its early beginnings. A large number of plays have come down to us but too little is known about the authors themselves, about dates of composition and publication, and about conditions of performance, to produce a reliably exact picture of how a theatrical tradition emerged and grew. Broadly speaking, however, there were, as we have seen, two readily identifiable, if overlapping, strands.

On the one hand was the humanistic drama, modelled on Torres Naharro's principles: mainly though by no means exclusively secular, it drew on classical, Renaissance and biblical material,[53] with the emphasis on comic and romantic intrigue; it was written normally in five acts (though there are examples of three, four, even seven-act plays), and for restricted consumption. We have reliable evidence for the performance of only one such play. In 1548 an Ariosto-based play was put on in Valladolid to celebrate the wedding of the King's daughter, Infanta María, with 'all the theatrical apparatus and scenery with which the Romans were accustomed to perform and it was a royal and sumptuous event.'[54] The magnificent processions and tournaments that characterized Renaissance festivities throughout Europe give an idea of what such a celebration might be like,[55] but it must be repeated that such secular festive performances seem to have been extremely rare in Spain.

On the other hand were the one-act plays in the Encina tradition written for performance on special days in the Church calendar, probably commissioned for the most part by Church and municipal authorities. Drawing on the Bible, legends and the lives of the saints as well as the liturgical and allegorical traditions, their popular appeal was in large part due to a generous admixture of profane festive elements which threatened at times to swamp their didactic content, and to the secular dramatic titbits, the singing and dancing, that accompanied them. Indeed the appropriateness of comedy and farce in religious plays became a subject of debate and one of the recommendations of the Council of Trent in the 1550s was that Corpus Christi entertainments should be more serious and dignified. The informative but decidedly unfunny introits to the plays in the Biblioteca Nacional collection mentioned above suggest that most of them belong to the Counter-Reformation period when these Tridentine strictures were making themselves felt. It is not clear who performed in this religious drama, though the fact that a touring company of Italian actors joined in the Corpus celebrations in Seville in 1538[56] suggests that by then Spanish professional players too were being hired to boost the efforts of lay and ecclesiastical amateurs. It was still common for the author himself to organize and direct performances, which presumably accounts for the lack of stage directions in most plays. Both fixed platforms and wheeled carts were used, but of their construction and decoration at this time little is known, although there is some evidence for the use on both of different levels or areas, representing, for example, Heaven and Hell.[57] The attraction of the wheeled stage was, of course, its versatility. It could both move along in the procession and link up with stationary stage extensions so that the performance itself could take place, in square or church precinct as appropriate. Religious plays continued to be performed on these carts throughout the sixteenth and seventeenth centuries in Spain.

These two categories, as might be expected, are by no means entirely separate ones, if only because the technical division between one-act and multi-act plays does not correspond invariably to a division of themes and techniques into the religious and the humanistic. The later plays of Encina himself are humanistic in content if not in form, and a number of one-act plays in this mould were written, and possibly performed in private houses. Conversely Palau's plays, as we saw, although religious in theme adhere to Torres Naharro's technical principles. López de Yanguas's *Farsa nue-vamente compuesta* (*Newly-Written Farce*) similarly has a five-act plot but uses pastoral and allegory like the school of Encina. While Carvajal's *Tragedia llamada Josefina* is unique in that it is a five-act play on a religious theme written for public performance and shows all the unconcern for unity of time and place of the popular religious drama. Both categories, furthermore, used songs and both utilized the introit with its protean comic rustic figure, though the humanist drama tended to append an *argumento* as well, as Torres Naharro himself had done. Many playwrights tried their hand at both kinds of play and the humanist plays in verse were for the most part written in native Spanish metres like the popular works (again following Torres Naharro's lead). The terms *auto*, *farsa*, *comedia*, *representación*, and *égloga* were used virtually indiscriminately for both, though the label *tragedia* seems to have been the preserve of the full-length play. Nonetheless, the two categories are helpful in that they identify the traditions that will mingle and eventually merge in the second half of the sixteenth century to form the national drama – on the one hand the popular tradition rooted in ceremony and rite and Church instruction, unclassical in that it makes no obeisance to rules and theories; on the other the classicizing, literary tradition of drama as a self-contained art form.

2

From drama to theatre

The next phase in the development of the Spanish stage spans the four decades or so from the 1540s, by which time both the popular and the humanistic drama were flourishing in their different ways, to the late 1580s, when Lope de Vega established his immensely successful national theatre in the form of the *comedia nueva*. This phase is a complex and somewhat confused one: partly because it was a period of theatrical development and dramatic experimentation – the public playhouses came into existence and the drama, in response to a wide range of influences, moved tentatively in a number of very different directions – but also because our understanding of the way in which all these developments interacted is incomplete. Yet by the end of it, a single-minded, coherent and distinct amalgam of many of these different tendencies was emerging which was to dominate the Spanish theatre for a hundred years.

The first companies of players

Until the middle years of the sixteenth century Spain could be said to have a drama but not a theatre. Plays were written for private consumption, plays were performed in public during Church festivities and, as in the rest of Europe, plays in Latin were performed by students in their rhetoric classes.[1] Drama was perceived as literature, ritual, instruction. The crucial change came in the 1540s and 1550s when a number of men responded to the Spaniard's growing appetite for dramatic entertainment by forming companies of players which took their own plays and those of others to the public. These actor-manager-playwrights were no more Spain's first players than they were its first dramatists. Small groups of strolling players had for years toured the country singing, tumbling and performing sketches, taking on musicians and extra actors as and when necessary. That they were regarded as a disreputable element of Spanish society is clear

41

from a decree published in Toledo in 1534 stipulating that they should wear distinctive clothing. But Lope de Rueda and his colleague and fellow Sevillian Alonso de la Vega were theatrical entrepreneurs in the true sense, who recognized a gap in the market and proceeded to fill it, creating the first organized theatrical companies to take dramatic entertainment in a systematic way to a waiting audience.

Not ony did they write much of their own material but they were ambitious enough to want to expand on the existing public repertoire of religious *autos* and comic farces and to turn for inspiration, in their endeavour to write actable plays, to humanistic drama and the cultured drama and *novelle* of Italy. With them Italianate intrigue plots leave the study and the gentleman's hall and move out into the public arena. It is in their work that the popular and literary strands that characterized the early Spanish drama begin to merge. It is not surprising, therefore, that subsequent dramatists, Cervantes and Lope de Vega included, regarded this generation as the real initiators of the Spanish theatre. We have seen that Rueda and Navarro were far from being the 'first inventors of the art' in Spain as Lope claimed;[2] but they were regarded thus not just because Lope de Vega and his contemporaries could themselves remember no further back and seem to have known very little about Spanish Renaissance drama[3] – though this undoubtedly played its part – but because they were thinking of the theatre as they by then knew it, as a living tradition of secular entertainment performed before a public audience.

It ought to be said at once that as theatre and drama the activities of this important generation were still fairly primitive. Both Cervantes, who as a boy saw Rueda perform, and Juan Rufo, a contemporary of Rueda's, bear witness to the paucity of costumes and props – a few sheepskin tunics, a few crooks, wigs, beards, a couple of flutes and a tambourine. His repertoire consisted of only one or two plays at a time, performed on a low, improvised stage of planks which the company carried with them, in courtyards hired for the occasion that were freezing cold in winter and burning hot in summer. An old blanket pulled by cords served to hide dressing room and musicians alike.[4] Childhood memories are notoriously unreliable and we have no way of knowing how many times the two men saw Rueda's company in action. It is clear from what he says of rustic sketches and pastoral colloquies that Cervantes saw none of Rueda's more ambitious Italianate romantic drama. It is also clear that Rueda could, when required, put on more elaborate performances: he performed twice before the court, the first time in 1554 at Benavente, when Philip II stayed the night there on his way to England to marry Mary Tudor.[5] But, nonetheless, between them Cervantes and Rufo give what must have been a reasonably faithful picture of the ordinary diet that Rueda, and his contemporaries and disciples, served their audiences.

Since these men were in a sense 'jobbing' playwrights writing for immediate performance by their own companies, much of their material has not survived. What we know of Rueda's and Alonso de la Vega's work we owe to a fellow playwright, the enlightened Valencian printer Juan de Timoneda. He not only wrote for them himself – his *Comedia llamada Cornelia* (*Comedy called Cornelia*) is his best-known play – but did them the favour of publishing their own plays as well, clearly believing that the new popular drama was important enough to merit preservation. Thus three of Vega's were rescued for posterity, including the *Duquesa de la rosa* (*The Duchess of the Rose*), one of the first plays in Spain to adapt Bandello (Novelle II, 44). In the case of Rueda's younger contemporary and disciple, the enterprising Pedro Navarro, only one play, *La comedia de la marquesa de Saluzia*, based on Boccaccio's story of patient Griselda, has survived. A major source of inspiration for all three playwright-managers was Timoneda's own collection of versions of Italian stories, *El patrañuelo*, though other collections in Spanish were also available. By far the most important figure of this generation, however, is Rueda himself, both as playwright and theatrical manager.

Lope de Rueda (died c. 1565)

Rueda was a goldbeater by trade, but he was probably acting by the 1530s (it is thought he might have performed in Seville at Corpus Christi with an Italian company that visited the city in 1538) and by the early 1540s he was running his own company. Such was his success that in 1552 he settled in Valladolid at the request of the city council, which engaged to pay him an annual salary to write, perform and direct plays during Corpus festivities – surely one of the first municipal theatrical enterprises in Europe. Six years later he sought building permission for some houses, probably for use as a *corral de comedias* (theatre yard) since the site was certainly functioning as a playhouse a few years later. He travelled the country widely, performing religious and secular plays.[6]

His own literary production was not large – five *comedias*, five colloquies and a dozen or so comic sketches called *pasos*, apart from a few attributed pieces[7] – and was not distinguished for its originality even when new to Spanish audiences. Apart from one short verse play strongly reminiscent of Encina and Italian pastoral, with shepherds, unrequited lovers and guest appearances by Cupid and Diana, the *comedias* (*Los engañados* [*The Deceived*], *Medora*, *Armelina* and *Eufemia*) are in prose and all very similar. Three are heavily indebted to recently published Italian plays which themselves drew on the *novelle* and deal in the common currency of long-lost children, separated twins, and transvestite disguise, and the mistaken identities and other complications to which these give rise. The fourth, *Eufemia*, is, like *Cymbeline*, based on *novella* IX of Part II of the *Decameron*.[8] Structurally they are very weak: like their models they depict not a complete action but selected episodes in the unravelling of complications the full background to which is given in an initial *argumento* in the Italian fashion. Rueda cut down his source plots, themselves already thin, to intensify and speed up the action for performance, often leaving out important scenes in the process. That his intention first and last was to entertain is clear. Not only does he stress the diverting nature of the plays in his *argumentos* but he lards them with extra comic scenes and characters whose relevance to the plot is often marginal; many such scenes, indeed, are effectively self-contained *pasos*. This comedy, provided by stupid servants, sharp lackeys, foolish old men, gypsies, negresses, beatings and disguises, constitutes the principal business of the plays. There is no attempt to produce dramatic suspense or even surprise – the *argumento* ensures the audience knows too much from the start – and there is no indication that Rueda was even clearly aware of what was needed in structural terms for a dramatic intrigue: he divides the plays arbitrarily into scenes (six, eight or ten) which have no logic either in terms of length or plot. Everything is grist to the comic mill – mythology itself is not sacred, as we see in *Armelina* where Neptune and a Fury appear at the end as incongruous *dei ex machina*. It is hardly surprising, therefore, that it was in comic roles that Rueda – who as leader of his troupe would have had the pick of parts – chose to make his reputation as an actor. That his 'negress' was famous is evident from what Cervantes later said of him.[9] And the strength of these *comedias* does indeed lie in their robust humour. The most successful scenes tend to be the energetic comic episodes more or less extraneous to the action, the nonsense can be very funny (*Medora* is the best example) and the dialogue, as befits the Punch and Judy-type violence of emotion and incident, is lively and emphatic, often with special linguistic effects.

There is no need to linger long over Rueda's *Coloquios* of which two are mere fragments and one a short pastoral dialogue. The remaining two are effectively plays, though somewhat shorter than the *comedias*, with an *introito* and *argumento* but no scene divisions. They graft romantic comedy

on to pastoral, presenting foundling plots in humble rustic settings. They
are complete hybrids: fantasy, allegory and rustic humour bed down
together and shepherds, herdsmen, simpletons, barbers and negresses rub
shoulders with mythological figures, magicians and supernatural beings.
Rueda was quite clearly ready to exploit Renaissance literature and culture
without feeling in any way constrained or overawed by it, and herein lay in
part the secret of his commercial success. His *pasos* – the independent ones
and those embedded in his *comedias* – were, of course, of native stock,
building as they did on a long tradition of rustic farce. His long-term
reputation as a dramatist rests on them, because he took the comic sketch,
cast it into the prose of everyday speech, enlarged its comic range and then
passed it on to that master of the short farce, Cervantes himself. It is a genre
difficult to judge fairly on the printed page since so much of the play's
comic effectiveness relies on the performance, but their quality is very
variable. They are simple pieces which for the most part rely for their
humour on the tricks played on specific targets – a gullible simpleton, a
boaster, a stupid husband – and there is little sense that observations are
being made on human gullibility or stupidity as a whole. The aim is to
amuse and the appeal is direct and basic. The dialogue is not usually
particularly witty, some of the little plots are rather lame and the banter is
of the vaudeville variety. But they are emphatic and dynamic with a simple
coarse appeal and the repartee is vigorous and natural. *La carátula* (*The
Mask*) is probably the funniest independent farce, but by far the best is *Las
aceitunas* (*The Olives*), which gives a glimpse of a larger talent than most of
Rueda's other works suggest. The sketch is gently ironic, capturing human
absurdity very nicely in a vivid emblematic way.

Lope de Rueda's importance has in the past been somewhat misre-
presented. It would be idle to pretend that his plays have great literary or
artistic merit. His aim was simply to combine the sort of dramatic humour
already popular in Spain with elements from the fashionable Italian drama
to produce a commercially successful theatre. He never had any intention
of preserving his works for posterity – after his death they were revised and
published in 1567 by Juan de Timoneda. The enormous reputation Rueda
enjoyed in his own time was largely for his skill as an actor and his success as
a theatrical manager; those successors who called him a 'gran poeta', which
he certainly was not, were merely according him the automatic accolade
given at the time to successful playwrights. His contribution to the Spanish
theatre was not one of quality or originality but one of entrepreneurial
innovation and example. It was his whole enterprise and not the plays
themselves which proved influential. His emphasis on the actable and the

entertaining, his unfettered and irreverent exploitation of literary material, his combination of rustic farce and urban intrigue, his use of romantic plot ingredients, his recreation of truly popular speech, but above all his readiness to experiment and his desire to put his talents unreservedly at the service of the theatre-loving public – all these helped create a new sense of what theatre was and what paths it could take. Like Torres Naharro before him and Lope de Vega afterwards, Rueda thought of the theatre not in terms of rules and constraints, not as literature, but as a live and fluid interchange between stage and audience. It is a measure of the sweeping success of this new concept of theatre that within twenty-five years Lope de Vega, a 'gran poeta' as well as a great playwright, was able to pursue the same course without setting foot on a stage himself.

The Italian theatre companies

With Lope de Rueda and his generation, Spanish interest in Italian drama and literature generally was given new impetus. This interest was stimulated not only by the import of Italian texts and their publication in translations or adaptations, and by the contact made with Italian drama by Spanish residents in Italy, but by the arrival in Spain of Italian theatre companies. So important and far-reaching was their impact that it is essential not to view Rueda and his Spanish contemporaries in isolation from them. There had almost certainly been sporadic visits by Italian players in earlier decades but their influence on the Spanish drama seems to have been negligible. In September 1548, however, a company of Italians performed Ariosto's *i Suppositi* in Valladolid as part of the celebrations for the marrriage of Charles V's daughter, María, to his nephew, the future Emperor Maximilian. Thereafter, as a result probably of Prince Philip's visit to Spain's Italian possessions in 1548–9 and his early accession to the governorship in 1552, a number of Italian actor-managers were attracted to Spain by the prospect of rich, even royal patronage.[10] In the thirty or so years that followed (the last recorded Italian visit was in 1603) Spanish companies had to compete on their own ground with the Italian companies, including in due course, the *commedia dell'arte*, and it was probably these Italians who to a large extent helped fill the gap left in the commercial theatre by Rueda's death in the mid-1560s until the advent of Lope de Vega and the *comedia nueva*.

The impetus the Italians gave to the Spanish theatre in terms of material, presentation and organization must have been enormous from the early 1550s on. This was the period when the financial basis of the theatre underwent a permanent change and with it the very nature of the theatre itself. Earlier, Church, municipal and private commissions had been the crucial factor in the financing of performances. Now companies started charging systematically for entrance to performances, opening up the theatre to anyone who could afford it. The market potential of the new public theatre was soon recognized by the authorities who, from around 1568, granted monopolies on the performance of plays to *cofradías* (charitable brotherhoods) for the maintenance of hospitals for the poor. The *cofradías* received a share of the proceeds in return for the hire of the *corral* (the yard in which plays were performed), which was leased for this purpose from the owner by the brotherhood concerned. The first permanent theatres in Spain were established in the late 1570s and 1580s by the *cofradías* and even when the municipalities later on took over their administration the proceeds continued to be used for the charity hospitals. This connection between the theatre and charity might well have been initially an Italian influence, for in Italy theatre companies had for some time been compelled to give a percentage of their proceeds to charity.

The impact of the Italians can be gauged from the success of the first important actor-manager to tread the boards after Rueda – the earliest recorded actor to play the *zanni* (comic servant) Harlequin, Alberto Naseli. Naseli, or Ganassa as he called himself, arrived in Madrid in 1574, performed in Seville the following year, presented an *auto* before the royal family in 1579 and in 1581 took part in the wedding celebrations of the brother of the Duque del Infantado; in 1584 he played in one of Madrid's two new permanent theatres, the Corral del Príncipe. He performed, in other words, to the full spectrum of the Spanish theatre-loving public. Even his exorbitant fees, which got him into trouble with the authorities, did not deter Spaniards from flocking to see him; he later quipped that he had made his fortune 'corralling sheep'. The high proportion of ordinary people in his audiences prompted adverse criticism from contemporary commentators who saw the new public theatres as a threat to the common good and initiated what would become a campaign of opposition to the commercial stage which would last as long as the Golden-Age drama itself.

If Rueda had been an able entrepreneur, Ganassa was a master of the game. It was he who first requested and was given permission to put on plays on two working days each week, as well as the usual Sundays and feast days. Spanish companies then followed suit and soon even these restrictions were relaxed, though the worry that the theatre would keep people from their work occasionally led to a tightening up in some places. In February 1580 Ganassa gave eight performances in a row in Madrid before

Lent closed the theatres down as usual, and so did a Spanish manager, Juan Granados, almost on the same days – the theatre was ceasing to be a special occasion entertainment and was well on the way to being a permanent feature of daily life, its activities determined largely by public demand. Ganassa's six-month stay in Valladolid from March to September 1580, a stay at last terminated by the authorities because of the 'inconvenience' created, suggests a striking change in the pattern of supply and demand in the theatre. Hitherto travelling companies had moved on after a week to ten days and their activities therefore constituted little threat to the rhythm of city life.

Ganassa's contribution to the development of the playhouse itself was also important. After his arrival in Madrid in 1574, unused to the makeshift stages of the Spanish *corrales* he asked the Cofradía de la Pasión, whose *corral* he was renting, for a permanent stage with a roof and instructed that a removable canvas awning be provided to protect the audience. Not only did he give the *cofradía* some financial assistance but he also persuaded the *cofradía* to guarantee their tenancy by leasing it from its owner for nine to ten years. In 1582 he again gave an advance on his rent to help with the construction of the second of Madrid's permanent playhouses, the Corral del Príncipe (the first, the Corral de la Cruz, had been inaugurated in 1579 and completed the following year).

Inspired by Ganassa's success, a steady trickle of Italian companies visited Spain from the late 1570s. By now, however, the Spanish companies were beginning to rise to the challenge and competition for the market became fierce; in 1581, for example, when an Italian company and that of Jerónimo Velázquez coincided in Valladolid, the ensuing squabble was settled when the Cofradía de San José agreed to allow them to perform on alternate days.[11] Municipal authorities tended to favour the native companies and the language barrier inevitably caused problems (there is no record of the Italians ever having played in Spanish). Consequently, Italian companies were occasionally squeezed out. Nonetheless the very ferocity of the competition ensured that the Italians exerted an influence disproportionate to their numbers. They had something new and glamorous to sell and their Spanish rivals had to take notice in order to compete.

What did the Italians have to offer? It is thought that in addition to the religious *autos* they presented at Corpus Christi, the Italian companies drew on both classical and Renaissance drama, performing a mixed repertoire of tragedies, tragicomedies, romantic comedies and pastoral pieces, as well as plays in the new *commedia dell'arte* style. Thus they kept Italian and classical material to the forefront of attention, they popularized the comedy of intrigue and with their new style of improvised drama they introduced schematized situations and characters which were to have a marked effect on the *comedia nueva* of Lope de Vega. Their emphasis on language as well as action – their humour was the humour of wit and clever dialogue – was to pay rich dividends later on in the Spanish theatre which, devoid for the most part of scenic effects, depended on words to hold and inform its audience. Their carefully contrived plots provided an invaluable example of dramatic craftsmanship. Their *commedia dell'arte* masks and colourful costumes (Bottarga, the most famous Italian actor-manager after Ganassa, was particularly famous for his extravagant costumes as Pantaloon and gave the word *botarga*, clown, to the Spanish language) do not seem to have been taken up by the indigenous Spanish theatre, though they remained great favourites for celebrations and processions; but their combination of Italianate plots with Spanish music and song was one which did take root. Furthermore, they almost certainly introduced the idea of using professional actresses. Lope de Rueda's wife was a dancer but there is no evidence that she ever acted, and the Council of Castile's 1586 decree banning the public appearance of women on stage probably referred to singers and dancers. It is difficult to believe that actors' or actor-managers' wives were never used even if actresses were not hired specially,[12] but it remains the case that in 1587 an Italian company called *Los Confidentes* had to seek special permission for their women to act. The licence, when granted, stipulated not only that the actresses be married and that they were not to dress as men (a ruling promptly and thereafter consistently ignored) but that boys were no longer to dress as women. Actresses were obviously seen as representing the more normal of two evils, and thereafter became an established feature of the Spanish stage, apart from a short period in the 1590s after the Council of Castile changed its mind in 1596. In England and France, by contrast, it was not until the second half of the seventeenth century that women were licensed to act in public, and even in Italy, where women did appear on the stage in the second half of the sixteenth century, boys continued to play female roles into the 1620s and 1630s. Where the performances themselves were concerned, the Italians were limited by the simple structure of the *corral* stages – no front curtain, no backdrop or wings, no lighting – but they did introduce more sophisticated stage effects involving trap doors, machinery and noises off. It was their example that Rueda's successor, the innovatory actor-manager-playwright Pedro Navarro, followed in his use of such effects and also in his discarding of the beards until then standard for actors in Spain.[13] The influence of Italian designers and engineers in the subsequent development of the court theatre was to be as paramount in Spain as it was elsewhere in Europe.

The Italian example had important less tangible effects as well. In the Italian theatre of the day, a play was not just a script but a complete performance in which costumes, sets, effects and acrobatics were as important as words. In the *commedia dell'arte*, of course, the text itself disappears. This inevitably led to a downgrading of the importance of the playwright. This, together with the democratization of the Spanish theatre, must account to a large extent for the hostility expressed towards the popular theatre by cultured writers and theorists and for the equivocal feelings it evoked even in its practitioners, such as Lope de Vega. The transformation of drama into a commercial venture inevitably affected the whole business of being a playwright – the speed at which he wrote, how and what he wrote, what happened to his text when he sold it outright to the actor-manager who had commissioned or bought it and who might then lend or hire it out to a colleague,[14] the lack of copyright which later led to pirate printings – all these conditions determined the sort of drama that was produced and the state in which it has come down to us. A striking example is the way in which comedy assumes a dominant role from Rueda and the Italians on. It is admittedly comedy now with a wider register than hitherto and it becomes in time more sophisticated – Ganassa himself was credited with raising the standard of comic entertainment by suppressing the crude and obscene; but it persistently intrudes even in serious or tragic plays sufficiently to subvert the overall tone of the whole. This deliberate avoidance of the unadulteratedly solemn or gloomy in response to what was presumably seen as public demand helped determine the nature of the Golden-Age drama, creating an enduring taste for tragicomedy as opposed to tragedy and, in the early years, a disconcertingly ambiguous approach to material normally regarded as deadly serious.[15] Lope de Vega's eventual triumph was to be the reintroduction of art into this new business of writing custom-made plays for the commercial theatre.

The school drama

At this point mention must be made of a form of drama, hitherto scarcely alluded to, which also had its influence on the formation of Spain's national theatre – the school drama. Latin comedies had been performed in rhetoric classes in some universities from the early years of the sixteenth century: it seems to have been normal practice at Alcalá de Henares, Spain's centre of humanist studies, from its foundation in 1508.[16] At Salamanca University a statute of 1538 stipulated that a comedy by Plautus or Terence or a tragicomedy be presented at Corpus Christi and on the Sundays following, with a prize for the best performance.[17] With the establishment of the Jesuit schools in the 1540s this teaching aid was used much more systematically by the Jesuits in Spain, as elsewhere, for moral as well as rhetorical instruction and, probably, as a means of propaganda and recruitment.[18]

The school drama proper was custom-made drama, mainly in Latin, written by schoolmasters to meet this increased demand for actable material. Every course opened and closed with a performance, and performances were given as well on major feast days and saints' days, including those of local patron saints and the founder of the order, Ignatius de Loyola. This attracted local patronage and served to integrate the drama and hence the schools themselves, into the life of the community. Occasional performances by travelling companies apart, the school drama was the only theatre available to most people in the provinces and many dramatists received their first exposure to theatre in the Jesuit schools. Competition between Jesuit dramatists and others who wrote plays for religious festivals was keen,[19] for school plays were performed not only in the schools themselves but often in churches, in the open air in public places, or even at court, depending on the audience and the occasion. The municipalities sometimes subsidized more lavish performances and played a part in their organization, but at the other extreme parents often made or paid for costumes and the public lent clothes, jewels and other props. The audience varied with the venue: semi-literate audiences in the small towns of Castile, more select and worldly spectators – officials, nobles, men of letters – in the big prosperous towns of Andalusia, in Madrid aristocrats and royalty; and the level of sophistication, the amount of comic relief, the balance of Latin and vernacular dialogue and the use of, for example, mythology and allegory, varied with the audience. Nonetheless, generally speaking, the material remained essentially the same, with a strict adherence to accepted standards of morality and decency and the equally strict exclusion of the love intrigues already becoming so popular in the commercial theatre – in many school plays the only female roles were allegorical ones. The plays tended to be anti-Protestant, ideologically elitist celebrations of the struggle between good and evil, traditional virtues and the role of free will and grace. Their protagonists were martyrs, saints, national heroes or classical heroes or gods whose stories lent themselves to Christian teaching. Unlike the more purist French and Italian school dramas which followed and propagated the model of classical tragedy, the Spanish drama, like the German, made more concessions to public taste, tending towards tragicomedy and often mixing popular and cultured elements from classical drama, medieval didactic literature and allegory, pastoral, rustic farce, national history and popular festivity.

The first schoolmaster to fix the norms of this drama was P. Pedro Pablo Acevedo, twenty-five of whose sober plays survive for the period 1556–72.[20] Each play was preceded by a prologue recited first in Latin then in Spanish, a summary in Spanish was given at the beginning of each act and the entertaining interludes between the acts were all in Spanish. When appropriate, Spanish was also used in the text itself, for example in dialogue spoken by rustics. In time, in response to the growing sophistication of audiences fast becoming addicted to the commercial theatre, the drama became more complex and more action-packed, the use of Latin declined, the emphasis on entertainment grew – from 1566 even Acevedo's plays contained at least one song – until in the seventeenth century the influence of the court theatre produced in Madrid a school drama lavishly adorned with music, song and dance.[21] In 1640, for the centenary of the Order, the famous Italian stage engineer Cosme Lotti devised the elaborate stage effects for the performance of *Las glorias del mejor siglo* (*The Glories of the Best Age*) put on by the Colegio Imperial in Madrid.[22] In short, the school drama rapidly became a flexible drama which adapted readily to a wide public within the confines of the aims it set itself. It set an example early on of adaptability and variety within a given formula, of initiative in the use of a wide and heterogeneous range of source material, which the commercial theatre first learnt from and then later influenced in its turn. Furthermore, not only did it help prepare the public for the religious and doctrinal drama which was soon to flourish on the secular stage of the *corrales*, but, ironically, it helped create and educate an audience for the very commercial theatre which the Jesuits were to oppose so fiercely on moral grounds.

The literary expansion of the commercial theatre

The interest in drama generated by this widespread dramatic tradition in the Jesuit schools, and by the touring Italian companies, led in the late 1560s to the establishment of regular playhouses not only in Madrid but in the prosperous provincial capitals of Seville and Valencia. In all three the basic *corral* stage seems to have been in use from early on – that is, an apron stage at the end of the yard, almost certainly without painted scenery and with an entrance on either side (either doors or curtained openings). The windows and galleries of the surrounding buildings provided higher acting levels such as walls and battlements, there was probably a small inner stage at the back covered by a curtain for indoor scenes and 'discoveries', and a trap door. Machinery of a sort was an early innovation. Certainly this was the kind of stage that the Sevillian poet-dramatist Juan de la Cueva was writing for by the late 1570s. Between 1579 and 1581 his plays were performed by three different companies in three of the eight or nine playhouses by then in use in Seville.[23]

Juan de la Cueva (c. 1550–1610?)

Cueva is an interesting transitional figure in the development of the theatre at this time. Seville was an important centre not only of the school drama but of humanist learning and, as a young man, Cueva was one of many enthusiasts who frequented the informal but high-powered literary gatherings at the home of the renowned classical scholar and schoolteacher Juan de Mal Lara (1524–71).[24] He was exposed, therefore, to the classicizing tendencies of both humanist and Jesuit dramatists. Mal Lara himself, according to Cueva, wrote many plays in the classical mould, none of which has survived. Shaped as he was by these influences, however, Cueva's aim was to write plays for public performance. His theatre, therefore, is a compromise between his humanistic training and his theatrical instinct. A playwright of greater ambition than talent, he had a nose for the way the Spanish commercial theatre was to go, and it is he more than any other dramatist at this point who spans the gulf between literary drama and commercial stage, between the erudite and the popular traditions.

He was an experimental playwright who despised imitation and admired novelty and his plays suggested a number of significant new ways forward for the theatre. Whether any of the other dramatists of this period whose works have not survived were moving in the same direction it is impossible to tell. Cueva himself stated that Mal Lara had in some respects adapted ancient practice to contemporary taste – he does not explain how – but he also stated that the Sevillian dramatists as a group, including Mal Lara, observed the classical rules.[25] Cueva was neither the initiator nor *the* precursor of the *comedia nueva* – the influences on Lope de Vega were multiple – but an important precursor he certainly was. It would be unwise to claim any direct influence on Lope in view of the disappearance of so many contemporary texts and the fact that Cueva and Lope studiously ignored each other's existence in their writings on the drama. On the other hand it is inconceivable that Cueva was entirely unknown to Lope, who in the early 1600s became well-acquainted with Seville and its literary circles.[26] Personal or literary animosity might well explain the silence but, on Lope's part at least, so might virtual ignorance of Cueva's contribution; Cueva's plays had been published, but by the 1600s the memory of their performances must have faded. Contemporary references to dramatists, even by other dramatists, are not a reliable indicator of their relative importance: hearsay, reputation, the mutual massaging of egos, chance meetings, readings and viewings, an inevitably patchy knowledge of the drama's early, even recent, history, led to arbitrary mentions and capricious judgements.[27] Lope's failure to mention Cueva, therefore, cannot be taken as an indication that the *comedia nueva* owed him no debt.[28]

Cueva continued writing plays certainly into the 1590s but only the fourteen performed between 1579 and 1581 and first printed in 1582 have survived. Of these, four deal with episodes from national history or legend; three with classical subjects and the remaining seven with novelesque themes. Four are labelled *tragedias*, ten *comedias*. In fact his approach to genre and generic nomenclature, like that to the formal elements of the classical tenets, was cavalier, not least because the classical categories were not equal to the range of material he wished to treat. In his plays high- and low-born mingle promiscuously, the unity of time is blithely disregarded and the 'comedies' are often as grim and gory as the tragedies. The only consistent distinguishing feature is that in the tragedies the protagonist is high-born *and* ends up dead. When he came to write his *Ejemplar poético* (*Guide to Poets*) in 1606 Cueva suggested somewhat firmer criteria, along neo-Aristotelian lines, for the drama than his early plays would lead one to expect, but whether this reflected the practice of his later plays we cannot know. The tone of *Ejemplar poético* is in any case curiously timid and ambivalent. Cueva's support for the by then successful new drama is warm and unreserved and he is eager to present himself as a significant contributor to its, in his view, unrivalled inventiveness, wit and skill. Yet at the same time an intellectual nostalgia for a more ordered dramatic art form is detectable.

The claims he makes for himself as an innovator in his guide were, whether he knew it or not, only partly justified. He was not the first to depict gods and kings on stage (Encina and Torres Naharro were, and Lope de Rueda had depicted gods even on the commercial stage); he was not the first to call his acts *jornadas* (Torres Naharro again); and neither did he introduce the four-act play (Micael de Carvajal did in his *Tragedia llamada Josefina*); although he was probably instrumental in helping these practices take root in his own time. On the other hand he neglects to mention important lasting contributions which, wittingly or unwittingly, he did make. He was responsible for a major technical innovation which would become a lasting feature of the *comedia nueva* – polymetry, consistently mixing different metres of both Spanish and Italian provenance to suit different situations and characters.[29] He was the first playwright to exploit national history (including recent history) and legend systematically for his plots and to insert ballad fragments into his verse – both distinguishing characteristics of the *comedia nueva*. He was probably the first to introduce Seneca to the Spanish stage,[30] to dramatize a subject from Greek history, to exploit the theme of the sentimental Moor, to use the drama for political allegory,[31] to dramatize belief in the divine authority of kings, and to write a two-part play. He took a lead in breaking with past and recent practice, too, in presenting plays as self-contained representations of reality, employing neither the comic *introito* or prologue spoken before the action by one of the characters, nor the *argumento* designed to help the audience follow the plot.[32] The conviction that a play must stand on its own feet was part of his classical heritage, born of a conception of drama as a self-sufficient art form; but it also, significantly, indicates confidence in the audience's ability to accept the play on those terms. The practice of 'warming up' the audience would continue, but by means of a separate *loa* unconnected with the play itself. Technically the banishment from plot to side lines of all overt humorous pandering to the audience – such as the virtually disconnected comic scenes in Rueda's *comedias* – was a major advance. It freed the playwright of that part of his obligation to the audience and licensed concentration on other things, both of which helped the creation of plays of high literary and dramatic value for the popular market. The attention and good will of the more restless element in the audience would from now on be captured with *loas* and between-act farces and dances.

Attempts in recent years to direct attention away from Cueva's role as precursor towards the intrinsic merits of his work have met with only very partial success. He was not, it has to be said, a very accomplished craftsman. His sense of the dramatic was insecure, and as a result the narrative demands of his material sometimes escape his control, leading to badly integrated scenes and acts: the fourth act of Cueva's most popular play, *El saco de Roma* (*The Sack of Rome* – by the imperial army of Charles V in 1527) is a postscript of only 208 lines which merely ties up the ends of the story. Too often dramatic considerations yield to moral and thematic imperatives, while the dialogue has a tendency to the declamatory and wooden. He also lacked a sense of the modally and tonally appropriate and his promiscuous insertion into novelesque plays like *El infamador* (*The*

Defamer) and *El viejo enamorado* (*The Old Man in Love*) of furies, fates, gods, infernal shades, personified rivers, allegorical figures, magicians and sundry magical happenings, muddy the water of what otherwise could have been very effective urban intrigues.

However, it must also be said that he was no less gifted a playwright than most of his contemporaries, whose work is marred by many of the same flaws. Lope de Vega's own early plays are often a ragbag of motifs. Cueva does show some skill in handling epic material, his characters are occasionally if not normally well delineated, he can use dramatic irony to good effect and many of his acts have considerable dramatic power. Furthermore, his treatment of themes like the conflict between inclinations and morality or duty – *La libertad de Roma por Mucio Cevola* (*The Liberation of Rome by Mucius Scaevola*), *La muerte de Virginia y Appio Claudio* (*The Death of Virginia and Appius Claudius*), *La libertad de España por Bernardo del Carpio* (*The Liberation of Spain by Bernardo del Carpio*) – and the primacy in political affairs of justice, law and restraint – *La muerte del rey don Sancho y reto de Zamora* (*The Death of King Sancho and the Challenge of Zamora*) – are by no means without interest. For all the chaotic tendencies of his drama it has a strong intellectual and moral underpinning. And there are plays which stand out: *La Constancia de Arcelina* (*The Constancy of Arcelina*) for its attempt at psychological complexity and its interesting reversal of traditional gender roles; the hybrid *El infamador* for its unprincipled libertine protagonist;[33] *Virginia y Appio Claudio* for its good construction and its tragic force.

But Cueva's real importance lies, and will continue to lie, in his role as a creator of dramatic possibilities, as a playwright with the energy and vision to try to fuse the traditional with the humanistic,[34] to channel aristocratic Renaissance drama towards the popular stage. His talent was not up to the task, for he lacked precisely the synthesizing genius with which Lope de Vega would soon create a national drama out of a morass of disparate trends and traditions. But his imaginative expansion of the theatre's horizons constituted a crucial precedent which, if not a direct influence on Lope, was assimilated into current dramatic practice to help make the creation of a national theatre possible. Apart from his use of polymetry, Cueva's biggest single contribution was his catholic use of sources. Classical authors, medieval chronicles and ballads, Italian *novelle*, Renaissance romance, humanistic comedy, the *commedia dell'arte* – all lent themes, plots and characters. Many of these were to become part of the regular theatrical diet of the seventeenth-century theatre-goer – the conflict between duty and inclination, the claims of honour, the power of love, sexual harassment and victimization; national heroes (Cueva was the first to bring the Cid to the stage), spirited women, corrupt and manipulative servants, glamorized Moors, brave soldiers, heroines in masculine disguise. Some did not – lustful old men, Senecan horror (as in Cueva's two-part play *El príncipe tirano* (*The Tyrant Prince*), men in drag, the nasty 'come uppances' with which his plays of urban intrigue are larded,[35] the indiscriminate use of the supernatural, the mythical and the magical. But it was in the sheer willingness to exploit and experiment that the true example and value of Cueva's drama lay. This love of novelty and variety was to become one of the theatre's major driving forces. And while it is possible, even likely, that dramatists other than Cueva were responsible for this or that innovation, it is virtually inconceivable that a body of plays written by a single playwright and comparable to his in range and novelty could have just disappeared from sight. On the other hand, a sprinkling of mentions of anonymous plays now lost suggests that there was in the 1580s what one might call a Cueva school of dramatists, who followed him in seeking parallels in their own country's history and legends for the heroic and tragic tales of antiquity. The early publication of his plays would itself have promoted such a following. Certainly a Cueva-type tendency in the mid-1580s has to be posited to help account for the emergence shortly afterwards of Lope's new drama, a tendency, that is, to move away from the norms of literary drama without inhibition or reluctance.

The classicizing tragedians

The other trend of these years was in one sense to prove a dead end. This was represented by a group of playwrights whose ambitions for the Spanish stage were largely moulded by the achievements of classical tragedy, although they did not all limit themselves to writing tragedy. Classical tragedy had been introduced into Italy early in the sixteenth century by Trissino and Giraldi Cinthio, but Spain had been slow to follow their example. Some university scholars had tried their hand at translating Greek tragedies, and humanist interest in classical drama generally had been boosted by Robortello's commentary on Aristotle's *Poetics* (1548) and had then grown with the Jesuit school drama. As we have already seen, playwrights outside educational circles (Carvajal, Alonso de la Vega) occasionally produced plays they called tragedies. In the late 1570s and 1580s, however, there was a concerted erudite effort in Spain to cultivate the tragic mode, possibly as a result of the surge in interest in tragedy created by the translation of the *Poetics* into Italian in 1570.

Although not all by any means committed to a strict adherence to classical rules, these tragedians may be called 'classicizing' in that they shared the conviction that drama had to be subjected to some principles of art, principles which were necessarily classical in origin, and the belief that tragedy was the principal path to a Spanish drama of comparable importance to that of the classical past. For the most part, like Shakespeare and Cueva they took as their model not Greek tragedy but Seneca or, more accurately, a combination of Seneca and a debased Seneca imported from Italy mainly via the plays of Giraldi, who had made Seneca more palatable to Italian audiences by the addition of novelesque elements. The first of them was the most purist – the Galician Dominican Jerónimo Bermúdez (1530?–99), whose two 'primeras tragedias españolas', as he called them, were published in 1577.[36] In labelling them the first Spanish tragedies, Bermúdez presumably meant that they were the first original tragedies in the classical mould. They were certainly the first to be published.[37] *Nise Lastimosa* (*Piteous Nise*) and *Nise Laureada* (*Nise Triumphant*) have five acts, a chorus, a plot of Aristotle's simple kind and they observe the unities. They provoke terror rather than pity to promote their moral message of *vanitas mundi* and show a streak of independence only in their use of a subject from Portuguese history – the famous story of Inés de Castro, murdered for reasons of state at the instigation of her lover's father, King Alfonso IV, and later disinterred and crowned Queen of Portugal. For the most part, the other tragedians were all aware of the need to produce a tragedy in keeping with the times and therefore made concessions of some sort to 'la moderna costumbre'[38] – often taking mild liberties with the unities, reducing the number of acts to speed up the action and dispensing with obvious anachronisms like the chorus and, to a large extent, the supernatural. What they retained almost to a man was the Senecan emphasis on horror and obvious moralizing, and the consequential exclusion of humour. Murders, suicides, martyrdoms, visions, auguries, reported atrocities, are the common currency of their works. A. Hermenegildo names no fewer than fifteen tragedians of this period whose works have not survived.[39] Of the others the principal figures were the Valencian soldiers Andrés Rey de Artieda (1544–1613) and Cristóbal de Virués (1550–1609), the Aragonese courtier and poet Lupercio Leonardo de Argensola (1559–1613), the Salamancan Diego López de Castro (of uncertain dates), the Madrid poet and courtier Gabriel Lasso de la Vega (1569–1623?), and Miguel de Cervantes (1547–1616), also based in Madrid.[40]

Most of these men in the pursuit of their duties led mobile lives, but the geographical and professional range of this list is nonetheless an interesting indication of the breadth of the classicizing onslaught on the theatre. One of the main centres of impetus was that city with a long and rich tradition of religious drama, Valencia. In spite of the fact that the regular public theatre seems to have got off to a more promising start in Seville, Valencia, with only one playhouse and an annexe between 1584 and 1619,[41] was to produce far more dramatic talent immediately before and during the early years of the *comedia nueva*. Rueda and Alonso de la Vega's popular theatre with its emphasis on humour and romantic intrigue had had connections with Valencia through their friend Timoneda and through their stays in the city, and Artieda and Virués now introduced the city to tragedy, contributing to a broadening dramatic tradition that was before long to help nurture Lope de Vega himself. Both Artieda and Virués were soon to be pushed aside by the new drama and bitterly resented it,[42] but they retained the respect and admiration of that drama's practitioners. Both are good examples of the way in which even the classicizing tragedians, who would later complain of the facility, extravagance and independence from the rules of the national drama, were forced often reluctantly but inexorably to give way before the pressure of public preference.

Rey de Artieda's *Los amantes* (*The Lovers*), a tragedy in four acts published in 1581,[43] deals with a recent Spanish legend taken originally from the *Decameron* (4, viii) and has love for its theme.[44] It is only partially faithful to the unities, its characters are not high-born and it even has a witty servant reminiscent of the type of the *gracioso* soon to become so familiar in the *comedia nueva*. The play is a workmanlike piece. It is structurally rather clumsy and there is too much narrative, but the dialogue in shorter metres can be quite brisk and convincing and the play does present a real conflict of interests rather than a mere accumulation of effects. Its main interest lies in its attempt to make passion, rather than horror, the axis of tragic emotion.

Artieda wrote at least three other plays which have not survived, two of them with chivalric subjects which almost certainly were not tragedies, and he was clearly something of an experimenter. But even Virués, probably the most celebrated tragedian of his day, is increasingly being seen by critics as a transitional figure rather than as an incompetent tragedian or the failed promoter of a lost cause.[45] We have no certain chronology for his plays, written probably between the late 1570s and mid-1580s,[46] but they do seem to trace a pattern of increasing liberalization. His *Elisa Dido*, in five acts, represents the second (after Bermúdez's) and last attempt to write a Spanish tragedy 'in the old style', as Virués felt the need to define it when his plays were published in 1609. Written possibly at any time as an exercise in, or tribute to, a tradition he admired, its logical place artistically is at the beginning of his output. One of his models here was the Italian Trissino, whose plays were based on the Greeks, and the work has an un-Senecan restraint that he never repeated. His Dido is the chaste Dido of Justinian, a queen torn between her vow of chastity to the shade of her dead husband and her desire to save her people from a suitor who offers her marriage or war, and the play, for all its stiffness and slowness, makes the dilemma seem entirely convincing. It is by common consent the only play of the five he wrote which has a real tragic vision. For all that it has a sub-plot, *Elisa Dido* is indeed a tragedy on the classical model. By contrast, the play that was almost certainly his last, *La infelice Marcela* (*Unhappy Marcela*), is, for all its label of tragedy, to all intents and purposes a *comedia* in the style of Lope de Vega. In his attempt to provide tragedies for his time Virués, perhaps without even fully realizing it, had moved gradually into a different ethos, effectively into a new genre. The plot, which is based on episodes in Ariosto's *Orlando furioso*, could be straight out of Lope; it is complicated romantic intrigue with a shipwreck, bandits, love affairs, rivalries and misunderstandings. (This development of the intrigue, due largely to the theatre's mining of the *novelle* for source material, was the biggest single factor in the drama's evolution, in the 1570s and 1580s, towards the *comedia nueva*, involving as it did the inevitable abandonment of the unities of time and place.) Not only are two of the main characters, for the first time in Virués, not noble,[47] but much of the dialogue is in the traditional ballad metre that will become a favourite of the national theatre – eight-syllabled lines in alternate assonance; indeed it is the earliest example of its use in the drama that has come down to us.[48] The play's only, rather dubious, qualification for tragedy is that all the principal figures, including poor Marcela herself, end up dead.

This wholesale slaughter is Virués's hallmark. The spirit of excess stalks through all four of his three-act tragedies, scattering incest, licence, catastrophe and atrocity in a successful attempt to outdo Seneca that suggests on Virués's part, as on the part of his like-minded fellows, a crucial misreading of the requirements of drama, let alone tragedy. Even his use of intrigue can be overdone to the point of obscurity and collapse (*La cruel Casandra* [*Cruel Casandra*]). The piling up of horrors, however, was not in Virués merely a short cut to terror and pathos. Virués, who came from a cultured family, his father an eminent physician and friend of the humanist Luis Vives, was in his writings a severe moralist and didact, and his plays are bitter attacks on human wickedness and folly. Indeed, they might

better be viewed as political moralities than as tragedies.[49] He identified
love (or lust), ambition and fortune as the main obstacles in life and by the
depiction of vice and its punishment sought to exhort his audience to
virtue. It is an extreme form of instruction by negative example, of
education through catharsis: a Renaissance grafting on to Aristotelian
theory of Horace's principle of pleasure with profit.

We do not know when, where or to whom Virués's plays were performed. He spent much of his life in Italy and it has been suggested recently
that his plays were written for performance there.[50] However, his use of the
three-act format and of ballad metre, his mixture of Spanish and Italian
strophes, and his gradual inclusion of romantic and novelesque motifs
heavy with complications, surprise and suspense (all unclassical elements)
suggest that he had a popular Spanish audience at least partly in mind.
Certainly the pre-publication fame of his plays in Spain and his references
later on to their unpopularity with the public indicate that they were
performed there. Lope later attributed the introduction of the three-act
play to Virués,[51] as indeed did Virués himself, but the fact that the same
claim was also made *for* Artieda and *by* Cervantes shows again how careful
we have to be with these contemporary attributions. For all his eventual
rejection by the public, Virués did anticipate its tastes in other ways as well.
His predilection for outstanding women, good and bad but mainly bad[52]
(four out of the five plays have a woman's name in the title, a fashion taken
from Giraldi), his introduction of the subsequently popular if rather
bizarre type of the female bandit in *La infelice Marcela*, his use of the
titillating Italian device of the female page in *Atila furioso* (*Furious Attila*),
his investigation of the themes of power, passion and vengeance – all these
added to the rich compost which would feed the imagination of Lope de
Vega and his disciples. It was the recipe essentially, and not the ingredients, which was wrong for lasting success. Even in his most 'mixed'
tragedies Virués was trying to sell an already out-dated formula – Giraldi's
fusion of horror and intrigue – to a public that wanted something new and
entirely in keeping with its own time. Imitations, even updated imitations,
of an ages-old drama inspired by a different view of the human condition,
did not meet the need. Technically too staid and tonally too gloomy, too
severe and too pessimistic, it did not offer the Spaniards the vision of
themselves they wanted. There are moments of grandeur in Virués's plays,
and the verse can be vivid and powerful, especially when it treats of things
he had himself experienced, like the trauma of battle – he had fought at the
battle of Lepanto and, interestingly, never glorifies war. The basic material
of his plots was not at all antithetical to public taste; it all reoccurs in

different disguises in the *comedia nueva* and the source legend of *La gran Semíramis* (*Great Semiramis*) would be turned by Calderón later on into one of his greatest plays. But the ethos of Virués's drama and that of his fellow tragedians was not the optimistic, humorous, self-congratulatory ethos demanded by the mood of the moment and shortly to be supplied by the national theatre. It would take a far greater dramatic talent than any of these possessed to know how to please discriminating and undiscriminating alike and to educate the taste of the new Spanish theatre-going public in the cause of art.

Of the other tragedians of the time the closest to Virués in spirit was Argensola, whose *Alejandra* (nicely described as a combination of *Hamlet* and *Othello*)[53] and *Isabela* both end with a full flush of deaths and an empty stage in the best Virués manner. These two plays (together with *La Filis*, now lost) were probably written in the early 1580s when Argensola was still a student[54] and show some skill in the handling of plot and characters (particularly *Isabela*), though once again they depend too heavily on their cataclysmic endings for their status as tragedies. Cervantes later claimed in *Don Quixote* (chapter 48) that Argensola's three tragedies, in spite of their respect for the precepts, were not only successful in the theatre but extremely profitable and he went to some lengths to stress that they were enthusiastically received by discerning and undiscerning alike. However, Cervantes was by no means an unbiased observer and one imagines that had the plays indeed been that successful Argensola would not have stopped writing for the stage.

Of his own plays during these early years Cervantes also spoke favourably if ironically. In the prologue to his *Ocho comedias y ocho entremeses* (1615) he asserts he wrote twenty or thirty plays during the eighties (probably 1581–7), all of which were staged (in Madrid) and received 'without cucumbers or other missiles' and 'without whistles, shouts or uproar'. He claims to have reduced the number of acts from five to three and to have been the first to introduce personified abstractions into the theatre 'to the general and delighted applause of audiences' (neither claim is true of the drama but both are possibly true of the commercial stage). Subsequently, he says ruefully, he had other things to occupy him: 'I abandoned my pen and the theatre; and then appeared that monster of nature, the great Lope de Vega, and he made off with the theatrical crown.'[55] Cervantes later tried to resume his career as a dramatist but he never had another play performed. Cervantes might well have been inspired to venture into the theatre by Virués's example. On his way home in 1580 from five years of captivity in Algiers he stopped off in Valencia for a month to put his affairs in order and perhaps there saw a Virués play performed. Certainly he praises Virués as early as 1583 in his pastoral romance *La Galatea* (which was finished by late 1583 and published in 1585), making it clear, without specifically mentioning his plays, that he was familiar with Virués's disenchanted view of the world.

Like all serious, aspiring dramatists during the early to mid-1580s, Cervantes wrote at least one tragedy. *El cerco de Numancia* (*The Siege of Numantia*) is the most impressive tragedy the Spanish drama before Lope de Vega produced and one of the best in Spanish literature as a whole. The play has a slight Senecan cast to it (auguries, famine, mass suicide, a resurrection), but like Cueva (whom Cervantes also praises in *La Galatea*) Cervantes recognized the appeal of national legend, and chose as his subject the citizens of Numantia's heroic defence of their city against Scipio in 133 BC. Both this play and the only other that has survived from this period of Cervantes's career, *El trato de Argel* (*The Traffic of Algiers*), draw on a deep well of intense patriotism in the veteran of Lepanto which itself virtually guaranteed their success with contemporary audiences. Since then *Numancia* has been performed in Spain at moments of national crisis – during the Napoleonic wars and during the siege of Madrid in the Spanish Civil War with the Romans dressed as Italian fascists.[56] The tragedy, in four acts, has qualities which in the nineteenth century attracted the praise of Goethe, Schlegel and Schopenhauer. Its theme of patriotic heroism and self-sacrifice is handled with assurance and skill, the characters, Romans and Numantians alike, are convincingly human and the play has moments of truly tragic grandeur and pathos. But it suffers, like all Cervantes's plays, early and late, from an inability to create and sustain a properly paced full-length plot, to capture a world of complexity in that emblematic reduction of real space and time to theatrical space and time called a dramatic action.[57] The dialogue is often wooden, the action is too slow and stately and, like many contemporary plays, overweighted with characters. Furthermore, the cast list contains the personified abstractions – Spain, the river Duero, War, Disease, Hunger, Famine and Fame – of which he was so proud but which were for good reasons to find no permanent place on the commercial stage. Here they appear as commentators intended to give an epic dimension to the play and raise its emotional temperature. Clearly their rhetoric could work for an audience in particular historical circumstances, but outside such special conditions the rhetoric impedes rather than promotes the play's psychological impact, threatening to transform a powerful and moving human dilemma into a nationalist tract.

In *El trato de Argel*, a largely autobiographical dramatic documentary about slavery in Algiers (of compelling interest, obviously, to contemporary audiences), the personified abstractions Necessity and Opportunity, while representing an interesting experiment in the externalization of feelings and motives, are singularly out of place. Again some of the scenes work well enough, the dialogue on the whole here has suppleness and pace, and the play's themes are allowed to flow from the action; but there is once more that quintessential lack of a sense of what constitutes drama which explains why Cervantes's career as a dramatist came to a premature end. There is little in the way of conflict or climax, its concerns are mainly ideological and the ending, albeit uplifting, is dramatically a damp squib. Five years of real-life danger, hardship and anguish enough for ten plays[58] had been served up in insufficiently digested form as an episodic plot that limps earnestly along relying on exalted religious and nationalist sentiment for its effect.

Although Cervantes was one of those playwrights soon to be rejected by the public, it would not be wise, given the substantial number of his plays from these years now lost to us, to align him unreservedly with those dramatists whose work is distinctly pre-Lope in feel and form for all the concessions they made to modern taste. Close as he was in time to Cueva and Virués, Cervantes's output, if he did indeed write as many as twenty to thirty plays, must have overlapped with Lope's early work, and his references years later to those titles he can remember seem to reveal them as a mixed bunch of romantic intrigues and stirring dramas of contemporary history, many of which could easily have been close in spirit to the emerging *comedia nueva*. He even refers to one of them as a *comedia de capa y espada* (cape and sword play),[59] although the label itself did not achieve wide currency until later on. Nonetheless, Cervantes's subsequent criticisms of the *comedia nueva*, as well as his own failure to compete with it, clearly indicate that however willing he might have been to follow contemporary fashion in his choice of subjects, his technique was significantly different, influenced more by neo-classical notions of artistic propriety and restraint and less by the desire to give a wide playgoing public the entertainment it wished to see. Unlike Cueva but like Virués and the other tragedians, he was at best a reluctant and half-hearted swimmer with the tide of change.

The collapse of resistance to the new mood, of course, took different forms. In Gabriel Lasso de la Vega's tragedies, *La honra de Dido restaurada* (*Dido's Honour Restored*) and *La destrucción de Constantinople* (*The Fall of Constantinople*), published in 1587 in his *Romances y tragedias*, the usual atrocities and large cast lists reflect one trend still not quite dead, while the technical format – three acts, no chorus or unities, little narration, a chronological sequence of events – looks firmly to the future. As F. Ruiz Ramón has pointed out, the plays, for all their label and their obeisance to Seneca, are nearer to Lope's historical dramas than to classicizing tragedies.[60] The erosion of learned assumptions about and learned ambitions for the drama affected form as well as content, and the erudite drama was consequently a comparatively short-lived affair.

The emergence of the *comedia nueva*

The late 1570s and 1580s, therefore, witnessed a period of growth and change only partially monitored by the texts that have come down to us and what we know of their performance. In the mid- to late 1580s erudite tragedies, semi-erudite historical drama, the Italian *commedia dell'arte* and the emerging *comedia nueva* all competed for the favour of Spanish playgoers. It is fruitless, therefore, to conjecture overmuch about influences, to insist on according primacy to Cueva or Virués, to divide playwrights rigidly into partisan groups. All of those, from Cueva on, whom we have been looking at were reformers whose vision of a more or less erudite drama was to be unceremoniously discarded but whose practice at once revealed the very imperatives which were to swamp them and offered new fields of inspiration for exploration. They wrote in a period of transition and experiment and their common aim was to provide the theatre with an alternative to its haphazard popular diet of farce and largely imported romantic comedy, tragicomedy and novelesque intrigue – a dignified alternative which would recognize the claims of art, which would be formally and thematically ambitious and which would be morally instructive, humour being excluded, for the most part, as unworthy. Their efforts did not go entirely in vain by any means. By taking themselves and their art seriously, they established the idea that what was being performed in the *corrales* could aspire to being something more than mere entertainment. Their verse drama probably helped establish verse firmly as the medium of the Spanish drama; and their use of historical or legendary material and their treatment of serious moral concerns gave an air of respectability and solidity to the theatre which actor-managers were not slow to draw attention to when the *corrales* were attacked as being a disruptive and immoral influence.[61] Their problem was that they could not get the balance of art and amusement right. They wrote for an audience that did not really exist, hoping that their efforts would create one. They were young, or relatively young, men and the circumstances of the theatre's growth prevented their talents maturing because they seem to have wanted no part in the national theatre when it started to emerge. Those whose views we know were united in refusing to admit the *vulgo* (the people, with the pejorative sense of 'the common herd' or 'the mob') as the arbiter of dramatic taste and in contemptuously denouncing what they regarded as the stage's sell-out to commercialism. Virués stated that he set out to write for the knowledgeable and discriminating but that the 'vain mind of the common herd raised the sea against him'.[62] If Cervantes is anything to go by, the spurned playwrights blamed the entrepreneurs and middlemen of the theatrical world – the theatre-company managers and the actors – rather than the successful playwrights themselves, 'for since plays have become a commodity, they claim and they claim truthfully that the managers would not buy their plays were they not written in the usual way; and thus the poet tries to fit in with the requirements of the manager who is to pay him for his work.'[63] And they were partly right. As a result of the introduction of printing and the rise in literacy there had been an extraordinary expansion in prose fiction in the sixteenth century, but the level of literacy was still low and the theatre, accessible as it was to all, inevitably became the area where the commercialization of art and leisure took root most obviously and most powerfully in the major cities. In the earliest stages of the *comedia nueva* art was indeed sacrificed to profit. What the judgment, to save face, leaves out of the reckoning, however, is that without a catalyst the whole process would have been neither so sweeping nor so sudden. If there had not arrived on the scene a playwright of genius prepared to espouse the cause of a popular national theatre, the dramatic careers of men like Virués and Cervantes would have been more successful and the development of the Spanish drama substantially different. Lope de Vega took the theatre by storm in the mid-1580s not just because Spanish playgoers were eager for entertainment and he was prepared to give it to them, but because he was an incomparably better dramatist than any of his predecessors or contemporaries. Although the Spanish and Italian theatre companies had paved the way, it was he who effectively created, through the success of his plays, a public of a sort that had scarcely existed before – a large public of regular playgoers from all walks of life prepared to pay for their pleasure. Madrid, created capital in 1561, with an expanding population that would increase almost fivefold during Lope's career, provided him with all the raw material he needed.

His drama did not spring into being fully armed like Athena from the head of Zeus. He took what captured his fancy from popular and erudite drama, from rustic, religious and Renaissance traditions, from classical antiquity, Italy and Spain, and moulded these elements into a different and distinctive whole which exactly suited the spirit of the age, firing and fuelling the imaginations of audiences and fellow playwrights alike to form a prodigiously successful national theatre. At the beginning the recipe was by no means faultlessly executed and only with time, experience and chivvying from the theorists did the best results come. But it had a vitality and a panache, unlike anything that had gone before, which stemmed from two outstanding qualities which Lope possessed from the outset: an astonishingly fertile poetic gift and an infallible instinct for the stage – the ability to weld a dramatic action and its controlling ideas into a dynamic whole, never in practice haunted, as his erudite predecessors had been, by the ghosts of the classical past. Without the enormous expansion in dramatic activity in the sixteenth century and the growth of the commercial theatre there could have been no Lope de Vega, but without Lope there would have been no national drama. As Lope said in a letter to Antonio Hurtado de Mendoza, 'Necessity and I brought the theatre into fashion.'[64] The exact timing of the emergence of the *comedia nueva* is difficult to pinpoint. Lope probably started writing plays for the stage rather than for amusement around 1583. By 1585 Madrid had eclipsed the other theatrical capitals of Spain and by 1587–8 Lope was established as Madrid's leading playwright. In 1588 Juan de la Cueva observed that the tragic and comic had united to form a new genre and that Euripides and Terence, Plautus and Seneca were now all one.[65] The *comedia nueva*, a mixed drama that represented the culmination of a long, slow process of democratization of the Spanish drama since the days of Encina's court plays, had been born. In the 1590s a flourishing, well-organized national theatre which had a strong sense of its own identity and which was an integral part of the social and ideological life of the capital came fully into existence.

In considering the development of the drama and the birth and growth of the theatre I have drawn no direct lines of descent from Encina to Lope because, quite simply, such lines are impossible to draw given the state of our knowledge of the period; much of what was printed has been lost and much of what was written never saw print at all. Even were our information fuller, only tentative genetic relationships should perhaps be attempted, for the evolution of the drama must have been a largely haphazard affair, involving influences as often indirect as direct, as often unconscious as deliberate – the result of circumstances as disparate as a chance meeting, a direct suggestion or vague mention, a literary argument or a rambling discussion over a pitcher of wine, the desire to emulate a respected model or the need to write something by next week. New ideas can materialize out of thin air and old notions can be reinvented. Most inspiration is a combination of novelty and a rich mulch of influences experienced and forgotten. The greatest danger of trying to establish an evolutionary pattern lies in the in-built assumption that the evolution is *towards* something, which then inevitably provides the perspective from which what has gone before is judged. Thus if we look at sixteenth-century Spanish drama purely as the breeding ground for the *comedia nueva* we not only neglect much that is of interest and value but we run the risk of underestimating the confused complexity of the *comedia*'s background and origins.

Our understanding of what was going on in the Spanish drama immediately before or as Lope de Vega started writing for the stage is, as we have seen, still very inadequate. The old, romantic view that Lope broke with the past and created his own theatre virtually out of nothing but the stuff of his own genius has given way to a more realistic and objective assessment of his great debt to both popular and erudite strains in the dramatic tradition he inherited.[66] But the exact nature and working of that debt remains conjectural and controversial. It is clear that what Lope started doing he did better than anyone else; what is not at all clear is who, if anybody, was already doing it.

An important, possibly crucial, area of uncertainty concerns Valencian dramatists writing in the 1580s, not Artieda and Virués so much as a group of somewhat younger contemporaries until recently regarded simply as relatively minor members, for the most part, of the Lope school and often ignored or swiftly passed over in histories of the drama.[67] To a large extent the relationship between them and Lope was in all probability one of mutual influence; Lope visited Valencia in 1598 and 1617, the Valencians presumably turned up occasionally in the capital and the activities of the theatrical companies ensured that plays got around. But Lope first went to Valencia as early as 1588, when he was exiled from Castile for two years and from Madrid for a further eight years for libelling a former mistress and her family – Elena Osorio was the daughter of one of the most successful actor-managers of the day, Jerónimo Velázquez. After six months away with the Spanish Armada he spent the remainder of his two years' exile from Castile in Valencia, before leaving for Toledo to sit out the rest of his sentence. His choice of Valencia was entirely understandable. The city was a thriving commercial capital with a lively cultural life, close ties with Italy, a flourishing printing trade and, perhaps most important of all in view of Lope's developing interests, a rich dramatic tradition latterly being carried on by playwrights such as Artieda, Virués, Francisco Tárrega and probably

Gaspar de Aguilar. It was in Valencia that Lope, for good financial reasons, started working seriously and intensively for the stage, sending plays every two months to Madrid.[68] He had been writing plays since he was a youth and circumstantial evidence exists that works of his were being performed regularly in Madrid in the mid-1580s. But only one authentic, datable play has survived from this early period, *Los hechos de Garcilaso de la Vega y el moro Tarfe* (*The Deeds of Garcilaso de la Vega and the Moor Tarfe*, 1579–83?).[69] It is from the period 1588 on, when he was writing from Valencia, that his other earliest surviving plays date. The problem will be immediately apparent. Are we to assume that Lope brought with him to Valencia something recognizable as the new *comedia* and inspired the Valencians to emulation? Did he encounter it there, albeit in embryonic form? Or did he evolve it in that city, partly in response to what he found there? If the Valencians were indeed already cultivating something akin to the *comedia nueva*, was it because they had already been exposed to Lope's influence through visits to Madrid or by the travelling companies?

Unfortunately Lope's *Hechos de Garcilaso* does not throw much light on this. It is a patriotic, episodic historical drama in four acts with an allegorical character – Fame – and although based on a sixteenth-century ballad it does not use ballad metre. The dialogue and movement of the action have in places a pronounced Lope flair and it incorporates traditional poetry, but there is little typical of the *comedia nueva* about it. Indeed it smacks of Cueva and Cervantes. That the Valencians' work is recognizably close to Lope's is obvious from their traditional inclusion in the Lope school, but where do the initial debts really lie? Ought we, perhaps, to think in terms of an uninterrupted Valencian tradition from Artieda and Virués through Tárrega to Aguilar, Ricardo de Turia and Guillén de Castro, with the last four forming a subsidiary group within the mainstream of the *comedia nueva* which some of them were themselves instrumental in founding? The question is unanswerable, in spite of some recent attempts to answer it,[70] since the necessary chronological evidence just does not exist, but it is a question that has at least to be asked.

If there is any substance at all in the possibility, then the playwrights who would emerge as being responsible for the *comedia* are to some extent Virués himself but principally Tárrega, who has hitherto been consistently omitted from surveys of the theatre, but who was a notable figure in cultured circles in Valencia and a founder-member of the influential literary club the Academia de los nocturnos in 1591. Virués's *La infelice Marcela*, for all its label of tragedy, is very close in spirit to the *comedia nueva* as we saw. Tárrega's plays, which seem pretty run-of-the-mill if viewed as Lope imitations, seem quite accomplished if perceived as trail-blazers. Three-act comedies of romantic intrigue and adventure with a heavy debt to Italian literature, a generous dash of history and a sensational streak reminiscent of Virués – plays such as *El prado de Valencia* (*The Meadow of Valencia*), *La perseguida Amaltea* (*Persecuted Amaltea*) and *El cerco de Pavía y prisión del rey de Francia* (*The Siege of Pavia and Imprisonment of the King of France*) – they are technically quite adroit and have considerable vigour and pace. If the *comedia nueva* is to be laid at the feet of some known dramatist other than Lope, then that dramatist might well have to be Tárrega, for he was almost certainly writing plays in 1588–9 and probably before, but the facts are just not there to prove it. It is interesting at least and presumably significant, if not conclusive, that no contemporary of Tárrega's and Lope's ever suggested that Tárrega played a crucial role in the launching of the *comedia nueva*, even allowing for the probability that the exact nature of the new genre was at first only dimly perceived.[71] Lope himself seems never to have been in any doubt that the *comedia* was his (and he was not ungenerous in acknowledging the contributions of other playwrights) and Cueva's observation in Seville in 1588 that a new genre had materialized does not readily suggest a source as tangential as Valencia. There is evidence to show that plays by Lope were being performed in Seville and Granada in or by 1588,[72] and while by no means fully typical these plays by any standards are early examples of the *comedia nueva*.

All this confused uncertainty originates partly in dubious assumptions about the birth of the *comedia nueva* and a great deal more sense could be made of it by taking a less glamorized view of the whole process. There is a strong case for seeing the *comedia nueva* as a genre given impetus, definitive form and fashionability by Lope but at the same time as a genre which in the earliest stages evolved in different parts of the country simultaneously. The Valencians, after all, were as subject as Lope to the influence of all that was already going on in the *corrales*, schools and studies of Spain. With the establishment of the permanent playhouses the demand for actable material was growing and the public was making it abundantly clear what sort of drama it wanted. The success of the Italian companies and their influence on their Spanish rivals provided clear models to be followed and the work of Spain's more literary playwrights opened up further vistas of experimentation. The travelling companies ensured the circulation of new trends and ideas. In the circumstances it would have been extraordinary if only one playwright, however gifted, had followed the clearly marked path towards the *comedia nueva*. The three acts, the varied metres, the romantic plots, the mixing of high and low, comic and tragic, the emphasis on the humorous or lighthearted – all these features had emerged or were emerging, largely in response to public demand, and public demand guaranteed their adoption and continuation. The *comedia nueva* was not a theatrical package dreamed up by one man and then handed over as a gift to other playwrights. It was a crystallization of trends operating on a wide front which did not achieve a definitive identity until the mid- to late 1590s. Lope's early plays are still exploratory; they are structurally loose, they show a marked predilection for the fashionable literary modes of the sixteenth century – the chivalric, the epic, the pastoral – their character range is wide and eclectic and their humour is not centralized in the comic servant, the *gracioso*. In other words, the typical formula of the national drama – a formula essential to playwrights supplying a voracious theatrical market – developed over some years in response to the conditions in which the drama operated. Nonetheless, Lope's role was crucial. He may well have benefited from the Valencians' example, indeed may well have learnt from the inventiveness and metrical skill Tárrega was credited with by writers of the period;[73] he would have been as receptive to this influence as he was to any other. But all this does is expand the already generous list of formative influences that operated on him. It does not alter the fact that the *comedia nueva* in its typical, fully fledged form was his. It was he who stabilized the assumptions on which it was based, he who popularized it and gave it identity and status, and he who turned it into great theatre.

3

The *comedia*: some definitions and problems

In the 1580s the learned and popular strains of sixteenth-century Spanish drama merged to form the *comedia nueva*, or *comedia* as it came to be called, a genre which produced that comparatively rare thing, truly popular great art. Under the auspices of Lope de Vega, Spain's commercial theatre became probably the most successful theatre ever in terms of the number of plays written and the number of people, proportionate to population of course, who flocked to see them. From the late 1580s on, the two permanent playhouses in Madrid had each to be supplied with three or four plays a fortnight for much of the year, for a run-of-the-mill play only lasted about three to five performances and it was an exceptional one that lasted as long as twelve. Lope claimed to have written around 1,500 plays. In 1604 he actually listed the 448 he had up to that point written in his prose romance *El peregrino en su patria* (*The Pilgrim in His Own Land*).[1] His protégé Juan Pérez de Montalbán later put the number at 1,800 *comedias* and 400 *autos sacramentales*. Losses and misattributions make it extremely difficult to determine how prolific Lope really was, but his productivity was by any standards astounding. The authentic plays of certain provenance which have come down to us amount to 331; almost two hundred further extant plays are attributed to him of which twenty-seven are almost certainly his and seventy-three may be. A total of about 800 plays might be a realistic estimate.[2] Lope, however, was not the only dramatist driven to a prodigious rate of composition by the capital's voracious theatrical appetite. Tirso de Molina claimed more than four hundred plays, of which eighty survive, in spite of the fact that his dramatic career was cut short by his expulsion to a distant monastery of his order. Even Calderón, the consummate craftsman, wrote around 180 plays and 80 *autos*. Many minor playwrights were also extraordinarily prolific: Montalbán himself wrote over 150 plays, while even a now-forgotten dramatist like Alonso Remón, with five extant plays to his name, reputedly wrote well over 200 *comedias*.

It has been estimated that the total production of the seventeenth-century Spanish drama was in the region of 10,000 plays and 1,000 *autos*.[3] Even if this is an overestimate, it will be clear that, taking into account not only full-length plays and *autos sacramentales* but all the short dramatic pieces that accompanied them in performance, we are dealing with a phenomenon unequalled in the history of the stage, fascinating not only as theatre and as literature but as an extraordinary example of the interplay between market demand and supply. It will also be clear that such a drama presents almost insuperable problems for the literary critic and historian.

The Spanish theatre during this time was able to exploit a broad and rich seam of dramatic talent – three great dramatists, a clutch of very gifted runners-up and a host of craftsmen and poetasters of varying competence. But there was no way in which such massive productivity could have been possible without a basic formula to write to. This formula, evolved primarily by Lope, is readily characterized. The *comedia* is always in three acts and roughly 3,000 lines long (though Calderón's plays tend to be longer) and it is polymetric, with the stanza form chosen, generally speaking, to suit the situation. The range of subject is hugely varied, taken from history, legend, mythology, romance, town life, country life, the Bible, the lives of the saints, and virtually any permutation of these. Lope himself borrowed liberally from traditional lyrics and ballads, taking not only themes and motifs but snatches of verse or whole songs which he weaves skilfully into the fabric of his plots and often glosses. The neo-classical unities of time and place are rarely observed.

The immediate world of the *comedia* is characterized equally readily. In accordance with Aristotle's definition of drama as the imitation of an action, the emphasis is on plot rather than character and, significantly, few plays are named after individuals (compare Shakespeare). Almost every play, whatever else it may have in the way of distinguishing features, has at least one pair of lovers or potential lovers and some comic servants, the *graciosos*, who usually echo, sometimes parody, the words and antics of their employers; in rural settings the servants are replaced by comic rustics. Then there are 'complicating' characters: figures of authority such as fathers, husbands or brothers, or figures of subversion such as rivals, jealous suitors, enemies, even the Devil. Often there are representatives of law and order – dukes, princes, kings – who contribute in some way to the solution at the end. Each character is defined, at least initially, by social or biological role rather than by personality and cast lists tend to be stereotyped accordingly – young heroines, maids, young gallants and their friends, older men (fathers, uncles) and sundry servants, though in historical plays the range is inevitably wider. This is not to say that the *comedia* was not interested in characterization – many of its characters are shown to have complex motives and reactions to the pressures that affect them. The *comedia* does have characters torn by doubt and does dramatize internal crises. This is not common but fictional characters do not have to be beset by existential angst to seem convincingly three-dimensional. The heroines often appear in masculine disguise and older women are conspicuous by their absence. Both schematized characters and masculine dress for women were originally Italian imports.[4] Plots tend to be complicated, usually action-packed; as a result the events they depict are inevitably compressed, and accelerated. Emotions are correspondingly intense, even exaggerated. Love and honour are the two overriding matters of immediate concern. The tone is varied, with comedy and danger or disaster promiscuously rubbing shoulders. This mixture is capable of ending happily or tragically, but a tragic ending is the exception rather than the rule. As a result, the tragicomedy (for want of a better term) – usually a play heading for tragedy which is finally resolved in some satisfactory way – becomes a high art form in the Spanish theatre, not least because there is often a sting in its tail which compromises the satisfactory nature of the ending.

This formula, made necessary by market forces, represents in its detail as well an adjustment to the preferences of audiences and the circumstances of the contemporary theatre. The provision of humour, 'happy' endings, a strong love interest, dashing heroines in doublet and hose, exciting, accelerated action with little pause for reflection and heroic events, met the desire of the public for a theatre of escapism which would lead them out of the world of everyday reality into a world of romance. For like any popular literature of entertainment the Spanish drama is in a significant sense romantic or escapist; that is, it typically depicts protagonists who are able eventually to impose themselves upon the obstacles or difficulties which threaten their well-being and to win through to some satisfactory solution. In addition, there are good reasons for seeing the seventeenth-century Spaniard's predilection for a drama of optimism and exultant heroism as the outcome of his particular psycho-social circumstances.[5] At a time when Spanish military hegemony was beginning to yield to outside pressures and social tensions and economic decline started to gnaw at the vitals of Spain's self-confidence, the *corrales* responded with a national drama of epic achievement and individual self-assertion which allowed the Spaniard, when he gazed for a while into its mirror, to burnish his self-image and go away reassured.

The practicalities of theatrical organization, too, played their part in the formulaic nature of the drama. Plays were commissioned by companies of players and had to suit their needs and capabilities. The constitution of the companies no doubt evolved originally partly in response to the requirements of their material, but the pattern once established, they had to be supplied in their turn with suitable texts. Leading ladies (often actor-managers' wives) had to be given appropriately prominent roles, which goes some way to explaining the dominant role played by women in so many *comedias*. There had to be parts for older men, for comic actors, for supporting players. The non-appearance of mothers in the plays (the subject of solemn critical inquiry in the past) is probably due to no more sinister a confluence of reasons than the older woman's limited attraction for a predominantly male audience and the fact that in a theatre where generational conflict bulks large the only older characters necessary are those officially approved authority figures – fathers. The omission of mothers is originally a novelistic element inherited from Italian comedy,[6] but the persistent ignoring of her existence illustrates how far the theatre was shaped by practical imperatives.[7] Even the availability of props could determine the formula's variations: it has been plausibly suggested that a spate of lion plays might be explained by the fact that during this time some company had a tame lion or a lion skin at its disposal.[8]

It is important to realize that the formula developed by Lope as a sort of kit of characteristics and ingredients which worked for both dramatist and audience was basically an enabling device. Its genius resided in its elasticity, in the ease with which it could be imitated and adapted. It offered guidelines and at the same time variety and flexibility; it allowed speed *and* inventiveness; it could accommodate a whole range of situations, tones, moods and emphases and therefore enabled dramatists of diverse abilities and temperaments working within its parameters to make great and distinctive contributions of their own. Born in the *corrales*, it matured effortlessly later on into an elaborate court drama.

To describe the *comedia*'s formulaic identity, therefore, goes only part of the way to characterizing it fully. In the hands of its ablest practitioners it might better be described as a form of play whose structural principle is normally dramatic causality, whose unity, for all the dynamism of its action, tends to be thematic,[9] and which uses imagery as a major instrument of structural and thematic cohesion. It utilizes the love intrigue and the honour plot as popular strategies to dramatize a wide range of aspects of human behaviour and experience, and is committed above all to an exploration of the relationship between the individual and the society in which he lives. Its inner voice can be counter-factual (the play's sub-text operating against the facts of the plot) and its implications can be adversarial (counter to or critical of the values or expectations of its audience). It is a drama fascinated, in both serious and light-hearted plays, by the relationship between reality and pretence or illusion and therefore with role-play, assumed identities and plays within plays. It is self-conscious and often self-referring. Irony and language are the two principal ways in which holes are punched through the ideas the action seems to endorse. Most important of all to grasp is the fact that the *comedia* of the *corrales*, written for a stage without curtains, scenery, wings or lighting, was directed at the ear as much as or even more than at the eye. Lope, in his prologue to *Las almenas de Toro* (*The Battlements of Toro*) refers to having 'heard' a play of Guillén de Castro's and the phrase was normal usage at the time. Audiences, illiterate and literate alike, were accustomed to absorbing information by listening; it was for this reason that a public which could tolerate five or six-hour long sermons had to be gradually weaned to the idea of reading extended prose fiction by means of frequent digressions and interpolations to keep their interest alive. Not only was essential information (for example references to night to set the scene) conveyed orally but words would have to carry a weight of sustained responsibility for radical changes of scenic atmosphere, for example from martial exploits to rural calm. Furthermore linguistic subtleties and signals, which we who have lost much of that ability to listen might easily miss in performance, would have been picked up by a contemporary audience, particularly, of course, its educated and cultured element. We have it on Lope's own authority that theatre audiences loved plays on words.[10] With the text before us it is easier to listen to its words, and the more we listen the better we understand its complexities.[11] The technique of writing plays that move in strikingly different directions at once, with the action leading one way, the language bearing us off in another, is one of the *comedia*'s distinctive achievements. It was the way the playwrights reconciled their art with their livelihood.

What this latter description does, of course, is move the emphasis from the *comedia* as *theatre* to the comedia as *drama*, from its visible, formal characteristics to its inner movements and energies. Clearly the division is an artificial one, but the two-fold emphasis is necessary because the *comedia* presents a very real but unique problem. The formula as a highly successful promoter of productivity generated a drama whose sheer size swamps our perception of individual plays and colours our view of that drama's achievement. The *comedia*, therefore, must be seen in two distinct ways if we are to understand it properly.[12]

First the *comedia* has to be viewed historically as a genre, as a theatrical and social phenomenon involving numbers so huge that at first glance it can indeed look like the theatre of limited range, or repetitiveness and conformity, that some have claimed it to be. Its formulaic nature did impart a very strong family resemblance to all the Spanish plays written over a period of almost a hundred years. But it is only when we stand back and view the texts generically that their distinctive configurations become hazy and they begin to appear monolithic. When the plays are experienced and examined individually their variety and their multivalence become apparent.

Secondly, therefore, the drama must be viewed as a body of separate texts for performance, each of which must be evaluated in its own right, independently of the others. The process is an unsettling one for the literary historian for the best plays are always the least typical and the most resistant to the generalizations which have to be used in describing a theatre so vast. But the rewards are enormous. Calderón's three famous wife-murder plays, which have in the past been lumped together and read as if they were virtually the same play, then appear as highly distinctive creations. Even Lope's earlier plays yield up unexpected secrets. Shakespeare's comedies and his histories bear a family resemblance and acquire in the memory something of a shared identity, but they are not in consequence regarded as monotonous; the situation is the same with the *comedia* but on a much larger scale. Shakespeare, too, wrote for the popular stage and he, like Lope, was in his own day and for long after regarded as 'a happy imitator of Nature', an instinctive genius with his finger on the pulse of life who ignored art. The reassessment has been slower to come in Lope's case, largely because of the way perception of him has been obfuscated by his prodigious creativity, but he is now increasingly being shown to have been not only a 'monster of nature' but a great literary artist who could produce intricately crafted, multi-faceted and often tonally complex and ambiguous works. This is not to deny that there was an 'automatic' Lope, who wrote at times with his full powers only half-engaged. In view of the extraordinary nature of his writing life, this was inevitable. We cannot ignore these works of his for they are part of the social and cultural phenomenon that constituted the *comedia*. Given the numbers involved, the average quality of his dramatic writing is in fact remarkably high but in the last analysis we make our value judgements on the basis of those plays which reveal the heights he was capable of reaching. Had we been left with only his forty best plays, traditional perception of his qualities would have been very different.

The *comedia*'s double identity, as a generic phenomenon and as a body of individual texts, it must be emphasized, is not merely a matter of critical concern. This corporate identity very quickly became implicated in each play's individual identity from inception to reception. For as the *comedia* developed, conventions were established which not only authorized the effects subsequently used by Lope himself and by other dramatists but which conditioned the responses of audiences to them. Each *play* also had both a corporate and an individual identity, therefore, and its impact on its audience was compounded at once of its similarities to and its differences from previous plays and performances. Its differences, indeed, would have derived added force from familiarity with the composite norm. That the self-influencing nature of the *comedia* was acknowledged in its own day is clear from the remarks made on this topic by the playwright Ricardo de Turia in his defence of the new genre, *Apologético de las comedias españolas* (1616).[13]

If the status and recognized value of the *comedia* have been adversely affected by the distorting effects of its numbers, they have also fallen foul of the confusion and uncertainty created by its lack of clear generic divisions. There are two principal reasons for this. First is the use of the label *comedia* for both play (genre) and comedy (form). Spain is not alone in this, of course: both the French *comédie* and the Greek *komödie* can mean 'play', but the use of the term in seventeenth-century Spain was indiscriminate and caused confusion even at the time – a contemporary commentator, Cristóbal Suárez de Figueroa, called the situation 'a fine old headache'. Second is the stubborn unwillingness of Lope and his followers to produce plays which fitted snugly into the traditional categories of comedy and tragedy, or even into the recently developed hybrid category of tragi-comedy. Labels other than *comedia* were used by playwrights and printers but in an inconsistent, often even contradictory way.[14] And while there is no real contradiction in labelling a play both *tragedia* and *comedia*, given the latter's generic meaning, the simultaneous description of a work as both *tragedia* and *tragicomedia* does become baffling.

The reason for this apparent capriciousness is that the playwrights' awareness of, and residual allegiance to, existing genre divisions conflicted, if only in the area of nomenclature, with their total commitment to a new form of drama.[15] It is not just that the Spanish tragic plays are often significantly different from Greek, Shakespearean and French tragedy and indeed for this reason have in the past been denied for the most part the very label tragedy. It is not just that the comedies contain more of danger, threat and disaster than is perhaps popularly associated with comedy – comedy has always been a capacious form. The main problem is presented by the large body of plays which are neither tragedy nor comedy and which do not conveniently fit some other instantly recognizable category such as historical drama. The term *tragicomedia* was used in seventeenth-century Spain to designate a tragic play with a satisfactory ending or a light-hearted play with a tragic ending, and tragicomedy is the label resorted to still by many critics, not only for such plays as these but for those tragic plays to which they deny the status of tragedy. As we have seen, the term was used very inconsistently in seventeenth-century Spain and it is therefore fairly meaningless – an unhelpful pigeonhole for plays which do not fit anywhere else.[16] Spanish usage did not even fit exactly the definition of tragicomedy given by the Italian theorist of the controversial genre, Giambattista Guarini, whose *Il pastor fido e il compendio della poesia tragicomica* (1599) lent authority to the practice of the *comedia* but who himself insisted that tragicomedy must end in joy not punishment.[17] The trouble is that some of the best Spanish plays are in this indeterminate category and, as serious plays on serious themes which provoke 'grave silence' or 'speculative sadness' at their close,[18] the term tragicomedy is singularly inadequate and misleading.

It is not a problem peculiar to the Spanish drama. In 1963 Lionel Abel identified a type of play which while not a tragedy possessed comparable philosophic stature and should therefore be recognized and named. His chosen designation was 'metaplay'. Into this category he placed a number of masterpieces from the past (including some from seventeenth-century Spain), many contemporary works and – since tragedy is difficult, if not impossible, for the modern imagination according to his strict, Greek-based definition of the genre – 'the plays which will occupy us in the future'. But the problem does assume serious proportions in the history of the Spanish drama because so many outstanding plays are involved and because the Spanish seventeenth-century theatre was generally far less constrained by generic difference. Even Abel's metatheatre, the two basic premises of which are that the world is a stage and life is a dream, is inadequate for the varieties of serious drama produced in Spain.

In dedicating himself to a naturalistic theatre that ignored the rigid shaping of art, Lope embarked on a mixed drama which by definition resisted the tidy orderings of old labels. The *comedia* was an original and distinctive creation compounded of variable but inseparable proportions of light and dark and susceptible of a comic or a tragic outcome, and its supplantation of all other forms of full-length play in a way made other terms redundant. At the same time the equation of the word for comedy with the word for play does also reflect, at least in part, the normative triumph in the drama of comedy as opposed to tragedy, of optimism as opposed to pessimism, if only at the surface level of the plot. Comedy has always been a more mixed, capacious and less specific genre than tragedy; furthermore it has great popular appeal and in the Golden-Age drama is certainly quantitatively dominant. Even so, the use of the verse traditionally associated with tragedy rather than the prose of comedy for all full-length plays without exception, is an indication of just how thoroughly mixed a drama it was; it also reveals Lope's ambitions for the *comedia* despite its popular orientation.

The greatest single consequence of the *comedia*'s identity as a unified but protean genre is the absence of tragedy as an autonomous form obeying its own rules. As a result, it has often been claimed, the Golden-Age drama is a drama without true tragedies. The charge is significant because it is the existence or non-existence of tragedy which has tended to be the criterion for great drama. To assert that the seventeenth-century Spanish theatre has few, even no tragedies is therefore effectively to downgrade it. Two responses suggest themselves: why privilege tragedy? and what is true tragedy anyway? These are self-evidently questions of huge scope and general import which cannot be answered here, but they are highly relevant to our view of the Spanish theatre and a few observations are therefore appropriate.

There seems in fact to be no good reason why great plays which engage with serious issues in the life of man should be intrinsically less great than great tragedies, just because they do not conform to certain formal requirements or to a specific vision of the human condition. Plays to be great must clearly move or otherwise affect us, but why should the nature of that emotion be prescribed? Life in any case runs its course on the whole somewhere between the tragic and the comic, so the privileging of tragedy is not a consequence of its greater relevance to man. Tragic endings are no more realistic than happy ones – life deals out both. Have we therefore perhaps been culturally brainwashed to accept these comparative values, to regard tragedy and its cathartic function as sublime, oblivious to the fact that their effect is indeed perhaps to reinforce the status quo, as Brecht suggested? The philosophy behind Greek tragedy is a philosophy of impotence. Conversely, perhaps comedy has been downgraded precisely because it is subversive. The huge upheavals of tragedy have to end in destruction to attain release and the hope of new beginnings, but the milder upheavals of comedy and its accommodations suggest alternative, perfectly valid, if unruly, forms of living. Which, therefore, is the more truly disturbing?

Dissatisfaction with the idea of tragedy as described by Aristotle on the basis of the only body of tragic plays known to him, plays linked directly to a specific view of the universe and man's place in it, has led to generally acceptable adjustments in the genre from Seneca onwards,[19] in spite of the fact that *Macbeth* is still regarded by purists as Shakespeare's only real tragedy.[20] These adjustments, it must now be recognized, include the adaptations of the Spaniards, who taking Seneca's violent, moralizing tragedies as their basic model produced tragic plays for their own time. Rather than judging plays by a narrow, exclusive definition of tragedy and banning from its sacred purlieus the majority which do not qualify, it is surely legitimate to allow our responses to a play to dictate to us whether it is a tragedy or not, and to re-establish our definition accordingly. Better, after all, to 'lose a definition rather than a tragedy'.[21] The only alternative is to restrict the use of the label to the Greek originals themselves and those plays modelled exactly on them, which would be a great impoverishment of dramatic nomenclature. Comedy is persecuted by no such rigidity (entirely because Aristotle's extended discussion of comedy did not survive to inhibit future generations), so it seems illogical not to legitimize the same generosity for tragedy. Recent common-sense efforts to do so have produced common denominator definitions of tragedy which do embrace a significant number of seventeenth-century Spanish plays, for example Geoffrey Brereton's endorsement of the common understanding of a human tragedy as 'a final and impressive disaster due to an unforeseen or unrealized failure involving people who command respect and sympathy'.[22] If we ignore formal requirements and take the essence of tragic feeling as that 'paradoxical continuation of a fearful sense of rightness (the hero must fall) and a pitying sense of wrongness (it is too bad that he falls)',[23] then again there are Spanish tragedies.

This is not to deny that the popular nature of the Spanish theatre and the particular ethos of the Spanish society of the day militated against tragedy or, more specifically, unequivocally tragic endings. They clearly did. Lope may have been himself temperamentally predisposed away from tragedy but some of his plays reveal him to have had a fine tragic sense. Yet it was not a sense he indulged very often and the popular imperatives of the *corrales* must have played their part in this. Nevertheless, there are, contrary to traditional wisdom, some very fine tragedies in the Spanish drama – plays that deal with the misfortunes and ultimately disasters which befall human beings worthy of our compassion who are incapable of avoiding destruction (that of their lives or of their happiness and well-being – even Aristotle did not insist on the death of the protagonist) and whose fate is therefore inevitable. Disconcertingly a number of them have dualistic endings which represent at the surface level of the plot an accommodation to the public's desire to see the hero triumph,[24] which is why their tragic nature has in the past been overlooked. The destruction of the protagonist's well-being is strongly implied in these plays but not explicit. Some tragedies were given that label in their own time. Eleven of Lope's plays were called tragedies by him or by his contemporaries and these conform closely to the essential requirements for tragedy as he conservatively understood the term – lofty characters, great and terrible events, a great fall, historical or at least not invented subject matter, deeds of violence and an elevated style – although the tragic stature of some of them has even so proved controversial.[25] Others were denied the name of tragedy because they did not conform closely to the prescriptions of Aristotle and his Renaissance interpreters – the term tragedy was understood conservatively and used sparingly in England as well – but nonetheless fall squarely within my working definition of tragedy given above. We sense them to be tragedies, we react to them as tragedies and it seems only sensible to call them tragedies. If the tragic plays of Ibsen, Strindberg, Synge, O'Neill, O'Casey, Eliot, Lorca, Tennessee Williams and Miller can be called tragedies then we can certainly include those of the Spanish seventeenth-century playwrights. What they were doing was experimenting more radically than playwrights elsewhere with the tragic mode, and they made some major departures: the apparent dislocation of tragic focus (the apparently triumphant executioner can also be seen as the tragic protagonist) or its extension (arguably no single tragic victim), the fracturing of tragic responsibility, the often uncathartic ending. The tragic status of such plays has been revealed as part of a radical reassessment in recent decades of the seventeenth-century Spanish drama and its procedures.

The old *canard* that there can be no tragedy within the context of Christian belief now commands less allegiance than it used to. There are splendid plays of tragic force in the seventeenth-century Spanish theatre which can be seen as resolving themselves into non-tragic endings with an implicit or explicit Christian message (Tirso's *El burlador de Sevilla* and *El condenado por desconfiado*, Calderón's *El príncipe constante, La vida es sueño, El alcalde de Zalamea, La devoción de la cruz*). But there are others (some of the wife-murder plays, for example) which end in a human desolation for which no real comfort on this earth is offered, which reject the balm of catharsis and the glimpse of hopeful new beginnings. As Helen Gardner pointed out, tragedy deals with the fate of human beings in this world; the fact that the heroes of Greek tragedy were apotheosized in no way attenuated the impact of their downfall.[26] Clearly tragedy produced in a Christian context is going to be very different both from that of the Greeks and from the not so dissimilar tragic vision of much modern philosophy, and there is no reason to suppose that all tragedies must share the same view of the human condition. The drama of the Golden Age is deeply imbued with irony, ambiguity and conflict and with a painful awareness of the complexities of human life and behaviour. Its tragic sense therefore resists monolithic unities and tragic certainties. The singleness of vision found in Greek tragedy and even in the modern view of man's powerlessness in his cosmic setting[27] is impossible in a world where the individual is believed to have a God-given free will, yet that free will is circumscribed not only by his human frailty and the workings of Providence but by his social identity: the *comedia*'s tragic protagonist typically creates his own tragic dilemma.[28] The *comedia*'s unequivocal commitment to the pulse of life in its own time is at the root of its dissatisfaction with neo-Aristotelian tragedy.[29]

Adaptations of classical tragedy were attempted, sometimes very successfully (for example, Calderón's *La hija del aire* [*Daughter of the Air*]) but many of the Spanish theatre's memorable tragedies are those which are faithful only to the presumptions of the *comedia* form and to their author's own inspiration. The results can be immensely powerful and very disturbing. Calderón was much more disposed to see the serious side of life than Lope and the other dramatists and it is mainly though by no means exclusively around his plays that recent attempts to define and evaluate the seventeenth-century Spanish theatre's contribution to tragedy have revolved. The most influential has been A. A. Parker's argument that Calderón developed a consistent and distinctive tragic vision based on the idea of diffused responsibility for human suffering.[30] Lately the relationship between tragedy and the *comedia* has been illuminated by the claim that some of Calderón's tragic plays constitute a contemporary Baroque tragedy which springs from the warping or alienation of the movements of comedy.[31] In this respect it is interesting that Calderón, unlike Lope, seems not to have bothered with the label 'tragedy' but got on instead with writing *comedias* which incorporated his tragic view of man's condition.

In the face of the expanding tragic horizons of the Golden-Age drama it would be inappropriate to argue here for the tragic status of particular plays. I shall take it for granted that the possibilities for tragedy are indeed wide and that the 'problem' of Spanish Golden-Age tragedy is rapidly ceasing to be one. I shall therefore use the term where I feel it to be suitable or helpful in the discussion of individual playwrights and works.

4

Lope de Vega

The son of an embroiderer, Félix Lope de Vega Carpio (1562–1635)[1] was that rare thing in his day – a professional writer. After a few years at the University of Alcalá he set himself to earn his living writing for the theatre, supplementing his income at times by the secretarial duties he performed for a succession of nobles, latterly the Duke of Sessa who became a life-long admirer and patron. Writing for Lope, however, was not merely a profession but a compulsion. He tried his hand at most of the fashionable literary genres – prose and verse, history and fiction, epic, pastoral, allegory, contemplative and burlesque. Amongst the most notable of these works are his pastoral romance *La Arcadia* (1598), his 22,000-line imitation of Tasso's *Gerusalemme Liberata*, *La Jerusalén conquistada* (1608), a brilliantly original 2,800 line burlesque poem about the loves and adventures of a cat, *La Gatomaquia* (1634), which is a parody of Italian epic, and his best prose work, *La Dorotea* (1632), a largely autobiographical novel in dialogue form. The theatre apart, however, Lope's greatest gift was for lyrical poetry. Essentially an extrovert impelled to exteriorize his feelings, poetry was his outlet, his safety valve. His every crisis, his every significant experience, became the stuff of poetic experience and he left behind him in his ballads, sonnets, eclogues, epistles and elegies a register of psychological and emotional experience that is possibly unique. He introduced into cultured poetry in Spain a greater sense of the realities of love and living than had hitherto been allowed by the courtly and neo-platonic conventions, and was responsible for the revival of interest in Spain's popular poetic tradition towards the end of the sixteenth century after decades of fashionable dedication to Italian metres and themes. Much of his most exquisite verse is in this traditional vein.

This compulsion to write verse was what made his drama possible. His freakish facility for it became a legend even in an age when the ability to versify was an accomplishment expected of everyone with pretensions to culture. For him verse came almost as naturally as prose does to most other writers. Even on board ship to England with the Armada he wrote over a thousand lines of *La hermosura de Angélica* (*The Beauty of Angelica*), based on Ariosto's *Orlando furioso*.

The briefest biography – imprisonment and exile for libel, two wives, three long-term mistresses, innumerable affairs, fourteen children (of whom only four survived to maturity), a position as familiar of the Inquisition, another as love-letter writer to the Duke of Sessa, and finally the priesthood concurrent with his last mistress, Marta de Nevares, and their child – gives some indication not only of the gargantuan appetite for life of this extraordinary man, but also of the tempestuous tensions and contradictions that informed his character and therefore his writing. An unregenerate womanizer tied irrevocably to the demands of the flesh, he was at the same time a sincerely devout man attracted relentlessly to the orthodox spirituality that Spain, since the Council of Trent, had made its heritage. With his sacrilegious last affair this conflict reached crisis point as he pursued his liaison in defiance of public opinion, but his religious poetry throughout his life is racked with remorse. It is a remarkable poetry, rooted in the sadness of the flesh, with a tenderness and passion as strong as any to be found in his love poetry. For all the spontaneity and openness of his writing Lope was, therefore, a very complicated human being. A man of intense passions, impetuous, sometimes silly and often irresponsible, he was capable of great loyalty, sensitivity and honesty. His infatuation for Marta survived the loss of her sight and reason, and when she died his poetry screamed his anguish.

Acutely aware of the tensions in his own nature Lope was further sensitized to life's contradictions by its treatment of him. Acknowledged as a genius in his lifetime, he was a charismatic national hero whose picture hung in every house and whose very name became a synonym for excellence on the grand scale; when he died his funeral obsequies lasted nine days. On the other hand, his humble origins, aided and abetted by his scandalous life, ensured that he never became a regular court dramatist and never attracted patronage from within the court's narrow confines. Mingling with the rich and the great but never of them, Lope felt insecure enough to devise a family escutcheon with no fewer than sixteen towers and to pretend to an erudition he did not possess, exposing himself on both counts to the derision of his enemies. Eager for respectability, social and literary, stronger compulsions always pulled him away. The tug-of-war can be seen in his drama, for, totally committed as he was to the *comedia* he launched and popularized, he could never quite shake off his respect for classical theory, which explains his apologetic often contradictory excuses for his own practice. The circumstances of his life and work nurtured in him complex and ambivalent responses to many aspects of the world he lived in. Not a man of intellectual or philosophical bent, he took for granted the larger, transcendental patterns of seventeenth-century belief, but he approached man's passions and problems, his human and social identity, with a deep compassion and a keen sense of irony born of the irreconcilable contradictions in his own nature. His life and his work show the impulse to self-expression and self-fulfilment triumphing over the pull of orthodoxy and convention. The opposing claims made on him by the urge to rebel, to innovate, to follow his instincts, on the one hand and the need to conform on the other, equipped him perfectly for his task of creating a commercial drama which had to contend with the requirements of audiences, theatrical companies, censors and critics, but which nevertheless breathed an energy and an excitement unmistakably his.

The plays[2]

I shall look first at Lope's three famous socio-political plays about peasant honour, not just because they figure amongst his most memorable works but because they provide an excellent example of his formula of variety within a pattern of proven theatrical success. Written over a span of some eighteen years in Lope's mature period, they reveal a continuing interest on his part in that subject which so obsessed seventeenth-century Europe – power. The theme of all three is the democratization of honour perceived in terms of class conflict and dramatized in terms of sexual aggression. All three have some degree of historical underpinning. All three at the same time reflect the powerful nostalgia for a highly idealized country life felt by an increasingly urban society, a nostalgia to which the thoroughly urbanized Lope was particularly susceptible. All three follow the tragi-comic pattern of harmony–discord–harmony of so many of Lope's plays. For all this, they are strikingly different creations.

The earliest, *Peribáñez y el Comendador de Ocaña* (*Peribáñez and the Commander of Ocaña*),[3] set in the fifteenth century, portrays the idyllic marriage and life together of the prosperous and ambitious young peasant Peribáñez and his lovely bride Casilda, and the attempts made by their overlord to seduce her. When Casilda remains impervious to his blandishments, the Commander makes Peribáñez a captain and sends him off to fight the king's war. He enters his house at night intending to take Casilda by force if necessary, but aware by now of his intentions Peribáñez returns

in time to prevent the rape of Casilda and the destruction of their lives by
killing his lord. His action is subsequently pardoned though not condoned
by the King, he is given a full captaincy and sent off to fight in the Granada
campaign.

The play, which is unusual in having a single plot, is about many things –
about true love and the trust it engenders, about the wholesome joys of
country life, about false ideas of honour and nobility, about the abuse of
power and privilege, about the right of every man of integrity to the respect
of others regardless of class, about the relationship between law and justice,
between individual and society, about the power of passion to destroy. It is
the story not of one but two young men whose happiness and well-being are
threatened, one from without, the other from within. One rises to the
occasion and, despite some initial mistakes, by dint of prudence and good
judgement asserts himself over the circumstances which threaten him,
while the other shows himself to lack the moral resources necessary to bring
under control the irrational passion which threatens what it claims to love.

It is rich in imagery which creates the joyous world of marital love in a
bountiful nature that is the play's special dimension but which also feeds
and develops the play's various themes and motifs, binding present events
and actions to their future consequences. It is a play of telling visual,
structural and thematic parallels, most strikingly between the Commander's almost lifeless figure after falling from his horse while fighting the bull
during the wedding festivities at the beginning, and his soon-to-be lifeless
body after passion has destroyed him at the end; the play's larger
movement and its ending are prefigured iconographically in the very first
scene. It is a play of great visual contrast between nobles and rustics,
peasantry and soldiery, imagined always in their clothes and trappings. It is
a play rich in the variety of its mood and tones, from the tender intimacy of
the young couple's life of harmony and simple plenty, of embraces in the
manger and quietly bubbling garlic and onion stew, to the splendour of the
court, from the joy of love and life to the sombre ugliness of aggression and
deceit. It is a play laden with dramatic irony where tension is skilfully built
up by means of a series of opposites – peasant/noble, true love/destructive
passion, harmony/discord – and then cunningly delayed. It is a play of
powerful dramatic conflict, considerable tragic force and intense lyricism,
its progress punctuated by songs which are themselves tightly integrated
into the development of mood and theme.

Its major source of excitement and suspense for a contemporary audience
would undoubtedly have been the confrontation between two apparently
hopelessly unequal adversaries – the social distance between them and the

Commander's power over Peribáñez, for all the latter's prosperity, are emphasized visually and aurally throughout. Peribáñez cannot act against his lord and yet he has to – self-preservation and his good name demand it. The question is, how is this impasse to be resolved? Lope's strategy is an interesting one. When the Commander makes Peribáñez a captain, he is really mocking the peasant he thinks he is deceiving in sending him off at the head of a band of men ill-equipped for and unused to war. The stage direction spells this out: 'Enter a company of peasants, comically armed' (2210). The dramatic irony is heavy here, for the Commander's assumption that he can trick Peribáñez in this way is rooted in his perception of the social difference between them. His social contempt for the peasant automatically unmans Peribáñez in his eyes. Peribáñez, however, sees through the charade and exploits it. Having spared no expense in rigging himself out for his new role, he obtains an admission from the Commander that he now looks the captain (emphasizing once again the importance of dress in assumptions about status and identity) and asks him to gird on his sword for him. The Commander has been outmanoeuvred: Peribáñez has exploited the Commander's eagerness to get him out of the way to have himself made a gentleman, making it possible, should the Commander betray the promise Peribáñez extracts from him to look after his honour and his wife, to seek redress as an equal. The Commander sees Peribáñez's ennoblement as the farce he intends it to be; but farce or no, it frees Peribáñez psychologically from his position of subservience and enables him to act. He himself recognizes the change in himself now that he is dressed like a gentleman and wears a sword. Confronted with his crime later on by the King, Peribáñez rejects all special pleading and knowing his ennoblement to have been a charade makes no mention of it. He wants the case to be judged on its own merits. When the King grants Peribáñez a real captaincy he is rewarded for his integrity with the social rank deemed to be commensurate with his self-respect and his concern with his reputation. To endow a peasant with a sense of honour the equal of any noble's and then feel it necessary to lend verisimilitude by actually ennobling him would seem, perhaps, to undermine Lope's point. But rewards are in the tradition of happy endings and the play's conclusion is not in any case without its irony, as we shall see later.

Like *Peribáñez*, *Fuenteovejuna*[4] also deals with the relationship between honour and noble birth by presenting sexual aggression in the context of class relationships. Here, however, the conflict is not the cat and mouse game played by the Commander in *Peribáñez*, but open confrontation from the start between a brutally predatory overlord and the entire village of

Fuenteovejuna which he tyrannizes in the name of his seigneurial rights; the tension is created not so much by how he will be stopped but by whom. The village's sense of impotence and fear is encapsulated in its name, *Fountain of the sheep*: the men are emasculated, almost dehumanized, by their overlord's grotesque abuse of power and privilege and it is a woman, Laurencia, who eventually shames them into action in the play's major speech. In the name of their communal self-respect the men and women of *Fuenteovejuna* kill the Commander and, when tortured for the truth by the King's men, answer only 'Fuenteovejuna did it'.

Fuenteovejuna moves us in a different way from *Peribáñez*, appealing more blatantly to our sense of outrage, playing more strongly on our perception of right and wrong, stirring us to righteous excitement with the downfall of evil and the triumph of the underdog. Its ways are bold and direct, not delicate and subtle. Its dramatic axis is that of confrontation and open conflict, not of surprise, uncertainty and evasion; its language is the language of threat and impotence not of hint and intelligent caution. It has less of poetry and more of humour, for the peasants here view the world with a greater irony than Peribáñez and Casilda – a reflection of the different seigneurial ethos in which they live. Songs punctuate the action to give the feel of an authentic rural setting and the same sort of tender caring love is portrayed between Laurencia and Frondoso as between Peribáñez and Casilda – indeed the guiding idea behind the play has been seen by some to be true love as a reflection of cosmic harmony. But the two worlds are very different: one is a world of outstanding individuals where an obsessive love distorts nobility into oppression, the other is a world which acknowledges the existence of evil so great that no single man can meet the challenge. *Peribáñez* with its genesis largely in Lope's imagination is a world of poetry, while *Fuenteovejuna*, which has its roots in chronicled fact, is a world closer to history.

The historical dimension of *Fuenteovejuna* is very important in that it has a thematic function. The Commander has aligned himself with the rest of his military order alongside the Portuguese and against the Catholic Monarchs in the War of Succession (1475–79), so that his tyranny against his vassals is identified with his rebellion against the Crown. When the villagers eventually rise against him they do so in the name of their Queen and King as well as of their village. The political burden of the play is that seigneurial feudalism has yielded now for good to the central authority of monarchy; historically, never again would the barons rise in revolt against the Spanish Crown.[5] The ending has once more the cautious realism of *Peribáñez*'s – the villagers have to be pardoned since no evidence of individual guilt is forthcoming. Any justification of their action has to be implicit, for the royal authority to which seigneurial authority yields depends no less than any other on the recognition and acceptance of hierarchical order and harmony as the mainsprings of society. Like Shakespeare's historical plays, seventeenth-century Spanish plays which depict rebellion or civil war derive their meaning from the ruling idea of cosmic order against which they unfold.[6] That the play's enduring spirit is not cautious, however, is plain from the way in which it has been performed in this century in order to make a political statement, most notably by Lorca's theatre company La Barraca.

The third play, *El mejor alcalde, el rey* (*No Greater Judge than the King Himself*),[7] in its procedures unites the two worlds of poetry and history, for when Lope returned to the theme of the noble's abuse of his privilege of power he made the role of the monarchy even more crucial than it is in *Fuenteovejuna* and more theatrical than in either. The Galician peasant hero, Sancho, does not take the law into his own hands but invokes the law's majesty by appealing to the King himself for aid. The noble, for his part, don Tello, not only transgresses against the principles of duty and responsibility on which the social contract is founded but defies the King himself, refusing to accept his monarch as ultimate arbiter of law and justice on earth. The play is set in the twelfth century, when seigneurial rights were only just beginning to yield before monarchical power and this gives credibility to don Tello's reckless anarchy. The King in the guise of a judge travels to the village and hears for himself don Tello's defiance. Revealing his identity he marries don Tello to Sancho's bride-to-be, whom he has raped, and then executes him so that Elvira, now a rich widow, can marry the man who loves her. Justice is done not by meeting force with force but by recourse to the processes of law. The play, therefore, marks in a sense a more mature and a more serene stage in Lope's exploration of the theme of power and its relationship to justice.

The King's personal intervention is a highly dramatic one, beautifully handled by Lope who delays the confrontation of noble and king with a scene of rustic plenty in which the disguised monarch is regaled by the villagers with food and in which the *gracioso*, Pelayo, who is in the know, keeps almost letting the cat out of the bag. Confident that a peasant will never gain access to a King's ear, don Tello rejects the judge, claiming that only the King can arrest him. The King in a moment of intense drama reveals his identity with the words 'But I am the King, peasant' (311). The insult is deliberate and precise: don Tello's behaviour has de-graded him; he is the true peasant. Sancho, on the other hand, has like Peribáñez behaved with a dignity and prudence that convinces the King he must have noble blood in his veins (an echo of the fact that since the far north had been the cradle of the Reconquest a disproportionately large number of its inhabitants were still in the seventeenth century regarded as being of noble birth). Whether we see this as an elegant compliment or a shameless idealization of the peasant, the association of nobility of behaviour with nobility of birth is firmly there. Sancho and Peribáñez, like their women and the inhabitants of *Fuenteovejuna*, are peasants who rise above their station in their behaviour and their perception of reality. Yet kings, we are constantly reminded, are flesh and blood too (and not made of velvet and damask, as Casilda says she once believed), and Peribáñez's gentrification and Sancho's possible noble origins do not invalidate the point Lope is making about the mutually dependent nature of the social orders or the right of every man and woman to dignity and respect. The contemporary aristocratic view that social and economic superiority necessarily implied moral superiority was not one that met with Lope's consent. In *El mejor alcalde* we even sense a powerful nostalgia for a more personal ideal of kingship, when kings did wear plain clothes and were involved in the processes of justice. The Hapsburgs had made of monarchy in Lope's time a very different thing.

El mejor alcalde combines something of the richness of *Peribáñez* with much of the vigour of *Fuenteovejuna*. Elvira and Sancho speak the language of courtly love (appropriate to the situation if not to their station) and there is an intimate association of natural beauty with the beauty of Elvira. Elvira herself has Laurencia's spirit and courage but she has at the same time more traditionally 'feminine' qualities of contrariness and elusiveness which frequently lead to misunderstandings. The humour of *Fuenteovejuna* is here much stronger. Pelayo is a full-blown *gracioso* who is inseparable from his master Sancho and therefore frequently on stage. He is a simpleton who sees the world entirely in terms of pigs and his language is thickly rustic. Crude as the humour is, it is skilfully deployed, and very funny.

Pelayo of course would more plausibly be Lope's rustic model, not Peribáñez or Sancho, were he intent on realism, but he is not. The plays of peasant honour are plays which construct bold, exciting situations to dramatize concerns in a way that will bring them vividly to life before the audience's eyes. For all their individual identities they are one in depicting the triumph of good over evil, of harmony over discord, of the underdog over the powerful aggressor. Their ethos is the ethos of romance and it is the ethos of by far the majority of Lope's plays. The prevailing mood of his theatre is one of optimism.

This mood found its typical dramatic expression in his many comedies or light-hearted plays. Seventeenth-century Spanish romantic comedy as a whole might very broadly speaking be divided into two groups: the urban comedies which depict the love tangles of city gentry and came to be known as *comedias de capa y espada* (cape and sword plays) and the romantic and adventure comedies (including the aristocratic *comedias de fábrica*)[8] which deal with more extravagant and further-ranging escapades and cover a social range from cowherds to kings. Later in the seventeenth century a preference for the urban love comedy becomes noticeable, particularly in Calderón, but Lope's range is wide and ebullient and resists ready categorization. His preference was always for variety and inclusiveness.

El villano en su rincón (*The Countryman in His Corner*), is an interesting example of Lope's exploitation of the pastoral idyll for light-hearted theatre. There are virtually no plot complications and the action is heavy with gentle rustic humour and song and with the aura of monarchy; indeed it smacks of royal festival drama. Its protagonist is a memorable and rather daring variation on the theme of the noble peasant. Juan Labrador is so contented with his prosperous lot and so immune to the attractions of the world outside his village that he has sworn he will die without ever setting eyes on the King. His son and daughter have different ideas and Lisarda falls in love with a nobleman. The plot portrays how the King, intrigued and irritated by this man who regards himself as king of his own castle, goes in disguise to his village to meet him, is struck with admiration and envy by his words and attitudes, and eventually orders him to court to reward him with a royal stewardship. Lisarda gets her noble and the brother is made governor of Paris (the play is set in France). The play skilfully manages at one and the same time to seem to exalt rural life and all that Juan stands for, and to pay extravagant compliments to the virtues of monarchy and, by implication, court life. And it is the tension created by this equipoise which prevents the play being the delightful time-serving nonsense it might at first sight seem. The King's admiration for Juan is balanced by his son and daughter's impatience with his parochialism. His crusty integrity has more than a little complacency and his declared motives for not wanting to see the King (he is an accomplished smooth talker) are nicely equivocal. It is an interesting characterization generally, for he is both a dignified and a slightly comic figure. There is, too, a major irony in the fact that the very values Juan stands for are betrayed at the end by his absorption into a court life previously criticized in no uncertain terms by one of the comic rustics. Juan's fears are realized: seeing the King does indeed lead to the end of the life he loves. The countryman is forced to abandon his corner on the order of a King who, for all his envy of the old man's contentment, insists on destroying the idyll in the name of a higher glory – royal favour. This ambivalence towards court life and social advancement also informs the ending of *Peribáñez*, where the King's favour effectively ends another life of rural perfection. It reflects the genuine tension that existed in the seventeenth-century Spanish imagination, beneath the orthodox vision of a harmonious state, between the values of an idealized rural existence and the irresistible charisma of the court, the focus of so many ambitions and desires.[9]

El villano en su rincón shows off admirably one aspect of Lope's rich talent – his ability to write with silken ease undemanding comedies which exude elegance, humour and grace. Another example, this time in an urban setting and altogether more complicated and energetic, is *El arenal de Sevilla* (*The Strand of Seville*). The play is a charming piece of candyfloss, packed full of movement and life, in which a wonderfully intricate love intrigue takes place against the bustling background of Seville's cosmopolitan port. Lope probably wrote it after one of his several stays in the city in the early 1600s; it might even have been written for performance in Seville. Its extra-large cast includes sea-captains, Moorish galley-slaves, soldiers and bully-boy cutpurses (there would certainly have been a lot of doubling of parts) and for most of the play one of the two heroines passes herself off and speaks as a gypsy. There is a great deal of not really necessary material but it is all welded together very attractively and by making Seville itself the play's real protagonist Lope unites action and incident in a coherent whole. The characters all share the insouciant amorality of literary creations whose existence is determined and circumscribed by their comic roles and the conventions of strict sexual morality that operate in the tragic honour plays are gaily suspended for comic purposes. Lucinda not only chases a man across Spain disguised as a gypsy and then earns her living telling fortunes, but Laura takes into her house a wounded gallant with whom she is soon clearly living on intimate terms.

Lope's provocative disregard for propriety on this score contributed to the charges of immorality soon being levelled against the *comedia*. In *El acero de Madrid*, a sparkling comedy of manners with a sharp cutting edge, the heroine's ruses to avoid an unwelcome match even end in pregnancy. Later seventeenth-century comedy, as a result of the criticisms, would become far more decorous. Lope's motives were undoubtedly partly commercial – the daring and the titillating were good box-office; but implicated too were his profound belief in love and freedom in love and his frequently stated conviction – hardly surprising in view of his own life – of the need for indulgence with regard to youthful passion. Love between the sexes was an enduring source of intense concern for Lope and this concern seeps into all his plays, whatever their nature.[10] He had a shrewd insight into the psychology of love and jealousy and he was clearly fascinated by the positive and negative workings of passion. Love for him was an uncontrollable, irrational force that drove the young to seek each other out irrespective of practical considerations. This process of mutual discovery brings the lovers into conflict not only with love's own obstacles – jealousy, misunderstandings, rivals – but with those man-made conventions which seek to regularize the disruptive force of sex. The confrontation is essentially that between nature, man's natural instincts without which the human race could not survive, and society, man's need as a social animal to rationalize those instincts. Thus Lope's love intrigues, even when elaborated comically, have a basic seriousness at a time when marriage was primarily a family and social consideration.[11] As a result of his example, the *comedia* in general must have made a significant contribution to the audience's familiarity with the idea beginning to gain ground in Europe that love and free choice had a role to play in marriage.

The power of love is the theme of one of Lope's most famous comedies, *La dama boba* (*The Idiot Lady*),[12] a charming play that deftly uses a wide range of comic devices – misunderstandings, unlikely coincidences, letters getting into the wrong hands, the technique of looking at one person while actually speaking to another, and so on. The eponymous heroine, Finea, has a highly intelligent and learned sister, Nise, who is as sharp as the retarded Finea is gentle. However Finea, because of her disadvantage, has the larger dowry. Finea's betrothed discovers she is a fool and decides he would prefer Nise. Nise's suitor, Laurencio, for his part decides quite separately that as a poor man he would prefer the rich Finea for all her lack of wit. Finea's love for Laurencio becomes the power that brings her to intelligence and maturity, and it is her new-found ingenuity that finds the solution that guarantees everybody's happiness. There is more to the play than meets the eye, for it has a strong neo-platonic underpinning in its philosophy of love as superior to the intellect and there is a lot of literary satire at Nise the blue-stocking's expense. But although Lope is in a sense here dramatizing an idea, the play functions brilliantly as comedy.

Finea at the start of the play is an eccentric figure, and there are others in Lope – all women. Seventeenth-century Spanish comedy on the whole does not go in for the purely ridiculous figure – this is reserved for the realm of farce – and Lope himself did not exploit the idea of the *figurón* – the exaggerated personification of some comic vice like Molière's *Tartuffe*. He did however come close to it with his *mujer esquiva* (disdainful woman), an enduring popular *comedia* type of his own invention;[13] scarcely a year passed between 1590 and 1660 without a new *mujer esquiva* play. The *mujer esquiva* tries to revolt against the way in which the authority of Nature is invoked by men to justify their relegation of women to an inactive, inferior role in life, by refusing to fall in love and marry. She is invariably punished by falling for an apparently unobtainable or unsuitable man and ends up accepting willingly the 'sweet yoke' of matrimony. The very convictions about the nature of love that led Lope to defend woman's right to choose her own mate and to champion the young in their struggle against restrictive social conventions led him to insist on love as an inalienable condition of human existence. The range of dramatic treatment is wide, with the programme for reform designed to suit the individual heroine's character within the inescapable general pattern. In *Los milagros del desprecio (The Miracles of Scorn)*[14] the vain and haughty Juana is publicly humiliated by being caught on a wet night, dishevelled and covered in mud, in pursuit of a man. In the later *La moza de cántaro (The Pitcher Maid)*, recently called a 'perfect play',[15] the plot takes a subtler twist, for María not only defies nature by refusing to marry but society as well by usurping her brother's role when she avenges an insult to her father. The murder makes her a social outcast and forces her to serve in an inn at the beck and call of a foul-mouthed master who eventually tries to rape her. Social degradation and sexual violence impress upon her the fact that she is a dependent female. María eventually falls in love and gets her man and is pardoned by the King, but the play's thesis is clear – unnecessary self-assertion in a woman is improper.

Lope's capacity in this respect for a harshness generally alien to his temperament and his work is evident in *Los melindres de Belisa (Finicky Belisa)*, an interesting play which traces the complex process by which Belisa, a hysterical, spoilt and violent girl, is chastened into responsible womanhood. No conventional happy ending here: Belisa, having capriciously rejected the chance to choose a husband for herself, loses the man she loves and has to make do with one chosen for her. The play's comic mood dissolves into an accommodation which is in effect a punishment. Its significance is clear in the light not only of Lope's views on love and marriage but of the usual stage convention whereby the heroine rarely fails to get the right man. The *mujer esquiva* plays are Lope's distinctive contribution to the theme of the taming of the shrew.

The comedies we have looked at so far are romantic comedies with varying degrees of underlying seriousness – Lope's preferred comic vein.

His comic register was wide, however, as *El castigo del discreto* (*The Discriminating Man's Punishment*) illustrates. Lope took the basic story from Bandello (1, 35). In Bandello Cassandra falls in love with a friar and uses her maid Biga to send him a letter. This is intercepted by her husband who makes an assignation with her in the friar's name. When he meets his unsuspecting wife, he beats her up and humiliates her sexually. Lope turned this unpleasant little tale into an extremely complicated intrigue, adding numerous novelesque and conventional comic devices to enhance the action and maintain interest. He adds a sub-plot involving new characters – a second hero and heroine, another villain figure and a brother – as well as additional love affairs. He adds the comic parallelism of the servants' actions and speeches; he adds sword play, *double entendre*, crossed notes, disguise (woman as man) and he adds the betrothal of Felisardo (who replaces the friar of the Italian original) to Hipólita, the extra heroine. More significantly, he embeds the plot in a firm framework of psychological plausibility: Casandra is susceptible to Felisardo's charms because she is a neglected wife – her husband is courting another woman, Hipólita herself – and this serves in some degree as an extenuation of her folly. The play constitutes an unusual treatment of the theme of conjugal honour in that it is the only play of Lope's where the husband does not decide on death as the proper punishment for an erring wife (whatever action he subsequently takes).[16] But Ricardo's motives are strategic, not moral or humane. Beating his wife into fidelity in the guise of the man with whom she is infatuated (and in the play it is just a beating, which takes place offstage) is the only way of ensuring that her infidelity remains a secret and never recurs. As Ricardo's servant so vividly remarks, murder merely turns blood into oil and the dishonour spreads. Casandra may be a silly fool but Ricardo is a ruthless, unprincipled philanderer who cynically operates a double standard of conjugal morality and gives no indication at the end that he intends reforming his ways. The expectations raised by the play's title and the plot's hint of a 'sauce for the goose is sauce for the gander' theme are upturned finally in an ironical reaffirmation of conventional sexual values. For all the unpleasant taste it leaves in the mouth, however, the play is extremely amusing with a comic range of astonishing virtuosity. Its huge complexities are kept under control and held in tension in a masterly fashion, and the action for all its ramifications is tautly developed without superfluities or dispensable parts. Its technical perfection and harsh humour reveal a Lope who was neither slapdash nor unfailingly benign in his treatment of human folly.

The comedy that is arguably his best, the sharply satirical *El perro del hortelano* (*The Dog in the Manger*), reinforces both these observations. The dog in question is the young and wealthy widow, Countess Diana, much sought after by eligible suitors but haughty and aloof as becomes her carefully chosen classical name,[17] because without realizing it she is in love with her secretary Teodoro. Jealousy of her maid Marcela, Teodoro's girlfriend, alerts her to her impossible situation and drives her alternately to pursue him and then withdraw. The rival claims of desire and class, of social prescription and the natural self, are beautifully portrayed, with wit and accuracy. The impasse is finally resolved by Tristán, Teodoro's servant and in a sense the director of the play's action, who convinces an old count whose son was abducted twenty years before that Teodoro is the long-lost heir. Diana's caste loyalties and the ruthlessness that embodies them, the Count's gullibility, Teodoro's heartless treatment of the loyal and forgiving Marcela – all are satirized. But it was with the contrived ending that Lope made his sharpest thrust. The romantic solution would have involved the discovery of Teodoro's true identity as the long-lost son; there are many distinguished dramatic parallels, after all, not least in Shakespeare's *The Winter's Tale* and *Twelfth Night*. If Lope chose to maintain the blatant deception then it was presumably to ridicule the values of a society whose hollow proprieties could so easily be satisfied. Social decorum is revealed as a pretence and a deceit in which individuals compliantly play their selfish parts. The subject was not an academic one: seventeenth-century Spain was obsessed with the pursuit and retention of social status and the large-scale sale of titles and privileges by the Crown meant that, like Teodoro, many a social climber indeed paraded a rank acquired rather than inherited or earned.

El perro del hortelano is a very polished example of the artistry and craftsmanship Lope lavished at times even on his plays in lighter vein. The sexual charge in the prudish Diana's volatile relations with Teodoro is powerfully conveyed by sexual symbolism laced with violence in the dialogue and the action. The play is carefully constructed with nine strategically placed sonnets monitoring the hearts and minds of its principal characters. This use of sonnets or songs to provide moments of lyrical pause during which the play gathers itself together before proceeding is typical of Lope. The broad movement of the play's theme is traced in elaborately-worked Icarus imagery which enriches the plot and its meaning. Teodoro is literally a courtly lover aspiring to the love of a woman literally his mistress. It is a love, however, that he seeks to remove from literature into life. He is therefore flying high towards the dangerous sun. Yet here it is the sun who descends first to Icarus; so although an image redolent of disaster and failure as well as bold ambition, it is diverted by Diana into the realm of the possible. It is Diana herself who then urges acceptance of the borrowed plumes that allow Teodoro to take his place in the sky alongside her. The equivocal portrayal of Diana and Teodoro, the action's theatrical dimension – the characters are constantly acting out charades and end up living one – and the rich texture of the language, all these make of *El perro del hortelano* one of the most studied and variously interpreted of Lope's comedies.[18] But whatever else it is or does, the play certainly serves as a useful paradigm of Lope's attitude to that authority he was so fond of invoking – nature. A hymn to the promptings of desire, *El perro del hortelano*, like the *mujer esquiva* plays, represents the triumph within the self of nature over the artificial restraints placed upon it by society and socialized individuals. At the same time it illustrates that in his own writing the control and embellishment of artifice was invoked and accepted by Lope as a legitimate and necessary adjunct to the promptings of natural inspiration.

Lest it be thought that Lope's belief in the supremacy of nature in human affairs was entirely patriarchal in its implications for women, mention ought to be made in passing of another favourite female type popularized by him and taken up by others – the sensational *bandolera*, or female bandit. The *bandolera* plays, for example *La serrana de la Vera* (*The Mountain Maid of La Vera*) and *Las dos bandoleras* (*The Two Bandoleras*),[19] form a separate group within the body of saints and sinners plays which are so distinctive a feature of Golden-Age drama. They can also be seen as contributing significantly to Lope's democratization of the whole issue of honour. The *bandolera* is a rebel against the double standard of morality, that patriarchal convention which dictates that upon the seduced or raped woman must fall the humiliation of society's scorn. By her rebellion she tries to reaffirm her worth as a human being, showing that women are not utensils to be used and discarded but that they too share that sense of self-respect, that desire for the respect of others, that men call honour. The criminal acts are inevitably condemned and punished, but there can be no doubt that the motives for the revolt are understood and sympathized with. Lope was intensely interested in the nature and role of women and dozens and dozens of his plays concern themselves with some aspect of this interest. His characterization of women is by and large enormously favourable – his heroines are spirited, resolute and full of initiative. His treatment of them consistently reveals a lack of confidence in the justice of prevailing attitudes towards them and invariably champions women's rights as long as they exercise them within the parameters established by their 'natural' role as lovers and wives. Lope in this respect is far more conservative than Tirso de Molina, but since he does not exempt men either from this shared human destiny, he can hardly on this score be pronounced a chauvinist.

Of course, by the standards of today the attitudes of the Spanish dramatists of the time are deeply imbued with a patriarchalism which a feminist critique could deconstruct with ease. And the *mujeres varoniles* – 'masculine' women – of the Golden-Age drama of course for the most part represent a violation of real-life norms designed to amuse and entertain.[20] Nevertheless, no one could contend that the *comedia* presents women as inferior or unimportant. It accords women considerable prominence (partly of course for commercial reasons), it portrays women in untraditional roles and with untraditional attitudes, even if verisimilitude demands that they eventually conform or compromise, and it does engage with the tensions created in and for women by that conflict between self and system which so preoccupied seventeenth-century Spanish playwrights. Indeed, since the *comedia* normally dramatizes the contemporary concern with honour (that is with self-esteem and social reputation) in terms of sexual relationships, and since woman was traditionally the repository of male honour, the very mirror and measure of that potent component of masculine identity, she tends to be the focus of the dramatic conflict even in plays where she is not nominally at the centre of theatrical attention. Woman's predicament in a patriarchal world is therefore always at issue in these plays.

As popular with audiences as Lope's comedies were the large group of what might be called 'mixed bouquet' plays, although they are ostensibly historical. In these Lope daringly but surely combined comedy, romance and epic to give the Spaniard a mixture of sentiment and heroism laced with humour that perhaps above all else typifies the *comedia* during Lope's heyday. Contemporary history was by no means ignored but particularly attractive to a Spain involved increasingly in defeats as well as victories were the glories of the historic and legendary past that had forged its identity. Two areas of special attraction were the heroic years of Castilian expansion and the battles with the Moor, reduced in the Spanish imagination to an emasculated yet noble and glamorous figure by the end of the medieval period when the last vestiges of Spanish Islam were obliterated with the conquest of Granada (1492). *Las almenas de Toro* (*The Battlements of Toro*) is a good example of the former. A play about leadership, it deals with Sancho II's devious attempts to regain for Castile the independent city of Toro inherited by his sister Elvira, and with Sancho's murder by the infamous Bellido Dolfos outside the walls of Zamora. Off-setting Bellido Dolfos is the legendary hero the Cid in a relatively minor role – the only surviving play of Lope's, strangely enough, in which the Cid appears. The sub-plot is set on a farm in the neighbouring countryside when Elvira has to flee from Toro. There is therefore something for everyone: characters to hate (Bellido Dolfos is a villain of hissing status) and to love; treachery and loyalty; martial excitement and conspiratorial suspense; royal dignity and rural simplicity; romantic tangles and even disguises – both Elvira and the Duke of Burgundy, whom she loves, turn up at the farm disguised as peasants. For the women in the audience there is plenty of vicarious heroism as Elvira, dressed in armour, repels invaders on the city battlements; the play was put on by Juan de Morales, whose wife, Jusepa Vaca, one of the leading actresses of the day, specialized in such roles. For the men there is the comforting intervention of the Duke of Burgundy whose marriage to Elvira legitimizes her sovereignty over Toro – Elvira's sex has been Sancho's excuse for trying to take the city from her.

Structurally the play gives an interesting insight into the bold way in which Lope blended such disparate materials: Act I has one rustic scene completely unrelated to all the others, which take place in or near Toro. With the audience's curiosity thus whetted, Lope picks up this thread at the very beginning of Act II and then proceeds to weave the unlikely pair of plots together until their relationship is fully revealed. At the end he frustrates expectation, however, by disentangling the two plots once more and leaving the rustic characters frustrated in love and dangling. Lope's skilful manipulation of elements of expectation and surprise is evident too in his treatment of a somewhat delicate historical topic. Sancho was a king with concerns for the integrity of his realm which could be seen as either legitimate or predatory. His reign was brief, he was killed in mysterious circumstances and he was succeeded by a monarch with a much stronger historical and legendary profile – Alfonso VI. Lope can thus make his portrayal of Sancho's leadership suitably equivocal, and equally equivocal are the attitudes towards him of the other characters including the Cid. Lope manages to suggest that loyalty to the authority of monarchy is a necessary prerequisite of ordered government while at the same time portraying a Sancho who is insecure, duplicitous and lacking in judgement. In the battle for the leadership of Toro there is no doubt that Elvira is the better man. Her appearance, at one stage while she is living on the farm, covered in flour from kneading bread, seems a striking example of Lope's lack of inhibitions in sacrificing plausibility to effect. But neither plot nor character is in fact compromised. Just as the action accommodates without strain its unlikely variety of strands, so the portrayal of Elvira is all of a piece; she is depicted as a woman prepared to do what it takes, whether that involves bread or battlements.

El remedio en la desdicha (*The Remedy for Misfortune*) is another imaginative reconstruction of historical material. It is the best of Lope's plays about *moros y cristianos* – Moors and Christians, a phrase not far removed in meaning and tone from 'cowboys and Indians'. By the sixteenth century the Moor had become in Spain the symbol of a romantic as well as heroic past. Aristocrats whiled away their leisure time playing elaborate jousting games of *moros y cristianos* which acted out the famous skirmishes and battles of the later Middle Ages and old ballads and chronicles were rifled for tales of Moorish heroes and lovers. There are several versions of Lope's plot in sixteenth-century Spanish prose but Lope's source was a story called *Historia del Abencerraje y la hermosa Jarifa* (*Story of the Abencerraje and the Beautiful Jarifa*) interpolated in the 1561 edition of Jorge de Montemayor's enormously successful pastoral romance, *La Diana* (1559). The story tells how the noble Moor Abinderráez is taken prisoner in a Christian ambush and prevented from keeping an assignation with his beloved Jarifa. Moved by his plight, his captor, Rodrigo de Narváez, gives him his liberty to see Jarifa on condition he returns within three days. Both lovers return to deliver themselves to Narváez, who shows his generosity again by freeing them. It is a touching tale of love and chivalry in the idealized setting of the Andalusian frontier wars between Moors and Christians, where neither side has the monopoly of honourable and generous behaviour. A comparison of story and play reveals Lope as a script writer adept not only at dramatizing narrative but also at grafting on to the plot further complexities of the sort demanded by a theatre which prized ingenuity and inventiveness above all else.[21] Thus the play opens with a troubled Abinderráez and Jarifa, who believe themselves to be brother and sister, hesitantly revealing the passionate love they bear each other – an anguished situation which in the narrative is merely described in retrospect by Abinderráez to Narváez after his capture. Then again Lope involves Narváez in a complicated love intrigue of his own which is deftly knitted into the events that concern Abinderráez; the play effectively has a double plot.

Unusually for this sort of theme the play does not exploit traditional ballads and lyrics. But its tone is very much that of the *morisco* ballads of the fifteenth century with their emphasis on the exotic and sentimental rather than the martial. The atmosphere of the play is a romantic one laden with the pulsations of passion and self-absorption; the heroism it celebrates is the heroism of gentlemanly self-denial and generosity rather than that of physical courage. The work is not without its faults. Narváez's misdirected passion for the married Mooress Alara is ultimately unconvincing, although thematically it is clearly intended to round out the play's portrayal of noble generosity and selfless love. Nonetheless the work has tremendous vitality and a seductive charm that injections of irony and realism prevent from becoming cloying. The love poetry and the scenes of introspection are superb – notably the robing scene, the garland scene and Abinderráez's speech of exultation when he discovers Jarifa is not his sister – and there are excellent examples of Lope's gift for exploiting prosodic effects for dramatic purposes. There are felicitous psychological touches too, among them the way in which Jarifa's former eloquence dries up into inarticulate self-consciousness when she realizes that Abinderráez is not her brother and that consummation of their love is now possible; the presentation of Narváez as a man of practical, humane concern as well as of high principle and self-control; and Abinderráez's descent into hypochondriacal literal-mindedness when Narváez asks after his injuries and instead of receiving some nonchalant disclaimer is told that they are just a little swollen. Even Lope's most shamelessly romantic plays never lose sight of the realities of the flesh and human nature.

It has already been observed that Lope's tragedies – those which we might now regard as tragedies as well as those given the label in their own day – form a small island in the ocean of his dramatic writing. For all that, they include some of his greatest theatrical achievements.

El caballero de Olmedo (*The Knight of Olmedo*), an extraordinary poly-valent work, is a devastating reversal of the very presumptions of comedy in which it appears to be rooted. It is a play where light turns to darkness, where discord finally prevails, where true love leads to desolation. It was written when Lope was approaching sixty – it is a play therefore not merely of his maturity but of maturity's riper and wiser end. Not an old man's play by any means – many fine plays including his greatest, *El castigo sin venganza*, were still to come – but a play that combines the vigour of a still powerful talent and a still youthful imagination with the mellow complexity that came to Lope with age.

The play is based on, and includes, a haunting, early seventeenth-century popular song, but it draws heavily too on the plot of the *Celestina*. Don Alonso, a valorous knight of Olmedo, falls in love with a lady of Medina, Inés. In order to circumvent her official suitor, don Rodrigo, Alonso engages a bawd who dabbles in witchcraft, Fabia, to help further his affair. Inés conspires with them by pretending to have a religious vocation. Alonso saves Rodrigo's life in a bull-fight, but this humiliation only fans the flames of Rodrigo's jealousy and he plans to murder Alonso. On the road to Olmedo to visit his parents, the terror-stricken Alonso meets first his own ghost and then a peasant who sings of his death as if it has already taken place. When Inés's sister finally reveals all to their eminently reasonable and understanding father and Inés receives his blessing for her marriage to Alonso, it is only to learn what the audience has already witnessed – that Alonso has been foully struck down on the road at night by four assassins.

The action unfolds against the background of the schisms of the fifteenth century when the Castilian aristocracy of the reign of Juan II was divided into two factions, based respectively on the towns of Olmedo and Medina.[22] No exact parallels are drawn but the rivalry between the two knights of Medina and Olmedo and the contrast they represent between two very different types of nobility are central to the working of the play. Alonso dies in a sense because he is an anachronism, at once too reckless and too guileless to survive in a world that no longer conducts itself – if indeed it ever did – in accord with the chivalric code of honourable conduct. The contrast is captured with pitiful pathos in the murder scene. When Alonso, like the stage gallants of a thousand plays, draws his sword to resist his assailants, he is gunned down on the order of Rodrigo who declares brutally that he is there to kill and not to duel. Alonso is a literary hero who thinks and behaves like the chivalrous knight, the passionate lover, the courageous gallant, of literary convention. His manufactured world of love and chivalry obeys only its own imperatives and takes no cognizance of the real world of jealousy, envy and humiliation, or of moral obligation and social duty. As he lies dying alone on the road he guiltily protests that his love was directed towards marriage but he has not, alas, behaved as if it were. In comedy love is licensed to spurn such considerations with impunity. But tragedy always lurks in the wings of comedy, waiting for authority to enter and destroy the hero for the very compulsiveness and assumed invulnerability which in comedy escape retribution, and Alonso and Inés realize, too late, that they have been acting in the wrong play. Inés's pretended vocation for the nunnery becomes a bitter reality. Lope conceived of passion as an irresistible force which carried within itself the seeds of its own destruction. Here he allows those seeds to flower.

The movement into tragedy is carefully prepared. The play's title and the specific references to the *Celestina* would have sensitized a contemporary audience to the signals and suggestions – chance ironies, warnings, misgivings, premonitions and omens, platitudes of speech that are revitalized into their literal meanings – which accumulate remorselessly to form a powerful undercurrent of impending disaster. Central to the themes of love and its potential for destruction is Lope's use of the love/death metaphors of the courtly love poetry of the fifteenth-century song-books, a poetry that used paradox, antithesis and ellipsis to convey a love blinkered and intense to the point of unreason. As the play proceeds this imagery sheds its conventional skin and acquires a truly tragic force. By the time Alonso at the end of Act II expresses his own presentiment of death in his description of the symbolic episode of the goldfinch and the hawk, our disbelief finally crumbles and we begin to realize that this time there will be no happy ending. In Act III the omens acquire a substance of their own as Alonso's fears and doubts now come to meet him in the form of the ghost and the peasant's song. Both come to warn him, but the song is in the past tense – Alonso is already dead. The death-in-life paradox of the play's love poetry is hideously resolved in this moment of utter terror when the future becomes the past.

For all the gradual intensification of the play's tragic mood, the ending when it comes still has a sickening impact. Far from providing the play with an explicit prologue like *Romeo and Juliet*'s to prepare us for the outcome, Lope deliberately plays on our expectations of romantic comedy and exploits our reluctance to believe the evidence of our ears. We grow to realize Alonso's folly but his recklessness and self-involvement serve to humanize for us this paragon of knightly virtue whose death moves us so deeply. The phoenix allusions, the joyfulness of the Petrarchan love poetry with its images of fire and beauty, Alonso and Inés's unstinting expressions of true love as something fateful but strong and freely given, the fun of the scenes between Tello the *gracioso* and the sinister Fabia – these for all their essential ambiguity help throughout two acts to preserve our confidence in love and romance. The play's very special identity lies precisely in its cunning manipulation of the springs of comedy to produce tragedy; its power to affect us comes from the disconcerting and disturbing way it deliberately speaks to us with a voice we hear but which we are conditioned by other works, other plays, not to recognize. There is danger in Alonso and Inés's conduct of their love affair but like them we allow literature rather than life to dictate our responses to that danger. *El caballero de Olmedo* is a brilliantly original play which necessarily assumes full tragic force only after it has ended and our sense of outrage has subsided, for that is when we realize that through the lips of comedy it has all along been telling us a tragic tale.

If *El caballero de Olmedo* is perhaps most safely described as tragic poetic drama, Lope's controversial masterpiece *El castigo sin venganza* (*Punishment Without Revenge*) is generally acknowledged to merit the title of tragedy Lope gave it in the autograph manuscript which has survived.[23] For all that, it has presented critics with severe problems of interpretation, including the crucial question of who the tragic protagonist is. The plot speaks for itself: the libertine Duke of Ferrara, realizing that his beloved bastard son Federico will one day succeed him only at the terrible cost of civil war, decides belatedly to marry. When his young bride Casandra and her stepson meet, they fall in love and when the Duke, after one night in the marriage bed, returns to his former philandering Casandra begins to see in her love for Federico a terrifying form of revenge. The Duke leaves to fight the Pope's wars and the young couple become lovers. On his return, covered in military glory, the Duke claims to be a reformed man. At this, the height of his fortunes, he receives an anonymous letter accusing his wife and son of adultery. Rejecting the idea of vengeance as inappropriate in a father, he plots the lovers' punishment. He bundles Casandra up after tying and gagging her and then orders the unsuspecting Federico to kill her as a traitor plotting the Duke's own death. When the deed is done he denounces Federico for murdering his step-mother to thwart the legitimate succession and Federico in his turn is killed on the spot by a courtier.

Two premises of this gruesome story, which is based on Bandello's novelization of a historical incident that took place in Italy in 1425, *Il Marchese Niccolò Terzo*, need to be emphasized. First, the lovers are guilty of adulterous incest and have to be punished. Second, the Duke as head of state as well as cuckolded husband has no choice but to see that punishment administered. It is the Duke's motive in killing the guilty pair secretly – in the original the husband has them publicly executed – which has inspired fierce critical disagreement. The only general consensus that has been reached is that if there is a tragic protagonist then it is probably the Duke himself, for all that he is on stage less than the lovers. He has killed the son he adored, destroyed his chance of a legitimate heir and is left to live out his life alone surrounded by people who in fact know the truth of his dishonour. Even so the judgements passed on the Duke, his final solution and indeed the nature of the whole play, have in some cases been so contrary as to be irreconcilable.[24] The reason for the various readings – many very persuasive – to which the play has given rise is that it is an extremely ambiguous work. It is a play shaped by and infused with irony and full of smaller ironies that reflect this broader vision.[25] Deceit, dissimulation and misrepresentation, conscious and unconscious, are its common currency. On the level of the action the deception reaches its climax in the last act in the scene between father and son, where Federico in his attempts to paper over the terrifying cracks appearing in his life pretends to want to marry Aurora and the Duke, pretending to be taken in, proceeds to the deception that will end in Federico's death. The death itself is the harshest deception of all – Federico the deceiver is deceived into killing the woman he loves and dies for it. But the theme of concealment infuses every aspect of the play, not merely its plot.[26] All three main characters conceal, misrepresent and deceive for reasons of varying degrees of respectability, and ambiguity becomes not just something that arises out of the sympathy with which their motives and their actions are presented by the dramatist but something in which they themselves become ensnared. Part of the time they are trying to deceive themselves, to convince themselves, to conceal from themselves the true nature of what they do.

This ambiguity is not a side effect of the play, not a device used by the dramatist to make a moral point, it is the play's very substance. And the ambiguity is substantive in a highly specific way, for it is the very stuff of which the play's language is constructed. The language itself mirrors the play's presentation of the truth as something shifting, partial and con- trived. We need not even see this in moral terms – in terms of people being deliberately deceitful or hypocritical – or as sophistry. We need see it only in terms of the way speech relates to the psychology of survival and self-respect, to the psychology of coping. The very first scene – a night scene in which under cover of darkness and disguise the Duke wanders the streets perpetrating sexual deceptions, behaving in a manner inappropriate both to the light of day and to his real identity – reveals that we are entering a world of part-truths and specious arguments, and primes us for the way in which its characters will exploit the elasticity of language in the creation and manipulation of perspectives that relate only to their own self-interests. The Duke's famous speech of self-justification in Act III in which he rejects vengeance in favour of punishment, a punishment in the event indistinguishable from vengeance, is an unconscious attempt to render the unthinkable (the death of his son) acceptable and to keep under control the urge for revenge that confuses his understanding of his public duty. His quibbling with words and his obsession here and elsewhere with the idea of punishment – an obsession reflected in the play's title – are attempts to placate his own tormented conscience but they also reflect his conviction that the son he loves, who has imaged him so faithfully in *everything*, as he ironically observes to Casandra, is the instrument of his own punishment. The play's emotional axis is the relationship not between a man and his wife but between a man and his son.

El castigo sin venganza explores and presents the protean and partial nature of human truth and, since language aids and abets that truth, its power is circumscribed by the tongue that speaks it. The Duke's, and effectively the play's last words, conclusive as they seem, leave us only with a strong sense of the dualism that characterizes human experience: 'he has paid for the evil his inheritance drove him to'.[27] The Duke intends the world to understand that Federico has paid for the crime he committed through his desire to be his father's heir. He knows only too well that Federico has in reality paid for the crime he committed through inheriting from his father the legacy of a misspent life that has made it possible for him to meet Casandra as his father's wife and fall in love with her. Language's own ambiguity has the last words in the ambiguous presentation of an ambiguous world.[28]

El castigo sin venganza is a very spare and concentrated play of intense power in which nothing distracts from the young couple's headlong rush towards disaster. Casandra's headstrong defiance, Federico's anguished reluctance, their helplessness in the grip of complex emotions, the taboo theme of incest, are superbly handled. But over them and the whole play, even when he is not on stage, looms the menacing figure of the Duke, as husband and head of state the representative twice over of the principle of law which they have fatally defied and which will crush them. The pattern has its reflection in the play's broader movement: the law that the Duke defied so long, the law that prescribes how a head of state must behave and what duties he must perform, ends up crushing him too. Here, in a complete inversion of the ethos of *El perro del hortelano*, the symbolic order triumphs.

It will be clear by now that there is much red meat for Lacanian interpreters of the Golden-Age drama to get their teeth into. The explicit concern with the relationship between the individual and his role in life at various levels is a constant in the *comedia* – a natural progression from the role play which itself constitutes theatre. Lope was particularly interested, in comedy and tragedy, in the man or woman torn between natural instincts or personal preferences and the authority of social role or duty. The fact that Spain itself from 1621 to 1665 had in Philip IV a king who combined a public presence of rigid formality and self-control with a highly irregular personal life, can be no coincidence. Indeed in the 1620s Philip IV himself, like the Duke of Ferrara, roamed the streets of his capital on nocturnal excursions accompanied by the Count-Duke of Olivares, who was accused of corrupting his monarch.[29]

Of Lope's other tragedies, *El Duque de Viseo* (*The Duke of Viseo*) is a much earlier but nevertheless very accomplished work which deserves to be far better known. It is a powerful tragedy of palace intrigue that explores the meaning of loyalty to that ultimate temporal authority, the Crown, in the face of an unworthy monarch. It serves to illustrate that tragic dilemmas are not experienced only by heroes torn by internal conflict. The Condestable of Portugal against his better judgement reveals to Inés why she should not marry the otherwise eligible Don Egan – he has Jewish blood in his veins. Egan, the King's favourite, finds out and swears vengeance on the Condestable and his brothers by the same means as he has been dishonoured – with his tongue. From the moment he activates the fears of an unreasonable, ungrateful and insecure king by telling him the brothers are conspiring to put his brother-in-law, the universally admired Duke of Viseo, on the throne, Viseo's death becomes inevitable – necessary, even, for the King's peace of mind. The sense of something with small beginnings getting completely out of hand, with an honourable and innocent man being sucked into the maelstrom and destroyed, is extremely effectively conveyed. The characters and their motives are convincingly complicated, the unadorned dialogue conveys anger, hurt, indignation, bewilderment and duplicity with a rawness which underscores the dreadful injustice of events as they unfold, and the treatment of the theme of loyalty to God's representative on earth is interestingly multivalent. Truth is again shown here as an elusive thing which recedes further and further before an array of different views and interpretations of what is going on. When Egan is killed by Viseo's servant in revenge for the 'execution' he in fact tried to prevent, the audience is left in sole possession of the facts and their terrible ironies. The way in which a concatenation of ignoble acts and chance accidents produces a disaster which need never have happened but which, once the first step has been taken, is absolutely inevitable because immovable forces come into play, anticipates Calderón's tragic technique later on. The avoidance of any simplistic apportioning of responsibility is, if anything, even more marked: motives are murky and acts of spite, malice, imprudence and irresponsibility are committed, but blame and doubt and regret are acknowledged and apart, perhaps, from the shallow and feckless Inés, the only character who consistently eludes our sympathy is the King himself, driven to an act of cruel injustice not by calumny but by his own fear. When none will obey his command to execute the 'traitor' Viseo, he is reduced to taking his own dagger and striking him down himself.

These three very different tragic plays reveal how absurd is the received wisdom of largely Anglo-Saxon tragedy-criticism that seventeenth-century Spain's attempts at tragedy were doomed from the start by the ever-present shadow of divine forgiveness or an acceptable retribution,[30] or by resounding devotion to God, King and Country[31] – another legacy of the 'black legend' of Spain. Jacob Burckhardt even blamed Spain for *Italy*'s failure to produce great tragedy.[32] Unquestionably Christian as the Spanish dramatists were, they were not so naive as to think either that their faith provided instant answers for all earthly dilemmas or that human beings, even religious ones, act always in accordance with that faith. Above all they were artists not theologians, moralists or philosophers, more concerned with portraying and exploring than prescribing, with questions rather than with answers. There is a considerable body of plays, in addition to the sacramental *autos*, which were written in the interests of the faith for theatre companies eager to cater for devout audiences who took great delight in being thus instructed and entertained. The year was punctuated with religious celebrations, regular and extraordinary, which the companies were quick to exploit – they often had to compete, after all, with the public festivities themselves. But this does not mean that the whole of the Golden-Age drama is a form of covert hagiography or a protracted sermon. The dramatist who writes tragedies is not thereby disqualified from writing comedies. Shakespeare wrote plays with the interests of the court clearly in mind and others where his allegiances are imponderable. Similarly the Spanish playwrights confine themselves to no single dramatic register or stance. Lope in particular was a protean writer of elusive views, less readily identifiable than Tirso de Molina or Calderón with any consistent tone or outlook.

The literary controversy

If Spanish tragedy is by and large different, rather than non-existent, it is different partly because it is rooted in a paradoxical world view and partly because it obeys the dictates of a changed concept of drama. In his prologue to the 1634 edition of *El castigo sin venganza* Lope asserts that the play is written in the Spanish manner, not the Greek or Latin, justifying this by invoking contemporary public taste, which has the power to modify art. Specifically excluded are 'the shades, messengers and choruses' of classical drama, but the point is the one he makes about his theatre in general in other prologues and in his 389-line literary manifesto, *Arte nuevo de hacer comedias en nuestro tiempo* (*New Art of Writing Plays in Our Time*). This was written for a literary gathering, the Academia de Madrid, sometime between 1604 and late 1608, probably at the invitation of the Count of Saldaña who ran the group, and was published in 1609.[33] This opportunity to defend his drama from its neo-classical detractors did not lead to as firm and illuminating a statement as one would have wished. The occasion and Lope's own lingering regard for classical authority produced a somewhat inhibited and contradictory document which is at once a survey of the history of drama culled mainly from the Italian classical commentators Francesco Robortello and Elio Donato and a practical guide for its contemporary practitioners. Lope defends his own theatre by presenting himself as the slave of a public he professes to despise but whose authority is absolute, and there is a lot of respectful hat-doffing in the direction of the classical precepts. But the note of irony, even flippancy at times, is marked and certain firm and serious principles based on his already considerable theatrical experience do emerge. Not least significant is the title itself: Lope may say that he writes 'without art', meaning here the classical precepts themselves, but in the title to his address he makes it clear that what he is proposing is not an abandonment of art in the wider sense but a new artistic recipe, suitable for the times.

This new recipe for art, however, while claiming to accept Aristotle's definition of drama as a mirror of the times and Horace's emphasis on the instructive function of art, puts the pleasure of audiences above the concerns of the academics and therefore privileges nature rather than theory and artifice. His belief that in poetry no less than in love what is natural must be granted the upper hand was largely responsible for his hostility to the difficult, obscure poetry of Góngora.[34] As far as the theatre was concerned, since nature involves variety the logical outcome for Lope was the mixed drama that provides it – an argument already used by the Italian Giambattista Guarini to justify his tragicomedy *Il pastor fido*.[35] For all his disclaimers Lope makes it clear that he has deliberately abandoned the restraints of neo-classical art – restraints which six of his early plays show he was perfectly capable of applying – in favour of his own theory that dramatic poetry is life not doctrine. The practical advice he gives is shaped by artistic as well as commercial considerations and reinforces the impression of a discriminating and thoughtful rather than anarchic attitude to dramatic theory and practice. Not only does he recommend the delights of mixed drama, plots in three brisk acts dealing with the popular themes of honour and 'virtuous actions', masculine disguise for heroines, suspense and surprise, and stages never left empty for long, but he advises verisimilitude, convincing propriety of speech, decorous treatment of women, versification suitable to the subject, and plots without superfluous elements which unfold in as little time as is feasible, with any inevitable temporal jumps taking place between the acts. He recommends, in other words, a dramatic recipe which takes major liberties without renouncing artistic control. And while his plays, particularly his earlier ones, by no means invariably comply with these strictures, the manifesto represents Lope's considered views of contemporary drama twenty or so years after he started writing for the public playhouses, views that are, underneath the rationalizations and disclaimers, brilliantly original and daring. He is claiming artistic legitimacy for a public theatre which has cast itself adrift from the authority of the past and makes enjoyment a priority – a claim only fully understood in the context of an age characterized in Spain by a huge expansion in two genres still on the border of art, drama and prose fiction, when the whole idea of a secular literature of entertainment was still fighting for recognition. Towards the end his tone becomes proudly defiant – 'I stand by what I have written' (372) – and in later years the growth in confidence is sometimes even more marked: 'Great writers are not subject to rules', he claimed in a prologue of 1621.[36] Yet even in 1625 we still find him apologizing, as he had done in 1604 in his Byzantine romance *El peregrino en su patria*, for his rejection of the classical rules and claiming that he was merely obeying the dictates of a commercial theatre already in existence when he started writing.[37]

His ambivalence towards his art (and therefore towards his public) was probably real. The compulsion now to claim the *comedia* as his own, now to disown it by insisting on the tyranny of public taste, is a reflection both of his own highly ambivalent attitude to all authority and convention and of the power of the classics' grip on literary Europe's thinking. It also suggests a lack of intellectual confidence understandable on the part of a man of insecure scholarship with an inordinate respect for erudition who was constantly under bitter attack from the theorists. In his work, as in his life, Lope did what he pleased and then grappled, often inadequately, with the consequences. There was nothing inevitable about the *comedia* at the time Lope chose to develop it in the direction he did. In Elizabethan England, a public theatre with a not dissimilar background and an uncannily similar stage produced a different sort of drama, for all that Shakespeare too has his mixed plays.

The campaign against Lope's new drama was a protracted one. By the late 1580s, the battle with the neo-classicizing tendencies in the theatre itself had been won, but the theoretical debate really only got under way in the 1590s with the publication in 1596 of a major commentary on Aristotle's *Poetics* called *Philosophia Antigua Poetica* by Alonso López Pinciano.[38] The first treatise on the classical theorists produced in Spain, it is a less rigid and altogether more reasonable document than the contemporary Italian treatises from which Spaniards for the most part had hitherto culled their knowledge of the classical authorities. In particular it has interesting comments on the association of comedy with tragedy, and on the tragedies with happy endings recognized by Aristotle for all that he denied them the label of 'pure', which could be seen as having important implications for the *comedia*. Nonetheless as a cogent and informed defence of the classical rules it constituted a significant threat to the legitimacy of the *comedia*, if not to its success, and authorized the fierce debate which prompted Lope's *Arte nuevo*. The *comedia*'s popularity naturally added the fuel of envy and resentment to the fire of academic indignation, ensuring that discarded dramatists like Cervantes weighed in behind the theorists to accuse Lope of being a literary barbarian and prostitutor of art. The principal targets of literary censure were the *comedia* itself as a dramatic form which abandoned the formal distinctions of the past, its cavalier use of the theatrical dimensions of time and place (essentially neo-classical rather than classical concerns), and its untidiness, extravagance and inclusiveness – offences summed up in the descriptions of 'hermaphrodites' and 'monsters' given the new plays by Francisco Cascales in his *Tablas poéticas*, 1617.[39] Such criticisms were further fuelled by the moral indignation provoked by what critics considered the theatre's lack of social decorum and general irreverence. Cascales's relatively benign treatise, which combines Aristotelian and Horatian theory, acknowledges the talents of contemporary dramatists while berating them for their neglect of the rules, but not all the theatre's critics were so fair-minded.

Lope and his *comedia* did not go undefended by his admirers and disciples. Poems, prologues, plays, miscellanies, letters, travelogues, tracts for the time and purpose-written treatises became the battleground for a struggle of vested interests that dragged on for years. Lope's own chosen authorities – nature, the changed imperatives of the time and the educational function of art – were the defence's main ammunition. In 1617 Lope was subjected to a virulent, last-ditch attack in a tract called *Spongia* written by a lecturer in grammar and rhetoric at Alcalá, the Aristotelian Pedro de Torres Rámila.[40] The treatise, whose text has not survived (all copies purportedly destroyed by the Lope lobby) prompted Lope and his supporters (Alonso Sánchez de Moratalla, Professor of Greek and Hebrew at Alcalá amongst them) to produce a reply, the *Expostulatio Spongiae*, the following year. It defended the *comedia* on substantially the same grounds as Lope had used in the *Arte nuevo* – that it was a new art suited to its time. This concerted and authoritative defence effectively put paid to the opposition. By now in any case the passage of time and the beneficial effect gradually exercised on the *comedia*'s wilder excesses by criticism over the years had already given the *comedia* a large degree of literary respectability. In 1615 in his prologue to his *Ocho comedias y ocho entremeses* (*Eight Plays and Eight Interludes*) Cervantes himself had graciously conceded a just victory to the *comedia*; in 1617 Cascales wrote to Lope, whom he obviously greatly admired, defending the theatre against the attacks of the moralists, the *comedia*'s other enemy, in terms which now seem to take the *comedia* as an art form for granted.[41] A conclusive and very penetrating defence and explanation of the *comedia* was delivered by Tirso de Molina in his miscellany *Los cigarrales de Toledo* (*The Countryhouses of Toledo*, 1621). Here he expounds the idea of art as an imitation of nature, specifically the problem that playwrights had created by claiming to imitate life while writing plays where the action was accelerated and intensified to the point of extreme implausibility. He dissipates the contradiction, normally fudged by other champions of the *comedia*, by explaining that a play is not life but an artistic construct, 'an image or representation of its theme' (in modern critical terms a sign). It is a living painting and like a painting in the way it represents reality by compressing it. The pen must therefore not be denied the licence unquestioningly given the brush.[42]

From this point on, the *comedia*'s literary credentials were more or less secure. Awareness of its distinctive nature did not fade, however, and this, together with the controversies that surrounded the theatre as an institution, ensured that the *comedia* continued to be a subject of commentary and concern throughout the seventeenth century. In the last important treatise of the period on the theatre, *Theatro de los theatros de los passados y presentes siglos* (1689–94), Francisco Bances Candamo, significantly, felt both compelled to defend the *comedia* in terms of art, and able to do so, ordering and classifying a theatre which had been born of the impulse to reject traditional orderings and classifications but had in the process of time acquired stable artistic procedures and presumptions of its own.

It would be idle to pretend that the theatre's critics had no grounds for complaint. In the early decades of the *comedia*, and throughout its career in the case of many minor practitioners, it was often untidy, slipshod and sensationalist. It was after all in a sense a theatre of improvisation in the way it worked to given patterns and themes and became a self-nourishing, self-perpetuating activity – existing plays were frequently cannibalized or completely reworked by other dramatists (including Calderón) – and in its sheer theatricality it owed much to that theatre of true improvisation, the *commedia dell'arte*. The triumph of its major exponents lay in their ability to retain this theatricality while turning the *comedia* into a fully literary art form. Lope may have constantly evoked the authority of nature for his writing but, as we have seen, his work can in fact be highly literary, reflective and self-conscious, using all the resources of rhetoric, metaphor and allusion to create different levels of meaning. However, just as his verse dialogue gives a convincing impression of spoken language and carries without strain its burden of literary charges, so his plots always work as exciting 'life-like' entertainment. Lope was writing for an audience whose members ranged from the illiterate to the cultured and he succeeded brilliantly in catering for all. He knew exactly how to serve them the delight that comes from a balance of anticipation and surprise, now fulfilling, now frustrating their expectations of plot, characters and codes of behaviour, expectations largely created by the *comedia* itself. As time went on, his work revealed an increasing sense of order and verisimilitude – a move away from the world of romance into a socially recognizable world – but the energy and the excitement of his drama never waned. Although not an actor himself he knew the theatre intimately and never betrayed its needs and imperatives. This ability to combine the compulsions of art with the demands of commerce was his greatest legacy to his pupils and successors.

The main difficulty in characterizing Lope's drama within the established framework of the *comedia* is that his range is extremely wide and his interests and preoccupations form no insistent patterns. The antinomies of life/death, light/dark, truth/illusion, art/nature, fiction/reality are not absent from his drama but he was not consistently preoccupied with them as were Cervantes and Calderón; he does not have that overwhelming sense of the illusory nature of reality they shared with Shakespeare. He was much more interested in people and the way they lived their lives in society than in abstractions, ideas and ideals and even then he was happier working within the range of normal human psychology. His privileging of nature is of a piece with this imaginative and intellectual involvement with the representative and the normal. More original than Tirso and even Calderón, his imagination lacked the grandeur of theirs, weaving patterns around the essentially naturalistic rather than around the exceptional, the extreme, the supernatural or the transcendental. *El caballero de Olmedo* is one of relatively few plays where we see his imagination take off and enter a world larger than man's day-to-day experience.

5

Tirso de Molina and the other Lopistas

Tirso de Molina's world, by contrast with Lope's, is a world peopled by the unusual and the extreme, even bizarre. Tirso de Molina was the pseudonym of a Mercedarian monk called Fray Gabriel Téllez (c. 1584–1648).[1] The greatest of Lope's disciples, although their personal relationship was neither close nor particularly good, he was writing plays by the mid-1600s and within a few years had become one of Spain's major dramatists. He more or less dominated the Spanish stage along with Lope in the early 1620s. This period of maximum productivity coincided with his transfer to the house of his order in Madrid at a time of great intellectual activity. Góngora, Quevedo, the ageing Lope and the young Calderón all lived and wrote there and other dramatists gathered from elsewhere – Guillén de Castro from Valencia, Luis Vélez de Guevara and Mira de Amescua from Andalusia, Juan Ruiz de Alarcón from Mexico. Tirso entered with gusto into this exciting literary world with its academies and controversies, its friendships and its animosities. For him, sadly, it was not to last. On 6 March 1625 the Council of Castile's Committee for Reform declared his dramatic activities scandalous in a man of his calling and recommended that he be exiled to a remote monastery. Why Tirso was singled out for this treatment is not clear – there were other men of God involved in the theatre, including Lope who even as a priest more or less openly kept a mistress – and his own order seems not to have taken exception to his activities. Tirso himself thought envious fellow writers were responsible – he even implied that Lope was involved.[2] Whoever his enemies were, he somehow through their intervention managed to attract the animosity of Philip IV's first minister, the powerful Count-Duke of Olivares, who directly influenced the findings that virtually ended Tirso's dramatic career. He wrote few plays after his departure from Madrid.

It is not surprising that Tirso made enemies who saw insults or supposed insults to themselves in his plays, for he is a hard-hitting dramatist who tackled the social and political questions that interested most dramatists at the time in an unusually direct way. Technically all his plays are cast in the mould established by Lope and in the literary and moral controversies that surrounded the *comedia nueva* he was resolute in its defence. In *Los cigarrales de Toledo*, a framed miscellany in prose in which a group of lords and ladies entertain one another with stories and plays, he states that times change and inevitably bring with them legitimate changes in the way drama is written. The new genre is quite as praiseworthy and respectable as the old classical forms of drama, he claims, especially now that it has matured and improved, and contains nothing corrupting. On the contrary it delights and instructs simultaneously.

Tirso brought to the Golden-Age stage an intellectual turn of mind and a psychological range and penetration absent in Lope. He was interested in the extraordinary and possessed a greater tolerance and understanding of human oddity and variety than the other dramatists. Owing perhaps to his observer status, he had a broadness of outlook with regard to women's role in the scheme of things which Lope, for all his passionate interest in women and his sympathy with their problems, lacked. His particular contribution to the Spanish theatre's often vaunted feminism was to allow women something which other playwrights tend to overlook – Lope's women have courage, passion, daring and determination but Tirso's have intelligence. If Lope's women rise to the occasion, Tirso's create it. Their intelligence, furthermore, is invariably greater than that of their men. The heroes of Golden-Age plays habitually pale in comparison with their female counterparts, but in Tirso the discrepancy is striking. In his comedies of intrigue the often mind-boggling complexities of plot are, typically, the way the ingenious heroine contrives to get herself out of trouble and on to the happy-ever-after path. Except that Tirso's comic vision is not that complacent. The selfishness and ruthlessness exhibited by seemingly nice people in pursuit of their own ends are embedded in the humour of the plays like a gently gnawing toothache, and their endings have an astringency which stays with us and subtly subverts the plot's conventional unravelling.

The controlled complexity and ingenuity, the wit and unique sparkle of his comedies of intrigue have rightly led to his acknowledgement as a master of this genre which was so popular in seventeenth-century Spain. In *El vergonzoso en palacio* (*The Shy Man at Court*) one of the three main characters, the wayward, narcissistic Serafina, falls in love with a picture of herself dressed as a man, not recognizing it as her own. *Don Gil de las calzas verdes* (*Don Gil of the Green Breeches*) is a hilarious romp so complex that in the final scene, in spite of the fact that no real don Gil exists, no fewer than four turn up, all in green breeches. In *La celosa de sí misma* (*Jealous of Herself*), don Melchor falls so passionately in love with an unknown lady's hand at Mass that he refuses to go ahead with his arranged marriage to Magdalena, whose hand it is. Mysteriously depersonalized, the hand attracts him, openly attached to his betrothed's arm it loses its mystery and therefore its appeal: Tirso is almost certainly sending up the neo-platonic cult of an ideal love that leaves the body and reality behind in its pursuit of perfection. In *Marta la piadosa* (*Pious Martha*) the eponymous heroine pretends to have a religious vocation to avoid an unwelcome match and once out of the marriage stakes is allowed to roam around the streets at will – an ironic comment on contemporary attitudes to women. The quirkiness of Tirso's imagination, his fascination with role play and illusion, and his uncompromisingly realistic view of human nature will be immediately apparent. Human vanity and gullibility, the capacity of human beings to deceive themselves and others, the lack of honesty and realism in the way man and society conduct their affairs, are all strongly predicated in Tirso's comedies, but the attractive thing about them is that they never preach and rarely judge. Tirso manages to establish that perfect equilibrium between exposure and understanding which we expect of the best comedy, provoking an ambivalence of response that is entirely satisfying. We warm to Serafina's non-conformity but laugh at her self-preoccupation; the notion of falling in love with a hand appeals to our sense of the absurd, yet its attraction for a man faced with an arranged match strikes a chord with our belief in the legitimacy of romance; we can accept the logic of allowing a prospective nun to do as she likes, yet deplore the hypocrisy of the rationalizations used to prevent marriageable girls from doing the same.

The originality in these comedies lies in their ingenious or unusual treatment of themes and situations already introduced by Lope and this is true of much of Tirso's theatre. But he is not always successful in his use of established motifs, tending to pack too much too breathlessly into his plays which can then end up seeming rather hasty and predictable. His trump card was his ability to produce memorable characters. Thus his enthusiastic adoption of the type of the forceful woman produced heroines like *La gallega Mari-Hernández* (*Mari-Hernández from Galicia*) and *Antona García*. Mari-Hernández is a fusion of two distinct *comedia* types: the rumbustious country wench and the quick-witted miss who for the sake of love poses as a dashing gallant (a particular favourite of Tirso's). Hers is a double image: the hoyden looks into the mirror but it is the charming Galician aristocrat who gazes back and only Tirso could have successfully synthesized the two.

Antona García, based on a woman who in 1476 conspired to oust the Portuguese from the Spanish city of Toro, is reminiscent of certain East European shot-putters with her herculean strength and fondness for horseplay. But in this dominating, idealistic peasant woman, compounded as she is of masculine and feminine qualities, Tirso almost succeeded in creating a masterpiece. He fails because, once again, he embarks on something more complex than he has time for – he allows his attention to be divided between historical theme and protagonist. Indeed Tirso often strikes one as a dramatist interested above all in characterization but trapped by historical accident within what was primarily a theatre of action.

His most memorable heroine and without a doubt the noblest female figure on the Spanish stage is María de Molina in the historical play *La prudencia en la mujer* (*Prudence in Woman*). María was regent of Castile during the minority of her son and Tirso portrays her fighting to protect her son's interests from unruly nobles who, because she is a woman, think she is easy prey. Here the combined emphasis on character, historical events and moral idealism works because all three are inseparable. María proves to be a supremely able ruler and Tirso with the utmost care draws her in her threefold majesty as perfect wife, queen and mother in an age and society dominated by men. It is a characterization both grand and nuanced. Tirso shows the human doubts and misgivings beneath the Queen's surface control and at the same time reveals in her an astuteness, a realism, an intelligent sense of strategy which nicely leaven her sublime virtue and nobility. In spite of the disadvantages of having a model protagonist, therefore, the play is entirely gripping and believable. It is essentially a *de regimine principum* in dramatic form in that it has direct relevance to the situation created in Spain by the death of Philip III in 1621.[3] The accession of a sixteen-year-old boy to the throne of the world's largest empire at a time when its future was seen by Spanish intellectuals to be in the balance understandably intensified Spanish concern with the concept of kingship and delegated authority. It is a concern that informs many Spanish plays of the period. Tirso repeatedly chose to dramatize this preoccupation using woman rulers, though I doubt whether this has any particular significance in terms of sexual politics. The Empress Irene in *La república al revés* (*The Republic Turned Upside Down*) is a lesser María de Molina, the very model of the wise and just monarch by which her son Constantine is measured and found wanting; but in the character of the biblical Jezabel in *La mujer que manda en casa* (*The Woman who Rules the Roost*) he depicts a female tyrant. Tirso could readily conceive of woman as possessing the qualities necessary for leadership, but essentially he was tackling a contemporary preoccupation in a way which was congenial to him, which was theatrically attractive and which at the same time diplomatically deflected the plays' overt relevance to the Spanish king.

The importance of the seventeenth-century political background for our understanding of many Golden-Age plays is only gradually emerging, but it is already clear that Tirso was probably the most politicized of the Spanish dramatists of the age. In the years before his banishment he wrote a number of plays, *La prudencia en la mujer* and *Privar contra su gusto* (*The Reluctant Favourite*) amongst them, which are critical of government and corruption at court and which pointedly reflect contemporary misgivings about the new reign and its *éminence grise*, Olivares.[4] It has recently been persuasively argued that even his Pizarro trilogy, apparently fairly run-of-the-mill plays written between 1626 and 1629 while Tirso was head of the Mercedarian convent in Trujillo founded by Francisco Pizarro's daughter, is an audacious indictment of the failings of centralized government and delegated power.[5]

Some of the most successful of Tirso's plays are those which dramatize biblical events. *La mujer que manda en casa* is one of the most memorable, in spite of its structural weaknesses, because of the explosive and beguiling presence of its protagonist, Jezabel, an incarnation of the medieval Vice figure. The sexual relish she exudes, her unexpected inhibitions, her rages, her unquenchable belief in her own attractions, give the play a sexual charge which threatens at times to swamp its exemplary aspects. The best of these plays, however, is *La venganza de Tamar* (*Thamar's Vengeance*) which is closely based on the account in Samuel II of Thamar's rape by her half-brother Amnon and the latter's murder by her full brother Absalom. No hasty craftsmanship here – the play is an extremely accomplished piece of writing. Structurally Tirso makes three memorable additions to the familiar story. First is the charade scene where Amón, feigning to be mourning a lost love, persuades his unsuspecting sister to 'cure' him by acting the part of his mistress in a courtship scene. The sinister discrepancy between Tamar's understanding of the situation and the obsessed Amón's intentions in this play within the play is dramatically very potent. The flower scene in Act III where the peasant girl Laurela presents the brothers Amón, Adonías, Salomón and Absalón with a lily, a larkspur, a saxifrage and a narcissus is rich in dramatic irony and prophetic symbolism. While the pathetic hallucination scene where old King David, fearing for his beloved first son Amón who is in fact already dead, goes to embrace him, is extremely moving. The outstanding feature of the play, however, is its characterization. The disintegration of Amón's self-control, his disgust for Tamar after the rape and his outrageous shrugging off of responsibility after he threatens to rape her a second time when she is disguised as a peasant girl – a betrayal of his vow to behave that is crucial to our judgement of him and his father – these are magnificently portrayed. Explained as melancholy in terms of the medical theory of humours of the age, his obsession is in fact presented as an integral part of a characterization which is convincingly all of a piece. Absalón too – narcissistic, urbane, plausible and self-justifying – is drawn with care and consistency, while Tamar is superb in her anger and her scorn. Through her verbal quickness and the consistently witty and metaphorical language she uses to convey her predicament she dominates the play intellectually.

As the play proceeds, however, it is the old King who emerges as the tragic figure, torn between his love for his children and dismay at their behaviour, incapable any more of exercising either his judgement or his authority. We are left at the end with the poignant image of the once great and powerful king lamenting the murder of his beloved first son, a murder precipitated by his own partisan compulsion to put mercy before justice. The last line of his speech, invoking as it does the murderer Absalón, reminds the audience that the full course of this tragedy is not yet run.

It has been suggested that the action of *La venganza de Tamar* unfolds against a contemporary political background characterized by the upheavals that surrounded the succession of Philip IV to the throne of Spain in 1621; Tirso undoubtedly saw the death of Philip III as marking the end of stability and prosperity for Spain.[6] But a contemporary audience's interest would have been captured mainly by its powerful handling of a particularly gripping, familiar biblical story. The full-length plays on biblical and doctrinal themes by seventeenth-century Spanish dramatists constitute a significant proportion of the theatre's total output. Lope proved their popularity and other dramatists followed his example in providing the *corrales* with plays which could unequivocally boast of providing instruction along with entertainment. The theatre as a result became in a way a self-appointed instrument of the faith, providing an extra dimension to the religious life of Spain that at once reflected and stimulated popular devotion and afforded the theatre some protection from the attacks of ecclesiastical and moral reformers. This allowed churchmen to become enthusiastic patrons of the *corrales* and of course a significant number of dramatists were themselves men of God: of the three major playwrights both Lope and Calderón became playwright-priests, while Tirso was from the start of his career a friar. Technically the religious plays they wrote do not constitute a category apart. They were performed in the *corrales* before the usual audiences and were written to the familiar *comedia* pattern. They speak the standard language of love and honour, they are full of action, excitement and passion, with *graciosos* who provide touches of comedy, and they employ all the conventions and devices of the secular plays. They even use sexual excitement as a legitimate channel of moral instruction, as can be seen in Tirso's *La mujer que manda en casa* and Calderón's *La devoción de la cruz* (*Devotion to the Cross*). To all intents and purposes they take place in a world whose ethos is recognizably that of seventeenth-century Spain. The liberties they took with their material often attracted the opprobrium of the theatre's critics but their audiences, of course, loved them.

The *comedias de santos*, saints' plays, form a coherent group within this larger body. These normally portray, with considerable artistic licence, the conversion or martyrdom of famous figures from hagiographic history and legend, but the special dramatic potential inherent in the theme of conversion inspired bolder, freer creations as well. There are as a result a number of very striking plays which depict not only the conversion and salvation of criminals but conversely the descent into crime of men and women who have been travelling the road to sainthood. This chiastic movement between the two poles of criminality and sanctity baffled, even shocked commentators until A. A. Parker convincingly argued that the plays present problems which are in fact psychological and social (in the widest sense) rather than religious, and therefore essentially moral not dogmatic.[7] Banditry in the Golden-Age drama is unquestionably a means of personal self-assertion and not of sociopolitical reform as it tends to be in other literatures. The psychological and philosophical justification of the apparently melodramatic plots, Parker claimed, is to be found in the proverb 'The greatest sinners make the greatest saints', which implies that temperamental energy is a prerequisite both of great good and great evil, and in the aphorism 'Corruptio optimi pessima' which encapsulates the Thomist principle that evil follows from the inversion or distortion of good.

The most famous and the finest of these plays is Tirso's magnificently grim *El condenado por desconfiado* (*Damned for Despair*),[8] a complex play which seems to confirm Parker's interpretation of the psychology of the saints and bandits plays but which has in addition an important contemporary theological dimension. Tirso uses the psychology of sin and repentance to confront in an unusually direct way for the theatre two of the dominant religious problems of the age – the question of justification by faith or good works and the related question of free will and divine grace. Even within Catholicism there was such fierce disagreement between Jesuits and Dominicans over the relationship between free will and divine grace that in

1611 the exasperated Inquisition forbade the publication of any more works on the subject of grace. In 1607 the Pope's pronouncement that both sides were free to defend their opinions had been jubilantly greeted in Madrid with fireworks and bull-fights. When Tirso dramatized these problems some years later he was dealing not with some technical squabble over abstractions but with a topic of still passionate concern.

The play tells the story of two young men. Paulo is a hermit who to save his soul has spent ten years of penance and prayer in the wilderness. One night he has a terrifying nightmare of Hell which impels him to beg God to reveal his spiritual fate. Seeing his chance, the Devil appears in the guise of an angel to tell him that his fate will be that of a certain Enrico. Paulo complacently assumes that Enrico must be a saintly man and is horrified to discover that he is a dyed-in-the-wool villain. Overwhelmed by bitterness and despair he avenges himself on God by becoming a murderous bandit himself. Unable to believe that either Enrico or he himself can now be saved he meets a violent death at the hands of the law and goes unrepentant to Hell. What he did not know was that Enrico himself has never lost faith in the possibility of redemption; just before Enrico's execution his ailing father, whom he loves, respects and supports, prevails upon him to repent and he is saved. The Devil's ambiguous prophecy has proved both true and untrue; whether or not the Devil himself knew that Enrico would in fact escape his clutches remains an intriguing question mark.

The play's theological position vis-à-vis the De auxiliis controversy is elusive, perhaps intentionally so; in a way it compromises by emphasizing both faith and responsibility. Its practical message of faith, hope and charity, however, is clearly spelt out. So, too, are Paulo's sins: doubt in the efficacy of repentance, arrogance in trying to preempt his own fate and lack of charity in his judgement of Enrico. The power of the play comes from Tirso's masterly ability to give dramatic life to these ideas by showing us two men gambling for the highest stakes of all – eternity. Even for us now the play succeeds in making this issue as dramatically real and immediate as any threat of physical death; its impact on an audience of seventeenth-century believers is not difficult to imagine. The work's fascination lies partly in the startling outcome,[9] partly in the understandable uncertainty and confusion generated in Paulo, and in Act III in Enrico as well, by the difficulty of telling the real from the counterfeit, of distinguishing between false voices and true. There is fascination too in the contrary characters of Paulo and Enrico, both psychological adolescents, the one rebelling against an apparently unjust God, the other against all restraints upon his own will. Our reactions to each are complicated. In Paulo we recognize the rational intellectual, eager to know, incapable of blind faith and irrational hope, believing in fair and logical connections between crime and punishment, effort and reward. We understand the insecurity, self-doubt and almost pathological fear which lead to his calculating attempt to buy himself salvation and then erupt into the fateful nightmare. At the same time we lose patience with his meanness of spirit, his wilful over-interpretation of the Devil's prophecy,[10] his obdurate rejection of hope in the face of all encouragement and, above all, his refusal throughout to accept responsibility for himself and his fate. As for the presumptuous Enrico, we detest his mindless violence and bully-boy ways, but we respect his spiritual courage and are moved by his tenderness towards his father and most of all we admire his complete acceptance of responsibility for what happens to him. He recognizes that forgiveness is there, that it is up to him ask for it or not. Paulo, on the contrary, is guilty even at the end of a crucial failure of understanding: when assured that Enrico has been saved he sees no need to repent, confident that he will automatically share the same fate.

The abdication of control over his own destiny, together with his incapacity for love – love of God, his neighbour or himself – makes of Paulo the lesser man, for all Enrico's wickedness. Not only theologically but psychologically and dramatically as well, the play's outcome is entirely convincing and consistent. The fact that it leaves us harbouring more sympathy than we probably ought to feel for the pessimist, the man temperamentally incapable of faith, is a reflection of Tirso's tendency to create characters which overflow the containing ideas of the age. It is certainly the inadequate, anguished Paulo, unable to the last to see that the salvation he hungers for lies all along within his own grasp, who remains most vividly with us; the scene in Act III in which he dons his hermit's garb once more and desperately tries to persuade an impatient Enrico to repent has a quite extraordinary intensity.

As becomes its subject the play is sparely written. Dramatically and theatrically it operates entirely through the stark power of its parallel enactment of two conflicting ideologies and two opposed temperaments in a situation where Hell's flames await the one who has misunderstood the nature of redemption. There are virtually no concessions to public taste. Both men are in their different ways insufferable and apart from the stricken Anareto, Enrico's father and for him a sort of God-figure, the play is full of objectionable individuals. There is no real love interest – Enrico has a sharp but unsavoury moll who plays a minor role. Apart from a few intense speeches of Paulo's, more elaborate as becomes his intellectual and contemplative nature, the play's language is correspondingly pared down and direct. The work has as its structural basis an elegant symmetry, the symmetry of its protagonists, each with his servant, the symmetry of its supernatural adversaries – the Devil and the Good Shepherd – or inner voices, and the criss-cross symmetry of the saints and bandits theme. Its final theatrical effects are appropriately awe-inspiring and balanced: Enrico's soul soars heavenward supported by angels, Paulo disappears in flames through a trapdoor in the stage. The popularity of doctrinal drama in Spain was due in no small measure to such spectacular climaxes.[11]

The play that makes truly magnificent drama out of Christian ideas and reveals the eternal human preoccupations they contain was Spain's distinctive contribution to European drama. Tirso's most famous play *El burlador de Sevilla o El convidado de piedra (The Trickster of Seville or The Stone Guest)* is another masterly example.[12] Less openly dogmatic than *El condenado por desconfiado*, it is, for all that it gave Europe one of its legendary lovers, don Juan, another eschatological work. Here, however, presumption, bombast, and over-confidence end up not in Heaven but in Hell. The don Juan of popular imagination – compulsive, irresistible lover, intellectual and social rebel – is a composite figure, the result of many subsequent versions and variations. Tirso's original is very different – a brothel-creeper, a trickster, a predator, a betrayer of promises, friends and hospitality, a murderer even – who delights not in seducing women but, more sinisterly, in dishonouring and humiliating them. He wins their favours either by bribery or outright deception. He is not a rebel but a criminal within the system, exploiting his social privileges to further his own ends, believing in divine retribution but foolhardy enough to think that youth is an insurance against it. He prates about his honour when in fact he is everything that is dishonourable; he believes in the rules but regards himself as above them.

As the alternative titles of the play indicate, the work has two main strands which converge in don Juan's consignment to Hell: that of the trickster and that of the stone guest. We are shown four of don Juan's sexual japes. He makes love to the Duchess Isabela in the King's palace by pretending to be her fiancé; he seduces a fishergirl, Tisbea, under solemn promise of marriage (regarded as binding by the conventions of the theatre); he tries to take his best friend's place in his mistress doña Ana's bed when the lovers arrange a tryst to consummate their passion, and finally he desecrates a sacrament by seducing the bride, Aminta, on her wedding night under promise of marriage to himself – 'the choicest trick of all'. This essentially episodic plot is given cohesion and sustained tension by don Juan's obliviousness to the gravity of his actions. His catchphrase whenever he is warned that he will one day be called to account for his crimes, 'Tan largo me lo fiáis' ('You certainly allow me extended credit' – *fianza* being a financial and legal term meaning credit or bailbond) becomes the play's leitmotif, reminding us that while don Juan thinks time is on his side (penance, he thinks, is for the infirm and the aged) it is in fact rushing him onwards towards his doom. The time bomb is triggered when don Juan scornfully invites to dinner the sepulchral statue of doña Ana's father, don Gonzalo, killed while defending his daughter from don Juan's predations. That night a thundering on the door announces the arrival of the terrifying guest, who sits at the table but remains silent in the face of don Juan's flippant bravado and his servant Catalinón's hysterical attempts at conversation. Only when he and don Juan are left alone does he speak, to invite don Juan to dine with him in return the following night in his chapel and only after the statue has left does don Juan collapse into terror. Persuading himself that it was all a figment of his imagination and that not to turn up the following night would be a sign of cowardice, don Juan decides to go. After a meal of vipers and scorpions, vinegar and gall, during which don Juan remains defiant to the end, the statue offers don Juan his outstretched hand. He takes it, only to be fatally overpowered by its burning, crushing grip, refused the absolution he begs for and swallowed up into the tomb, never to re-emerge. As he disappears, the statue booms out, 'This is God's justice: as man sows therefore shall he reap.'

While Tirso took don Juan's catchphrase and the idea of the stone guest from oral tradition (the exchange of invitations between a living man and a corpse belongs to European folklore),[13] don Juan was his own creation. Tirso's conception of the character has a moral and ethical emphasis absent from don Juan the myth figure, symbol of sexual energy and individualistic self-assertion. There is undoubtedly an incontrovertible fascination in don Juan's brazen recklessness in the play, in his refusal of fear in the face of the supernatural, in his sense of himself as archetypal man; when he refuses to let Isabela light a lamp to see his face and she cries out in alarm '¿Quién eres, hombre?' ('Who are you, man?'), his answer is 'Un hombre sin nombre' '(A man without a name'). And herein the seeds of the myth lie. Tirso's don Juan, however, as bringer of chaos and confusion, with his sinister arrogance, his delight in power and control, his cynicism and slippery duplicity, assumes an aura that is more than human. When he appears in Aminta's bedroom and she remonstrates '¿En mi cuarto a estas horas?' ('In my bedroom at this hour?'), he replies 'Éstas son las horas mías' ('These hours are mine'). Night is his element; it is no coincidence that the play opens in the dark and that, like some earlier Count Dracula, don Juan resists the light. It is not only we who catch a whiff of the Devil: described by his uncle as a snake – the Devil's symbol – he is explicitly called Lucifer by that man of judgement and conscience, his servant Catalinón, when he commiserates with the wretched Aminta. Defiant to the end, he is greater in death than in life; it is in defeat that he commands our admiration. He is one of the few Golden-Age characters who swamp the action that contains them. He is too big for the play and hence has had to leave it behind.

His ultimate sin is Lucifer's own – he challenges God himself, unaware that he is playing with hell-fire. Fire consequently provides the play's dominant imagery, linking as it does the ideas of sexual lust and destruction. Don Juan uses vocabulary of fire to describe not only his passions but his contempt for the world – 'que el mundo se abrase y queme' ('Let the world burn and go up in flames') – and significantly he uses the same words in reverse when he is crushed by the statue – '¡Que me quemo! ¡Que me abraso!' ('I am in flames! I burn!'). When he disappears the whole chapel goes up in flames; the destroyer is destroyed, the consumer consumed; Hell has claimed its own. It is a cataclysmic ending to a cataclysmic struggle. Don Juan has defied God's law as well as man's, pitting the power of youth and noble birth against the power of time and divine retribution. He has scoffed at death and it is therefore a dead man who calls in the debts he thought he could pay at his own convenience. The relationships he has violated are, with a little manoueuvring and papering over the cracks, re-established in a socially acceptable way. But there is no complacency in this ending. Few characters emerge with honour from the events the play portrays, and peasantry and aristocracy alike are depicted with a pervasive irony.

This gives the play a unity of tone and vision which, together with the themes of deception and deferred payment, and the metaphors of the bailbond, fire and personified death, knits the four episodes into a dramatic whole. The work has not the structural perfection of *El condenado por desconfiado*. Of the women, the proud self-assertive Tisbea is the only one in whom any dramatic conflict takes place, and even so the thematic parallelism between her character and don Juan's – she delights in making men suffer as he does women – is never developed. Once more we see Tirso's imagination straining against the discipline of the *comedia* form. For all this, the work is a magnificent achievement, thematically and poetically tightly coherent, theatrically stunning, with a larger than life protagonist of extraordinary potency who was to step out of the work and capture the imagination of the world in a way unrivalled by any other dramatic creation. In consigning don Juan to Hell, Tirso ironically gave him the gift of immortality: the theologian in Tirso would have disapproved but the artist would certainly have rejoiced.

Tirso is the only seventeenth-century dramatist who compares with Lope and Calderón in terms both of sustained achievement and outstandingly memorable individual plays. Distinctive as their typical creations are, they habitually combine theatrical impact, thematic weight and mastery of language in a way not matched consistently by any other dramatist. Nonetheless, Lope's lessons were successfully applied and developed by a number of other gifted dramatists capable of producing plays of the first order. It must be emphasized that the drama during Lope's theatrical hegemony did not stand still. Not only was there a general move, led by Lope himself, towards greater artistic control, but there were as the years went by certain developments from which Lope remained aloof: a marked growth in the satirical content of plays, and the visible influence on some dramatists (not Tirso) of the complex, Latinate language of Góngora's major poetic works, the *Fábula de Polifemo y Galatea* (1613) and the *Soledades* (1614). There was a certain tendency, too, to sensationalism, exaggeration and stylization, a move away from realism into the fantastic and mannered. Satire apart, Lope's followers were walking the path that would lead to Calderón.

Guillén de Castro (1569–1631)

The lively Valencian theatre whose acquaintance Lope first made in the early years of his career flourished for several decades before fading away and leaving Madrid in uncontested control of the Spanish stage. For all its peripheral position it had in any case become an outpost of Lope's new drama, albeit a slightly idiosyncratic one, sharing its aims, ideals and methods. Its leading light was Guillén de Castro, gentleman and government and military functionary, whose move to Madrid in 1619 effectively marks the demise of the Valencian drama as a semi-independent entity.[14] A playwright with a predilection for stirring historical plays, for which he skilfully utilized traditional ballads, and for elegant comedies, he has a deservedly high reputation for the psychological and emotional finesse with which he endows his characters and for his somewhat unconventional approach to standard themes. He is regarded, with some justification, as rabidly anti-marriage and anti-woman, which itself marks him out from most other dramatists, and he generally ignored the *comedia*'s preference for self-assertive heroines. On the other hand some of his female characters are splendid and his plays reveal considerable insight into the psychology of love, which he saw not only as woman's proper sphere of activity but as man's strongest motivation.

His best-known play *Las mocedades de Rodrigo* (*Young Rodrigo*), the inspiration for Corneille's *Le Cid*, is interesting not only for its portrayal of Spain's greatest hero, El Cid, as a young man, but for the way it depicts a Jimena torn between love and a deeply felt sense of filial duty (Rodrigo has killed her father) which is deemed by king and court to be inappropriate and irrelevant in a woman. The direct conflict between love and honour (which is how the struggle is articulated) in a man is often dramatized in the *comedia* but is unusual to see it actively at work in the heart and mind of a woman and the play illustrates Castro's typical off-beat approach. His Dido, in *Dido y Eneas*, is likewise Virgil's impassioned lover rather than Justinian's chaste queen, the preferred version of sixteenth-century Spain. *Progne y Filomena*, his version of the gruesome Procne and Philomela legend, not only, incredibly, has a happy ending – made possible by the fact that Progne after serving Tereseo their son for supper, is able to forgive him when she discovers that he did not after all manage to rape her sister Filomena – but it dramatizes Ovid's tale as a straightforward revenge story without any 'Spanish' shaping in terms of honour. This might have something to do with its early date (probably pre-1600), but the theme of honour–vengeance was already gaining ground in the theatre in the 1590s, with Castro's fellow Valencian Aguilar playing no small part in its elaboration and codification, so it is probably another example of Castro's preference for a personal approach.

One of Castro's most original plays is a brilliant comedy, *La fuerza de la costumbre* (*The Force of Habit*), which depicts how a sister and brother separated as babies, the former brought up as a soldier by her father in Flanders, the latter tied to his mother's apron strings in Spain, are turned into a 'normal' young woman and man when the family is reunited. The parallel reconstruction of their correct gender identities is done with great wit, humour and charm; the play is a sharply eloquent illustration of social conditioning for all that Castro himself would undoubtedly have regarded the process as a rediscovery of the young people's essential selves. In Hipólita's case it is, predictably, love which accelerates the transformation, turning her from a loud-mouthed tomboy trying in vain to cope with skirts and high heels, into a maiden who starts at a mouse, but Castro unconventionally deploys too the precipitating power of sex. When Hipólita insists on challenging her lover don Luis to a duel for infidelity, he takes her to a spot where the grass is wet, she slips and falls and he makes love to her. As she admits later to her mother, 'And in truth, mother, since then I am a woman.' Ironically, Hipólita's masculinity is betrayed and subverted throughout, and her femininity revealed, by her 'masculine' directness, and the metamorphosis of both sister and brother is depicted with admirable subtlety for all the conventional assumptions on which it is based.

Antonio Mira de Amescua (1574?–1644)

Of Lope's fully-fledged disciples, Antonio Mira de Amescua and Luis Vélez de Guevara are the most prominent. Mira was a tempestuous priest of illegitimate birth who neglected his ecclesiastical duties in Andalusia in favour of a literary life in Madrid, where he wrote for the *corrales* and acted as official book censor.[15] He enjoyed a very high reputation as a dramatist in his day, deservedly so because he possessed a powerful and exuberant if somewhat unruly talent. He exemplifies the tendency of dramatists of the time to overstuff their plays with episodic incidents and motifs and to pursue ingenuity and novelty at the expense of credibility – common failings for obvious reasons of popular entertainment, particulary in the hands of lesser writers. Nonetheless he produced some excellent historical dramas – the tragedy *La próspera fortuna de Álvaro de Luna* (*The Good Fortune of Álvaro de Luna*) is an outstanding example[16] – and very accomplished comedies of intrigue characterized by lavish local colour. Amongst the best of these are *La fénix de Salamanca* (*The Phoenix of Salamanca*) about a woman who goes off in masculine disguise to search for her lover, and *Galán, valiente y discreto* (*Gallant, Bold and Discriminating*) about a duchess wary of fortune hunters who tests the love of her man by pretending to be her own maid. The extraordinary *No hay burlas con las mujeres o Casarse y vengarse* (*There's No Ridiculing Women or To Marry for Revenge*) may sound like a comedy but is in fact one of the many uncategorizable Golden-Age plays where seemingly predictable situations take unpredictable turns. The heroine, slapped in the face by her jealous lover, reacts with such ferocity to the insult that she does not rest until she has killed him. So ludicrous is the discrepancy between insult and revenge – no theatre husband, after all, kills his wife because she has hit him – that we assume that Mira is sending up the whole idea of honour–vengeance, for all that there is little humour in the play. In the play's closing lines Mira makes it clear that he realized his punctilious heroine was a novelty even in a theatre full of women who react positively to dishonour. *No hay burlas con las mujeres* is a disturbing play of uncertain tone where melodrama fails because it is deployed without cause or conviction. Yet Mira was a master of melodrama and his best-known play *El esclavo del demonio* (*The Devil's*

Slave),[17] which is one of the outstanding hagiographic plays of the period, is a vindication of melodrama as an art form.

Like his other famous saints and bandits play, *La mesonera del cielo* (*Heaven's Innkeeper*), *El esclavo del demonio*, the first play of the period to confront seriously the problems of social rebellion and free will, is a sure-fire combination of sex and religion. Based on a historical figure, its impact was enormous; it not only influenced Tirso's *El condenado por desconfiado* but was a major source for Calderón's *La devoción de la cruz* and *El mágico prodigioso*, and it was reworked by three dramatists, Matos Fragoso, Cáncer and Moreto, for their collaborative effort *Caer para levantar* (*Fall to Rise*), Act II of which lifts scenes verbatim from Mira's play. *El esclavo* portrays how don Gil, Canon of Coimbra, after dissuading don Diego from eloping with Lisarda, succumbs to temptation, himself climbs the ladder to her room and takes Diego's place in her bed. In an attempt to drag Lisarda down to infamy with him he tells Lisarda that Diego sent him thus to humiliate her. Cursed by her father for wanting to marry the man who killed her brother, deceived and dishonoured (so she thinks) by the man she loves and violated by don Gil, Lisarda decides she has no more to lose and joins Gil in a life of crime. The play ends in salvation for both of them but the way there is strewn with moments of intense drama and excitement. The desperately fatalistic Gil sells his soul to the Devil; Lisarda, at best a half-hearted criminal, repents and becomes a voluntary slave; the Devil and an angel battle for Gil's soul on stage; and finally Lisarda's corpse is revealed with those typical seventeenth-century emblems, a cross and a skull. There is a sub-plot involving Lisarda's obedient and sensible if somewhat coquettish sister, who ends up married to the Prince of Portugal.

For all that it proved a goldmine of fertile ideas, the play itself is a deeply flawed work. There is no real link between Gil's story and Lisarda's, they constitute effectively two different plays. The work is distractingly full, uneven in tone and mood and nothing is properly developed: the motivation is sketchy and changes of heart are hurried and unconvincing. It is a perfect example, in fact, of the disorderly exuberance critics were complaining of in the early years of the seventeenth century when it was written. Nonetheless it has considerable dramatic stature. As the story of man's difficult journey towards the truth and a resounding rejection of Calvinistic predestination it has tremendous force and conviction. The quality of the language is high, with vivid and original metaphors and excellent dialogue, the passionate intensity of emotion is entirely convincing (even from the lips of such intrinsically melodramatic characters), it has an endearingly worldly Devil, and the idea of the foil of the 'normal' sister is well-conceived and executed. The opening scenes are first-rate: the sense of happiness missed by a hair of fortune's head is very poignant and the power of deception, misinformation and temptation to create a situation where the well-being of all is prejudiced is chillingly conveyed. It is an unforgettable play for all its faults, an excellent example of the imaginative vigour of Spain's religious drama. In its gloomy view of man's existence and its emphasis on the need for faith and neo-stoic resignation it is typical of Mira's drama in general.

Luis Vélez de Guevara (1579–1644)

The list of Mira's fifty or so surviving plays reveals the standard diet of the *corrales*: history and legend – national, classical and foreign – comic intrigue and religion. His contemporary the Sevillian Luis Vélez de Guevara, a favourite of Olivares who became a gentleman-in-waiting at court in spite of his openly acknowledged *converso* (Jewish) origins, wrote across the same range, revealing in even greater measure the same preferences and tendencies – ornate language, larger than life characters, lavish, action-filled plots, a fondness for miracles and the supernatural, a passion for the extreme and the unusual, and for generous local colour, particularly in his case the colour of court life.[18] He had a predilection not only for energetic, stout-hearted female characters but for machine plays (plays in which mechanical devices were used to create illusions) and was largely responsible for popularizing them, first in the *corrales* and later at court. Much more prolific than Mira and equally popular in his own day, Vélez combines Mira's energetic imagination with a greater range of tone, even a certain delicacy at times, and a more ironic, detached view of the world. *La luna de la sierra* (*The Moon of the Mountains*) exemplifies some of these qualities.[19] It also illustrates the way in which familiar plot situations repeatedly turn up in different ingenious, even original, guises in the seventeenth-century theatre, for although the rural story it tells is similar in outline to that of Lope's *Peribáñez*, it is a very different work. It is an honour play of an unusual sort, with no hint of tragedy or disaster. It is romantic, amusing, lightweight and self-consciously contrived, with stylized characters and highly symbolic language. It even ends unconventionally – as the final lines take pleasure in pointing out – without the usual marriage. A theatrical portmanteau packed with familiar themes, motifs and episodes in which the heroine Pascuala, whose symbolic nickname figures in the title, is pursued by no fewer than four suitors, its sprawling, open structure is so deftly handled that one is tempted not to criticize it but to accept it as a perfectly valid alternative form of dramatic construction.

La serrana de la Vera (*The Mountain-Maid of La Vera*) is a play in a very different vein in which Vélez indulges his fondness for the inflated and extreme. A *bandolera* play based on a play of Lope's with the same name, it follows the pattern, established by Lope, of the woman who reacts to sexual victimization by becoming an outlaw and waging war on men in general.[20] Vélez, however, gives his play an atmosphere of savagery and violence of its own and his hoydenish heroine Gila – who kills a thousand men – is a brutal caricature of her dramatic prototype. So consistent is her characterization, however, and so carefully depicted the psychology of wounded pride and humiliation, that even these excesses are made to seem almost plausible. Indeed the play, which ends – exceptionally amongst the *bandolera* plays – with Gila being executed for her crimes, is the tragedy of a woman driven to her downfall by the excess of temperament and physique she was born with, a tragedy heavy with melodrama but none the less potent for that.

Vélez's finest play, *Reinar después de morir* (*Queen After Death*), one of the Spanish drama's best-known plays and arguably its finest tragedy along conventional lines, has not a hint of melodrama. Based on an episode of fourteenth-century Portuguese history, it portrays how the beautiful and virtuous Castilian, Doña Inés, who is secretly married to the heir to the Portuguese throne, is murdered for reasons of state to allow the Prince to marry his official bride. After her death, her distraught husband, now King, crowns her Queen. Vélez had the sense to allow this poignant tale to work for itself without added complications, creating a concentrated, linear plot which relies for its effect on the beauty and power of the couple's love, the intensity of the emotions portrayed and the pathos of the denouement. There is little action – emotion and mood and the words which carry them are all. It is a lyrical, elegantly constructed work which makes extremely effective use of symbolism, omens, parallels and symmetry. The play's outcome is rendered tragic rather than merely unfortunate by Vélez's skill in creating the sense of a real dilemma, a conflict of legitimate but irreconcilable interests. Although our pity goes out to Inés and the Prince we do see that duty has some claim, that it is indeed in Portugal's interest to arrange a dynastic marriage, that a Princess of Navarre cannot be sent packing after a dynastic marriage has been contracted. Doña Blanca's sense of outrage at her insensitive rejection by the Prince and the manipulated King's agonized indecisiveness, command our sympathies, as they are meant to. In this Hegelian conflict between two desirable ends the Prince himself, I think, must be seen as the tragic protagonist. Inés, for all her spirit, is an innocent, passive victim, her death a sickening outrage. It is the Prince who, with that singleminded intensity which in tragedy leads inexorably to disaster, forgets that as a Prince he is not his own man and fails to see the consequences of his actions and words, and who, having caused the suffering, is then left to live with it. His crowning of Inés's corpse at the end is at once the celebration of an enduring love and an expiation of guilt.

Juan Ruiz de Alarcón (1581?–1639)

Castro, Mira and Vélez were friends and self-acknowledged admirers of Lope. 'The remaining figure in this group of runner-up dramatists, however, remained personally aloof from Lope and his inner circle, although he was a friend of Tirso's. In the circumstances this was hardly surprising: a man of difficult character with a severe hunchback and unconcealed social and professional ambitions, he and his plays were at first ridiculed and attacked by most of the poets of the time, Lope foremost amongst them, though he did gain some acceptance later on.

Born in Mexico, Juan Ruiz de Alarcón came to Spain in 1600 and seems to have established a prosperous career for himself in legal administration, writing in between times some twenty successful plays.[21] Although he worked within the dramatic pattern he found in the Madrid theatres, Alarcón's drama has the flavour of something altogether more 'modern' than that of other playwrights – less heroic, less extravagant and fantastic, less romanticized and idealized, even more mundane. His characters in general have a basic urbanity and reasonableness. His fathers are not seen just in terms of generational conflict as authority figures, but stand for acceptable values and provide sensible guidance. Even standard *comedia* situations have in his plays a down-to-earth quality: in *El examen de maridos* (*The Husbands' Review*) Inés's admiration for the Marquis is maliciously deflected by the false assurance that he suffers from bad breath, while in *El tejedor de Segovia* (*The Weaver of Segovia*) Pedro frees himself from his thumb chains by biting off his thumbs. The impression of realism is intensified by the language. Although written in verse, Alarcón's is not a poetic drama; he does not habitually deploy imagery to create patterns of meaning and he avoided Gongorine complexity. His dialogue is brisk, naturalistic and efficient. Like Tirso, Alarcón is a sharply critical observer of contemporary society as well as of human nature. He is particularly good on social pretensions and on people's motives for falling in and out of love. There is a strong emphasis in his plays on the heroism of virtue and integrity rather than on that of noble birth (particularly noticeable in his historical drama) and on restraint, honesty and truthfulness. He is essentially a moralistic writer. Even his bandit play, *El tejedor de Segovia*, betrays a moderation foreign to the genre. Pedro has more the makings of a gentlemanly highwayman, a folk hero, than a desperate bandit; for all his threats of vengeance against society for the wrongs done him, he does not get around to murdering any innocent travellers and makes only a gesture towards robbery. At the end he is reintegrated into society and marries his faithful *bandolera*, even more untouched by crime than he.

Alarcón's plays are very stylish, are carefully, even elegantly constructed and move at a spanking pace. He is a master of tension and dramatic irony and of the unpredictable ending. His most famous work is *La verdad sospechosa* (*The Suspect Truth*), a satirical comedy with a strong moral thrust about a compulsive liar. Don García is a fantasist whose lies are motivated now by expediency, now by the sheer pleasure he takes in the art of fabrication. Both sorts of lies create intolerable difficulties and his unnecessarily devious manoeuvring to marry the woman he loves ends in frustration. Comedy does not wave its magic wand here to wrest happiness from the jaws of disaster. The play is a severely cautionary tale. For all that, it is enormously entertaining, with a beautifully orchestrated plot which turns on García's mistaken conviction that Jacinta, whom he loves, is Lucrecia. He is deceived to the very end, when both he and his rival move forward to claim their brides only to find that they are claiming the same woman. Until the very last lines the audience is kept guessing as to how the play will end and then its fond expectations are denied. The play that revolves around some comic vice, the *comedia de figurón*, was not a type favoured by the Spanish theatre particularly during the first half of the seventeenth century – although the plays which depict women who refuse to marry through vanity or pride come near – but here in *La verdad sospechosa* we have an outstanding example of the genre. García, however, is not Alarcón's only target: the court, the capital and the times at large come in for severe criticism.

The simplest calculation will indicate that the playwrights I have mentioned, for all the productivity of some of them, could not by themselves have supplied the voracious *corrales* with the plays they needed. During this first period of the seventeenth-century drama there lurk behind Lope, Tirso and the others a large band of shadowy figures, some very prolific and commercially successful, others only occasional playwrights, whose work for the most part has either not survived or has fallen into neglect, to be found only in inaccessible editions. Agustín de Rojas in the *Loa de la comedia* in his dialogue miscellany *El viaje entretenido* (*The Entertaining Journey*, 1603) lists a string of now forgotten dramatists; to one, Miguel Sánchez, dubbed in his day 'the divine', he devotes more space than to Lope himself. These playwrights adopted and adapted the themes and motifs of the more gifted dramatists, reworking plots and borrowing often from several plays at once so that some plays seem like nothing so much as dramatic collages. All the playwrights throughout the century did this to some extent – the *corrales* could not wait for original inspiration to strike – and the drama was in that sense a collective enterprise which drew on a common ever-expanding pool of material and where influence was often mutual; collaborative efforts by anything from two to (exceptionally) nine writers were not uncommon, especially in the case of plays written first for performance at court.[22] Originality was still not a prized feature of art in general in the seventeenth century and in the craft of the commercial theatre ingenuity, skill and novelty rather than originality were what counted; formulaic variation normally plays an important part in popular art. What now distinguishes the first from the second rank and these from the rest is the way the recurring themes are felt and treated: thus whereas some of Calderón's greatest plays are reworkings of earlier plays by other dramatists, what many a minor dramatist engaged in was a sort of painting by numbers.

Miguel de Cervantes (1547–1616)

A last name that must be mentioned again at this point, although no plays of his reached the stage after Lope became established, is Cervantes, because his failure as a dramatist is as revealing as others' success. It is clear that he did try to adapt to the new drama, writing new plays and modifying old ones in an attempt to supplement his meagre income.[23] But he was no longer taken seriously as a dramatist and his failure to earn a single *real* with his plays before he finally had them published in 1615 was a profound disappointment to him.[24] His plays in the new style, probably written in the decade or so from the late 1590s, are in fact as good as many which did reach the stage and it is difficult to believe that they failed to attract professional interest solely on grounds of incompetence. The animosity between himself and Lope – on one occasion Lope maliciously denounced Cervantes as the worst poet of the age – in all probability counted against him with theatre-company managers who naturally respected Lope's judgement and who could not afford to incur his displeasure.

Of the eight plays Cervantes had published in 1615, probably two are revisions of earlier works. Which ones these two are is uncertain, although *El laberinto de amor* (*The Labyrinth of Love*) is certainly sufficiently involved to have been a rewriting of the lost *La confusa* (*Comedy of Confusion*), while *La casa de los celos y selvas de Ardenia* (*The House of Jealousy and Woods of Ardenia*), a mixture of chivalric romance and elements from medieval morality and classical mythology typical of the *comedia*'s early years, shows signs of a somewhat hasty reduction of acts to the now standard three. A third play, *Los baños de Argel* (*The Bagnios of Algiers*) is a second attempt at dramatizing his experience of slavery in Algiers and an illuminating example of the problems he faced when writing for the stage. The play is less episodic than *El trato de Argel* and altogether more carefully crafted, but in the writing the emotional intensity and the documentary vividness of the earlier play have been lost. It is as if Cervantes could achieve one thing only at the expense of the other.

These later plays contain much of interest, as one would expect of a writer of Cervantes's calibre. *El laberinto de amor* and *El gallardo español* (*The Gallant Spaniard*), for example, make a significant contribution to the drama's favourite themes of women's freedom and the conflict between individual and society.[25] But Cervantes was never really at home with the full-length play and for all his major concessions to the *comedia nueva* – some of his plays have a geographical span which would have scandalized him years before – something in him continued to resist its tyranny. Aware of what was needed for success, he could not provide it. Not only was he temperamentally incapable of being a slavish imitator but, at the same time, as a naturally expansive writer he was unable to shape his inspiration to the demanding requirements of the tight *comedia* form, to combine artistic integrity with commercialism. The delightful *Pedro de Urdemalas*, an episodic mixture of pastoral, gypsy and picaresque motifs, contains some scintillating scenes with excellent dialogue and has a lovable rascal for a hero. But the plot lacks consistency, the pace is uneven, the ending undecided and, most disconcerting of all for a prospective buyer at this still early stage in the drama, the play is markedly self-conscious and somewhat iconoclastic in its characterization (the characters' world and the audience's overlap in places) and in its refusal to provide a 'real' ending. This tendency to misjudge his market is evident again in his hagiographic play *El rufián dichoso* (*The Fortunate Ruffian*) where, after a racy, character-packed depiction of low life in Seville in Act I, Act II opens with two abstract characters, Curiosity and Drama, discussing dramatic theory – hardly calculated to rivet the groundlings' attention – after which the play follows the fortunes of the now saintly hero. Since the conversion has taken place between the acts, it is hardly surprising that the pace flags quite badly after this. Cervantes seems not to have realized that the dramatic charge of his protagonist's story lies in the conversion itself.

Cervantes's main problem, however, was not an absence of an instinct for the dramatic but an inability to sustain dramatic interest and tension over the length of the three-act play; thus his scenes are better than his acts and his acts are more successful than the completed works. He was a master of the episodic and of accumulated episode, as his short stories and *Don Quijote* show. It is not surprising, therefore, that the dramatic form at which he did excel was the minor genre of the *entremés* or farcical interlude,[26] a descendant of the early pastoral farces.

The *entremés* and the *loa*

Performances of plays were accompanied by entertaining titbits which for many in the audience constituted the main attraction, keeping them in their places through the principal business in anticipation of the fun still to come. At a typical performance a comic *loa*, or prelude, preceded the play to settle and amuse the audience; an *entremés*, which often ended in dancing and singing, separated Act I from Act II; another *entremés* or a *baile* (dance dialogue) came before Act III, and then the afternoon's entertainment finished with more singing and dancing. Most dramatists contributed to the supply of this supporting material – of which a huge quantity was produced – and would often write a *loa* and an *entremés* to accompany a commissioned play. Some writers specialized in these minor forms; others not primarily associated with the stage, such as the satirist Quevedo and the poet Góngora, occasionally tried their hand at them.

It is unlikely that Cervantes's eight *entremeses*, some of which were written to go with specific plays which were never performed, reached the stage in his lifetime, but they were certainly performed later on in the century. He had them published along with his eight *comedias* in 1615, and in the absence of any effective copyright printed collections of plays were habitually raided by theatre-managers as well as by unscrupulous printers for pirate editions.

In his Prologue to his *Ocho comedias y ocho entremeses* (*Eight Plays and Eight Interludes*), where Cervantes concedes victory to the *comedia* in terms very generous to Lope, he reminisces about the primitive theatre of his childhood. It is clear that Lope de Rueda, 'a notable actor and a man of distinguished intelligence', made an indelible impression on him and his brilliant *entremeses* are in the tradition of Rueda's *pasos*. Six in prose and only two in verse (a consummate prose writer, his verse was never more than adequate), they cover a variety of enduring humorous themes: cuckoldry (*El viejo celoso*, *The Jealous Old Man*; *La cueva de Salamanca*, *The Cave of Salamanca*); divorce (*El juez de los divorcios*, *The Divorce Judge*); the conning of the gullible (*El vizcaíno fingido*, *The Sham Biscayan*; *El retablo de las maravillas*, *The Miracle Show*); ineptitude and ignorance in local government (*La elección de los alcaldes de Daganzo*, *The Election of the Sheriffs of Danganzo*); picaresque low life (*El rufián viudo*, *The Widowed Ruffian*); and sexual rivalry (*La guarda cuidadosa*, *The Anxious Guard*). Their comic range is wide but they all have pace, wit, sophistication and a sparkling realism. Without ever descending into cruelty or forfeiting one iota of their humour they take serious and not merely humorous swipes at the fatuousness and folly of human nature and of seventeenth-century Spanish society, exploiting the licence of farce to deal openly with topics like divorce, the contemporary obsession with purity of blood, and sex, which could be approached only obliquely in the *comedia*. His two best-known farces are for this reason probably *El retablo de las maravillas*, where the theme of the Emperor's clothes is employed to send up the contemporary Spaniard's desire for the social respectability guaranteed by 'old' Christian blood (only the racially pure can see the miracle show); and *El viejo celoso*, about a frustrated young girl married to a decrepit and jealous old man, which ends with her fornicating noisily off stage with a stranger, in a scene so bawdy that the censor must surely have been nodding when he passed it for publication, for all that it was easier to get away with such things in print than on the stage.

Cervantes, for all his reputation as a failed dramatist, is an acknowledged master of the *entremés*. The *entremés* occupied a rather equivocal place in Spanish dramaturgy at the time. It had the stamp of tradition and even distinction – Lope saw it as complying with the demands of art since it had a single action and dealt exclusively with plebeian folk.[27] At the same time it was for this latter reason regarded as inferior to other forms. For most successful dramatists, writing farces was a routine part of writing for the theatre, almost an afterthought, with their major energies going into their plays. It is significant in this respect that the most successful *entremesista* of the age – the lawyer-priest Luis Quiñones de Benavente (1589?–1651)[28] – did not attempt to write *comedias* at all. Different qualities were required for the writing of distinguished *entremeses* – a comic vision of undiluted intensity, a lack of interest in plot, a satirical eye, a sense of the ludicrous. Quiñones uses all the standard ingredients of contemporary Spanish farce – deceived husbands, old men in love, wily or lascivious sacristans, and stupid sheriffs abound – and the emphasis is always on the shortcomings or ridiculousness of society and human nature. But he deploys these with a satirical wit, an inventiveness, a sharply observant eye and a moral incisiveness that never seem to flag over the huge range of his playlets – he is thought to have written getting on for 900 short dramatic pieces in all. His reputation in his day was enormous. In 1645 it was said of him, 'The theatre-company manager with a bad play who added two of this wit's *entremeses* to it gave it crutches to walk with, and the one with a good play gave it wings with which to soar.'[29] Amongst his best-known *entremeses* are *Las civilidades* (*Civilities*), a satire on pedantry, *Turrada*, about a miser, and the two called *El guardainfante* (*The Farthingale*), which send up the huge, paniered skirt ladies wore at the time.

The *loa* was an even lesser genre that the *entremés* – usually it was not even given a title – but it is an interesting phenomenon for all that. Its length varied enormously – some were little plays, others short speeches. Its metre varied and its subject matter ranged from the play about to be performed, through women and the customs of the age, to flies. Some were funny, some serious, some religious, some profane. Some had literary origins – existing ballads were sometimes used instead of original pieces – while others consisted of jokes and anecdotes. They were used to settle the audience, to put it in a good mood, to ask for silence, to grind favourite axes, to attack the *comedia*'s detractors, to talk about the actors or other troupes, to explain the work to come when they preceded religious *autos*, or to stress the illusionist nature of theatre which, like life itself, is 'no more than a breath of wind'.[30] The *loa*, in other words, was an invaluable, infinitely expandable portmanteau into which playwright or theatre-company manager could tuck anything he liked. It is as a result a fascinating mine of information about theatrical practices, concerns and problems at the time.

6

The reign of Calderón

Although some of Lope's latest plays are his finest, in the ten or so years before his death his dominance of the theatre was challenged by a new and exciting force in the *corrales*. He was now the grand old man of the *comedia*; the new darling of the playgoers was a dramatist of great and distinctive talent as attuned to the mood of the day as Lope had been and as skilful at shaping the tastes he seemed to serve.

Pedro Calderón de la Barca (1600–81)[1] was descended from an old Castilian family, his father a government official, his mother apparently a gentlewoman of German descent. He attended a Jesuit school in Madrid and then studied logic, rhetoric, mathematics and law at the Universities of Alcalá and Salamanca, which enshrined respectively the humanist and scholastic traditions of learning. Abandoning the ecclesiastical career he had been destined for by his father he started to write plays, living the life of a fashionable young buck in Madrid and having at least one brush with the law. After serving, it is thought, as a soldier in Italy and Flanders he returned to the capital and rapidly began to make a reputation for himself as a playwright. By the late 1620s his plays were being performed at court as well as in the *corrales* and he soon became a firm favourite with Spain's aesthete king, Philip IV. He was made a knight of the Order of Santiago and then did military service again in the early 1640s during the revolt of Catalonia. In 1642 he was forced by war wounds to abandon the cavalry and lived thereafter partly on a pension. Some time in the early 1640s he fathered an illegitimate child. In 1651 he made what seems to have been a relatively sudden decision to enter the priesthood and gave up writing for the commercial stage, concentrating instead on his theatrical duties at the court. He died working on an *auto sacramental* on Pentecost Sunday 1681 and at his own request was buried in an open coffin to illustrate the transitory nature of the flesh. Three thousand citizens of Madrid are supposed to have followed the funeral procession. In brief, in spite of the religious orientation of his life in middle and old age, Calderón, like most seventeenth-century men of letters, was a man of the world who knew its ways extremely well.

His dramatic output can broadly speaking be divided into four: (1) The comedies or light-hearted plays, essentially love intrigues in an urban setting that purports to be that of contemporary Spain. (2) The dramas or serious plays, written for the secular stage though they are often on religious, moral and philosophical issues. These draw on the Bible, history, legend and devotional literature for their plots as well as on contemporary manners and recent events, and include the famous honour–vengeance plays. (3) The elaborate mythological plays with their pronounced musical element and special technical effects, which effectively mark the birth of opera in Spain. (4) The *autos sacramentales*, one-act allegorical plays elucidating aspects of Christian dogma commissioned for the feast of Corpus Christi. Most of the plays for which Calderón was best known were written early on, from the late 1620s to the 1640s, and it is on these that I shall concentrate here.[2] The 1640s were anyway something of a watershed in the history of the seventeenth-century Spanish stage, for during the second half of the decade the public and court theatres were closed because of two royal deaths – those of the Queen, Isabella of Bourbon, and Prince Baltasar Carlos – and the wars in Portugal and Catalonia. When Calderón was ordained in 1651 he had intended renouncing the theatre completely. In the event pressure from above led to his continuing to write for the re-opened court theatre, but from this time on he wrote exclusively for a proscenium stage with a front curtain and not for the old open stage of the *corrales*. Stimulated by these new stage conditions, the plays he wrote from the 1650s on are much more elaborate and less realistic than the earlier plays, moving freely into fantasy and through time, and are accompanied by music and singing – elements which reach their climax in the 1660s in the operatic works.

In Calderón's drama we find the consolidation and extension of tendencies already present in the mature works of Lope and in those of his followers. From the 1620s on there was a general move towards greater unity, tightness, control and restraint, a more overt attempt to claim the *comedia* for Art, and the fusion of all the different elements of a play into a coherent whole which we increasingly see in Lope becomes Calderón's hallmark. His is a highly intellectual, complex and artfully crafted drama where meaning moves at the level of metaphor and symbol rather than in the surface plot. Technically it is characterized by a classical emphasis on perfection, harmony, order and contained energy which is very different from Lope's freer, apparently spontaneous and inspirational approach. It is a more perplexed and more reflective theatre than his, more concerned with religious, moral and philosophical problems. In Calderón the action traces or explores some guiding dilemma or idea, whereas in Lope action is usually its own justification, the primary concern whatever the ideological underpinning or however complicated the characters. Novelty of plot is therefore no longer as important and there is as a result a narrowing of the *comedia*'s horizons, a falling off of interest in the novelesque and extravagant romantic adventure, a contraction of the dramatic space which reflects not only the desire to write more tightly crafted plays but also an interiorization and concentration of focus and interest. Even Calderón's comedies are played out inside the claustrophobic houses of the urban gentry, peopled by heroines who resort to ingenuity and veils to achieve their designs rather than to action and doublet and hose. Inspiration in the second phase of the *comedia*'s career was sought increasingly from within the theatre's own immediate past – old plays were rewritten, tried and tested themes revived and revitalized – and there is a significant increase in literary self-conciousness, in self-referral, in humour at the expense not only of the illusions and customs of the age but of the theatre's own practices. In Calderón repetition of themes, techniques and motifs – including favoured devices, omens and symbols such as knives, horoscopes, runaway horses, tripping or falling, abnormal upbringing – becomes a way of penetrating more deeply into persistent preoccupations.

Language becomes part of the process. Keenly interested in painting, Calderón employs words as a painter deploys his paints, repeatedly using the same colours, tones and textures to produce a wide range of different effects. A Calderón play is as distinctive as a Velázquez although no two plays or paintings are the same. Lope and Tirso both use master images which are then developed, elaborated and teased out to form a network of imagery which plays an organic part in the development of the theme. Calderón, however, largely as a result of the poet Góngora's influence, goes much further, elaborating this technique into a complex metaphorical and rhetorical system.[3] Series or chains of cosmic and elemental images – *air*: wind, birds, feathers; *fire*: thunder and lightning, volcanoes, guns, salamanders; *earth*: rocks, mountains, beasts, flowers, fruit; *water*: sea, fish, serpents, crystal, foam, pearls – are used to create a symbolic language which reveals what is taking place in the minds and souls of the characters, which plots the development of the theme, and which sends the audience signals that work on it emotionally and intellectually, subtly guiding and manipulating its responses. At the same time it extends the play's philosophical reach, linking the stage action with the cosmos and giving philosophical perspective to the troubled world of man. At a time when the hitherto accepted model of the universe was beginning to crumble, an intense need for patterns of order and meaning is reflected in this highly stylized dramatic discourse of Calderón's, as well as in his general predilection for linguistic and structural parallelism and symmetry. At the same time the almost obsessive self-repetition betrays a profound consistency of vision with regard to the human predicament which is in tension with this need, for the cosmic patterns his imagery sets out to trace are typically patterns of chaos and disruption, not of harmony and stability. The conflict that drama demands becomes a microcosm of the conflict that for Calderón lies at the heart of human experience. The idea of the theatre of the world is explored with no greater frequency and feeling by any other playwright.

The supreme dramatic craftsmanship and mastery of the poetic resources available to the theatre displayed by Calderón have encouraged, perhaps understandably, the view of him as a dramatist who authoritatively answers all the questions he poses, a master puzzlemaker whose intricate creations contain within them a piece of life's truth. Find the key, unlock the play and its lesson is revealed. But Calderón was a dramatist, not a theologian or a philosopher. In choosing to express himself in drama – and unlike Lope he restricted his literary activities to the theatre – he opted to explore dilemmas not solve them. In the *autos sacramentales* he dramatizes Catholic dogma because that is in the nature of the undertaking. But in his plays, even in his religious dramas where he overtly promotes Christian solutions and values, it is clear that life in this world was for Calderón a complicated, painful and bitterly ironical business. There are few villains in his universe and no glib, easy answers. To say that his drama is Catholic in its shaping is to say everything and to say nothing, for Christianity itself embraces highly problematic issues which Calderón continually addresses, directly or indirectly, in his plays for the secular stage. The difficulty, furthermore, of rendering appropriately to Caesar and to God was something that clearly preoccupied him; so too did the ethical and philosophical implications of a pre-Christian world. He did not challenge the major ideological assumptions of his age any more than Shakespeare did, but he certainly grappled with their implications.

It would be idle to expect all his plays to provide the same answers because like every great dramatist he uses his art as a scalpel to investigate the pathology of human experience, not as a prescription for remedies and cures. There is a consistency of vision and preoccupation in his plays but there is no complacency and in his secular dramas only at the most superficial level is there certainty. Even in Spain the seventeenth century was an age far more beset by division and insecurity than it chose to admit, and for all Calderón's position as an establishment figure the subtext of his drama is as riddled with tension, uncertainty and anguish as the subtext of his age. His practical view of human nature and the human predicament is by and large pessimistic, for all that his theological position was the optimistic one concomitant upon a belief in free will. And it is pessimistic precisely because he entertained no complacent belief in the easy application to life in this world of the prescriptions of Christianity. Calderón is above all the dramatist of the agony of choice – between self and other, social expediency and morality, this world and the next, life and death. Chance and circumstance intervene, other people interfere, upbringing and character influence, but all these do is complicate the game, changing the alternatives and forcing new choices. Like Theseus, man did not, in Calderón's eyes, enter the labyrinth entirely unequipped. He would not have held that one ball of string was an adequate guide through life's moral maze, nor would he have denied that the world is a moral obstacle course of Gargantuan dimensions. But he would have maintained that a way through existed, however precarious, however uncongenial, however costly; and his tragic vision flows from this deep sense that man is himself largely the creator of his own agony rather than from any conception of man as the helpless victim of a hostile universe.

It is to a large extent Calderón's constant concern with man in the face of the universe that gives his drama its majesty and power. He is an outstanding example of the way in which the imagination can be strengthened by ideology, rather than undermined or distorted. His plays do not have the lyrical grace, the apparently spontaneous charm, the irrepressible optimism of most of Lope's, but they have an intellectual rigour, an incisive intelligence and an imaginative grandeur entirely foreign to the older dramatist. Calderón by no means neglects man in his social context – the relationship between private and public morality is a constant in his work – but the imaginative, philosophical and spiritual dimensions of man's existence are central to his vision. While Lope approaches humanity from without, often working his way then to the core, Calderón's point of departure is the inner man. And this inner man is Man in all his vulnerable complexity. To describe Calderón as an intellectual dramatist is therefore accurate but inadequate, for alongside the artistic control, the intellectual brilliance, the transcendental thrust of his plays, is the ability to convey love, passion, sensuality and desire, to penetrate to the heart of feeling, of the true metaphysical. The very axis of his tragic vision is the oppositional pull that exists in man between the claims of reason and those of the passions, between intellect and instinct, understanding and will, thought and action. In his drama both sides are felt with equal intensity and paradoxically it is in this irreducible tension that the satisfying completeness of his great drama is to be found. The secret of his mastery of the *auto sacramental*, too, lies not just in his command of theology, or in the strength of his intellect, but in the equilibrium created by the keenness with which he responded to both sides of man's nature. In neither dramatic form is the opposition a simple one; reason and intellect can themselves be false gods, and the Devil's disguises are many and devious. But in his plays for the secular stage Calderón was under no constraints to provide the logical satisfaction of abstract solutions and does not do so. For all their structural coherence, their artistic wholeness, no plays are more open-ended, more susceptible of alternative readings, than Calderón's, as the critical controversy that has surrounded his work bears eloquent witness. An intellectual dramatist, the solutions he moves towards are not always intellectual ones. If there is one ingredient consistently and tragically absent from the world of confusion, selfishness and non-communication in which his characters act out their parts, it is not reason but emotion; not the emotion of anger and passion – there is plenty of that – but the emotion of compassionate love.

Of the dramas written in Calderón's first period *El alcalde de Zalamea* (*The Mayor of Zalamea*) is probably the most readily accessible because of its surface realism and its straightforward plot. It is written in a relatively unadorned style, it does not forge the elaborate chain of cause and effect found in many of Calderón's plays, the action is short and concise and all the attention is focused on the build-up of tension and the unfolding of Pedro Crespo's character in preparation for the dilemma he has to face – a greater degree of detailed characterization is to be found here, therefore, than is typical of the *comedia*. The play is a reworking of an earlier one with the same name by Lope and is a prime example of Calderón's gift for creating magnificent drama out of often commonplace borrowed material.[4] Thought to be based on a real event that took place in the village of Zalamea when Philip II's troops passed through on their way to Portugal to fight for the Portuguese throne, the play dramatizes the predicament of a rich peasant whose daughter is raped by an aristocratic army captain. Just as Pedro Crespo is about to avenge his daughter's honour he learns he has been made mayor of the village, responsible for law and order. Here then is his dilemma. First he tries the way of restitution, but after failing on bended knees either to persuade or to bribe the captain to marry Isabel, he opts for retribution: he makes his daughter file a complaint against the captain although this means publicizing her dishonour. He then tries and executes the captain, in spite of the fact that he has no jurisdiction over him, knowing that no military court would punish a caste brother for a crime against a peasant woman. Pedro, after some nimble self-justification, is made mayor in perpetuity by the King. Isabel, who, as a decent woman, is now through no fault of her own dead to the world, retires to a convent – the only place where society will allow her to live any sort of constructive existence. There, as Pedro bitterly observes, she will have a husband who pays no heed to social station.

The play is an excellent introduction to Calderón's drama because even here beneath the deceptive plainness lies the sophisticated structural and conceptual patterning central to his art.[5] It is in fact a complex, subtle and even highly artificial creation, elegantly constructed, threaded with light and dark symbolism, which concerns itself with the co-ordinating ideas of the rule of law, justice, nature and reason, and explores through the whole range of its characters the idea of honour as a social and moral concept. Even its forceful protagonist, who so disconcertingly manages to unite integrity with expediency and guile, would seem to embody that prized seventeenth-century virtue, discretion, which for Calderón denoted the habit of mind which enables man to apply his moral values, to navigate a virtuous and circumspect course through life. As we see in the play, discretion does not enable man to avoid dilemmas, but it does allow him to tackle them in the best possible way suggested by the circumstances. It is the working and triumph of Pedro's discretion that diverts the play technically from tragedy, but its impact is none the less tragic for that. For what this dramatization of the familiar seventeenth-century theme of the abuse of social and sexual power so uncompromisingly shows us, is that however well adapted virtue is to the ways of the world, it can never be sufficient protection against evil. Pedro stands up to evil and through his discretion ensures that the nearest thing to justice is done. Justice in this world can never be done to the victim herself, for the captain and society have conspired to rob her of her right to self-determination. The disturbing poignancy of the play's ending lies precisely in the fine equilibrium it establishes between triumph and impotent waste.

Calderón's achievement here and in his other plays is that he was able to breathe into the ideas that guide his creations the fire of dramatic life. Pedro's sparring relationship with the gout-testy old general, as honourable as he but rigid where Pedro is not, his loving support for the disgraced daughter who expects him to kill her, his tender affection for and firm guidance of his impulsive and conventional son Juan, his inspired handling of difficult people and situations, the predatory captain's ominous obsession, the foppish *hidalgo* suitor equally ready, given the chance, to use and discard Isabel at will, Isabel's self-loathing after the rape, the mounting sense of an unavoidable disaster, the wide-ranging irony of tone and situation – all combine to make of *El alcalde de Zalamea* an intensely moving and memorable play. And at the heart of it is the unforgettable figure of the man torn between the rival claims of duty, honour, paternal love and Christian forgiveness, who learns the hard way to distinguish false honour from true, self-interest from duty, vengeance from remedy and from punishment. Pedro Crespo's ability to get his priorities right is a lesson that few of Calderón's protagonists ever learn; the men in his world, above all the fathers, are not distinguished for their compassion, their humanity and their selflessness, which is why Pedro Crespo occupies a special place in our affections.

It is in this inability of man to make the distinctions and therefore the decisions that are right for himself and others that Calderón's tragic sense of life manifests itself. And none of his plays illustrates it more powerfully and more starkly than the three famous wife-murder plays. Like Lope's peasant-honour dramas they eloquently illustrate that plots are not plays, that the repetition of themes and plot-situations forced on playwrights by the commercial imperatives of the *corrales* could lead to artistic enrichment. *El médico de su honra* (*The Physician of His Honour*), *A secreto agravio, secreta venganza* (*Secret Insult, Secret Vengeance*), and *El pintor de su deshonra* (*The Painter of his Dishonour*) all dramatize the predicament of the husband who becomes convinced that his wife is unfaithful; in each case the marriage is an arranged one contracted after the death or departure of the man the wife previously loved, who then returns to pursue her. All three wives remain faithful – two in thought, all in deed – but the obsessed husbands cannot live with the threat they represent and end up murdering their wives and, in two cases, the lovers as well; the third lover is a royal prince and therefore immune. The plays have many features in common: the mounting tension as the women unwittingly commit the errors which ensnare them more and more inextricably in the web of events that will eventually destroy them; their haunted misgivings and imaginings as death approaches; the husbands' anguished protests against the self-imposed tyranny of an honour code which allows them to rationalize the jealousy they consider it degrading to feel; the irresponsible, importunate suitors who sacrifice the women they claim to love to a past which cannot be revived; the contributions to the tragic outcomes of other characters in the plays; the closing scenes riddled with irony and ambiguity in which the husbands' actions are ratified by authority figures who have already been shown to speak with compromised voices. Yet for all their similarities the three works have very separate identities. Not only are the murders themselves ingeniously diverse but each play has its own dramatic and poetic procedures, its subtle psychological and circumstantial variations, which create a distinctive dramatic whole that affects us very differently in each case.

El médico de su honra,[6] set in fourteenth-century Seville, is a chilling tragedy. Don Gutierre, who before the play begins has abandoned his fiancée, Leonor, on false suspicions of infidelity, marries doña Mencía, unaware that she has been courted and left by don Enrique, the King's brother. The play opens with a hunting accident as a result of which the unconscious Enrique is carried into Mencía's house to recover; when he does so, he embarks on his fateful campaign to win Mencía back. Gutierre's jealousy returns to haunt him, with the compromised Leonor's curse at the end of Act I working as a sort of Nemesis which seeks Gutierre out and makes him pay for his own broken promises. The evidence that his wife is unfaithful seems to grow: so too does Gutierre's pathological obsession with the notion that his honour is sick and needs a radical cure. Mencía's ghastly end – Gutierre hires a surgeon to bleed her to death – therefore has a crazed logic about it; as an actualization of the metaphors he uses to articulate his dilemma it represents a sickening fusion of poetry and action. The dreadful irony lies in the fact that Mencía all along is the victim of a wrong diagnosis, that the wrong patient has in fact been treated. Gutierre's tragedy is that he is driven to kill the wife he loves and is then forced by the King, who is aware that he has murdered an innocent woman, back into the situation he is least able to cope with – an unwanted match with his former betrothed Leonor, which will expose him all over again to his haunted imaginings. It is a contract both partners know is written in blood. The story ends where it began, and the stage is set for the same cycle of suspicion and suffering to begin all over again. The King, Pedro I, who throughout the play lives up to his double epithet of the Cruel and the Just, plays at the end with Gutierre as he has played with the *gracioso* Coquín, devising a solution which gives Leonor the justice she seeks and Gutierre, under cover of approval, the punishment he dreads. It is a disturbing end to a disturbing play. Gutierre's appearance of control over himself and his circumstances is throughout as illusory as the truth he thinks he has discovered about his wife; even his boast that he has marked his door with an escutcheon of blood is an idle one, for it was in fact the blindfolded surgeon who marked the house with blood in order to identify the place of the crime, bringing Gutierre's attempt at secrecy to nothing. Loss, desolation and a suspect honour are the burden he will have to bear; official silence is bought at the price of a second marriage which he knows will render him eternally vulnerable. Calderón's honour tragedies do not begin or end with the action; he uses dramatic narrative to integrate the past causally with the present, along with a variety of devices to suggest that the wife-murders are false solutions, bringing not peace of mind but a lifetime of psychological suffering.

Gutierre suffers and longs in vain for the death that alone would free him from himself. He knows that he is condemned to a life of vigilant insecurity. This self-awareness and the pity it engenders win the play for tragedy. The circumstances in *A secreto agravio, secreta venganza*,[7] set in sixteenth-century Portugal, are substantially different and its tragic force is, it seems to me, far less palpable. Doña Leonor has married don Lope by proxy after the reported death of her lover don Luis. The jewel scene in which Luis, masquerading as a diamond merchant, intercepts Leonor on her way to her new husband and they obliquely speak their love and anguish is extremely poignant, but thereafter our sympathy is increasingly alienated from the central characters. As Luis lays siege to her virtue, Leonor slides ever further into complicity, never honest enough with herself to recognize her true motives although her guilty conscience gives her away at every turn, signing her death warrant. Her intention to be unfaithful, when it crystallizes, is clearer even then to us than it is to her. Lope the husband, for his part, is a more controlled and rational man than Gutierre, without an ounce of passion in him. His council to himself to 'suffer, dissimulate and be silent' ('sufre, disimula y calla') monitors a duplicitous campaign of vengeance that progresses repellently from cautious suspicion to cautious murder. There is no evidence that Lope loves his wife, no sense of loss, no sorrow; he is an entirely self-concerned individual. His desire for death at the end – a wish soon to be granted, it is implied, at the famous battle of Alcazarquivir – has nothing to do with grief; it is simply the reaction of a man who cannot live with the knowledge that his wife was unfaithful. The irony is that the consummate tact of his revenge – Luis 'drowns' at sea while being rowed across the bay by Lope, Leonor then perishes when the house 'accidentally' catches fire – is all in vain. The story his friend don Juan related earlier on of his own experience of dishonour argued against vengeance: after he publicly killed a man who had accused him of being a liar, he says, he became known not as the man who had avenged himself but as the man accused of lying. Lope assumed the story argued against public vengeance and proceeded accordingly to devise a secret solution. But since vengeance will only confirm what people already suspect, Lope on the evidence of Juan's story will always be the man whose wife was unfaithful rather than the man who protected his honour.

At the end of the play the false promise of its title is clearly apparent, as the truth about the two deaths already begins to spread – murder indeed turns blood into oil, as Lope de Vega said.[8] The three wife-murder plays all show results inexorably following from certain patterns of belief and behaviour, for all that chance plays its part in nudging the characters towards their fate. The sort of men the husbands are and their complete subjection to certain social values inevitably leads to disaster and suffering. Our response to their plight is crucially affected by their own reaction to what has happened. In don Lope self-knowledge is never forthcoming and so the husband with the greatest excuse for what he has done moves us least. The fact that Calderón's most characteristic dramas are those which portray man's painful road to self-discovery invests don Lope's complacency with added point. The play is a chastening exposé of duplicity and self-deception. The lovers are Lope's dupes while thinking he is theirs; he in turn is honour's dupe, capable of recognizing its tyranny but incapable of either feeling it or breaking it. This tough, uncompromising play commands our admiration but not our affection, for our sense of outrage is never dispelled. It is not meant to be.

The same cannot be said of *El pintor de su deshonra*,[9] for this brilliant tragedy, the latest and finest of the three plays, calls on our emotional, intellectual and aesthetic responses equally. It is the easiest to like, since here the murder when it comes is an unpremeditated act of passion not a calculated display of cunning. Don Juan Roca's young wife, doña Serafina, whom he has married late in life, is abducted by her former lover don Álvaro, who has returned from the dead to pursue her and destroy her husband's peace of mind. Juan Roca discovers Serafina by chance months later in the hunting lodge that is effectively her prison, at the very moment when she wakes terrified from a nightmare in which her husband is killing her. Álvaro rushes in at her cries and takes her in his arms to comfort her. His worst fears confirmed, Juan Roca shoots them both dead, destroying the only witnesses to his wife's continuing fidelity. Serafina's pride and steadfast but helpless innocence, Juan Roca's terrible anguish at his wife's abduction and his sense of utter desolation at the end are deeply moving. So too is the play's sad vision of the human condition, for all the characters in the play conspire with varying degrees of blame to create a situation that leads remorselessly to a disaster that should never have happened and was never intended.[10] We see human nature to be as effective an obstacle to man's well-being as any notion of an implacable Fate and it is in this tendency for the theoretically evitable (through the exercise of the individual's free will) to become the inevitable (through individual wrongheadedness and the misguided collusion of others) that the essence of Calderonian tragedy lies. The characters, in E. M. Wilson's happy phrase, create their own impotence.[11] It is often maintained that there is no such thing as Shakespearian tragedy, only Shakespearian tragedies. The same could be claimed of Lope, but Calderón does project a consistent tragic vision in his plays, for all that the balance of individual responsibility and external influences varies from play to play.

The greatness of *El pintor de su deshonra*, however, lies not so much in its tragic insight as in the way in which action, theme and imagery are fused into a magnificent whole which is highly poetic, highly intellectual and at the same time intensely dramatic. In *El médico* Gutierre deliberately gives substance to his own metaphors. Here the entire play is the enactment, at once unconscious and inevitable, of a central symbolism initiated long before the action begins. Juan Roca's tardy marriage is due to his preoccupation hitherto with his books and his painting, yet when he eventually marries he is to his intense irritation unable to capture his wife's beauty on canvas. There is a basic incompatibility, in other words, in Juan Roca's life between painting and marriage, a disjunction between imagination and reality. In Act III, having disappeared from sight and living, now that his wife has gone, the life of a professional painter, he is hired to paint in secret a lady who turns out to be the missing Serafina. The connection between his two attempts to paint Serafina is an eloquent one. To paint is both to record and to create. The first time, Juan fails to paint the perfection he can see but does not really believe in. The second, he succeeds in painting the imperfection he imagines; the difference is that now the brushes turn into pistols, the paints into blood, the canvas into his own life and the lives of two young people. The creativity of art has become the destruction of murder. Since the murder prevents the truth about Serafina's innocence ever emerging, the painter of his own dishonour has not recorded (and then obliterated) his shame, he has actually created it. Dramatically and poetically the ending is perfect. Our pity is matched by our sense that the lovers' deaths are not only inevitable but aesthetically fitting.

The striking painting metaphor is the key element in a subtle, intricate network of imagery and symbol tied to the structural development of the play and the unfolding of its controlling ideas. There is the wood where the hunting lodge is situated, a traditional symbol of danger and uncontrol, of something outside the bounds of rational behaviour. There is the motif of disguise, role-play and deceptive appearances, as Serafina poses as a loving wife, Álvaro as a sailor and Juan Roca as a painter – so much is not what it seems or ought to be, and so too the ending where murder gives substance to a sin that has not been committed. But the principal supporting motifs are those of fire and sea. Fire runs through the plot – as gunshots which punctuate the action at crucial moments (ships' salvoes, hunting shots, the fatal explosions at the end), and as a real conflagration that enables Álvaro to abduct Serafina – as well as through the play's metaphorical language as an image of destructive passion. As for the sea, it not only plays a crucial part in the unfolding of events, but it also has a powerful symbolic role in the play. Dynamic and open, the sea is the element of the men as they come and go, disappear and reappear; the earth, static and enclosed, is the hapless Serafina's. As the men circulate freely in space and time, Serafina moves only from passivity to confinement and then to death. She is as powerless to prevent Álvaro pursuing her, or the Prince who has discovered her presence in the lodge having her secretly painted, as she is to prevent her husband shooting her dead. The hunting lodge that is her prison and her tomb is the concrete symbol of the enforced and helpless passivity of woman in a man's world.

One of the most sobering features of all three plays, in fact, is the impotence of these women, however great their virtue, their pride, their sense of themselves, to exert any control over their own fates. Their husbands and lovers form an unholy alliance to destroy them and in their case free will seems to be suspended. To be a threat to their husbands' honour it is sufficient that they exist and neither action nor inaction is of any avail. Conceived of as extensions to men, mere repositories of male honour, they are separated by marriage from their subjective selves, alienated even from their own emotions – as Mencía says, 'ni para sentir soy mía' ('not even my feelings are my own'). Their role as victims, as prey, as possessions, is constantly underlined in these plays, most brutally in *El médico de su honra* by don Enrique, who in Act I cynically observes that if Gutierre has taken his lady, then he at least has acquired Gutierre's horse in exchange. For their men, even those who love them, these women have no reality as people, as subjective individuals. There can be no more powerful statements in any literature of the way men have sacrificed women to the egocentric values of a phallocratic world.

Not all Calderón's women, by any means, fill the role of passive victim.

On the contrary many are gloriously their own. The legendary queen, Semíramis, in the magnificent two-part tragedy *La hija del aire* (*Daughter of the Air*)[12] is one of them. Conceived in violence when her mother, a nymph of Diana, was raped with Venus's help, and born of death – her mother killed her father then died in childbirth – at a time of eclipse and omens of cosmic destruction, she has been raised in isolation at Venus's command to protect her and the world from Diana's wrath. The two plays show how the beautiful and ambitious Semíramis becomes the battleground in a war that ends, as Venus predicted, with her destruction. The first depicts her release and her rise to power as King Nino's queen at the expense of the general, Menón, who freed her and wants to make her his wife. In the second, years later, the king having died in suspicious circumstances, Semíramis rules for her weakling son Ninias whose physical resemblance to her is striking. When the people rebel against her she initially accepts retirement. Her hunger for power, however, will not be denied: she locks the young king away, dons his clothes and rules in his place. The lapse of time between the two plays creates a difficulty for the second, in which the audience is brought up to date with events in the intervening years in a long narrative that slows the action down. But this is more than compensated for by the stunning emblemism of the opening scene, where Semíramis, who is combing her hair surrounded by her ladies-in-waiting, interrupts her toilet at the sound of trumpets to lead her people against an invading army. A few scenes later she is back in the palace completing her coiffure. Semíramis's is a beautifully engineered portrayal which captures our feelings in a fine balance of disapproval and sympathy. To achieve this – and not just for reasons of decorum – Calderón has cleaned up the traditional story; there is no incest and Semíramis's sexual appetites are minimized. The psychological and emotional tensions she triggers, her growing realization of what she might achieve, the pitiful plight of Menón, blinded by the jealous Nino, the irony of the scenes where Semíramis takes her son's place, the fickleness of the people and the self-interest, indistinguishable from loyalty, of her courtiers – all are handled with immense skill. Calderón was a consummate master of the significant ending, and the moment when her people race to find the queen they have spurned to save them, only to discover that it is she who has just died in battle and that they are left with their weakling king, is a telling one. After this the play closes on an empty rather than a serene note: the gap left by the woman who with her dynamism and her obsessive ambition has dominated the stage is almost too great to produce the sense of equilibrium traditionally associated with tragedy's end.

Prediction or astrology is the strategy commonly used by Calderón to explore the dramatic possibilities of the complex relationship between free will and the nexus of external influences that circumscribe it.[13] The treatment is very diversified, although the basic principle of self-determination is normally asserted.[14] In the plays set in the pre-Christian world the absence of Providence operating to rescue men and women from themselves is an important factor, and belief in a predestined fate is shown to lead to actions which can actually bring it about. Thus Semíramis is free to choose in full knowledge of the risks, and does so. But arguably she is not free to make the right choice, partly because her deprived upbringing – intended to circumvent fate – nourishes in her a lust for life and power that must be satisfied. She herself assumes that she can overcome her fate, but she misjudges what is necessary to make this happen. And her misjudgement is made to seem an inevitable outcome of her character. She has free will but not the understanding to apply it.

In *La vida es sueño* (*Life is a Dream*),[15] probably Calderón's best-known play, the paradoxical conviction that man's destiny is both predictable and avoidable is worked out more optimistically in terms of the traditional Christian proposition that the stars, as part of God's providential pattern, influence but do not determine, and that their working resists human interpretation. Segismundo is brought up in captivity by his astrologer father, King Basilio of Poland, to prevent him challenging his father's authority and plunging the country into civil war as the King predicts. When his son is twenty Basilio repents of his action and decides to give Segismundo a chance to prove himself worthy of freedom. Segismundo is drugged and brought to the court, but behaves so violently that he is drugged once more and transported back to his tower. When he wakes he is convinced that he has been dreaming. This experience and the eventual realization that his 'dream' actually happened, enables him to grope his way to self-discovery and to a grasp of the truth which allows him to rise above the horoscope. This is in fact fulfilled; Segismundo is released by a rebel, the people rally to his cause and he defeats his father in civil war. But the horoscope was in the first place the crystallization of Basilio's own fears and it has come about because Basilio has had the power to make it do so: twenty years of captivity in isolation have deprived Segismundo of everything necessary to rational, humane and civilized existence. What Basilio does not and cannot foresee is how Segismundo will then choose of his own free will to act. And Segismundo, able now to distinguish the essential from the inessential, reality from dream, chooses to forgive his father and accept his regal authority. The touchstone in his conversion is sexual awakening, then love, something which he has never been allowed to know. Rosaura, the thematic link between sub-plot and main plot, stumbles on him in his tower and it is her appearance both in real life and in the 'dream' which alerts him to the fact that the dream was true. His decision at the end to marry Princess Estrella rather than Rosaura, to follow the path of duty rather than that of inclination, marks his full entry into his princely inheritance. Segismundo knows now that life is *not* a dream – his famous monologue at the end of Act II which maintains that 'toda la vida es sueño/y los sueños son' ('for life is only a dream and dreams themselves are but dreams') is only the half-way stage in his journey towards the truth – but he knows too that it is folly to dream one's life.

The play represents Calderón's art at its most complex and symbolic. The conceits, the interconnected images, the circumlocutions, the parallels and accumulations, the constant reaching out of language to a philosophical world outside itself – all this is typical of Calderón's high style; so typical that Calderón at one point even uses the *gracioso* to send it up. In the three superb speeches – one in each act – which monitor Segismundo's progress from uncomprehending anguish through doubt to self-discovery, Calderón relies for his effects on the pain and passion of Segismundo's contemplation of his predicament. Stylistic effects are there, but they are techniques which on the whole aid the straightforward presentation of meaning and do not splinter it. We are required here to respond at once to the music and significance of the words, rather than search for conceptual patterns to establish their full implications. Elsewhere the play has its own distinctive tracery of imagery and symbol. At the very start Rosaura, who has come from Russia disguised as a man in pursuit of her seducer Prince Astolfo, is unseated by her horse – a familiar symbol of unbridled passion. Rosaura's reference, in the midst of a speech full of images of cosmic chaos, to her mount as half-horse, half-gryphon, a horse that gallops with the speed of wings, not only points to a Nature out of joint with itself but echoes her own hybrid identity, her masculinity an illusion that is the outcome of her fall from honour owing to passion. Rosaura's dress throughout reflects her predicament and her state of mind. Having lost her identity as a respectable woman she dresses as a man not only to give herself the freedom and mobility she needs to re-establish it by chasing after Astolfo, but as an indication that she has assumed the stance of the active, self-respecting male. At the Polish court she reverts to passive femininity in the guise of a lady-in-waiting, her honour now in the reluctant care of her long-lost father. In Act III, she combines her woman's skirts with masculine weapons to fight Astolfo and the King's army at Segismundo's side, defiantly and openly accepting responsibility now for her own destiny. The parallelistic speech to Segismundo in which she proudly asserts her identity as a woman but lays claim to the courage, resolution and self-respect traditionally associated with the male, is an extraordinary proclamation of female selfhood.

Segismundo's images are those of labyrinth, monster, tower, cradle and grave. In the man-created maze through which he must find his way to freedom he is a force for destruction, a creature out of the usual course of events. The pelts he wears signal his identity as a creature of instinct, the chains he drags stress the need for that instinct to be fettered. His tower, where he has been imprisoned since birth, is the sepulchre of a living corpse, the conceit that embodies the paradox of Segismundo's existence – alive and a human being, yet not alive *as* a human being. It is a tower scarcely reached by the rays of the sun, representing an existence from which the light of reason and truth has been excluded; yet within glows a flickering light, the tiny but unquenchable flame of humanity that will be fanned into the full radiance of reason. The tower is the representation not merely of confinement, of man's captivity within the walls of his imperfect nature, but the womb itself, the place from which man emerges to face the light of day, from which the child embarks on his hazardous road to recognition and acceptance of his human inheritance. At the end of the play the tower is still there and to its captivity Segismundo condemns the rebel soldier who freed him and unleashed civil war. It is a potent reminder that while it is within man's capability to triumph over himself, it is also in his nature to create his own destruction. Unless man can learn the lesson learnt by Segismundo, then the tower of darkness will indeed be his end as well as his beginning, his sepulchre as well as his cradle.

The life/death topos is a leitmotif that runs throughout the play. At one point Segismundo in his tower wonders whether man's greatest crime lies in having been born at all – a theme developed in some of the *autos*, where the question of whether man deserves to live in view of his capacity for destruction is pondered. The corresponding symbolism of light and darkness is carried even into the women's names: Rosaura, as becomes the association of her name with the dawn, is Segismundo's first glimpse of light and life. For him she becomes the sun, the centre of existence, and in settling at last for the lesser light – Estrella means star – Segismundo performs the ultimate in selflessness and self-control. The name symbolism further extends to Rosaura's assumed name as lady-in-waiting, Astrea – the maiden Justice whose return to earth, Virgil prophesied, would restore the

Age of Gold. It is justice that Rosaura seeks and through her a new era of peace is indeed established.

There is no weak link in this astonishing play – even the *gracioso*'s role is tightly woven into the fabric of ideas. It is a supreme example of Calderón's ability to make gripping and moving theatre of complex ideas and symbolic patterns. Segismundo's philosophical provenance is indisputable: he is Man. But he is not just a cypher: made flesh on stage he becomes a suffering, thinking, changing human being. He is at once himself and everyman, in his complexity another illustration of the considerable range of characterization the *comedia* has to offer. Thomas Mann in this respect described drama as 'an art of the silhouette' and only narrated man as round, whole, real and fully shaped. The notion that the only worthwhile dramatic character is the so-called three-dimensional individual is after all a strange one. Only the God-like narrator of extended prose fiction, arguably, can create such a thing. In life we normally experience people two-dimensionally from the outside not the inside, but we do not for that reason doubt their reality or their interest.

Amongst the most distinctive of Calderón's plays are those dramas for the secular stage which, without any loss of theatrical interest, overtly serve Christian ends. The religious message may be straightforward but dramatically the plays are as intricate and layered as any. *El príncipe constante (The Constant Prince)*[16] is the harrowing story of a Portuguese prince, Fernando, who is captured by the Moors at the siege of Tangiers and refuses to be ransomed in exchange for Ceuta. He starves to death in filthy squalor rather than allow Ceuta to fall into Moslem hands. After his death he appears to the Christian troops attacking Fez and leads them to victory. The plot is simple enough and so is its aim: to glorify the Christian virtues of steadfastness, humility and patience. The play's poignancy and its beauty derive from the way in which these ascetic values are contrasted with a very different way of life. The opening scene exudes sensuousness and beauty as the lovesick Moorish princess, the lovely Fénix (Phoenix – the name is symbolic but ironic) performs her toilet with the help of her maids and conjures up images of a once loved nature which, reflecting her new mood, no longer delights her. The love scene with Muley that follow throbs with a passion and a jealousy that are almost palpable. Totally sympathetic as she is, Fénix represents the hedonistic values of the pagan world. She has lived surrounded by the flowers of the palace garden in Fez, protected from the harsh realities of life. Terrified by thoughts of death, she is horrified when Fernando, now a palace slave, brings her flowers which he proceeds to present to her as images of life's brevity and decay. Later in the play she is so revolted by the sight of him dying that for all her pity she cannot bear to look at him and has to flee. The contrast between ascetic Christian prince and hedonistic Moorish princess lies at the very heart of the play's purpose. And this contrast becomes a crucial part of the working of the plot when the appalled Fénix learns from a soothsayer that her beauty is to be the price of a corpse. The prophecy comes true at the end, when Fénix is captured by the Christians and then exchanged for Fernando's dead body – the equivalence of beauty and death speaks for itself. The brevity of life, the illusoriness of beauty, the transitory nature of human happiness inhabit the play like the flowers that symbolize them. This proximity in the language and imagery of flowers, death and bloodshed is hauntingly effective – Calderón is at his most memorable as a poet when talking philosophically of life and death and the destiny of man.

The Christian emphasis, so dear to the seventeenth century, on the transitory nature of the flesh provides the dramatic core for another play that depicts the triumph of the human spirit, *El mágico prodigioso* (*The Wonder-Working Magician*).[17] *El mágico* is an excellent example of the great skill with which Calderón married a variety of religious and secular themes and motifs to produce instructive but entertaining theatre. It is a hagiographic play dramatizing the fates of the two Christian martyrs Cyprian and Justine which develops into a variation on the Faust legend. It grafts the theme of necromancy onto the typical *comedia* love plot with total aplomb – one of the Devil's guises in the play is that of a rival lover – and succeeds in putting across its message of free will and divine mercy with tremendous theatrical force. Cipriano is a student at Antioch in the early days of Christianity whose philosophical deliberations have brought him so near belief in the one God that the Devil decides to distract him with the beauty of the virtuous Christian Justina, whom the Devil also wishes to destroy. Cipriano sells his soul to the Devil posing as a necromancer in return for instruction in the magic arts which will enable him to enjoy Justina, and he retires with the Devil for a year to an isolated cave. In the meantime the Devil has contrived to discredit Justina's virtuous reputation. In Act III the Devil's attempt to corrupt Justina for Cipriano through the workings of her imagination fails and he has to settle for second best – the Justina whom an ecstatic Cipriano eventually embraces is revealed on stage to be a horrifying skeleton. When Cipriano prises out of the Devil the admission that Justina owed her triumph to her belief in the Christian God his philosophical search is at an end. He becomes a self-confessed Christian and is cast into prison. There he meets Justina, also imprisoned for her faith, and from the prison they set out together for the executioner's block. The Devil, at the last, bears forced witness to Justina's virtue and Cipriano's pact.

It is difficult to convey adequately in a brief treatment not only the complexity of this play but its intense drama. Its presentation of the archetypal struggle between good and evil is wonderfully vivid, requiring the complicated stage effects typical of religious drama in Spain at the time – thunder and lightning, a cloud bearing a shipwreck scene, a moving mountain, a rock that opens to reveal Justina sleeping, a hooded figure that becomes a skeleton and, at the end, the grisly executioner's block and the Devil revealed in all his true monstrosity on high, seated on a serpent. The play's first version was written for performance with carts in the village square at Yepes in 1637 on the feast of Corpus Christi and the adaption for the *corrales* retains some of the original *auto*-like flavour. In addition, there are less sensational highlights such as the cutting of the arm with a dagger to seal the Devil's pact with blood, Justina's physical struggle with the Devil (the outer representation of the struggle taking place in her mind and imagination), Cipriano's attempt to strike with his sword at an enemy he cannot hit and his horrified discovery of the reason why, and later his madman-like appearance, semi-nude, in the Governor's palace to bear witness to his new faith. All these are part of the theatrical language of the religious drama, the way in which abstract ideas were rendered not just comprehensible but entertaining. At the very core of the play's metamorphosis of theology into theatre is the figure of the Devil himself.[18] The Devil here is no 'Asse' but the traditional arch-enemy of God. Truth and virtue are anathema to him and his self-appointed task is to obfuscate the one and compromise the other. He does not wait for his victims to falter but creates his own opportunities. He seeks Cipriano and Justina out and – impresario as well as player – engineers the whole situation from the start. As he moves from part to part, as philosopher, magician, gallant and monster, he reveals himself as ingenious, inventive, adaptable and eminently threatening. For all the *gracioso*'s cracks about the smell of sulphur, there is no cosy domestication or trivialization of evil here. The Devil fails not because he is bound to fail but because Justina by a superhuman effort of will and with the aid of divine grace defeats him.

Justina's virtue and her beauty are the axis of the play's physical and spiritual conflict. Her human and moral perfection is the magnet that attracts desire (that is, love) in Cipriano and her other suitors, and envy (and therefore hatred) in the Devil. It thus becomes the instrument of chaos, as the Devil uses her beauty to try to destroy her virtue and gain Cipriano's soul. The extraordinary seduction scene – extraordinary because there is no seducer other than Justina's own imagination – in which her senses are ravaged by aural and visual representations of love that manage to be at the same time both delicate and extremely sensual, is the dramatic climax of the play. The point when, after weakening momentarily, she recovers her reason and her will and resists rock-like the Devil's attempt to drag her off to Cipriano, is one of the Spanish theatre's great emblematic moments. Justina's victory teaches Cipriano that he has not lost his right to choose and it is the exercise of choice which at the last turns tragedy into triumph for both of them.

We learn in the course of *El mágico* that Justina's mother, a secret Christian, was left by her outraged husband to die in childbirth on the mountainside. History therefore repeats itself, though unlike her mother Justina dies for her faith and not merely because of it. It is very Calderonian for situations to be repeated from one generation to another and one of the heaviest burdens his characters carry is the burden of the past. Through no will of their own they find themselves confronted with seemingly unsurmountable difficulties initiated before they were born. No play illustrates better than *La devoción de la cruz (Devotion to the Cross)*[19] the way in which the sins of the fathers are thus visited on the children.

La devoción de la cruz is Calderón's outstanding contribution to the saints and bandits theme. It has over the years provoked extremes of praise and abuse but its power and its passion have been recognized even by those who have found it difficult to understand and to like. It is a case-book example of the way in which Calderón traces effects to causes by means of an elaborate chain of causality which would seem to support the Parkerian thesis that Calderón believed in the idea of diffused responsibility for moral evil and human suffering.[20] Calderón's essentially tragic view of life suffuses even those dramas which may not be formally called tragedies; in *La devoción de la cruz* a human tragedy is deflected eventually into spiritual triumph. The play is also a prime illustration of how Calderón's essentially metaphorical drama operates. Superficially the play is the story of a wicked man, Eusebio, who is saved from damnation by the odd, seemingly arbitrary act of mercy and a talismanic devotion to the cross, and his equally wicked twin sister Julia, who repents in time to be borne off to a convent by a flying cross – religious plays freely exploited the licence offered by miracles to become the *corrales'* most spectacular plays. As far as the plot is concerned, the cross functions in two ways – through the medium of narrative as we learn how the cross has from the moment of Eusebio's birth played a crucial part time and again in his survival; and in the action itself, where we witness the cross continuing to exert its protective function. But clearly it is not meant by Calderón to be taken as a sort of rabbit's foot which if worn around the neck will protect the wearer from harm; purely superstitious belief in the cross's powers is actually mocked in the play when the *gracioso*, who has heard of the bandit Eusebio's devotion to the cross, sets out to collect wood on the mountainside weighed down with crosses in case he encounters him. Eusebio's recognition of the power and significance of the cross is presented as the chink in the armour of his criminality, the sign that he is not lost to grace. More important, the cross is a symbol of mercy and forgiveness, love and compassion, indeed of all the qualities lacking in the twins' harsh, repressive father, who is shown to be ultimately responsible for what they have become.

Because of Curcio's insane jealousy and outrageous treatment of his wife, the twins were separated at birth, brought up in ignorance of each other's existence and later fall in love; because of Eusebio's inferior social status Julia's brother Lisardo taunts him, is challenged to a duel by Eusebio and killed; because Lisardo is killed, Eusebio becomes an outlaw. In other words Eusebio becomes a criminal and dies for his crimes because his father does not think him good enough to marry his daughter. The twisted irony is devastating. In Julia's case Curcio's responsibility is twofold. Having squandered the family fortune he is unable to provide the dowry necessary to marry Julia to a social equal and forces her against her will to enter a convent. There the lover who is through Curcio's fault really her brother comes to find her. When he flees in horror at the discovery that like him she has a birthmark in the form of a cross on her breast, she feels belittled and despised. When she decides to follow him, then changes her mind only to discover that the ladder has been removed and she cannot re-enter the convent, she regards it as a sign that Heaven has abandoned her. She is now a social outcast; she becomes a social outlaw, like all her *bandolera* sisters, through a misguided desire to restore her self-respect in her own eyes and in those of the world. As a social and spiritual outcast she feels alienated from society and God, and therefore freed from all social and spiritual restraints.[21] Beneath the extravagant melodrama of the surface plot, the play's psychology is totally convincing.

Far from preaching a formalist Christianity as has sometimes been claimed, the play uses the energizing metaphor of the cross to convey a profoundly humane message of love and forgiveness. Its thematic axis is the contrast between the twins' treatment at the hands of men and their treatment by God. The eloquent parallel drawn between earthly and heavenly fathers is a significant one in Calderón's drama, which consistently depicts the father–child relationship as an extremely problematic one, possibly for autobiographical reasons; the role played by the family in fashioning individuals into responsible members of society is a continuing theme in his work. Curcio pays for his obsessive jealousy years before by living to see two children become criminals and all three children dead to the world. It is significant, however, that he never recognizes his responsibility. At the end he embraces the criminal son who absolves him of guilt for what he had always feared was murder at birth; but he rages towards the daughter who has dared defy him. He is as violent at the end of the play as he was at the beginning; grief and dishonour have taught him nothing. He is thus resolutely denied any claim to being a tragic hero.

The play's vision of human passion and divine compassion is articulated at the level of language in Calderón's favourite imagery of fire and light, imagery which as usual in Calderón contains contradictions without resolving them because contradiction is shown to be central to human nature and human experience. Perhaps the most memorable moments of the play, however, are two which feature Julia. The scene where she stands up to her father and in the face of his violent threats defends her right to freedom and self-determination is remarkable for the humanity of the sentiments expressed and for the fact that they are expressed by a woman, as well as for the powerful, unadorned simplicity, vibrant with truth, of the writing. It is one of Calderón's finest scenes. So too is that in which the desperate Eusebio, driven to sacrilege by his love, finds Julia sleeping in her chair. The passionate dialogue that follows, with Julia at first not sure whether or not she is dreaming, has a naked intensity unsurpassed anywhere in the Golden-Age theatre.

The renown of the plays that have so far been mentioned tends to mark Calderón out as a playwright preoccupied with religious and philosophical themes and with honour. His range, however, is wider than that and includes a number of works with a historical focus. In keeping with the *comedia*'s tendency in its second phase to move away from the quasi-historical exoticism of the medieval epic and the chivalresque, his interests centre on contemporary events or relatively recent history. The tragedy *Amar después de morir* (*Love after Death*) deals remarkably sympathetically with the *morisco* uprisings in southern Spain in the late 1560s. *El sitio de Breda* (*The Siege of Breda*) celebrates the taking of Breda by Philip IV's troops in 1625. *La cisma de Inglaterra* (*The English Schism*) offers a Spanish Catholic perspective on Henry VIII's decision to divorce his Spanish Catherine for Ann Boleyn and the latter's subsequent execution. *El postrer duelo de España* (*Spain's Last Duel*), on a more domestic scale, dramatizes the last official trial by duel in Spain. All are in their different ways very fine plays which adapt historical material freely and skilfuly for dramatic ends; in some cases, of course, national and political ends are also served. The lack of interest in evoking a simpler, more distant and glamorous national past was to be expected of Calderón's overriding vision of a complex and troubled world. When he did move out of the ambit of sixteenth- and seventeenth-century Europe it was only to rediscover its problems and preoccupations in biblical history and in classical mythology.

The mythological plays, seventeen in all, constitute Calderón's court drama (see also chapter 8) and represent a substantial proportion of his serious work. Lope wrote eight mythological plays and Tirso wrote one, but they are on the whole very tentative in their exploration of the myths' dramatic potential. Furthermore, mythological drama was not entirely suitable fare for the *corrales* or even for performance in princely or royal halls. It was the advent of systematic royal patronage and the creation of sophisticated theatres in the royal palaces, particularly the Palace of the Buen Retiro, which allowed the largely Ovidian myths to be staged with all the startling technical effects they required, creating the sense of wonder and awe central to the myth's purpose. The myths, however, were not dramatized merely to exploit their possibilities for theatrical spectacle. Their inherent allegorical significance had long appealed to late medieval and Renaissance scholars eager to claim them as prefigurations of Christian principles and values,[22] and Calderón, clearly, had recourse to the moral interpretations of the ancient stories given in Renaissance digests of classical learning such as Juan Pérez de Moya's *Philosophia secreta* (1585) and Baltasar de Victoria's *Theatro de los dioses de la gentilidad* (1620). The attraction for Calderón is obvious. The timeless quality of the myths allowed him to deal with those aspects of human nature and life that preoccupied him in an almost theoretical way devoid of any contemporary cultural shaping other than what he chose to introduce. His treatment is bold and imaginative. He selected the stories that interested him, then moulded them to his purposes by changing the sequence of events, inventing characters, altering personal relationships, collating identities and adding elements from pastoral, chivalresque, even the *commedia dell' arte*. The tone tends to be anachronistic: the heroes often act like stage gallants and the business of love, jealousy and honour is conducted in much the same way it is elsewhere in the *comedia*. The serious, or tragic, comes fused with humour in the by now time-honoured way. Without such concessions he would have forfeited the interest even of so sophisticated an audience as the court itself. Nonetheless, the essential remoteness of the myths, familiar as some of them were, aided and abetted by the atmosphere of fantasy conjured up by the spectacular staging, the various metamorphoses and apotheoses, and the intervention of gods and goddesses, freed him to explore his persistent preoccupations outside the overt political and religious imperatives of his own age and uninhibited by the constraints of verisimilitude. So that although as court theatre the mythological plays seem to represent the nearest thing he wrote to establishment drama – and do indeed recommend politically as well as morally acceptable values such as *desengaño* (constructive disillusionment), reason, order, harmony, duty, self-denial and responsibility – in artistic and intellectual terms they were a liberation, the logical outcome of what had all along been a strong inclination towards metaphorical and symbolic drama. Study of the plays is still in its infancy and although their broad allegorical meaning is readily grasped the full significance of all their detail is not yet established. We can be fairly sure, however, that just as all the details of stage scenery and proscenium decoration were ideogrammatic, all that takes place behind the proscenium also has its precise relevance.[23]

The mythological plays, therefore, work on different levels – as a festive spectacle and attempted synthesis of poetry, painting and music, as philosophical and moral symbolism, even probably as political allegory, though how extensive and exact has yet to be determined.[24] As a theatrical phenomenon they were a paradoxical fusion of supernatual fantasy and the high technology essential to produce it. They dramatize familiar *comedia* themes such as the abuse of power and the creative and destructive potential of love, as well as continuing concerns of Calderón's – free will, self-discovery and responsibility. Some end happily, others tragically. The proportion of music and singing varies but most of the later plays are *zarzuelas*, a mixture of spoken dialogue, recitative and song in the *stile recitativo* established in Florence in the 1580s and imported into Spain from Italy in the seventeenth century along with Italian scenography. Most are in three acts, though several are in one or two. The one-act exaltation of love, *La púrpura de la rosa* (*The Purple of the Rose*), a little gem in its perfect fusion of plot, allegory and scenic effects, is preceded by a *loa* in which Calderón explains that he is trying to introduce opera into Spain. The much earlier *Los tres mayores prodigios* (*The Three Greatest Wonders*) was an experiment with the three-act format in which each act has a distinct action, the first dealing with Jason and the golden fleece, the second with Theseus and the minotaur, and the third with Hercules and his wife Deyanira. There is, however, a narrative link – all three have been looking for

Deyanira who has been abducted by the centaur. Each act was performed by a different company on a separate stage, with the three casts combining for the final scene.

One of the finest of the plays and certainly one of the most spectacular is the tragic *El hijo del sol, Faetón* (*Phaeton, Son of the Sun*). The proud but noble Faetón, who ascends to heaven to seek his father Apollo, has to be killed by Jupiter to prevent him destroying the world when he loses control of the chariot of the sun. His mild but treacherous brother, Epafo, by default then wins Tetis, Faetón's love. The siblings motif is a recurrent one in Calderón. The idea of the rival brothers, or young men brought up as brothers, appears in the part-historical play set in the Eastern Empire in the early seventh century AD, *En la vida todo es verdad y todo mentira* (*In Life All is Truth and All is Falsehood*),[25] where it is bound up with another favourite Calderonian theme, the duties a father owes a son. It reappears in the mythological *La fiera, el rayo y la piedra* (*The Beast, the Thunderbolt and the Stone*), Calderón's version of the Pygmalion story, as a struggle between Cupid (discord) and Anteros (harmony). It turns up again in *La estatua de Prometeo* (*Prometheus's Statue*), about the man who brought fire (wisdom and enlightenment) from Heaven, where the conflict between the two brothers Prometeo and Epimeteo represents that between reason and passion, knowledge and action. Calderón's most overtly allegorical full-length play, it promotes the idea that the desire for knowledge is an essential part of the civilizing process, with the man of intellect eventually triumphing over the man of action.

Another familiar motif found in the mythological plays is that of the prophecy. There is a liberal sprinkling of Segismundos predestined to a fate which they attempt, normally through the intervention of a parent, to avoid. In *Apolo y Climene*, Climene, who has been imprisoned by her father, chooses, when she gains her freedom, to enjoy her forbidden love and pays the price. Narciso in the pastoral idyll *Eco y Narciso* is brought up by his mother in total isolation but mistakes the nature of the danger that threatens him, and in seeking to avoid it goes to meet it. *El monstruo de los jardines* (*The Monster in the Gardens*), in contrast, ends on a note of triumph. Achilles, at his mother's suggestion, dresses as a woman to avoid death at the battle of Troy. Discovered by Odysseus by means of a ruse and confronted with his shameful behaviour, he faces up to his destiny and prepares for glory in battle. The persistent message is that by fleeing or ignoring an adverse destiny man only goes to meet it; Fate has to be confronted not avoided and it cannot be conquered until man has conquered himself through understanding, self-knowledge and love. In Christian terms we can see that adverse destiny as original sin, in humanist terms as man's capacity for self-destruction. Each individual's destiny is the failing in his character which must be overcome. The prophecies are merely warnings of what will happen if the characters do not take control of themselves, and are often therefore self-fulfilling. Calderón's ideal is Senecan man, man who can master himself and his passions and confront his fate with equanimity. The essential role of love in this process is dramatized in *Fieras afemina amor* (*Love Tames Wild Beasts*), first performed in January 1670 when Calderón was seventy, which portrays an unexpectedly ignoble Hercules who is boorish, arrogant, ignorant, almost savage, who sees love only as a weakness and a distraction. He is taught his lesson by falling in love with Yole, whose affections lie elsewhere, and through the intervention of the three Graces he learns to see himself as he really is. Finally the *macho* beast is tamed by the supreme humiliation: Yole dresses him as a woman while he is sleeping and ensures he is seen by his men. The play ends with the apotheosis of love as Hercules is made its prisoner. The supremacy of love, understood clearly here as a reflection of the divine, is unequivocally stated.

Few would claim, I think, that the mythological plays, for all that they often contain moving or powerful scenes, capture our imagination and affection as well as our admiration, in the way many of his other dramas do. The very fact that they occupy a space somewhere between the human and the divine produces a crucial disengagement of our sympathies. But they are ingenious works of great literary, intellectual and often psychological interest essential to any serious, extended study of Calderón's art. His use of the myths stays, broadly speaking, well within the ideological parameters of his age, but there are many original and unusual elements which would repay close attention. One of the plays' most fascinating aspects is the way they show the preoccupations and interests of Calderón's earlier period metamorphosed into something strikingly different yet recognizably the same. Like Ovid's own metamorphoses they are a distillation, a crystallization, of hidden essences.

Calderón's reputation as a literary 'heavy' has tended to obscure, certainly outside Spain, the fact that he was a prolific writer of comedies, particularly *comedias de capa y espada* (cape and sword plays) which purport to depict the love antics of the urban gentry. The action normally takes place in or near a city, often but not invariably Madrid, and consists of a succession of ingenious variations on the intertwined themes of love, honour and jealousy; a few have a palace setting (*comedias palaciegas*) with intrigues complicated by the presence of a princely master or mistress.

Beneath the persuasive air of realism and vitality the plays are highly stylized and artificial, both in their artistic procedures and in the view they give of seventeenth-century upper-class life. To move from the wife-murder plays to the comedies is to walk into a completely different world of sensibilities, a world where social conventions are freely flouted for humourous ends. Both tragedy and comedy bend reality to their purpose and if we are so unwise as to use the *comedia* as historical evidence then it can as easily sustain a picture of an easy-going society as it can that of a narrowly regimented one. Danger and the threat of disaster are, of course, central to the ways of comedy, and in the *comedia de capa y espada* they are provided by the brooding presence in the background of a shared preoccupation with masculine honour which can at any moment erupt into violence. But the business of the plays is contained always within the comic limits of the genre and it is not useful to try and reconcile Calderón's honour tragedies with what are effectively honour comedies.[26] The circumstances are quite different and both obey the imperatives of drama and the particular dramatic form, not those of real life. The comedies utilize the more or less familiar objects and aspects of everyday existence – cellars, attics, double doors, concealed entrances, candles, veils, clever servants, dancing masters, human ingenuity and wiles – to construct complicated plots that are every bit as unreal as the Spanish theatre's more extravagant comedies of romance and adventure. Titles such as *La dama duende* (*The Phantom Lady*), *El galán fantasma* (*The Phantom Gallant*), *Casa con dos puertas mala es de guardar* (*The House with Two Doors is Difficult to Guard*), *El maestro de danzar* (*The Dancing Master*), *El escondido y la tapada* (*The Hidden Gallant and the Veiled Lady*), *El astrólogo fingido* (*The False Astrologer*) immediately convey the flavour of Calderón's comic world.

The question of whether the plays have an intentionally serious side to them has in recent years exercised critics of the *comedia*.[27] Some indeed see them as essentially serious works with a guiding moral purpose, only lightly caparisoned as comedy. Others feel that they are intended simply to entertain. Some regard them as socially subversive, others as entirely orthodox. The arguments are in reality arguments not so much about the nature of Calderón's comedies as about the nature of comedy itself, seen at one extreme as entirely lacking in transcendence, at the other as deeply symbolic of experience, even as the truly tragic mode.[28] But there is the added complication that Calderón does indeed strike one as the least frivolous of all Golden-Age dramatists and perhaps the least likely, therefore, to write meaningless comedy. Such an assumption has its dangers, but equally dangerous is the assumption that when a writer moves into the comic mode he necessarily abandons his habits of mind and attitudes to life. Calderón's comedies betray the same control and artifice, the same concern for shape and structure, the same love of contrast, symmetry and balance, the same predilection for complexity and causality, as his serious dramas.[29] It is hardly surprising, therefore, if they also betray the same preoccupation with truth, illusion and deception, the private and public self, inclination and duty, passion and reason, family relationships and the power of love. It is not difficult to find morals in the plays as the characters wilfully prejudice their well-being and that of others through their selfishness and imprudence, their indiscretions and infidelities. And the titles themselves are often an invitation to see the plays as encapsulating some lesson or some piece of proverbial wisdom: *Guárdate del agua mansa* (*Beware Still Waters*), *Cada uno para sí* (*Each Man For Himself*), *No hay cosa como callar* (*There is Nothing Like Silence*), *No hay burlas con el amor* (*There's No Playing With Love*), *El secreto a voces* (*The Open Secret*). That each of the comedies has a guiding theme there can be no doubt; neither can there be any doubt that human nature in general and Spanish seventeenth-century society in particular come in for close scrutiny, frequently for implicit criticism. Moral values often conflict with social values and the endings are not invariably as happy as they ought to be; indeed *No hay cosa como callar*, where the heroine has to give up the man she loves without being able to tell him why, is a poignant little tragedy masquerading as comedy.

But it remains the case that the plays are written as romantic comedies, albeit 'significant' ones and that they must be allowed that essential identity. The ingredients of tragedy and comedy, after all, are much the same; it is the treatment that counts. The cuckold is tragic or comic depending on the glass through which he is viewed. The characters of comedy are protected from the consequences of their actions by their comic status and are therefore further removed from the sphere of our sympathy. Even those who are married off against their inclination at the end accept their fate with the willing acquiescence required for happy endings; they know their parts and play them well. Our appreciation of the serious implications, the inner patterns, of Calderón's comedies constitutes a secondary, intellectual response. Our immediate instinctive reaction is one of delight and amusement, the sovereign purpose of comedy whatever its other aims. To seek to find for the plays alternative labels such as 'entertaining moral allegories'[30] is to misrepresent their undoubted comic genius.

It would be difficult to mistake a typical Calderonian comedy for one by Lope or even Tirso, not so much because of its ingenuity and complexity, for these qualities are not peculiar to Calderón, as because of its distinctive air of controlled chaos, of stuffy, convention-ridden genteel society threatened, if only temporarily, by the seething anarchy of human nature underneath. The excitement and tension thus generated are immense. For all their intricate plots and polished construction the plays move at a spanking pace and the dialogue is brisk and natural. The most fascinating are perhaps those with an element of manufactured mystery or fantasy, where the bewilderment of those characters not in the know adds to the general amusement. In *La dama duende*, for example, the existence of a hidden door allows Ángela, an impoverished widow kept in seclusion by her brother to prevent her getting up to mischief and compromising the family honour, to move freely between her quarters and those of an attractive guest of her brother's, don Manuel. The fear and confusion the 'phantom' spreads with her invisible visits and the letters she leaves behind reaches a hilarious climax in Act III when Manuel, invited to dinner by the sender of the notes, is led through the streets and then back to Ángela's room in the very house he has come from. He is of course discovered there by his outraged host. The way in which situations and people are shamelessly manipulated in these plays intensifies the impression of dramatic manipulation generated by the comedies as a whole, with their schematized characters and plots. If one of comedy's self-appointed tasks is to show people for the puppets of their needs and desires that they are, then Calderón succeeds admirably. In his plays even those who think themselves to be the puppet masters dance endlessly to the control of a superior hand.

Calderón's influence on the second phase of the *comedia*'s development was considerable without being overwhelming. By the 1620s Spanish drama, as we saw, was already becoming more carefully crafted, more self-conscious and more reflective. Calderón's arrival on the theatrical scene greatly reinforced these tendencies but he took them to lengths that other dramatists were incapable of imitating. As is usually the case with very complex art, the servile imitations of Calderón are tediously bad, reproducing only the superficial adornments and sensational elements without the conceptual depths that give them meaning. The ablest of his contemporaries, therefore, wisely ploughed their own furrows within the familiar outlines of a theatrical tradition that was still developing under the influence of the ageing Lope, Tirso de Molina and now Calderón.

Francisco de Rojas Zorrilla (1607–1648)

Rojas, a careful craftsman and stylish writer, was the most gifted of Calderón's contemporaries and also the most independent.[31] A close friend and collaborator of Calderón and other court poets of his day, he enjoyed the favour of Philip IV and it was a play of his that was chosen to be performed at the opening of the Coliseo theatre at the Palace of the Buen Retiro in 1640. Rojas, for all this, delighted in being unconventional, even provocative. He was at the same time a genuinely thoughtful, clear-sighted and humane man inspired much of the time by the desire to brush aside the deadening clutter of false social values and get at the real priorities of human life underneath. His method is not the subtle, allusive, accumulative campaign of Calderón but the bold, iconoclastic attack. He is the seventeenth-century Spanish theatre's most uncompromising and ablest satirist (the high-flown language of Gongorine verse was a favourite target) and its first real caricaturist: his entertaining *Entre bobos anda el juego* (*It's a Fool's Game*), about the pompous and avaricious don Lucas de Cigarral who wants to marry a young girl, initiated the vogue for the *comedia de figurón*, the play that satirizes the pretentious fool. On one occasion, at least, his unconventional approach earned him the severe disapproval of his audience. When *Cada cual lo que le toca* (*To Each His Own Concerns*) was performed in Madrid,[32] it was booed by its audience for depicting a wife who before her marriage was enjoyed and discarded by another man, and a husband so reluctant to kill his wife when her former lover returns to pester her that she has to take the family honour into her own hands and kill the man herself. Don Luis then forgives his wife her past and they settle down to married bliss. Not only was this resolution an affront to the audience's belief in the double standard, but it deprived them of the pound of bloody flesh to which they had become accustomed. That it is a deliberate twisting of the basic Calderonian pattern seems clear – the circumstances are the same even to the extent that Doña Isabel has married don Luis reluctantly on the rebound. Rojas's aim may partly have been novelty, but there can be little doubt that he is also confronting a real dilemma: what is a wife to do if, because of her but through no fault of hers, the conjugal honour is threatened?

It is Isabel herself who turns potential tragedy into triumph. Here we have a woman who sees her husband's honour not as a thing apart, waiting in a corner of her life like a wild beast ready to pounce, but as something which is hers to protect. When she kills don Fernando she avenges not only her past humiliation, but the present threat to her own and her husband's moral and psychological integrity. By revealing herself to be as conscious of their honour as he, and more capable in the circumstances of defending it (since Luis does not know the identity of her would-be seducer his only recourse would be to kill the wife he loves), she adopts a position of equality in their married relationship. The dagger that kills Fernando is her husband's, the hand that wields it is hers; they are one in the pursuit of honour. The play is a remarkable statement about female equality and Rojas must have realized that he was taking a risk with his audience.

That Rojas's interest was seriously engaged with the question of female honour is clear from *Progne y Filomena*. His treatment of the Ovidian myth indicates that he saw in it not only another opportunity to pursue his favourite theme of revenge, but an opportunity to explore the whole idea of female revenge in relation to the theatrical conventions of his time.[33] The sisters' motive is not just revenge without sanction of reason, but a concern for their honour which is analysed in considerable depth through the careful depiction of their mental processes. Filomena, violated and injured by her brother-in-law, chooses not to leave vengeance to her father and her lover. She is the cause of their dishonour; more crucially, she sees her own dishonour to be greater. In her eyes, therefore, the onus of revenge for both injuries, indirect and direct, properly falls upon herself. Like Isabel in *Cada cual* she uses her husband-to-be's dagger as a symbol of double satisfaction. Progne's part in the revenge is in a sense more revolutionary. She, after all, has not been physically injured. However, she feels implicated not only in her sister's dishonour but in her husband's vicious and adulterous behaviour. She feels as dishonoured by her husband's action as the husband is conventionally supposed to by his wife's, and decides that it is her right and duty to punish Tereo. The sisters' explicit assumption of that combined sense of selfhood and social identity called honour – normally in the seventeenth century the prerogative of the male – was a defiant challenge to the accepted values of Rojas's day.

Rojas, naturally, was no more a feminist in the modern sense than any of the other dramatists of the day. Like Lope he believed that woman's place is at man's side and his treatment of his women characters is variable, yielding now to convention, now to his iconoclastic urge, as well as to the liberal conclusions of his more serious moments. Thus *Lo que son mujeres* (*What Women Are*) is a clever, rather savage satire on the theme of the *mujer esquiva*, the disdainful heroine, and her admirers, in which the cruel and capricious Serafina is punished for her disdain by being reduced to proposing to her servants when her four former suitors in turn reject her. The changes in the familiar format, including the absence of marriages at the end, are typical of the delight Rojas took in refusing to follow convention and he uses them to paint an unattractive picture of men and women alike. He pokes fun at the *esquiva* again in *Sin honra no hay amistad* (*No Friendship Without Honour*), but here the whole ethos of the *comedia* and its preoccupation with love and honour is mocked. The disdainful heroine Juana falls in love eventually, not with any particular man but with love itself, and then is confronted with the problem of which man to choose. Her marvellously amusing account of the antics of the courting male, the two heroes' polite division of the duties of courtship, their inability to decide who is to kill the man attacking them, the continual falling in and out of love and hate – this is all good fun at the *comedia*'s own expense. The lack of moral concern, the absence of true emotion, the disregard for personal feelings, the humorous treatment of serious matters such as murder and rape, are all typical of the satirical method, but the play is a satire not on life but on other plays – a double treat for the habitués of the *corrales*.

Rojas in fact made irreverent send-ups of dramatic conventions something of a speciality. In the pseudo-historical romance *El desafío de Carlos Quinto (Charles the Fifth's Challenge)* he creates an extraordinary female character, Mari Bernardo, in whom he parodies both the *graciosa*, the comic servant girl, and the beautiful Amazon type beloved of theatre audiences. Mari Bernardo – the name is deliberately bisexual – has led a free and adventurous life not through any desire for independence but because her devotion to her man, Buscaruidos, drives her to imitate and surpass his every action. Weary of her mimicry, Buscaruidos becomes convinced that Mari Bernardo is a hermaphrodite and finally decides that the only way to rid himself of his shadow is to marry her. The stage direction that she be dressed in male and female attire signals her ambiguity and the whole situation makes for a brilliant theatrical romp. It is surprising in the circumstances that the *hic mulier* character, so popular in the *corrales*, was not used more often as a figure of fun, an interesting indication, perhaps, of the hold the type exercised over the romantic imagination of playwrights and playgoers alike.

For all the variety of his heroines and their fates, the lasting impression Rojas's drama creates is of a mind unusually receptive to the female point of view. Even when the plot requires its women to conform at last to what is expected of them, the logic and justice of their arguments are rarely toppled. Juana in *Lo que quería ver el Marqués de Villena (What the Marquis of Villena Wished to See)*, who since the death of her father has lived incognito as a successful academic in the highly competitive masculine world of Salamanca university, eventually falls in love, and love, running true to form, reveals the essential woman beneath the scholarly male exterior. But while Juana is not allowed to forget the conditions of her sex, she is allowed to make the point, and with considerable eloquence, that men are endowed with no monopoly of intelligence or courage, and that if women are different it is only because they have been brought up to be so. And this reasoning goes unchallenged.

Rojas, like most of the dramatists of the age, was deeply interested in the potential conflict between the private and public spheres of man's life. Their religion, their exposure to classical thought, their historical circumstances, all conspired to produce in them the profound conviction that man's first duty is not to himself but to God, king and society. At the same time they were not complacent about the ease with which this goal could be achieved or about the personal cost. Rojas's *García del Castañar o Del rey abajo ninguno* (*García del Castañar or None Below the King*) dramatizes the dilemma posed for the individual by loyalty to his sovereign, God's representative on earth, within the familiar cadre of conjugal honour. *No hay ser padre siendo rey* (*No King May Be a Father*) and *El Caín de Cataluña* (*The Cain of Catalonia*) demonstrate that the tension can be found at its most acute in the monarch or leader himself, as royal duty struggles with paternal feeling. The extreme difficulty of reconciling private and public personae is conceded in both plays and both come up with interestingly uncasuistic solutions. In the first the king can pardon his son for accidentally killing his brother only by yielding up his crown to him and forgiving him as a father. In the second, the Count signs his son's death warrant and then surreptitiously frees him; the young man, who has intentionally murdered his brother, is then shot by the guards – justice is done, but a father's conscience is saved.

There is a broad vein of tragedy in Rojas's work which contrasts vividly with his talent for sharp, irreverent comedy. The dualism is more marked than in any other dramatist of the time and is another example of his resistance to the authority of the typical *comedia*, with its distinctive blend of tragic and comic elements. This strong, clear note of tragedy has led in the past to the view that Rojas is seventeenth-century Spain's only true tragedian. This view is no longer acceptable to many who see in plays by Lope and Calderón an altogether more original concept of tragedy at work; and hindsight indicates that it was Rojas's more recognizable approach which made his plays stand out as tragedies. In fact, his handling of tragic material was not as sure as his reputation suggests. In his comedies, as we have seen, a very original and successful comic vision comes into play.[34] The tragic plays by no means lack originality but the originality has a tendency to frustrate the ends of tragedy rather than serve them. Good as they are, the tragedies or potential tragedies often lack the willingness to confront their own essential nature which we find in such abundance in the comic plays. Thus in *Del rey abajo ninguno* the tragic dilemma of a peasant faced by the prospect of being cuckolded by his King dissolves with the discovery that his enemy is not the king at all but a noble; since García del Castañar is in fact of noble origin himself he can then kill his enemy as an equal. This superb play has many virtues: it has moments of great tragic and lyric intensity, and the use of a split perspective on events – unlike García the audience know throughout who his prospective cuckolder is – is novel and interesting. While the ironic multiplication of points of view is dramatically extremely effective, however, it does serve to reduce the specifically tragic impact of García's dilemma, a dilemma which we know to be far less acute than it seems to him. The play involves us far more in pleasurable anticipation of the working out of this complication than in García's anguish. The possibility for sociopolitical conflict is posed twice over (García is a peasant, his enemy the king) and evaded twice over (García is in fact a noble and so is his enemy). Even before he learns the truth García has decided to solve his predicament with an evasion of his own: he tries to get rid of the problem by killing the wife he knows to be innocent, but fails.

Years before, a fine tragedy, *La estrella de Sevilla* (*The Star of Seville*) had been written by an unidentified dramatist on the theme of the predatory but untouchable monarch and in *Peribáñez* and *Fuenteovejuna* Lope had openly confronted the matter of class conflict in the sexual arena; *Del rey abajo* has in fact a great deal in common with *Peribáñez*. But García neither succumbs tragically to his dilemma nor imposes himself heroically upon it in the tradition of tragicomedy – he is merely rescued by circumstances. Rojas's evasion of the full tragic, as well as the sociopolitical, implications of his theme is the outcome of his desire to play a new tune on an old instrument, of his resistance to treading in the footsteps of others. The result is excellent drama and splendid theatre, but not, I would argue, successful tragedy or near-tragedy. The same is true of *No hay ser padre siendo rey* where the ending is admirable in human terms but something of a cop-out in terms of tragedy; and of *El Caín de Cataluña* where the King dishonestly if understandably tries to have things both ways and justice is done in spite of him. Both are moving and their ingenuity appeals; but as tragedies they lack the courage of their convictions. It is significant that one of Rojas's most poignant and successful tragedies is the more straightforward honour tragedy *Casarse por vengarse* (*To Marry For Revenge*), where female revenge goes sadly wrong. The tragic protagonist Blanca, abandoned by Enrique when he becomes king, takes her revenge by marrying someone she does not love. This pathetic attempt to punish Enrique, who still loves her, and herself, for allowing herself to get hurt, rebounds upon her with tragic intensity. She forgets that her husband too has feelings, that he loves her and that hurt in his turn he too, as a man careful of his honour, might wish to strike back. She forgets all this when on her wedding night she breaks down and cannot bring herself to accept her husband's embraces. She is the victim of her own revenge and by the time she sees the folly of the course her grief and jealousy have driven her to, it is already too late. In this play Rojas's tragic judgement is beautifully right; so it is too in the harrowing *Progne y Filomena* and his memorable love tragedy *Los áspides de Cleopatra* (*Cleopatra's Asps*). In others the love of the different and of the unexpected, which led him to the very heart of comedy, distracted him from complete fulfilment of the tragic potential of his material.

Of the other dramatists in and around the court who wrote in the shadow of Calderón, frequently collaborating with one another and sometimes with him – dramatists such as Antonio de Solís, Antonio Coello, Álvaro Cubillo de Aragón, Juan de Matos Fragoso, Jerónimo de Cáncer y Velasco and Francisco Antonio de Bances Candamo – the only one with a truly distinctive talent of quality was the courtier priest Agustín de Moreto y Cabaña.

Agustín Moreto y Cabaña (1618–1669)

The writer of many competent plays in most of the familiar modes,[35] Moreto is best known for his witty, stylish comedies. The polished and utterly delightful *El desdén con el desdén* (*Disdain With Disdain*) marks the culmination of the genre of the *mujer esquiva* plays created by Lope some fifty years before. Again the situation is that of the disdainful heroine won over to love by feigned scorn and betrayed by her own vanity. Diana's quarrel is essentially not with men but with love itself, which her reading has taught her is responsible for all the world's troubles. She adopts, therefore, a stance of intellectual disillusionment. The siege her disdain now undergoes is a subtler campaign than most. Carlos falls in love with Diana, in spite of her 'modest beauty', because for the first time in his life he is unable to have what he wants for the asking. Intelligently realizing that only the challenge which the unattainable represents for his own ego will succeed in shaking Diana's he poses as *un hombre esquivo*, daring Diana with his pretence of aloofness and disdain to try to reduce him to the same state of abject submission as her other suitors. Swallowing the bait, Diana resolves to conquer what she sees as his vanity, little realizing that she is passing judgement not on Carlos's motives, but her own. Wounded by Carlos's seeming immunity, she is slowly but surely drawn into the trap and when Carlos plays his trump card by pretending interest in Diana's

lady-in-waiting, she is irretrievably lost. Moreto was writing within a
well-worn tradition, with ready-made situations and ideas and a ready-
made phraseology to draw on, and like the other dramatists he upholds love
and marriage as the natural habitat of women. But the controlled elegance
of the symmetrical plot and the psychological finesse with which the lovers'
relationship is developed makes the play the best of its kind.

Another of Moreto's outstanding comedies is *No puede ser*, whose title is
half of the proverb 'No puede ser el guardar una mujer' – 'There's no
guarding a woman'. It dramatizes the idea that her own virtue is a woman's
best protection and it is effectively a plea for recognition of woman's dignity
and integrity and of her capacity for self-determination. The character who
incarnates these liberal ideas is the splendid Ana, a poet of culture and
learning who presides over a *salon* that meets regularly at her home. She it is
who decides to prove to her fiancé, don Pedro, that he is wrong to insist that
a woman, in this case his sister, can be guarded against her will. Ana's
outlook is so completely that of the emancipated woman that she is
determined not to marry don Pedro until he is cured of his prejudices and
narrow-mindedness. Part of the comic irony derives from the fact that poor
Pedro is not bright enough to be aware of the discrepancy between the way
he conducts his own affairs and the way he tries to conduct his sister's: he
treats his future wife as a responsible and mature adult yet fusses over his
sister like an indignant cockerel. Ana, needless to say, gets her way. Her
calm, firm assumption of female equality makes her the nearest thing to
modern emancipated woman to tread the boards of the *corrales* and Moreto,
of all the Spanish playwrights, might have been expected to produce her.
His men and women possess a moderation and urbanity reminiscent of
Alarcón's. Unlike Alarcón, however, Moreto was clearly interested in
female roles. His honour-conscious men lack the impetuosity and air of suppressed violence we tend to associate with stage *galanes* and his women
seem to take their men's behaviour very much in their stride. Such
characters do not yield high drama and Moreto's plays are altogether milder
and more credible than the average *comedia*; he was not at home with the
extreme, the extravagant or the sensational. He composed by preference in
a minor key, making his points in a neat, restrained hand and with a fine
and delicate nib. His comedy has not the romantic verve of Lope's, the
dazzling intricacy and ingenuity of Tirso's or the hot-house tension of
Calderón's, but it has a grace and a serenity which exert a great attraction
of their own. He took the comic traditions of his day, reduced them to
essentials and with his perfect control of the movement of comedy and his
fine grasp of human psychology constructed out of them a drama that has

quite a special flavour. His comedy is a distillation not of life but of comedy itself; the social and moral implications of his themes are there below the surface for those who care to look, but they are never allowed to disturb comedy's smiling mask.

7

The *corrales* and their audience

The *corrales*[1]

In the preceding chapters we have been concerned with the dramatic and literary nature of Spain's national theatre – its procedures, its assumptions, its preoccupations. However, since it was a theatre shaped and defined to a significant extent by external considerations and pressures, no real understanding of the *comedia*'s institutional identity is possible if these influences are overlooked. The time has come, therefore, to look at the circumstances of the plays' performance and their reception.

The entrepreneurial initiative shown by charitable brotherhoods from the later 1560s on in sponsoring performances of plays in hired yards led within ten years or so to the construction of Madrid's first permanent *corral* on a site in the Calle de la Cruz which was bought for the purpose in 1579. Three years later, in 1582, another site was acquired in the Calle del Príncipe. The new *corrales* depended heavily for their success on the good-will and co-operation of the authorities. Before long, therefore, in return for permission to hold performances more often, the brotherhoods were obliged to share their profits with other charitable institutions, including the city's General Hospital. To ensure their efficient running the *corrales* were placed under the general supervision of the hospitals' Protector, a member of the Council of Castile, although at this stage the brotherhoods still retained responsibility for their management.

Successful as the *corrales* were, their takings inevitably fluctuated with the weather, unexpected closures, rival attractions on feast days, and plays which proved unpopular. In 1615, therefore, the city of Madrid was required by the Council of Castile to guarantee the hospitals a maximum annual subsidy to supplement when necessary the proceeds from the *corrales*. The *corrales* themselves were henceforth to be run by lessee-managers, accountable to the Protector, on the basis of what became four-year contracts. At the same time marshals (*alcaldes*), paid by the management and attended by constables (*alguaciles*), were appointed to ensure decency and order during performances. In 1638 the city's control over the *corrales* was consolidated when it was decided that in order to streamline the whole operation, the lessees would in future pay the city treasury directly and the treasury would then hand over a fixed subsidy to the hospitals; the Council of Castile, however, retained general control over the *corrales'* activities. The complex hierarchical administration of the Madrid theatres which thus evolved has in the event proved a boon to theatre historians, since it guaranteed the survival from this later period of titles, leases, and contracts regarding the organization and repair of the *corrales* which would almost certainly not have survived in private hands.

The construction of the *corrales* was a slow business at first though it accelerated once performances got under way and funds started coming in. The Cruz and the Príncipe were very similar if not identical in lay-out and form, largely because their construction was determined by their location within existing blocks of buildings and therefore by their restricted possibilities for expansion.

Each playhouse consisted initially of a yard (*patio*) surrounded on three sides by the backs of neighbouring dwellings, with a stage at the far end and raked steps (*gradas*) with benches down each side. On the fourth or street side an entrance facade to the yard was built, with doors on to the street. Since this side was the brotherhoods' own property, expansion here was straightforward and fairly swift. A first-floor circle called the *cazuela* (stew pot) to accommodate women playgoers was soon built opposite the stage above the entrance passages to the yard. A second floor was added to the facade building shortly after, by 1602 in the case of the Príncipe, to provide balcony boxes, including a large central one for city dignitaries.

Along the sides expansion was necessarily slower and more piecemeal, as the owners of the adjoining properties over the years gradually opened up windows (*rejas*) and boxes (*aposentos*), for their own use, for rental or for sub-letting. The financial arrangements varied. Some owners paid a fee to the management, some handed over a share of their profits, while others received viewing rights in return for allowing access through their property to other boxes: most lateral boxes had no separate access, though a few probably had their own passageways to the street. In due course the management itself acquired property to enable it to build more boxes at second-floor level and then attic boxes (*desvanes*) above at third floor level. The *desvanes* were continued round over the second-floor facade boxes to provide extra attic seating, including a second, upper circle for the women

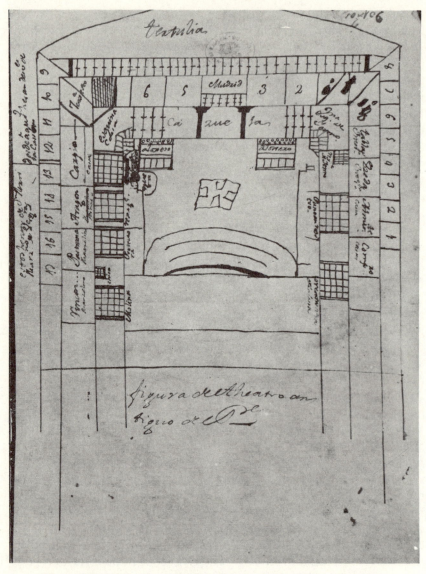

Plate 1 Plan of the Corral del Príncipe, probably eighteenth century

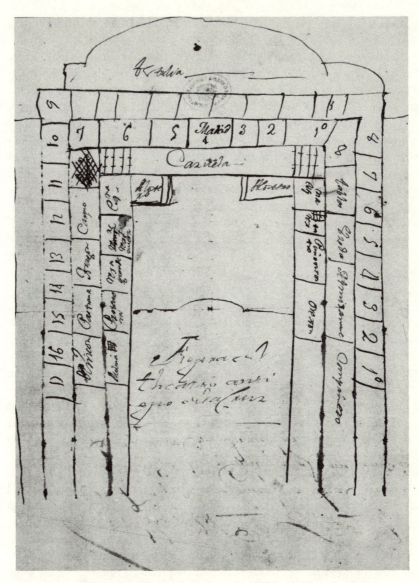

Plate 2 Plan of the Corral de la Cruz, probably eighteenth century

(*cazuela alta*). A section of the *desvanes*, called the *tertulia*, was reserved for the clergy.

The development of the stage wall of the yard is not entirely clear. There was at least one corridor or gallery with a railed balcony above the stage, possibly two, and since there is no evidence that these projected out over the stage it looks as if they were created within the rear of an existing building. Certainly in 1613 the house backing onto the stage at the Príncipe was bought so that the backstage area could be expanded. The third-floor *desvanes* extended over this side too, providing storage space for stage machinery (*los desvanes de los tornos*), though it is not certain when these were added; stage machinery (*apariencias* or *tramoyas*) was used from the beginning and soon became quite elaborate.

The *corrales* seem to have reached their full development, minor alterations apart, by the 1630s (see Plates 1 and 2). Since their construction was so piecemeal and is in some respects conjectural, it seems sensible for the sake of clarity to give a description of the one we know most about in its finished state. The Corral del Príncipe had a rectangular apron stage – probably six foot high but possibly as high as nine feet – with an understage area which it is assumed accommodated the men's dressing room and the wardrobe. Trap doors were built into the stage – as many as seven were cut into the stage at the Cruz when it was rebuilt in 1652. The back of the stage was probably curtained, with openings for exits and entrances, and had an inner acting area, flanked by two pillars, which could double as a women's dressing room. This too probably had curtains, which could part to 'discover' anything from a tableau of the Annunciation to a murdered wife.[2] Props were used but there was little scenery proper, though later on painted flats, possibly with doors, are thought to have been placed in front of the rear curtain, or behind it in the case of discoveries (also called *apariencias*). There was no lighting, although the inner stage, which would have been somewhat darker than that outside, gave a certain degree of lighting flexibility; performances therefore took place in the afternoon. Over the stage the gallery, or galleries, also curtained when required, provided more flexible acting space, serving as balconies, battlements, towers or mountain tops, as the action demanded. To the sides of the stage yet more flexible space was probably provided by lateral platforms which could either be used as stage extensions or as extra lateral seating. It has been suggested that the *alcalde*, who signalled for the play to begin when the audience had settled down, normally sat here with his men. It is likely that portable steps were also positioned on these platforms to provide access to the galleries and to serve as ladders, staircases, even hillsides, when required by the action. The stage machinery was operated from the *desvanes* above and behind the stage; by the late seventeenth century aerial effects had become so elaborate that in 1674 the boxes at the *opposite* end to the stage had to be modified so as not to get in the way.

Immediately in front of the stage was a raised row of stools (*taburetes*) for special spectators, separated by a railing from the groundlings (*mosqueteros*) standing in the *patio* behind. On either side of the *patio* were the raked *gradas* with bench seating; these rose to just below first-floor level, where the protruding railings (*rejas*) of the first-floor windows of the surrounding houses prevented their occupants from climbing into the *gradas* without paying. Above were the second-floor boxes, flush with the walls of the *corral*, and above them were the low-ceilinged *desvanes*. Opposite the stage was the entrance area, with a box on either side with a railed enclosure (*alojero*) in front, where water, nuts, fruit and *aloja*, a spiced honey and water mixture, were sold. At first-floor level was the *cazuela*, covered at least partially by a grill or railing, with corner boxes on either side. Above were more boxes with the Madrid box in the middle, and on the top floor were the upper *cazuela* and the clerics' *tertulia*. The strictly segregated women in the *cazuelas* had their own passageway to the street and in due course even their own law officer to protect them from being pestered by the men; in the boxes men and women sat together. The King had a separate entrance to a box in the Cruz and probably in the Príncipe as well.

The stage, sides and facade had projecting roofs at third-floor level which rested on pairs of support posts the length of the *corral* and which protected all but the yard itself. When the Madrid box was in due course extended outwards to increase its capacity it was given its own roof – to protect the occupants, apparently, from dust and urine. The spectators standing in the yard could be shaded from the sun if necessary by a canvas awning which was operated by boys who reached it by climbing through a trap door in the upper *cazuela*.

The total capacity of each *corral* with extra benching in every available space – for first performances for example – is thought to have risen from around 1,000 in the early days to around 2,000 in the 1630s, when they had reached their full expansion. Of the latter figure, there were almost 1,000 public places for men and around 350 public places for women; the rest represents preferential or private accommodation. Admission fees were controlled by the authorities. Spectators paid an actors' fee at the street door and another sum inside for entry to the yard. Bench seating was extra again. For the *cazuela* and the boxes, single but commensurately higher prices were charged.

The fully-developed *corral* was not a self-contained theatre. It was a curious and uneasy mixture of public and private seating, of theatre property and private property. This created financial and legal problems which were finally solved only in the eighteenth century, when the *corrales* were demolished and new proscenium-stage theatres were built in their place; these had walled-up sides which removed the offending intrusions of the privately-owned boxes. The English playhouses of the day did not suffer in the same way – the Fortune and the Globe were custom-built. In other respects, however, they were remarkably like the Spanish *corrales*. Developing at more or less the same time in similar circumstances, they necessarily responded to those circumstances in a similar way. Both started off as temporary inn-yard theatres, both were public theatres and both, thanks to the arrival on scene of a playwright of genius, enjoyed enormous popular success. Their overall shape, rectangular in Madrid, polygonal or round in London, no doubt obeyed the different restraints of their physical locations, but their general lay-out and functioning, particularly with respect to the stage, retained the stamp of their primitive, public inn-yard origins. The possible influence of the touring *commedia dell'arte* companies, particularly that of the entrepreneurial and innovative Ganassa who played an active part at an early stage in the development of the Príncipe, must not be overlooked;[3] but this influence was relatively short-lived and is not in any case necessary to explain the basic likeness between the two national playhouses. The inn-yard model with its apron stage met admirably the needs of the general public it served; the sophistication of the later proscenium stage was a response to a very different sort of theatre audience.

The organization of the theatrical world[4]

Lope's *comedia nueva* was a commercial theatre subject to the law of supply and demand which went all out to create the demand and maintain the supply. The gradual concentration of its economic and administrative organization in the hands of the municipality ensured the maximum stability, status and efficiency possible. The charitable work of the brotherhoods had enabled the theatre to become established in the first place and this continuing connection, particularly when placed on an official municipal footing, virtually guaranteed the theatre's survival in the face of all criticism. The two new *corrales* in Madrid provided an essential vehicle for Lope's talents and his plays soon guaranteed them a theatrical monopoly in the capital. In the provincial capitals – Seville, Valencia, Córdoba[5] – the theatre also became a fixed and well-organized if not quite so prominent feature of public life; indeed the theatres built on the same basic model somewhat later in Valencia (the Olivera) and Seville (the Coliseo and later the Montería) became famous for their luxury and comfort. Many other towns also boasted a permanent or semi-permanent courtyard theatre, as the reconstructed *corral* at Almagro near Ciudad Real survives to remind us, the precise shape varying with the physical location.[6] After performing for a time in the capital acting troupes would normally take their new productions on tour in the provinces.

With the establishment of permanent playhouses operating on a regular basis throughout the year, Lent apart, the activities of the players them-selves were gradually placed on a more professional footing, above all in Madrid. Heads of theatrical troupes (*autores* or actor-managers) were nominated by the Council of Castile every two years, and licences were required to form companies – in 1600 the limit was eight, in 1615 twelve and in 1646 eight again – and to enter the capital to perform. The constitution of each troupe had to be vetted; no company could in theory stay for more than two months a year in any one city, and only in Madrid and Seville were two companies allowed to reside at the same time; in these two major cities the use of the theatres had to be equitably shared out. From 1615 every new play had to be passed, and if necessary expurgated and altered, by a censor and a fiscal (the officer responsible for the implementation of censorship) who were answerable to the Protector. It was then licensed for performance by the Council of Castile, and even so remained vulnerable to Inquisitorial objection. A play by Lope about the conversion of St Augustine, probably *El divino africano* (*The Divine African*), was confiscated in 1608 by the Inquisition on account of its 'indecent arguments'[7] and there are several recorded cases of plays being suspended on the very point of performance pending Inquisitorial cuts. It is possible that on these occasions the licence had been granted against the advice of one of the examiners (a third opinion was usually sought in such cases) who then tipped off some official of the Inquisition. We know that occasionally material was added to or reinstated in texts of plays after they had obtained their licence.[8] The Protector therefore fulfilled a role similar to that of the Master of the Revels in Elizabethan England who exercised his prerogative of censorship to ban Shakespeare's *Sir Thomas More* twice. Whereas the emphasis in England seems to have been on sedition, in Spain the censors cast their net fairly widely, trawling for anything objectionable from slander or ridicule of private individuals, through coarseness and indecency, to irreverence and profanity. The Inquisition for its part concentrated on heresy and subversion and seems not to have been very interested in moral issues; indeed immorality on the stage was generally easier to get away with than profanity. Censorship was stricter at some times than others – normally when the theatre was under attack and above all in the 1640s, before and after new theatre legislation in 1644[9] – but in the second half of the seventeenth century a significant tightening up of the criteria for heresy, blasphemy or poor taste in references to religion led to cuts being made in revivals of plays which had been readily passed by the censors years before.

These regulations, which were not all enforced with equal success it has to be said, reflect not only an understandable desire to regulate the workings of a new phenomenon – the commercialization of leisure – in Spain, but a deep-seated suspicion that the whole business of play-acting was potentially a disruptive social and moral force. Like actors everywhere before the twentieth century, the Spanish players lived on the margins of social respectability, and the presence among them of actresses, albeit married women (actors were compelled by law to have their wives with them), inevitably reinforced the conventional view of their profession as a disreputable when not downright immoral one. The appearance of women on stage remained a target for moralists and detractors throughout the seventeenth century and a succession of regulations were introduced to meet their worries and objections: for example, no unmarried women or widows were allowed to act; costumes had to be seemly and doublet and hose were forbidden – although a compromise decree allowed masculine costume to be worn, if absolutely necessary, from the waist up;[10] while the only male visitors actresses could regularly receive in the women's dressing-room were their husbands. The frequency with which these decrees and certain others (such as those governing the movements of the troupes) were promulgated suggests that they were for the most part ignored.

For the players the advent of the new permanent *corrales* represented a great professional step forward in spite of the restrictions on their activities. For those who gained places in the accredited companies based in Madrid, it meant more, and more regular, work, including contracts to perform in other cities. By the 1620s they were employed on yearly contracts, with detailed stipulations about roles, for pre-agreed salaries which did not depend on daily takings. Recruiting took place mainly in Lent, when the theatres were closed. Furthermore, regular companies and permanent playhouses must have increased rehearsal time, professional co-operation within the group and familiarity with the stages and their facilities, and must therefore have led to more polished performances. Those players not chosen by the licensed companies joined one of the large number of more loosely organized *compañías de la legua* ('companies of the road') which went around the countryside performing when and where they could and sharing the day's takings – a survival from the days before the permanent playhouses were established. In 1646 they were officially disbanded because they had fallen into disrepute as a refuge for criminals, drop-outs and riff-raff generally.

Although some contracts were not specific and some, in the case of famous players, allowed first choice of parts, a hierarchical type-casting system was the norm. Actors and actresses were usually hired to perform particular sorts of roles for the year – first, second, third or fourth *dama*; male lead, second male lead and so on; the *barba* (beard) or older man; the *gracioso* (comic). The *autor* often played the *barba* and his wife the leading lady. Most players, particularly the women, were expected to turn their hand to singing and dancing, for the plays when required and for the between-acts entertainments. It has already been pointed out that since plays were commissioned by companies, the structure of these companies was a major determining factor in the composition of a play, with parts often being written with specific players in mind. For example, it has been suggested that Calderón wrote *La vida es sueño*, with its unusually important role for an older man (Basilio), for an *autor* who had become too old to play the first gallant and was not content to settle for being the *barba* (who would have taken the other old-man role, Clotaldo).[11] The recurring plot patterns shared by the plays were the result not of lack of inventiveness or of commitment to an aesthetic ideal, but of the need to write at speed and to meet the requirements of an existing professional structure, formed in the first place very largely to suit the needs of the Italianate comedies of the pre-Lope theatre.

In addition to the players themselves, the troupes had an infrastructure of wardrobe keeper, prompter, sometimes a money collector (to collect the actors' fee) and often musicians as well. They varied in size from ten to over twenty, but the doubling, even multiplying of parts, was usual. In 1631 the licensed companies set up their own charitable brotherhood, membership of which was compulsory for all players (including the *compañías de la legua*), and open to all those who had ever been connected with the profession and their families. Since players by now had their own career structure with contracts stipulating agreed conditions such as the minimum number of plays to be performed and regular attendance at rehearsals, the brotherhood effectively constituted an actors' guild.[12] Its funds, which derived from a performance tax levied on *autores* and an income tax levied on the players themselves, were devoted to helping the old, sick and poor amongst its members and to paying for burials. It also compelled *autores* to undertake to lend money to sick actors, repayable when they could work again, not to hire or fire without the company's consent, and to pay actors even when they chose not to use them. In return, players who broke their contracts were fined and, if necessary, arrested until the fines were paid.

The players, therefore, constituted the extraordinary anomaly of an organized, disciplined, hierarchical group which was recognized and controlled by the authorities but which nonetheless was not accorded social respectability.[13] The profession as a whole was regarded as disreputable, even despised, by the general public. At the same time, over the years many of its more prominent and successful actors and particularly actresses acquired the glamour and popularity of every entertainer who attracts and keeps the public eye. Some players found rich and powerful patrons amongst the nobility, many led perfectly respectable, humdrum lives: the range of personal behaviour was in reality as wide as the range of ability, professionalism and success. Those at the bottom of the hierarchy – the motley collection of actors, tumblers, dancers and musicians who travelled the countryside – had the worst reputation, though dancers in general tended to be reviled for the supposed lewdness of the dances they performed; the *zarabanda* in particular drove ecclesiastics to frenzies of moral indignation. Holy communion and Christian burial were in theory denied actors as 'public sinners', and the Council of Castile's 1644 report on the theatre, which established new norms for the profession, reiterated the stricture. In practice, however, and in accordance with the views of a number of liberal theologians, the rule was usually interpreted as not applying to accredited players with licensed companies. As their specially designated attic boxes in the *corrales* indicate, churchmen regularly attended performances in spite of ecclesiastical censure of plays and players alike, perhaps on the pretext of keeping an eye on what went on or perhaps instinctively recognizing that, in Cervantes's lovely phrase, actors are as necessary to the republic as flowers and trees.[14] As one would expect given the profession's standing, most actors came from the lower orders of society, though there were some gentlemen *autores* and some players who, for reasons personal or financial or merely seduced by the freedom of the player's life, chose to drop out of their proper milieu. A surviving early eighteenth-century two-volume manuscript – *Genealogía, origen y noticias de los comediantes de España*[15] – gives invaluable information of varying detail and depth about hundreds of seventeenth-century actors and actresses and makes fascinating reading. Amongst the more memorable entries are Antonia Infanta's (II, 254), which matter-of-factly records her fondness for sleeping between black satin sheets, and Juana Margarita Pinelo's (II, 141), which relates how the poor girl fell to her death while eloping from a convent when her lover and his companions, who were waiting below to catch her in a cloak, fled to avoid falling masonry. The catalogue reveals that a number of acting companies in the later seventeenth century were run not by men but by enterprising women, not all of whom, by any means, were widows merely stepping into their dead husbands' shoes.

The financial rewards were not negligible. In the early decades of the new theatres players were often paid partly in kind (food, clothing) and wages were less standardized, but from the 1620s on actors seem to have been paid a basic daily wage plus a higher rate per performance. Although bit players appear to have been paid about the same as a day-wage man (and the same as the *alguaciles de comedias*, the theatre constables), supporting players received twice that amount and leading actors and actresses three or four times as much, though clearly there were variations according to success and popularity. Married players were paid as couples, not necessarily at twice the individual rate. Performances during the celebrations for Corpus Christi and in private houses would have boosted their incomes considerably and there can be no doubt that the most successful players were quite prosperous. However, the profession had its risks; bad weather in winter made performances impossible and any enforced closure of the *corrales*, owing to plague, periods of royal mourning or the temporary success of the anti-theatre lobby, was a disaster. In 1644 the *corrales* and the court theatre were closed for six months because of the death of the Queen; in 1646 they were closed for what turned out to be five years owing first to the death of Prince Baltasar Carlos, then a general prohibition on moral grounds, the protracted wars with Portugal and France and the continuing revolt of the Catalans. This extended closure forced the companies to disband and caused great hardship. The profession had its responsibilities, too. Leading players provided their own stage clothes and clearly felt they owed it to themselves and to their public to live and dress well, with the result that their own extravagant expenditure, particularly on fine clothes, frequently got them into debt. For all the disadvantages, however, there was understandably no shortage of players in an age beset by economic difficulties when poverty and deprivation were at times intense and unemployment high.

The linchpin in the licensed companies and in the whole process of turning literary texts into theatrical performances was the actor-manager or *autor*, who was impresario, producer, director and actor rolled into one, exerting direct financial, administrative and artistic control over the company's activities.[16] He even turned his hand when necessary to writing *loas* and *bailes*. He was hired with his company by the management of the *corrales* to perform so many plays on certain dates, and it was he who then commissioned plays from the playwrights. On delivery of the script he acquired outright ownership of the text and did what he liked with it, cutting or altering it to suit his requirements; copies would usually have been made for players and prompter, but frequently the manuscripts themselves were cut up for use as actors' copies. The *autor* was responsible for submitting the text to the censor, meeting any objections he might have, and obtaining the licence. Since none of the Spanish playwrights had his own company, as Shakespeare did, and none of them acted, the responsibility for interpreting the text lay mainly with the *autor* and his conception of the play was by and large the one the audience saw, though it would be unwise to assume that no word about the plays ever passed between playwright and *autor*. In the lavishly-produced court theatre later on the situation was rather different – Calderón certainly played an active role in the production of those texts that were written as aural and visual spectacles. The dramatist's role as a commissioned writer working separately from the production team inevitably placed constraints upon his creativity. It is reasonable to assume, however, that established and successful dramatists possessed considerable room for manoeuvre. We have only to compare the plays of Lope with those of Calderón to see that even within this highly organized, commercially orientated system a great playwright could significantly change public taste. It was precisely the combination of external constraints and powerful dramatic talents which produced a drama with an outer and inner identity.

It was only the licensed *autores* who commissioned plays. Unlicensed companies got hold of material as best they could, bribing some company member to hand over a copy or presenting mangled versions of works they had seen performed; very probably licensed *autores* sub-let scripts after finishing with them for the time being themselves. It became actually illegal to perform a play bought by another *autor* unless he sold it but piracy was rife – not least because the pressures on *autores* and playwrights alike were enormous. Lope de Vega in the prologue to Parte XIII (1620) of his plays complains of two men – one nicknamed Memorilla, the other Gran Memoria – who stole plays by memorizing them. If there were three companies in Madrid at any one time, each might in the course of a fortnight give four performances, not necessarily consecutive, in each of the two *corrales* (no company stayed in the same theatre for more than a week at a time). Since the normal run for a play was only five or six performances – even the most successful rarely lasted more than twelve – a contract to play for several months in the capital,[17] although highly desirable financially, created an intense demand for new material. Any fall-off in takings and therefore in the *corral*'s profits meant that another play had to be substituted to bring the crowds back, and the *corral* management sometimes had to advance money to *autores* for the commissioning of plays. Inevitably, in the circumstances, unscrupulous *autores* passed off the work of the second-rate or unknown as that of the great and popular, though posters advertising the plays were supposed to set out the facts clearly, and it was obviously good business to sell or sublet plays to unlicensed companies outside Madrid. In the 1630s two capacity audiences of around 2,000 each (in a capital with a population somewhere in the region of 150,000)[18] made the *corrales* voracious consumers of creative talent. Little is known, unfortunately, about the compensations received by the *autores* for the risks they took, though as one would expect they seem normally to have earned somewhat more from the *corrales* than the actors themselves; like these, they received a financial boost from private commissions and commissions for Corpus, the latter being by far the best-paid occasions in the theatrical calendar.

We do have some information about what the playwrights themselves were paid. In the early decades of the seventeenth century Lope was getting 500 *reales* a play, about twenty times the daily income of a leading actor.[19] His fee for an *auto* was 300 *reales*. By 1647 inflation had driven the going rate for a play up to 800 *reales*. Writing for the theatre, therefore, was pleasantly profitable – by far the most profitable form of writing at the time – but the fees were certainly not high enough to permit extravagant living by the standards of today's rewards for entertaining and publishing success. Since payments were one-off, with no share in profits, no automatic copyright and no royalties,[20] income depended entirely on productivity and even Lope with his huge output was grateful for financial help and gifts from patrons, particularly the Duke of Sessa whom he served as unofficial personal secretary to the extent of writing his love letters. His life was certainly not a restrained or frugal one but neither was it very lavish by the standards either of today or of his own time, and he continued writing until he died at the age of seventy-three to support himself and his family. He was effectively the only career dramatist of the age in Spain; his fellow playwrights had other major sources of financial support – private incomes, ecclesiastical benefices, government appointments, pensions and the like.

Performances

The activities of the *corrales* were closely supervised by the Protector, who had ultimate authority over every aspect of their operation – repairs and accounts, the activities and constitution of the companies, what they performed, and the organization of performances. After the municipal authority assumed closer financial control in 1638 two Protectors seem to have been appointed, presumably to reinforce the voice of the central authority. The Protector's authority was represented at the performances themselves by the *alguaciles de comedias* who were on duty from the time the *corrales* opened until the last spectator had gone. At first officers were appointed for two months at a time; later on the job appears to have become in some instances a hereditary office, in others a purchased appointment. By 1641 there were two in each of the Madrid *corrales*, one to supervise the men, the other to protect and escort the women. When a new play was being performed and on other occasions when capacity audiences were expected, the officer to whom they were responsible, the *alcalde*, had to attend as well with his own *alguaciles*.

The policing of performances was not an unwarranted intrusion on the part of the authorities. The playwrights frequently complained of the high level of noise and disorder, not only in the *patio* but in the *cazuela* as well. In the *patio* the *mosqueteros* included self-appointed judges and critics who led the responses of an audience that freely expressed its approval or disapproval during the performance with applause, catcalls, whistles, barracking and even missiles. The problem seems to have grown with the years and it is likely that the *mosqueteros* were sometimes paid to orchestrate audience response. Up in the *cazuela* the women rattled keys against the railings and, if one of Lope's *loas* is to be believed,[21] never stopped talking and laughing; an important part of the *loa*'s function, as we saw, was to settle the audience for the performance. Before the play there were rows as people tried to get in without paying, there was quarrelling over seats and anger over late starts. Occasionally stink bombs were let off and mice let loose in the *cazuela*, and from time to time some bright spark took it into his head to put on skirts and cause consternation by joining the women in the intimacy of their box (there were severe fines for this). In 1656, even Philip IV, who should have known better, is said to have ordered a women-only day at the Coliseo, the palace theatre, so that over a hundred mice could be let loose amongst them while he and the Queen watched the fun from a screened window; fortunately the prank was abandoned for fear of causing pregnant women to miscarry.[22] On Sunday, 25 January 1642, there was a riot in the

Montería theatre in Seville when a capacity audience was told that the play about St Christopher that it had come to see had been temporarily banned by the Inquisition pending cuts, and would be replaced by another of the audience's choice. The theatre was vandalized and the players had to take to their heels.[23] A similar incident had occurred in Madrid in 1623, so it is hardly surprising that in 1621 a prospective lessee stipulated that he and his money collectors be allowed to carry daggers for protection.[24] If a play finished late, when it was getting dark, then fights broke out, pockets were picked and the women spectators were molested as they left – hence the *alguacil* appointed to look after them. In view of what the players had to contend with, it is hardly surprising that Lope's advice to playwrights was to keep the action going, maintain suspense and never leave the stage empty.[25]

Since there was no lighting in the *corrales* the starting times of the performances were dictated by the daylight and the climate – two o'clock in autumn and winter, four o'clock in spring and summer, though in the middle of the seventeenth century a three o'clock start was stipulated for the spring.[26] There is some evidence that in the seventeenth century torches were occasionally lit when performances which had started late finished as darkness began to fall. The full performance of *loa*, play, interludes and finale lasted around 2½ hours. There were performances most days except in Lent, when puppet shows were allowed but live performances were forbidden, but Sunday was the big theatre day. Attendance in winter was predictably higher than in the summer and usually rose with changes in the programme, particularly with new plays. The re-opening of the *corrales* at Easter was a major event in the social calendar. Performances were advertised with posters and boards and probably with vocal announcements as well given that the *corrales* often had to compete with other entertainments such as acrobats and jugglers, religious processions and other free public festivities. The entrance charges were not high, but neither were they negligible: in 1600 the *patio* cost almost 0.6 of a *real* when the labourer's day-wage was three *reales*; a man's bench seat cost half as much again and a place in the *cazuela* was one-fifth more than the *patio*. A box cost twelve *reales*. The audience represented a good cross section of urban society – nobles, prelates and the wealthy in the boxes, traders, shopkeepers and artisans on the benches and raked seating, manual workers, soldiers, servants, young bucks and those who lived by their wits in the *patio*. The King had a box, certainly in the Cruz, as did the Council of Castile, the Protector, and the City Council; their servants had designated benches. Friars and lesser clerics crowded into the *tertulia* although attendance for them was in theory forbidden by a succession of unheeded edicts, and those women prepared to put up with the rough and tumble of the *cazuela* squeezed in there – an *apretador* (pusher) was employed to pack them in. Those interested in the play's finer details and its poetry – writers, theorists, moralists, the learned – probably placed themselves well to the fore in order to hear clearly, perhaps monopolizing the benches and seats immediately in front of the stage.

The lack of lighting and scenery meant that the dialogue and costumes between them had to perform the functions which later on in the proscenium theatre were undertaken by the stage itself – fixing the action temporally (day or night) and spatially (setting, surroundings). Audience noise must have been a very real difficulty in this respect and it is little wonder that playwrights so frequently complained. There is some evidence to suggest that in the second half of the seventeenth century, perhaps under the influence of the court theatre, rather more elaborate scenic effects were used, in the inner stage in particular, which must have eased the problem somewhat. The use of mechanical devices for producing illusions increased as the seventeenth century got under way, in spite of the fact that some dramatists professed scorn for them, because such devices naturally thrilled audiences and were, furthermore, a useful prop for less talented poets.[27] They soon became an accepted part of the spectacle of theatre in the *corrales* although they were by no means a feature of all or even most plays. They were common in religious plays, where stage miracles were necessary, but given the expense of constructing and maintaining them, and the damage they did to the fabric of the theatre, such productions were probably concentrated round special occasions in the Church calendar. With Calderón's court drama later on, elaborate settings and effects would achieve full artistic respectability, becoming integrated so completely into dramatic procedure that spectacle at times threatened to overshadow the text.

It might be thought that the simple, bare *corral* stage would lend added importance and emphasis to stage costumes and in one sense this was the case. Leading actors and actresses supplied their own clothes and tended to enhance their performances and their reputations by dressing very lavishly. The sumptuary laws that controlled dress in real life (both for economic reasons and for the purpose of class definition) lent added glamour to stage finery, and attempts to restrict extravagant displays of apparel on stage seem to have been largely ineffective. So too were the attempts to restrict the use of masculine disguise – on moral grounds this time – by actresses. The heroine who dressed up as a gallant was one of the commonest and most popular stock types of the theatre, a frank exploitation of the attractions of an elegant female figure;[28] her hybrid identity, however, is often skilfully integrated into the play's theme – a perfect example of the marriage of commerce with art. Some actresses specialized in such parts and in the second half of the seventeenth century one actress, Bárbara Coronel, allowed art to infiltrate life to the extent of almost permanently dressing as a man.[29] While costume did have a role to play in the theatre's popularity, however, the attitude to any notion of accuracy was cavalier to say the least. As in the Shakespearean theatre, contemporary dress was normally worn whatever the period depicted, with vaguely distinguishing costumes or accessories for kings and queens, Moors, Turks, angels, devils and so on. That the differentiation was sometimes very makeshift is clear from Lope's *Arte nuevo* (lines 356–61) where he mocks the *comedia* for presenting Turks in Christian dress and Romans in breeches. However, ethnic and historical accuracy apart, a limited range of costumes and accessories was normally perfectly adequate for the drama's requirements – differences of age and social status could be readily reflected in dress, night scenes could be signalled at a stroke by a long cloak and hat. For supporting players and for particular recurring roles companies kept or hired wardrobes (crowns, turbans, angelic and demonic shifts) which served economically for most purposes.

As to the way players performed their parts, we know, alas, very little. It has been claimed that actors at the time made no effort to become the role or to draw the spectators into the illusion.[30] Yet the heated reactions of spectators cited by moralists as evidence of the theatre's detrimental effect on the Spanish nation do suggest that the players were at least sufficiently convincing to elicit a very positive public reaction, to create what Ernst Kris called a belief in the 'reality of play'.[31] Lope points out in his *Arte nuevo* (lines 331–7) that players were often identified in real life with the characters they played and treated accordingly, which says something for their acting ability and suggests a fairly natural acting style. The between-act entertainments must have disrupted the illusion and made the actors' task harder, but we cannot assume from this that no illusion was created. Not only does our own experience of a play in a modern theatre with intervals for refreshments or of a television play broken up by advertisements bear this out, but it must be remembered that the *corral's* neutral or unlocated stage meant that during each act nothing impeded the free and natural flow and speed of the action. Lope certainly saw it as part of the actor's role to move the audience: 'let [the playwright] depict lovers with emotions that deeply affect those who listen, let him paint soliloquies in such a way that the speaker is totally transformed and, himself being moved, moves the listener'; futhermore he recommends interior dialogue of a naturalistic kind.[32] López Pinciano in his *Philosophia Antigua Poetica* (1596) strongly recommended a natural acting style based on observation of the way people talk, act and react in real life so that the actor seems not to be acting at all; in this context he also recommends body movements to 'give force to the poet's words'.[33] At the same time, when referring specifically to facial gestures to convey fear, rage, hate, sadness and so on, he recommends expressions such as a lowered brow for sadness, a raised brow for joy, which does suggest a certain exaggeration and stylization although he insists that they are based on an observation of how people behave in real life.[34] We know that certain actors were admired for their facial effects. Pinciano suggested different arm and foot movements for different roles and situations, which again suggests a degree of stylization.[35] What we do not know, unfortunately, is whether these comments were descriptive as well as prescriptive, so the problem of what style of acting was favoured or even taught within the companies themselves remains largely unsolved.

The theatre and society

No theatre audience can ever have exerted more influence on the drama that served it than that of seventeenth-century Spain, and no theatre can ever have had a greater and more sustained impact on the society that produced it. Certainly no theatre can have been more effective in creating for a people myths that not only reflected but confirmed and even shaped its sense of collective historical and national identity. It was a theatre of contradictions – highly commercial yet at its best great art, enormously popular yet, with Calderón, highly intellectual, a theatre that had something for everyone from the illiterate poor to the cultured and wealthy. It was a theatre where the noise and disruption reached levels that would now be regarded as entirely unaccceptable, yet which demanded much more of its audiences than later audiences became accustomed to giving. The *corral* stage's limitations were compensated for in various ways: costumes to communicate not only day or night, but also town or country, road scenes, even scene changes; dialogue to refer to place, time and things supposedly happening off-stage beyond the audience's gaze; changes of metre to indicate scene shifts and changes of mood and tempo; two back openings so that a character could walk out of a scene through one and into a different scene through the other; symbolic scenery – a ladder here, some greenery there, a few pieces of transportable scenery, later on a painted backflat – to conjure up a whole world of different settings, with the stage balcony representing anything from a mistress's window to the throne of God. All these aids required the audience to understand and respond to the dramatist's intentions, to play a remarkably active role in the creation of the play's illusion even if they were not actually bidden, as Shakespeare bade his audience,

> Think when we talk of horses that you see them
> Printing their proud hoofs i' the receiving earth;
> For 'tis your thoughts that now must deck our Kings.
>
> (Opening chorus, *Henry V*)

Clearly many of those present, even in an audience trained to listen,[36] would not have caught, let alone properly understood, all the figures of speech, the classical allusions, the structural and metaphorical patterns; it has been suggested that rhetorical elaboration might actually have been pared away for provincial audiences.[37] The dramatists catered for this by incorporating enough pace and excitement into the plot to keep them happy;[38] the occasional live horse was even used to thrill the audience – one unfortunate actress, Ana Muñoz, miscarried when she was thrown by her horse when the unruly *mosqueteros* startled it. As we have seen, critics, scholars and academics probably sat on the *taburetes* in front of the stage in order to get the full benefit of the play's poetic and rhetorical dimensions, exerting an influence on the playwrights that was disproportionate to their numbers. Stage conventions established over the years were presumably a rather different matter, becoming part of the expertise of every regular theatre-goer and therefore relied on by the dramatists for their appropriate communicative effects. It is interesting, indeed, to see how in a self-renewing and self-perpetuating national drama the idea of a conventional signalling system could be exploited in more sophisticated ways. In Calderón repetitive motifs such as runaway horses, horoscopes, tripping or falling, abnormal upbringing, imagery of cosmic confusion, constitute signals which, although developed into a complex referential system fully appreciated only by reading the text, would have been readily picked up, at a superficial level at least, by seasoned spectators at the time. The very nature of Calderón's drama forced listeners and readers to participate more actively than ever before in the experience of theatre.

On the face of it the Spanish drama, in spite of its very varied audience, was ideologically monolithic, reflecting and supporting the aristocratic values which were by and large the values admired and aspired to by all in the society of the day – particularly Madrid society characterized as it was by its dependence on the court and its obsession with social status and advancement. This is what the socio-historical context would lead us to expect and this is what some social historians have recently asserted.[39] It is, furthermore, what a list of plot summaries would seem to confirm. The fact is, however, that plots are not plays and that the detail of the texts themselves, which historians understandably tend not to study in depth, do not by any means always bear out this assumption. The texts reveal that the drama was a much more complex phenomenon, which works on various levels and which is no more free of tension, strain and doubt than was in reality the age that produced it, for all that in Spain it preferred to try to ignore the fact. And the complexity of the drama suggests not only that the dramatists saw themselves as something other than conscious propagandists of an aristocratic elite, but that the attitudes of audiences, too, were rather more complicated than a surface appraisal of contemporary society would allow. Social dependence and social aspiration are by no means straight-forward psychological phenomena.

The Spanish dramatists, like all writers of the *ancien régime* in Europe, Shakespeare included, were intensely patriotic, and without a doubt shared the larger values and beliefs of their age. This does not, however, mean that they were complacent about the implication of those values and beliefs or about the way seventeenth-century man lived them. Tirso and Calderón, as we saw, probed the political and theological preoccupations of the day and Lope too engaged, if rather more obliquely, with social and political issues. The belief in patterns of universal order did not prevent Calderón and others depicting a succession of inadequate, indecisive and misguided kings and the drama abounds in plays which confront the problems of monarchic rule, though it goes without saying that plays commissioned for performance at court on national occasions are suitably diplomatic in this regard. The drama's role in this respect was recognized by Bances Candamo who in the second part of his *Theatro de los theatros* referred to plays written for kings as 'decir sin decir' ('saying without saying') – getting messages across without being obvious about it. At the same time the theatre's preoccupation with generational conflict and the tyranny of age, and its repeated confrontation of the past with the future, suggest that even in Spain a sense of development and change, of the old order yielding to new sensibilities, was being felt. The powerful charge of anarchy and rebellion contained in Calderón's drama is by no means entirely diffused by the restoration of harmony and order provided by 'satisfactory' endings. In the struggle depicted between individual and social duty, or Law, it is the latter which prevails, but only just. The sense of a legitimate individualism is very strong. It is perhaps as well to remember that the very theatre which might now seem to some modern eyes undesirably conformist was regarded as scandalous by many in the seventeeth century who were acutely aware of the ways, often invisible now to us, in which the drama departed from the respectable orthodoxies of the day. I wonder whether we are wise to assume that they were necessarily always the blinkered ones. Even Calderón, the most theological of dramatists, sometimes fell foul of the censor on some doctrinal point.[40] The fate of theatre regulations in Spain itself suggests that it is unwise to overestimate the ability of the authorities to enforce legislation, let alone something as nebulous as ideology. We must not forget that the Count-Duke of Olivares was so loathed for his authoritarian government that when Philip IV fell ill in 1627 and Olivares ordered public prayers, the churches, to the astonishment of foreign visitors in Madrid, remained empty. The nobles, too, were so disaffected in the early 1630s that they stayed away from court festivities to show their disapproval.[41] A leading historian of the period has recently criticized the tendency 'to overestimate the passivity of seventeenth-century societies and to exaggerate the capacity of those in authority to manipulate those societies for their own ideological ends', pointing out that 'the works of Spain's Golden Age contain sufficient ambiguities to suggest that subversive texts are there for the reading'.[42]

If the plays were merely variations on a repetitive pattern of ideological certainty there would be no joy now in reading or watching them. This is patently not the case. The critical controversy that has surrounded many of them in itself makes nonsense of the view that they are simplistically conformist. In a theatre of this vast size a distinction probably has to be drawn between the many plays which did, more or less hastily, merely replicate plots and patterns, and those whose dramatic identity is more intricate. I should not like to be the one to draw the line of demarcation, however, and suspect that closer study of more plays would swell the second category rather than the first.

The point is that a commercial and in theory closely regulated theatre like the *comedia* had inevitably to present a conservative if not prudish face to its public. At the same time, to please this public and ensure its own survival it had to provide a dramatic diet of romantic or heroic escapism. Accordingly any ideological criticism or doubts, any adversarial or subversive elements, at whatever level, it might contain would necessarily be covert and oblique: apparent enough to achieve the dramatist's aim and tickle the attention of the more thoughtful and alert members of the audience but not so obvious as to displease those who enjoyed the uncomplicated pleasures of witnessing heroes and heroines – with whom no doubt they liked to identify – winning out against the odds. The Golden-Age theatre was the servant of many masters – *autores*, actors, *corrales*, moralists, literary theorists, censors, municipal and central authorities and a socially and geographically heterogeneous public – all of whom had to be reckoned with. The result was a triumph of compromise, a balance of external pressures and artistic imperatives made possible by the production of richly complex, nuanced texts. We know that after the early years dramatists were writing with publication at least partly in mind.[43] We know that the audience included the cultured and learned. We should not be surprised therefore at the sophistication of what was written. Since a play is a combination of action, characters and dialogue, of text, subtext and context, its meaning cannot be found in the plot and its ending alone; the true identity of a play lies in the interrelationship of all its parts. The *comedia* in particular represents a type of dramatic shorthand; it is a compressed form that operates through the art of suggestion. It is only when we listen to the dramatic and poetic detail of the plays and read the signals that the dramatist is sending us that we see the plays for what they are. Cultural invisibility is obviously a problem – our inability now to see what is there, to assign to words and remarks their correct meanings and associations, to make the right referential connections, things which would have been instantaneously appreciated by a contemporary audience, especially with actors to give them the lead with gesture, expression or tone of voice.[44] Another problem is the danger of historical distortion of what *is* seen to be there – taking plays to be more or less accurate reflections of real life attitudes and *mores* and, in misconstruing the relationship between fantasy and reality, misunderstanding the plays' identities as works of art. An outstanding example is the way in which a handful of seventeenth-century wife-murder plays used to be taken as evidence that wife-murder was the common pastime of real-life Spanish husbands obsessed with a barbaric honour code, and then read back as dramatic propaganda *for* the code; the methodological flaw is self-evident.[45] What the Golden-Age theatre, like any great popular theatre, demands because of its double identity as national institution and individual artistic vision is an approach that combines social history, textual analysis and theatre studies. *Comedia* is, after all, a convenience term covering an extremely heterogeneous range of texts. It includes playwrights of different generations, different social and geographical provenance, different temperaments, aims and talents. Three elements give them their shared identity: a common language (with variations) that occupies the ground between the poetic and the natural, the dramatic identity of the form they used and the social identity of the theatre they wrote for. The plays remain, nonetheless, individual works of art. The development of a distinct form of tragedy which satisfied the public's desire for 'satisfactory' endings is, I would argue, an example of the playwrights' genius for coming to terms with the imperatives of the theatre they served, an honorable solution which, by harnessing the vast resources of poetic drama, succeeds in compromising neither artistic integrity nor tragic value.

The morals controversy

We know that audiences at the time reacted as positively to what they saw on stage as modern viewers and listeners do to television, film and radio, often failing in the same way, as Lope's remarks in his *Arte nuevo* reveal, to make a clear distinction between fiction and reality. This partly explains the fears of moralists that the theatre could mislead and even corrupt. That these moralists did not themselves distinguish clearly between reality and performance, or at least maintain them separate in their own minds, is suggested by their outrage that people who often led disreputable lives should depict kings, saints, even Christ himself on stage or that the actress who played the Virgin Mary in a play should then appear as an innkeeper or even as a prostitute in an interlude between the acts, kicking up her heels in some 'lascivious' dance.[46] The idea that the player can bring the part into disrepute may betray a fundamental innocence with regard to the nature and identity of theatre, but it also recognizes the mimetic power and effectiveness peculiar to enacted fiction. It has, furthermore, to be conceded that the theologians and moralists did in practice have a point. Because the audience itself failed to make the proper distinction between play and players, it reacted to incongruities in a way that in context must indeed have appeared unseemly. A memorandum of 1598, arguing against the Madrid submission that the theatres be re-opened after the mourning period for the King's daughter was over, cites an occasion on which the Virgin Mary's surprised response to the Angel's news – 'How can this be, seeing I know not a man?' – was greeted with hilarity by the audience who knew perfectly well that the actor and actress playing Joseph and Mary were living together. Any lack of professionalism on the players' part did not help either: the memorandum goes on to claim that Joseph, just as the play was reaching the climax of the Nativity, suddenly abandoned his role, heatedly accusing Mary of making eyes from the stage at some other man and calling her a whore. It offended the memorandum's author, too, to see God and sundry angels and saints drinking together in costume in the dressing room. It may not be a coincidence, of course, that the author is believed to have been the poet and classicizing dramatist Lupercio Leonardo de Argensola, who was one of those who abandoned the theatre after failing to halt the advance of the *comedia nueva*.

The moral campaign against the public theatres was a broad-based and sustained one waged by a succession of outraged commentators, secular and ecclesiastical. The latter included, interestingly, a preponderance of the very Jesuits whose own theatrical activities still played so important a part in religious festivities. Support was lent from time to time by the official committees set up by the Council of Castile to investigate the complaints and report to the Crown. The campaign's arguments were wide-ranging, frequently vituperative and often ingenious. The anonymous 1598 memorandum, for example, also claimed that actresses ensnared many gentlemen, causing public scandal and ruining them financially; that the theatre gave the public a distorted or incomplete view of history and great events; that it satirized other nations and earned their animosity for Spain; and that the companies led a dissolute life and were a haven for criminals. In support of its argument that the theatre's harmful effect was generally recognized, it pointed out that players were already banned from impersonating knights of the military orders (a ban readily circumvented by chronological displacement) and mentions Philip II's rule that he must never be portrayed on the stage. The committee of three theologians set up by Philip II in 1598 to investigate the effects of the public theatres came up with arguments that were, in the light of Spain's military and economic problems at the time, even more forceful. First they invoked the authority of the Church fathers and classical commentators in support of the time-honoured and still familiar argument that the theatre perpetrates evil and immorality by reminding the present of past wickedness, by encouraging evil thoughts with love intrigues (a prime target) and by corrupting the innocent by putting ideas into their heads, offering them examples of how to deceive husbands, suborn servants, and so on. The moral conundrum presented by the very idea that wicked actions could be a source of entertainment clearly worried them. They went on to claim, closer to home, that the *corrales* encouraged idleness by distracting people from their work and students from their studies, and extravagance by tempting people to spend their hard-won earnings. Pressing the point even further, they argued that the playhouses diverted men from military pursuits, making them effeminate and soft, and unfit for work and war. Such was the *corrales*' effect on Spain's military health, they concluded, that they might as well be a weapon of the Turk or the English. The report recommended that the theatres be permanently banned and that the hospitals should be financed in some other way.

Philip II found these arguments very persuasive and all performances, including those in private houses, were accordingly forbidden. His death a few months later and the period of national mourning that followed settled the matter. For all the theologians' rhetoric, however, the financial importance of the *corrales* to the city of Madrid and the now huge public demand for theatrical entertainment ensured that the municipal authorities eventually had their way and a year later the *corrales* were back in operation, although plays remained banned in Alcalá de Henares and Salamanca in term time so as not to distract university students from their studies. There must have been another closure very soon afterwards, for in February 1600 the reopening of the *corrales* was again under discussion.[47] Again the pro-theatre lobby won the day, though the re-opening was conditional upon certain restrictions, including the proviso that only historical subjects were to be used and no 'acts of religion or of saints' were to be performed. One interesting development was the rescinding of the 1596 decree banning actresses.[48] The Council had clearly been convinced that it was better for women to appear on stage than for boys to dress up and act as women; it is unlikely that much notice had been taken of the 1596 decree anyway in the two and a bit years the theatre had been open between 1596 and 1600. The edict went on to impose restrictions on actresses – no masculine dress, no extravagant dressing outside the theatre, no unmarried women – which were in the course of the seventeenth century to become as familiar as they were ineffective. As for the actresses themselves, they were now in the Spanish theatre to stay, perhaps for the reason offered by a member of Prince Charles of Wales' entourage during an official visit to Madrid in 1623 when the English guests were entertained with a play in the Palace: 'The Players themselves consist of Men and Women. The Men are indifferent Actors, but the Women are very good, and become themselves far better than any that I ever saw act those Parts, and far handsomer than any Women I saw. To say the truth, they are the only cause their Playes are so much frequented.'[49]

The 1598 battle set the pattern for many years to come, one side waging war on the *corrales* on moral grounds, with the inflammatory and corrupting nature of the plays and the life-style of the acting profession as its main targets; the other defending the theatre on financial and social grounds – the hospitals needed the money and the people needed recreation – although arguments both for the theatre's moral neutrality and its useful-ness as an instrument of instruction were deployed as well. The anti-theatre lobby by no means had a monopoly of ecclesiastical commentators. One of the most sensible and intelligent tracts written in defence of the theatre, for example, was the extended *aprobación* written for the *Quinta parte* of Calderón's comedias in 1682 by the censor Fray Manuel de Guerra y Ribera, Trinitarian friar, Professor of Philosophy at Salamanca and royal preacher. His view was that the theatre had no effect on the ordinary playgoer, ill effects on the foolish and beneficial effects on the discriminating, and that all in all it compared very favourably with that other popular entertainment, bull-fighting.[50] Earlier, the Jesuit writer Baltasar Gracián in his treatise on wit, *Agudeza y arte de ingenio* (1648, *Discurso* XIV), had praised Lope de Vega's writing in his 'moral plots', giving *El villano en su rincón* as an example. But the Church undoubtedly played a prominent part in the campaign to suppress the public theatres, for fairly obvious reasons. The *corrales* exposed a wide public, which included even the illiterate, to a succession of imagined worlds and a range of interpreted facts and ideas which many churchmen saw as dangerous even if not heretical. The desire to protect a public perceived as vulnerable from this potentially harmful form of entertainment was part of the wider contemporary concern with the effect of a secular literature of entertainment on the new reading public, and stemmed, of course, from the Reformation debate about the wisdom of allowing the direct dissemination of knowledge in the vernacular without the church hierarchy to act as intermediary. It was the overriding concern with the public's corruptibility which led the theatre's ecclesiastical opponents to concentrate on the ingredients of a play rather than its overall purpose. They presumably went very rarely, if ever, to the *corrales* they so disapproved of and when they did their indignation certainly blinded them to the artistic identity of what they saw. It has to be said that this indignation was not motivated solely by a disapproval of fiction or by the Church's traditional dislike of the activities indulged in during public festivals. Some of the songs being sung at theatrical performances during the early years of the seventeenth century were staggeringly lewd by any standards and even serious plays written well into the century were not always entirely free of bawdiness.[51]

In the event it was the popular and therefore financial success of the *corrales* which guaranteed their survival and the repeated piecemeal attempts to control their activities in ways uncongenial to public taste (by forbidding actresses to wear doublet and hose, for example) were for the most part blithely ignored. The playwrights themselves had no control over the companies but it was within their power, obviously, to anticipate criticism of the plays. Much of the time the imperatives of the box office prevailed – love intrigues were part of the *corrales'* staple diet and actresses pranced to their hearts' content in the masculine disguise indicated by the texts. But the emphasis on the heroic deeds and virtuous actions (albeit generously interpreted) recommended by Lope,[52] the frequent application, even if at times only superficially, of the principle of poetic justice, and the avoidance of the sort of on-stage violence found in the Elizabethan and Jacobean theatres (although gruesome discoveries[53] were fairly common and severely criticized) did go some way towards meeting the concerns of the moralists even if the first two of these three met with public approbation as well. The situation where the theatrical depiction of honour, especially where wife-murder was concerned, was rather more complex. Honour–vengeance plots were certainly immensely popular and the theatre indeed was seen by some as fostering an unhealthy concern with honour. But the battle lines here were drawn up in no neat pattern. Some supporters of the theatre were amongst those who deplored as unChristian the honour code it seemed to exalt, while some of the theatre's detractors were amongst those who excused the wife-murder plays on the grounds that they acted as a deterrent to potentially unfaithful wives. These complicated, even confused, reactions are explained at least in part by the extremely varied and even ambiguous ways in which the theme of honour – vengeance is dealt with in the plays themselves.

In 1644 the Council of Castile launched another concerted attack on the theatre, using the state of war with Portugal as an excuse for recommending that the *corrales* be closed indefinitely. At the same time it laid down new norms for the *corrales* should they be reinstated. These new norms stipulated that the number of licensed companies be limited to six or eight and that the *compañías de la legua* be abolished; that dramatic material should be exemplary and exclude love intrigues; that all previous plays be banned 'especially Lope de Vega's books which have done such harm to public customs';[54] that costumes be less lavish and less dictated by fashion; that only one costume per actor per play be permitted and that actresses be forbidden to wear masculine dress; that there be no immodest songs or dances; that no woman be permitted to dance alone and that mixed dances be decently conducted; that no unmarried woman should perform; that no visitors be allowed into the dressing rooms; that an *alcalde* be present at every single performance; and that the houses and streets where actors lived in Madrid should be patrolled to prevent scandal. It also stipulated that only one company should be present at any one time in Madrid and that new plays should be limited to one a week. Between them these restrictions give a clear picture of what went on in the theatres and the theatrical world, what excited the concern of the authorities and what they proved, and would continue to prove, powerless to control because of the conflict of interests involved. Obviously some regulations were easier to enforce than others, but the objection which could perhaps have been most easily implemented – that concerning the nature of the plays themselves – was in practice ignored. Every play had to be licensed yet hundreds of the sort of plays which the Council of Castile and moralists and theologians in general considered undesirable and harmful were declared unobjectionable by official censors who affirmed that they contained nothing contrary to morality or public decency. Throughout the period theatre legislation fell victim to a sort of official double-think where the *corrales* were concerned and it is interesting to compare the half-hearted attempts to clean up the theatre in Spain with the draconian measures of the Puritan Interregnum in England where the theatres were resolutely banned on moral grounds.

The controversy over the morality of the theatre did have some cumulative effect and there was as the century advanced a greater emphasis on moral and social decorum – ladies wearing masks instead of masculine disguise, somewhat more seemly love affairs with none of the provocative situations of some of Lope's early plays (for example, *El acero de Madrid*, *El arenal de Sevilla*), less bawdy songs. This suggests that those later critics who still harped on about inflammatory performances could not have been to the *corrales* themselves since the heyday of Lope de Vega, that 'wolf who devoured souls',[55] who had done 'more harm with his plays in Spain than Martin Luther in Germany'.[56] But the *corrales*' essential diet remained more or less unchanged, as did criticism of it. In a society so theatre-orientated that clerics and friars attended performances sitting in their own boxes and plays were even performed in religious houses, although both practices were forbidden, the public was the ultimate arbiter.

Within a few years of the 1644 suspension, the city of Madrid and the Cortes, the Castilian parliament, were exerting pressure on the Crown to allow the theatres to re-open. In 1648 the King instructed the Council of Castile to re-examine the matter. The result was a recommendation that the theatres be reinstated. Its arguments are extremely illuminating, moving as they do from the theoretical to the practical and the strategic, deftly turning some of the now traditional arguments against the theatre back on themselves. It pointed out that many classical commentators and many eminent theologians, including St Thomas Aquinas, had held that the theatre was not intrinsically evil and – hitting now below the belt – that the favour it had found as court entertainment proved that it could not be regarded as being in itself disreputable. It went on to argue that the country's protracted wars and other problems meant that the people needed and deserved some pleasure and distraction, and to assert that the suspension of 1644 had had no effect whatsoever on public morals and behaviour; on the contrary public unrest and disorder had never been greater and the ban had earned overt public disapproval for some of the ministers of the Crown, which in the circumstances that prevailed, it implied, was highly undesirable. It pointed out that the ban was being ignored in many places outside Madrid (which suggests that the *compañías de la legua* had not been successfully disbanded) and urged a policy of greater tolerance, therefore, towards the theatre. Finally it reminded the Crown that love comedies always ended very properly in marriage (generally if not invariably true) and realistically concluded that in any case contemporary *mores* were such that the theatre could not teach the public anything. Unfortunately nine Council members refused to agree to these eminently sensible arguments and submitted a report of their own urging that the ban on the theatres be continued. Faced with this division of opinion, the King diplomatically did nothing to resolve the matter officially, but a blind eye was henceforth turned to illegal performances and from 1650 they were openly tolerated. Companies were re-formed and in 1651 the *corrales* re-opened.

The closure had been the longest in the history of the *comedia* and it effectively divided into two the theatrical career of the man who was now Spain's greatest dramatist. In 1651 Calderón entered Holy Orders and never again wrote for the *corrales*, devoting his great talent exclusively to the re-established court theatre instead. For a while the *corrales* continued to flourish with no lack of dramatists to supply them with material. But these writers, gifted, individual and interesting as some of them were, were essentially second-order playwrights working well within an established tradition, making what were essentially minor adjustments and refinements and breaking no major new literary or theatrical ground. As the century advanced the pre-eminence of the court drama led, for good practical reasons, to a decline of the apron-stage *corrales* and to a marked drop in the esteem in which they were held. With Spain's greatest living dramatist now fully absorbed by his duties at court, there was no-one writing for the *corrales* to take the lead and revivals and reworkings proliferated. The great days of the *corrales* were over, although they would survive well into the eighteenth century, and the next developments in Spanish Golden-Age drama would take place not in the public playhouses which half a century earlier had been mid-wife to the birth of an original dramatic form, but in the Palace of the Buen Retiro. The separation between popular and court theatres, as we shall see, had always been and would continue to be more apparent than real; the crucial factor was that the court now replaced the *corrales* as the dynamic centre of seventeenth-century Spanish drama.

8

Theatre at court

As we saw in chapter 2, court plays were very occasionally performed in Spain in the sixteenth century – Ariosto's comedy in Valladolid in 1548, for example – and professional players from time to time were hired to give private performances in noble houses, as Lope de Rueda was in 1561 when Philip II was on his way north to England.[1] Plays of a sort also formed part of popular secular festivities: in 1559 in Toledo a representation called a 'comedia' was performed by a professional company as part of the celebrations for the Peace of Cateau-Cambrésis. Apart from these sporadic instances, however, festive drama flourished in Spain only as an element of the triumphal processions, pageants, masquerades, mock battles and tournaments, with their allegorical, mythical and chivalresque figures, that were typical of Renaissance festivities. Such festivities were held throughout Europe to celebrate victories, treaties, royal entries, births and weddings. In Spain, where the religious and the profane were never far apart, Corpus Christi carts were often borrowed to depict biblical and hagiographic scenes on these secular occasions, and *autos* were even performed atop triumphal arches. Gradually, and probably under the influence of the *corrales*, themes and figures from Spain's own history were added to the celebratory motifs; for example in 1571 at an entertainment at Alcalá de los Gazules the capture of Montezuma by Cortes was re-enacted. In 1599, at Carnival time, during the festivities in Valencia for the wedding of Philip III to Margaret of Austria, Lope de Vega himself took part in a *máscara* (masque) dressed in the red Pantaloon costume of the *commedia dell'arte* player Botarga to symbolize Carnival, and addressed a poem to the King, first in Italian and then in Spanish.

It was with the accession of Philip III to the throne in 1598 that the court drama proper got underway in Spain. Philip II's reign of austerity was over and the life of the Spanish court began to acquire a glamour and brilliance, even an element of extravagant frivolity, that it had never had before. The

Queen, who was still in her teens, was extremely fond of the drama. Since she was unable to attend the *corrales*, she started the custom of engaging professional players to give private performances (*particulares*) of plays from their repertoire at court, not only in the Palace in Madrid, the Alcázar, but in the royal residences at Aranjuez, El Pardo and Valladolid. The payment authorizations were all signed by the young Queen herself. The practice soon spread to the houses of nobles and prelates and even to monasteries, where religious plays were frequently performed in spite of the fact that representations in monastic houses were officially banned. In June 1605 Lope's *El caballero de Illescas* (*The Knight from Illescas*) was performed before the King and some English visitors in the garden of the King's first minister, the Duke of Lerma. The nature of the engagement offers a good indication of the somewhat vague way in which such performances were probably usually commissioned: the Duke asked the *autor*, Nicolás de los Ríos, for 'something about love or war', warning him to avoid religious subjects or miracles out of deference to the Protestant guests. Ríos came up with this play, written some years earlier.[2] Whether the plays were presented before the Queen in her private apartments at the Alcázar or as part of some larger court entertainment, the performances were at this stage presumably simple affairs along *corral* lines, with rudimentary scenic devices on hangings or frames. For the players these commissions were a welcome supplement to their incomes. The authorities, on the other hand, alive to the danger they represented to the *corrales* and therefore the hospitals, regulated these new activities by issuing licences for *particulares* and by stipulating that the public should not be admitted.[3] And indeed for half a century the *corrales* flourished virtually unaffected by these royal and aristocratic excursions into theatrical entrepreneurship.

The royal *particulares* soon overflowed the royal apartments. At first a removable stage was erected occasionally in one of the halls in the Alcázar for larger audiences. Then in 1606 the King and Queen attended two plays in the Casa del Tesoro (The Treasury) near the Alcázar, where the Duke of Lerma had an apartment, and in the following year one of the courtyards there was converted into a replica of a public playhouse to allow the royal family to see their plays in authentic *corral* conditions – a significant step in the integration of the theatre into court life.

Alongside the professionally-acted *particulares* amateur theatricals also thrived at court in the form of the court masque, which during these years and probably under influence from abroad enjoyed a brief vogue, with the King and Queen taking part in their organization. Special halls were sometimes built and quite elaborate machinery was constructed, with the use of a discovery curtain and an upper gallery revealing the inescapable influence of the *corrales*. Performances were given inside and in the open air, at court and in the houses of the nobility, with the royal children and the sons and daughters of the nobility and the local gentry taking part, as well as the ladies and gentlemen of the court. The future Philip IV was weaned on drama and the theatre became for him a life-long passion which developed unaffected by an unfortunate experience he had at the age of nine when he played the part of Cupid in a court play: the rocking of the chariot in which he came on stage, combined no doubt with excitement, caused him to vomit twice in front of his august audience.[4] In the event the masque proved a short-lived phenomenon in Spain, partly because the death of the Queen in 1611 brought performances before the King to an end for two years but mainly because no dramatist was interested enough to develop it. The leading playwrights of the day were already deeply committed to the home-grown *comedia* form and this was so flexible and so protean that it lent itself with consummate ease to development into a superior version of the court spectacle provided elsewhere in Europe by the masque. The close connection between the court and the public theatres, through playwrights and acting companies, must also have militated against a form of drama associated with amateurs, although after the court drama was reinstated full-length plays continued for a while to be acted by ladies and gentlemen of the court from time to time. Only the habit of ending court plays with a dance in which the audience took part remained as a survival of the short-lived vogue for the masque.

The emphasis in contemporary accounts of these court plays upon the element of spectacle at the expense of all else accurately reflects the ceremonial role of these extraordinary performances, which were written either by regular or by occasional playwrights and acted by amateurs, but produced with elaborate settings and machinery on which no expense was spared. For Lope's *El premio de la hermosura* (*Beauty's Prize*), performed on 3 November 1614 at Lerma, in which the royal children both took part, an open-air theatre with several simultaneous settings was built on the banks of the river, which itself formed part of the play's scenery. This included several paths, two mountains, a moving cave and temple, a palace, a second temple, and an enchanted castle, all elaborately decorated; a ship large enough to carry thirty people which foundered on a rock in the river; a cloud machine and a back curtain to hide the river when necessary. The whole was covered with a canvas awning, with dressing rooms, work-rooms and a machinery room. There were dances in the intervals and the performance ended with a dance by the Queen and her ladies. In October 1617 an equally lavish amateur performance of Luis Vélez de Guevara's *El caballero del sol* (*Knight of the Sun*) was organized on the banks of the river, again by Lerma who made drama one of the ways in which he sought to flatter and distract the king and keep himself in power. This time both banks were used with a projecting platform on each, one for the spectators and one for the play, and the scenes appeared one at a time by means of a revolving set. The effects included a storm with thunder and lightning, mist, hail and rain, a ship sailing round on the river, a grotto that opened and closed and aerial flights. The overall shape of the entertainment was similar to that of the *corrales*, with a satirical *entremés* in the first interval and a dance in the second. As part of the same festivities another play, *La casa confusa* (*House of Confusion*), and two *entremeses* were performed before the King in a church, this time by professional players, and the same company is said to have performed a third play the previous evening. By now plays, both amateur and professional, paid for either by the King or by nobles eager to honour him, had become not only an indispensable but a major part of court festivities along with the usual pageants, tournaments, fireworks and bull-fights organized by the municipalities. In 1621 Philip III even obtained a special dispensation for plays to be performed in Lent, by two companies combined, in order to entertain the visiting Maréchal de Bassompierre. With the *corrales*, the Jesuit drama, the *autos sacramentales* and now the court drama, the theatre had become so much a part of Spanish urban life at every level and in every sphere that it is not surprising that the theatre's opponents found it impossible to suppress for long the public playhouses which were their main targets.

The published text of Lope's *El premio de la hermosura* shows that it was modified subsequently, presumably for performance in the *corrales*[5] (given the play's effects and its mythological characters it is unlikely that it was written for public performance first). This seems to have been normal procedure when plays for performance at court were commissioned from regular dramatists – though it is not clear what the financial arrangements between original commissioner, playwright and *autor* would have been[6] – and is another example of the symbiotic relationship that existed between court and public theatres. The plays the public saw, the court itself saw either in the *corrales* themselves or as *particulares*; what the court saw, the public in its turn normally saw, albeit in simplified form. The productions varied but the texts remained substantially the same. With the reign of Philip III the public theatre received an invaluable boost from royal and noble patronage, while at the same time the demand for court spectacle pointed the drama in a direction that would lead in the next reign to the extraordinary flowering of a fully professional court theatre.

With the accession of Philip IV in 1621 dramatic activity at court intensified. Regular performances by professional companies were given at the Palace (one a week by 1623 according to a member of the entourage that accompanied the Prince of Wales on his visit to Madrid that year, but this was if anything an underestimate), and for a while court spectacles continued to be performed by amateurs. In 1622 the King expressed a wish for a *corral de comedias* to be built within the Palace but the Madrid Council, probably worried about the effect of such a theatre on the public play-houses, seems not to have taken the hint. By 1623 the great hall of the Alcázar was being used for plays and other festivities regularly enough to be called the *salón de comedias*. Described as 'an indifferent fair Roome' by another of Prince Charles's entourage[7] it nonetheless became the centre for the dramatic performances to which the King and his court were so passionately addicted according to the testimony of many visitors, although performances in royal chambers and other royal and noble houses con-tinued as before. For Carnival 1623 all four companies working in Madrid at the time were hired to perform *entremeses*, songs and dances, and the court was to its great delight further entertained by an impromptu burlesque play acted by various courtiers and court poets, including Vélez de Guevara and Alarcón.

In 1622 a landmark in the development of court spectacle occurred with three brilliant amateur performances at the royal summer palace at Aranjuez – entertainments described as *invenciones* rather than *comedias*, to emphasize the element of spectacle and their difference from ordinary plays. For the Count of Villamediana's *La gloria de Niquea*, the story of an enchanted princess based on the chivalric romance *Amadís de Grecia*, which was performed at Whitsun in retrospective celebration of the King's birthday, a stage 115 by 78 feet was built, with arches on Doric columns and galleries with gold, silver and blue balustrades. Effects included a mountain fifty feet wide and eighty feet in circumference which divided into two for discoveries, a flying gold eagle, an enchanted wood, two huge statues of Mercury and Mars, sixty torches and other lights reflected in four glass spheres, all covered by an awning painted with stars. Trees opened to reveal nymphs, Dawn descended on a cloud, columns turned into giants and nymphs into lions, and a lady-in-waiting rode on a flying dragon. The entertainment took place in the evening in the middle of the river Tagus and was open to the public. The daughter of the Count-Duke of Olivares, Philip IV's first minister, spoke the prologue while the Queen played the

Goddess of Beauty (a non-speaking part) and the Infanta the enchanted princess. The production was designed by Julio César Fontana, chief engineer of the fortifications of the Kingdom of Naples. The reign of the Italian set designer in Spain had begun.

A similarly elaborate festival play about another enchanted princess was performed by the royal ladies-in-waiting later on to celebrate the Queen's birthday. This was *Querer por sólo querer* (*Love for Love's Sake*) by Antonio Hurtado de Mendoza, a favourite of Olivares who became secretary to the King and resident court poet and dramatist, writing some dozen plays for special occasions.[8] Interestingly, the spectacle was performed again a year later as a *particular* by a professional company, although it is not known whether this performance was able to reproduce the effects of the original production, for these included a raised castle that descended to the stage and opened to reveal the princess covered with flowers, a black fire-breathing giant leaping from a serpent's mouth, Mars in a lion-drawn cart bearing a flaming lance, and Diana rising out of the ground on a throne.

The third play performed at Aranjuez that year was a specially adapted version of Lope de Vega's *El vellocino de oro* (*The Golden Fleece*), a play already performed in the *corrales*. Presented on 15 May along with *La gloria de Niquea* in honour of the King's birthday, it had been shortened by Lope for the occasion. He also added some lines relevant to the royal celebration together with a special *loa* spoken by Fame seated on a winged horse, Envy astride a second horse and Poetry descending from above. The play had the usual quota of production tricks designed to amaze and delight: a gold ram on wheels, a rock which opened to reveal a silver dolphin with a nymph on its back, a temple that opened to reveal Mars, a cloud that concealed a god, and a ship sailing away with Jason aboard which then reappeared to allow the God of Love to descend on his cloud to sit on the mast. In the event, however, the audience was cheated of at least some of these delights, for during the performance the whole set caught fire and the audience fled, with the King, we are told, carrying the Queen and the Infanta to safety. The rumour grew that the fire had been deliberately started by *La gloria de Niquea*'s author, the Count of Villamediana, not out of professional jealousy but because he wanted to have the opportunity of rescuing the Queen, with whom he was generally thought to be in love. A few months later Villamediana – a flamboyant court poet, satirist and wit who wilfully lived on the edge of notoriety – was killed by an unknown assassin. His murder is thought to have been the result of a homosexual intrigue, with the true facts of the matter being lost when the scandal was suppressed by order of the King. The story that spread, however, was that the murder was connected with his suppressed love for the Queen, and in the course of time the fire itself came to be associated not with Lope's play but with Villamediana's own *La gloria de Niquea*. As the fiction grew, this was then said to have been performed not at Aranjuez but in the garden of his own house, all as part of his plan to engineer a situation whereby he could hold the young Queen in his arms.[9]

The court was undaunted by the alarming experience of the fire, as the July performance of *Querer por sólo querer* indicates. The Queen's fondness for the drama certainly remained undiminished: between 5 October 1622 and 8 February 1623 no fewer than forty-five *particulares* by at least a dozen dramatists, most of whom wrote for the *corrales*, were performed by five different companies in her apartments, Sundays, Thursdays and feast-days being regular play days at the Alcázar. As far as one can judge, these plays were a fairly representative selection of what was being seen in the *corrales* at the time,[10] though a few might have been written to order and released to the *corrales* subsequently. This programme of private performances at the Alcázar, which continued through the years that followed, must already have been putting considerable pressure on the companies working the *corrales* who would have had to drop everything to answer a call from the Palace. In time the constant demands made upon them by the court would have a gravely deleterious effect on the public theatres.

The next festival play of major importance took place on 18 December 1627, when Lope's 700-line pastoral eclogue *La selva sin amor (The Lovelorn Forest)* was performed before the King and Queen and the King's sister the Infanta María in the *salón de comedias* at the Palace; two days later it was repeated, presumably for the sake of court and government dignitaries.[11] The occasion was significant for two reasons. First, although music and singing had played a substantial part in earlier court productions, *La selva sin amor* was the first Spanish play entirely set to music, modelled on similar entertainments in Italy; in other words it was Spain's first attempt at opera. Second, the play was the first major spectacle produced at court by the Tuscan hydraulics engineer, Cosimo (Cosme) Lotti. Brought from Italy in 1626 to construct fountains and garden water-works at the request of Olivares and through the good offices of the Grand Duke of Tuscany, Lotti soon proved himself a highly skilled and inventive designer of stage scenery and machinery and became chief *tramoyista* to the court. His production of *La selva sin amor* greatly excited an audience already accustomed to spectacular machine plays, for as well as concealed lighting it featured stunning scene changes, detailed perspective settings not before seen in Spain, and a seascape with fish that rose and fell with the waves. These scenographic innovations outshone the novelty of the play's music – Lope himself remarked that the spectacle had the effect of making 'the ears defer to the eyes'[12] – and it would be another twenty-five years before the operatic formula was tried again. The new staging techniques, however, were there to stay. Lotti's remarkable mechanical transformations were to become his trademark and under his direction perspective scenery and *trompe l'oeil* effects became normal features of court drama. His success, however, did not stop the Palace works committee allowing his salary, theoretically a handsome one, to get seriously into arrears on various occasions, in 1624 by no fewer than fourteen months. Not all court plays were as lavishly produced, of course, as *La selva sin amor*. The staging at times was probably relatively simple, with scenery and props being re-used to cut down on time and expense. But the arrival of Cosme Lotti marked a significant advance in theatrical professionalism and sophistication.

The hiring of professional companies now began to be the norm even for festival plays. *La selva sin amor*, one imagines, was beyond the reach of amateur performers, but even plays with spoken dialogue must have stretched the abilities of the ladies and gentlemen of the court to the limit, while the ever more ambitious stage effects constituted an increasing risk to limb and even life. Thus professional companies were engaged for the three outdoor plays with which Olivares, himself an enthusiast of the theatre at this time, entertained the King and Queen in the summer of 1631. Two, the first on 1 June, the other on Midsummer Night, were produced on a specially constructed stage in the garden of the Count of Monterrey, the Countess of Olivares's brother, on the outskirts of Madrid. On the second occasion, after seeing *Quien más miente medra más* (*He Who Lies Most Prospers Most*) by Antonio Hurtado de Mendoza and Francisco de Quevedo, the royal party moved to the Duke of Maqueda's garden next door to watch a different company perform Lope's *La noche de San Juan* (*Midsummer Night*). Both plays were accompanied by *loas* and *bailes*. Lope's play seems to have been performed again in Valencia the following year by the same company, though this time at royal expense. Such entertainments, it ought to be said, were not necessarily the responsibility of their hosts; the Midsummer plays were directed by the Duke of Medina de las Torres while the construction of the stages and settings was supervised by the Superintendent of Palace Works, the Marqués Juan Bautista. It is not clear whether Cosme Lotti was involved in these festivities, but he was certainly the designer for three more plays performed by professional companies before their Majesties the following year. These were paid for largely by the Countess of Olivares as part of the festivities held to celebrate the Cortes's oath of loyalty to the heir to the throne, the three-year-old Infante Baltasar Carlos, who unfortunately for Spain was to fall ill and die years later at the age of sixteen. The plays concerned were *Júpiter vengado* (*Jupiter Avenged*) by Diego Jiménez de Enciso, at the Alcázar, and two *capa y espada* plays, one by the Prince of Esquilache, the other by Antonio Hurtado de Mendoza. The Enciso play was performed by actors from the best two companies currently in Madrid, for three days in succession: on Carnival Sunday before the royal family, on Monday before members of the councils of state and on Thursday before the Cortes, the Madrid Council and other dignitaries. This was the normal way of allowing court and government officials the privilege of attending palace plays without compromising the dignity and remoteness of majesty cultivated by Philip IV and his first minister Olivares.

While the festivities of these years came and went, a development of outstanding importance for the court drama was already underway. The Count-Duke of Olivares was set on creating round the King a brilliant, cultured, ceremonial monarchy which would redound to the glory of Spain but at the same time leave him in peace to get on with the business of government himself. He had therefore conceived the idea of creating a new centre for this glittering court life on the eastern outskirts of Madrid, on the site of the royal church and monastery of San Jerónimo. There the royal family could escape the gloom of the old Alcázar and enjoy the benefits of country life without depriving the capital of the royal presence. Accordingly, in 1629, the Palace of the Buen Retiro was begun, amidst much hostility and derision from Olivares's enemies who condemned the project as an unnecessary extravagance in hard times and dubbed the place, because of its rapid and rather flimsy and haphazard construction, *El Gallinero* (chicken-coop), after an iron aviary on the site. Since festive drama had become an indispensable feature of the cultivated charisma of the Spanish monarchy the plans for the new palace included a full-blown, custom-built theatre – the first permanent home for the court drama. The Buen Retiro itself was ready for use some time in 1632 or 1633, and was inaugurated with lavish splendour at the end of 1633. The Coliseo del Buen Retiro, as the theatre was called, was not completed until 1640. Nonetheless plays were performed at the new palace in the 1630s, both indoors on portable stages in the *saloncillo* (little hall) and the palace courtyard, and outdoors on the great lake in the Buen Retiro park which was in the years to come to witness some of the most spectacular productions in the history of the theatre; Quiñones de Benavente in his sung *entremés Las dueñas* (*The Duennas*), which was written it is thought to accompany Calderón's *El mayor encanto amor* (*Love the Greatest Enchantment*), refers to the lake as the place 'where fire and water have made friends'.[13]

The theatrical inauguration of the lake took place on 2 July 1635 with a stunning production on a special stage built seven feet above the water, produced by the combined genius of Cosme Lotti and Calderón. The collaboration did not go entirely smoothly. Excited by the new challenge, Lotti produced ideas for the spectacle which Calderón rejected as unactable since they were in his view 'more concerned with the ingenuity of the machines than with the pleasure given by the performance'.[14] The effects Lotti had planned included artificial lighting which could brighten and fade, a raised stage with a parapet, waterfalls and a staircase leading up to it, a silver chariot drawn across the lake by two gigantic fish spouting water, an urn spouting not only water but live fish, nymphs who were to pass dry shod over the surface of the lake, a golden ship arriving to the sound of gunshots and trumpets, a mountain that exploded into a palace, stars rising from the water, a flying Mercury, six more ships, and Virtue riding on a turtle, in addition to a host of the more familiar devices used in pageants (triumphal cars) and in the *corrales* (trapdoors, aerial machines). Little wonder that Calderón was afraid that these pyrotechnics would swamp his text! In fact Calderón did retain many of these effects and also added several of his own, playing an active part in their execution. Nonetheless, what he wrote was a play and not a mere dialogue to accompany a spectacle and the work, *El mayor encanto amor*, which dramatizes the Circe legend, marks an important development in grand festive drama, firmly putting the writer in control and establishing a proper balance in the court drama between spectacle and literary worth. The complete performance lasted six hours, finishing at one in the morning; it was given by professional players on several days in succession, with the public being admitted on the last days on a paying basis. This became normal procedure with performances on the lake, though many spectators could have heard very little of the dialogue from the banks or the more distant boats. The surviving text of the play suggests that it was later performed in the *corrales*, and since the work was a full-blown *comedia* with a dramatic identity independent of spectacle there was no reason why it could not have been acted in a simpler production in the playhouses. The creation of the Buen Retiro, far from separating public and court audiences, brought them closer together, as we shall see.

The new palace, while by no means the exclusive home henceforth of the court theatre, became the centre of court entertainments on the grand scale, its facilities creating an intensification of interest in lavish, ambitious and experimental productions. On Midsummer Night 1636 Calderón's *Los*

tres mayores prodigios (*The Three Greatest Marvels*), with its three independent acts with different characters in each, was performed by three
different companies on three separate stages, one for each act, which came
together at the end. Quiñones de Benavente wrote two *bailes* (dance-
dialogues) for the occasion, which was greatly admired by the English
Ambassador. In July of that year another play, *La fábula de Dafne* (*The
Fable of Daphne*), whose author is unknown, was produced, with
machinery by Lotti. Ordinary *comedias* too were frequently performed – for
example Calderón's cape and sword play *Casa con dos puertas* on Ascension
Day 1635 on a portable stage in the small hall – with the difference now that
such plays seem increasingly to have been written specially for the court
and released subsequently to the *corrales*. Burlesque court entertainments
on feast days apart,[15] amateur performances had become a thing of the past
and with the increasing professionalism of the productions recognized
playwrights appear for the most part to have ousted the literary courtier
who wrote the odd, one-off play for a specific occasion. Like the regular
playwrights, those occasional writers include names which are now
virtually unknown; Philip IV, for example, much to the chagrin of
other dramatists especially favoured a government lawyer, Jerónimo de
Villayzán y Garcés, who as a result acquired considerable popularity with
the public as well.

It was Calderón, however, whose name occurs more and more frequently
in accounts of theatrical activities at court. At Carnival 1637, as part of the
protracted festivities held to celebrate the King of Hungary's election as
Holy Roman Emperor, the visit of the Princess of Carignano and Spain's
recent victories in Italy,[16] three plays were performed in addition to the
usual burlesques and masquerades: one by Vélez de Guevara (*El amor en
vizcaíno*, *The Biscayan Way of Love*), one by Rojas Zorrilla and Juan and
Antonio Coello (*El robo de las sabinas*, *The Abduction of the Sabine Women*)
and one by Calderón – *Don Quijote*, alas now lost. Two companies
reinforced by *sobresalientes* (supernumerary players) were engaged to
perform them. Another play by Calderón was possibly planned and then
cancelled. It is not known whether the various machine plays – one with no
fewer than thirteen scene shifts in one and a half hours – planned for
Midsummer 1637 or those performed at Carnival 1638 included works by
Calderón, but on the nights of St John and St Isabel 1638 two Calderón
plays were presented in the small courtyard of the Buen Retiro for which
the dramatist was paid the handsome sum of 2,200 *reales*, the equivalent of
fifty pounds at a time when in England an income of one hundred pounds
per annum represented considerable comfort. The payment is an indication

of the esteem in which court dramatists were now held (1,100 *reales* seems to have been the going rate for a court play by a leading dramatist[17]) as well as a glimpse into the huge sums of money being spent annually on court plays: on playwrights for new or revised plays, on designers, on players and their food, on copyists, music and musicians, on materials and machinery (vastly expensive – two mechanical devices constructed in 1637 cost 66,000 *reales*), on heating and lighting (a recurring item in palace records is large quantities of expensive wax), on costumes, and on various incidentals including the transport of the playwrights to the palace. The increase in sophistication and professionalism did not come cheaply, but the plays were all part of a calculated demonstration of the wealth and power of Spain. Calderón received 1,500 *reales* for a play (*La fábula de Narciso, The Fable of Narcissus*), a *loa* and an *entremés* probably commissioned for Carnival 1639, and in June another play of his with its *loa* and *entremés* was performed four times by two companies combined. Plays on the lake seem to have been fairly frequent, though even in Madrid in summer open-air performances were not without their hazards: in June 1639 a performance of a Lotti play (possibly Calderón's June play) was abandoned when a strong wind blew up causing the boats and gondolas (brought specially from Naples), from which the royal party were watching, to collide. In July 1640 Calderón collaborated with Antonio de Solís and Rojas Zorrilla on another lake play for the night of St Isabel, the Queen's birthday.

On 4 February 1640 the Coliseo del Buen Retiro, designed by Cosme Lotti, finally opened with Rojas Zorrilla's Romeo and Juliet play *Los bandos de Verona (The Factions of Verona)*, which was no doubt specially written for the occasion. A few weeks later, on Shrove Tuesday, a machine play by Calderón was performed which lasted from five in the afternoon until midnight; preparations for this auspicious occasion must have been very tense, for on the Sunday during rehearsal there was a quarrel during which Calderón was actually wounded. Although it was part of the fabric of the Retiro and although it enjoyed special status as a royal theatre, the Coliseo was in the full sense a playhouse. It was open to the public and in this capacity came under the jurisdiction of the Madrid Council. Furthermore it was designed to reproduce the conditions of the *corrales* (it was often referred to as a *corral de comedias*), partly so that the royal family could derive amusement from watching the public as well as the play – a nice inversion of the usual theatre of the court whereby the court watched the royals watching the play. To give the Queen the full flavour of a public playhouse arrangements were even made in the early performances for the audience to jeer and whistle and for the women to insult and scratch one another.

Plate 3 Scene from court play, *c.* 1680, showing royal spectators

It is not clear how different the Coliseo originally was from the other
playhouses. However, a ground plan of 1655, by which time the Coliseo
had fallen into disrepair and been restored, shows that the seating
arrangements in the roughly rectangular auditorium were similar to those
in the *corrales*, with three tiers of four boxes on either side and a *cazuela*
opposite the stage with the semi-circular royal balcony above. The acting
space, however, was quite different, with an architectural proscenium
providing a picture stage, a drop curtain, visible-change stage machinery,
and wings and a backcloth to provide perspective settings. At some later
date the stage was considerably deepened to give more scope for perspective scenery, with a window being constructed at the back to allow the
gardens of the Retiro itself to form part of the setting; by the beginning of
the eighteenth century the stage was deep enough to accommodate eleven
wings on either side. For court and private performances the royal
spectators sat, not in the royal balcony, but on thrones on a yard-high
canopied dais at ground level opposite the stage, so as to enjoy the
perspectives from the perfect vantage point (see Plate 3). The court ladies
seem to have sat facing the stage on the ground on either side of the dais

with the gentlemen standing behind, while other spectators stood along the sides looking inwards behind a row of royal guards; invited guests and dignitaries occupied the boxes.

The new Coliseo, therefore, was extremely versatile, providing a home both for lavish productions commissioned for special court occasions and for the private performances of plays from company repertoires which were an established feature of court life. It also provided a third playhouse for the theatre-going public of Madrid. The city's past misgivings about the effect of a royal theatre on the *corrales* seems to have been allayed by the knowledge that what income the hospitals might lose from the Cruz and the Príncipe would be recouped from the Coliseo. When court plays at the Coliseo were opened to the public they proved very popular and enjoyed long runs.

The creation of the Buen Retiro and its theatre did not lead to the neglect of the palace at the Alcázar, where the royal family still lived much of the time. Between 1639 and 1641 the great hall of the Alcázar, where plays had for many years been performed, was lavishly renovated and refurbished, with a new moulded ceiling painted gold which gave the hall its new name, the *salón dorado*. To provide the Alcázar with theatrical facilities comparable to the Coliseo a low framed stage, also painted gold, with front curtain, machinery and perspective scenery, was constructed for use at one end of the hall, for court plays and for *particulares* (see Plates 4 and 5). In this case, however, the stage was removable since the hall continued to be used for other purposes as well, and the proscenium, which had bold, flowing lines, did not reach the ceiling to create a fourth wall. The royal family sat under a canopy opposite the stage at the other end of the hall to get the optimum view of the sets – the King on a throne, the others on armchairs and cushions; the ladies of the court sat on rugs on the floor along the sides, leaning against two rows of covered benches behind which the gentlemen stood. Special guests might be given raised, shuttered vantage points at the side from which to view the spectacle.[18]

This spectacle included the royals as well as the play. The arrival and departure of the King and his family on these court occasions were conducted with the utmost ceremony and the extremely formal behaviour of the monarch throughout was that of a man who knew that he was the true centre of the theatre of court life. Once seated Philip IV, with cramp-defying control, apparently moved nothing but his eyes. Since the play itself was merely a spectacle within a greater and more significant spectacle, the picture stage of the *salón dorado* and even that of the Coliseo only partly succeeded in creating the illusion of theatre normally associated with the

Plate 4 Frontispiece (with curtain raised) for *Los celos hacen estrellas*, 1672,
probably in the *salón dorado* of the Alcázar

Plate 5 Stage set for *Los celos hacen estrellas*, 1672

proscenium stage.[19] Not only were the Royals, seated outside the theatrical space, the prime object of attention, but the theatrical space itself reached out to participate in the symbolic ritual of monarchy. *Loa*, *entremés* and *bailes* usually related in some way to the occasion which the performance was designed to celebrate and the iconography of the special curtains, scenery, even on grand occasions the special frontispiece, which were designed for court plays over the years[20] were often an extension of the themes and symbolism of the play itself, or otherwise a celebration of monarchy or of some particular royal personage. In the *salón dorado* the play even overflowed the stage when the players swept down to dance in the long space in front of the royal party. In the Coliseo with its raised stage the sense of separation must have been somewhat greater but even here, with the King and Queen on raised thrones, the element of court ceremony was still strongly present. The auditorium in both places remained illuminated throughout the performance to allow the principal protagonists to remain visible, and this again blurred the distinction between the world of the stage and that of the court which contained it. The *loa*, often performed, in part at least, in front of the drop curtain, served as the link between the dramatic text and the occasion, gradually drawing the audience into the matter and illusion of the play.[21]

Clearly the proscenium stages of the *salón dorado* and the Coliseo did create a theatrical experience that was different from that of the *corrales*. The formal picture stage and the perspective scenery must have created some illusion of entering a different world, albeit at the same time emphasizing the artificiality of that world, while scene shifts altered the pace of the action and effectively divided each act formally into constituent scenes. Performances were therefore longer than the simple, fluid *corral* performances. The crucial difference between court and public theatre, however, lay in the nature of the occasion. In the presence of the monarch, the audience observed rather than participated, and observed in an atmosphere of formality and silence quite foreign to the *corrales* and much more akin to our modern experience of the theatre. The new stage and the royal actors between them had changed drama from something to be listened to and watched into something to be watched and listened to. The *oyentes* (listeners, as the audience was called) of the *corrales* had in the new theatres truly become spectators.

In spite of the vast expenditure of money and effort on the Coliseo and the *salón dorado*, the 1640s were not to prove a propitious decade for the court drama, or for the theatre in general. Scarcely had the Coliseo been inaugurated when first the revolt in Catalonia and then the war with

Portugal brought an end to court festivities, though *particulares* continued to be performed at court for a while on a much reduced scale. Olivares, at one time an enthusiastic instigator and supporter of court drama, was dismissed in January 1643. Cosme Lotti died later that year and when the Queen herself died the following year even performances of *particulares* ceased. The *corrales*, too, closed for a time, and performances were suspended again in 1646 after the death of Prince Baltasar Carlos. They remained closed for the rest of the decade. Court festivities, however, began to revive somewhat sooner: on 21 December 1647 a masque was held in the *salón dorado* to honour the birthday of Philip IV's niece and future bride, Mariana of Austria. Performances of plays in the King's presence started up again in June 1649 and two plays, one acted by professionals, one by royal servants, were presented in the *salón dorado* in November 1649 in honour of the new Queen. Indeed it was with her arrival that the drama started up again in earnest. She had been fêted on board ship off Tarragona with a play performed by professional actors; her meeting with the King at Navalcarnero on 7 October 1649 had also been marked with a performance and further plays were presented subsequently in the Escorial, both in the palace and the monastery.

In 1650 the Coliseo, which had fallen into disrepair during the long closure, was restored and modified – to what extent it is not known – in time for a Carnival play in the Queen's honour. Far less is known about the court theatre in Spain than in England and France and how much of the ground plan of 1655 predates the restoration of 1650 is unclear, though the backward extension of the stage almost certainly dates from that year. In 1651 the Coliseo was opened again to the public and the yawning gap left by Cosme Lotti's death was filled by another brilliant Florentine designer, Baccio del Bianco, who was sent to Spain at the King's request by the obliging Grand Duke of Tuscany. With Bianco, who had a great fondness for mechanical figures, the machine play came into its own again, with effects of even more dazzling ingenuity. His production of Calderón's *La fiera, el rayo y la piedra* the year after his arrival had seven scene changes and took no fewer than seven hours to perform; it was obviously something of a national event, for over a period of a whole month a series of performances was given to audiences from royals to ordinary citizens who, according to contemporary accounts, flocked to see it from all over Spain.

Some idea of just how impressive such productions were may be gained from the recently discovered set of eleven drawings of the staging in 1653 of Calderón's *Andrómeda y Perseo*, which were sent subsequently to the court in Vienna and did not therefore perish, as it is assumed most documents relating to the court theatre did, in the fire that destroyed the Alcázar in 1734. These exquisite drawings[22] depict beautifully executed perspective sets engineered by means of wings and flats set in grooves in the stage and mechanically operated from beneath, with stunning transformations and aerial effects. These included a fall of Discord from the stage sky that was so precipitous as to cause the poor actress concerned almost to break her neck; it is little wonder that the court now left acting to the professionals – in 1660 another actress was badly hurt when she fell off a machine. In the opening set a half-hidden colossal automaton Atlas, on one knee and bearing a gigantic globe on his shoulders, was fully revealed to the astonished audience when the curtain was raised (see Plate 6). Atlas then rose, no doubt to the even greater astonishment of the audience, and sang. This awe-inspiring opening was followed by scenes which included a snowy village setting (see Plate 7), the grotto of Morpheus, the chamber of Danae with a perspective down a series of rooms that seemed to stretch on for ever, a blazing inferno, a forest scene with Pallas in an aerial chariot and Mercury on a cloud that flew round the stage (see Plate 8), a palace and garden scene with a flying Pegasus, a rocky seascape in which Perseus on Pegasus rescues Andromeda from the monster and a finale with a triumphal arch, receding colonnades, statues and crowds of people, real and painted, while the gods look benignly down from their aerial perches (see Plate 9). If the reality was as effective as the drawings then the total effect must have been by any standards breathtaking.

The period from Bianco's arrival in Spain to the death of Philip IV in 1665 represents the heyday of the Spanish court theatre. Performed in the Coliseo, the *salón dorado* and in various other rooms and courtyards of the royal residences, plays not only became once more a regular and indispensable feature of court life but were produced on an unprecedented scale of extravagance. One 1653 production, probably *Andrómeda y Perseo*, required sixty-six players. A June 1655 production in the hall of the Buen Retiro of a burlesque play, *La restauración de España* (*The Restoration of Spain*) by Francisco de Monteser, Antonio de Solís and Diego de Silva, with *entremeses* by Jerónimo Cáncer and others, required no fewer than seventy actresses; four of them appeared in a coach drawn by two mules which had to be winched up to the first floor where the performance was held. The machines for one play had to be robust enough to carry twenty-four women. The costs of all this were enormous. One machine play in 1655 was said to have cost 50,000 ducats, twelve and a half thousand pounds at the time – a prodigious sum of money. To pay for the lead used as counterweights for the machines for Carnival plays in 1656 a special tax was

Plate 6 Opening stage set for *Andrómeda y Perseo*, 1653

even levied on olive oil. Such blatant extravagance at a time of imperial and military decline and economic recession did not go uncriticized by the Church, contemporary writers or public opinion. The censure, however, had no effect. As Spain's credibility as a wealthy and powerful nation waned, her concern to maintain an appearance of power and wealth grew. The court theatre was an essential ingredient of this hollow splendour. For all its impressive technology it was a poignant charade that symbolized the later Hapsburg dynasty's flight into a world of illusion and make-believe, a vast exercise in the *trompe l'œil* effects used on the stage of the court theatre itself. In 1655 no fewer than twenty-two plays were prepared to celebrate the birth of the child the Queen was expecting, and in the spring of 1656 the King sent to Italy for extra machine experts to help Bianco impress the Queen of Sweden on her forthcoming visit to Madrid with more spectacular plays. When Bianco died the following year he was promptly replaced by yet another Italian scenographer.

Inevitably this intense theatrical activity at court began to take its toll of the old *corrales*. Not only was the court absorbing the energies of the leading

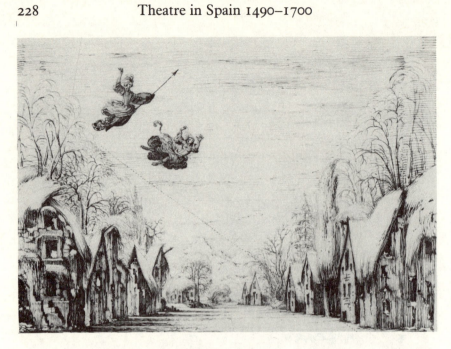

Plates 7–9 Stage sets for *Andrómeda y Perseo*, 1653

dramatists and *entremesistas* of the day, offering them opportunities and status with which the *corrales* could not compete, but demands were being made on the acting companies which created serious difficulties for the public playhouses, where plays frequently had to be cancelled at short notice. Two companies at a time were often engaged for the court theatre, sometimes with supernumerary players as well, in order to ensure the best possible results – doubling, making do, inferior singers and dancers were obviously not acceptable for court spectaculars. The resulting unreliability of *corral* performances lost the public playhouses the vestiges of public esteem left them after the opening of the Coliseo. Not surprisingly the lessees of the *corrales* began to request and receive compensation for loss of income due to the demands made by the palace on actors' time, and provision for discounts from hiring charges even came to be built into the leases.

Writing for the court drama had very positive professional advantages, apart from the obvious ones of money and status. The court's sophistication and eagerness for novelty and its no-expense-spared approach made experimentation more feasible. Plays continued to be performed at the palaces of El Pardo and its hunting lodge La Zarzuela outside Madrid, and it was at the Zarzuela in January 1657 that what is thought to have been

Calderón's first musical comedy was performed – a one-act piscatory eclogue called *El golfo de las sirenas* (*The Gulf of Sirens*) followed by a one-act *mojiganga* (farce) which parodied the machine play. Music and singing had always played a significant part in festival plays and Calderón had experimented with both earlier on in *El mayor encanto amor*, the two-act *El jardín de Falerina* (*Falerina's Garden*, 1648), and probably *La fiera, el rayo y la piedra*. But in this new distinctive mixture of spoken dialogue and alternating arias and recitative (probably in the Italian style), the musical element was more important. The short experiment was an instant success. Other dramatists, including Solís, Juan Bautista Diamante and Juan Vélez de Guevara competed to follow Calderón's example and within a short time the brief, stylized musical play on some mythological subject had acquired a name of its own – the *zarzuela*, after the place associated with it. So favourable was the reception of Calderón's play that it seems to have been transferred with its machinery to the Coliseo in time for Carnival, so that it could be enjoyed by a wider audience. Its author, meanwhile, had been rewarded not only with prompt payment but with elevation to the coveted rank of *grande* (grandee) of Spain. For Carnival the following year Calderón wrote another *zarzuela*, this time in two acts, *El laurel de Apolo* (*The Laurel of Apollo*), for a new production in the Buen Retiro.

Encouraged by the success of his *zarzuelas*, Calderón now went a step further and wrote a one-act opera on the legend of Venus and Adonis, *La púrpura de la rosa*, in which the dialogue was wholly sung. Written originally to allegorize the peace treaty with France in November 1659 and its outcome – the forthcoming wedding of the Infanta María Teresa to Louis XIV – it was performed on 5 December 1660. Music was provided by the Royal Chapel and singers from two companies of actors were engaged; no doubt more emphasis was now being placed, in the hiring of players, on the ability to sing. It is clear from the *loa* that Calderón was eager to compete with the Italian and French courts where opera was already in vogue, but he also makes it clear that he had his doubts about a Spanish audience's ability to tolerate a wholly sung play. The court spectacular, with its poetry, its music, and its visual effects, was considered the consummate fusion of the arts and opera represented the logical and complete development of this synthesis; yet Lope's experiment with opera in 1627 had not really caught on, as Calderón would certainly have remembered. He was sufficiently committed to the idea to write another opera around 1660, this time in three short acts, *Celos aun del aire matan*, about the myth of Cephalus and Procris. Enough of the score of the first act has survived to indicate that the music was in the Italian style; apart from the *gracioso* and the chorus all the parts were sung, as was usual in these plays, by female voices. However, his misgivings seem to have been confirmed by this second venture and in 1661 Calderón abandoned the operatic formula and returned to writing full-length, three-act *comedias* with the now well-established *zarzuela* mixture of spoken dialogue, Italianate recitative and song. The *zarzuela* fared better than the experiment with full-blown opera, becoming an immensely popular feature of Spanish theatrical life and evolving in the nineteenth century into full-length operetta.[23]

Apart from the experiments with the musical play, court drama during the last years of the reign of Philip IV continued as before, with the emphasis on machine plays performed indoors by professionals and with no lessening of enthusiasm for the theatre. When the English Ambassador Sir Richard Fanshawe came to Spain in the mid-1660s he and Lady Fanshawe were entertained with plays at each major stage of their journey from the south to Madrid (in Seville, Córdoba and Toledo), and Lady Fanshawe in her journal remarked on the Spaniards' fondness for 'stage plays'.[24] The immense prestige enjoyed by the court theatre and those connected with it can be gauged from an extraordinary incident in 1662 involving the departing Director of the Court Theatre, the Marquis of Heliche. Heliche was an enterprising man who seems to have put the duties involved in his position on a profitable footing: when Solís's splendid *Triunfos de amor y fortuna* (*The Triumphs of Love and Fortune*) was produced in the late 1650s, with seven actresses representing stars on a cloud machine and six more on wires as flying birds, Heliche purchased the rights to the profits from the eleven performances arranged. His pride in the theatre, however, became excessively proprietorial. When Calderón's *El hijo del sol, Faetón* was performed at Carnival 1662, special scenery was built for the Coliseo. The day before the opening, a workman came upon a trail of gunpowder, and a plot to blow up the scenery was uncovered. Heliche himself was arrested and subsequently confessed to his uncle, the President of the Council of Castile, though not before he had attempted to have the slave who actually committed the act for him murdered to protect his own skin. His motive, it transpired, was that he did not want his successor, the Duke of Medina de las Torres, to get the credit for scenery and machinery planned under his direction. He was tried and sent to prison, from which he made two unsuccessful attempts to escape, one dressed as a woman. He had clearly developed a histrionic turn of mind.

On Philip IV's death in 1665 the public theatres were closed for over a year and no more court spectaculars were produced for almost five years. In January 1670 this court mourning finally came to an end with the performance at the Coliseo of Calderón's *Fieras afemina amor* in honour of the birthday of the Queen Mother, Mariana – appointed Regent during the minority of her physically malformed and mentally backward son, Charles II, who would reign without governing for thirty-five years. There was a specially designed frontispiece and front curtain, with motifs connected with the theme of the play, which opened with a *loa* spoken by three nymphs riding an eagle, a phoenix and a peacock respectively, which then flew up beating their wings and carrying the curtain with them. A masque followed; the masque indeed, seems to have enjoyed something of a revival at this latter stage of the court drama, becoming a regular feature of the performance of court plays. Then came the play, with the usual discoveries, transformations and aerial effects. One innovation was the use of a removable backdrop to reveal further backdrops with entrances and exits – the stage by now appears to have been deepened – while hidden stars and variable lighting enabled an ingenious background-perspective of Heaven to be used for both day and night scenes.

Thereafter the court drama returned to normal with a mixture as before of *particulares* and court spectaculars – new ones from time to time but, increasingly, revivals of existing plays as well. Not only was Calderón now in his seventies but there was a marked scarcity of able playwrights to support him and no new stars, even minor ones, were emerging to take his place. The decline of the *corrales* had been caused by the diversion of literary and theatrical energies into the court theatre and now the court theatre itself was running out of talent. With that great enthusiast of the theatre, Philip IV, gone, the drama continued more or less of its own momentum without a patron at the top to revitalize it by encouraging new playwrights. Furthermore, the demoralized, intrigue-laden atmosphere at court in a Spain now in full political decline was certainly not conducive to cultural buoyancy of any sort. The court theatre, which had been so strongly exploited in the reign of Philip IV as an instrument of Spain's grandeur and political power, was, appropriately, waning with them. Only Calderón still breathed life and greatness into it and with his death the court drama as a vital expression of literary and theatrical talent would effectively come to an end in Spain.

One notable sumptuous production in the early seventies, in the *salón dorado* of the Alcázar, was that of Juan Vélez de Guevara's two-act *zarzuela Los celos hacen estrellas* (*The Stars of Jealousy*), written to celebrate the Queen Regent's birthday. An elegant, light-hearted burlesque on the Ovidian theme of Jupiter's infidelity with the Arcadian nymph, its import-ance now lies in the fact that it is the only seventeenth-century Spanish court production for which we have not only the complete texts – *loa*, play, *entremés* about an *autora*, and a humorous sketch as *fin de fiesta* which ends in singing and dancing – but most of the music (by the Spaniard Juan Hidalgo) *and* five drawings of the stage and sets with costumed figures.[25] Our knowledge of what the stage of the *salón dorado* was like comes from these.

What the court theatre lacked in originality during the remaining years of the seventeenth century it tried to make up for in lavishness. Under the direction of the two designers of the day, the Italian Dionisio Mantuano and for the first time a Spaniard, the Valencian architect José Caudi, productions became if anything more elaborate, with revivals surpassing the original performances in extravagance and ingenuity. The 1690 performance in Valencia of Calderón's *La fiera, el rayo y la piedra* (see Plates 10 and 11) had no fewer than twenty-four perspective sets compared with Baccio del Bianco's original seven in 1652. Not until 1675 did detailed accounts of expenditure on court plays begin to be kept and even then they were not kept systematically for all performances. But the exercise seems to have given sufficient food for thought for half-hearted efforts at least to be made from the late 1670s on to limit the cost of palace productions, above all behind the scenes. In 1680 even Calderón received only 3,300 *reales* of the 5,500 *reales* originally promised him for his new play *Hado y divisa de Leonido y Marfisa (The Fate and Emblem of Leonido and Marfisa)*, and debts incurred during the production of this still remained outstanding ten years later.

In 1679–80 a number of Calderón's existing plays had been performed along with others in the *salón* of the Buen Retiro and in the Alcázar on various royal occasions.[26] For the production of *Siquis y Cupido*, better known as *Ni amor se libra de amor (Not Even Love Can Escape Love)* Calderón seems to have modified his original text. For the King's wedding in 1680, however, something special from the leading court dramatist was obviously in order, even though he was now in his eightieth year. Accordingly on 3, 4 and 5 March 1680, the King's marriage and then Carnival were celebrated with Caudi's brilliant production at the Coliseo of *Hado y divisa*, which was to prove Calderón's last play. The theatre was specially redecorated in green and gold with a frontispiece representing marble pillars. The roof of the Coliseo was painted in perspective to represent a dome surrounded by corridors underneath which hung the royal arms. The opening scene depicted a royal hall of fame in Corinthian style with a canopied throne and portraits of the King and his French Queen, with Fame herself seated above on a cloud: a blatant rupture of the

Plates 10–11 Stage sets for *La fiera, el rayo y la piedra*, Valencia, 1690

theatrical illusion intended to fuse occasion and performance, to incorporate the royal principals into the play's fictitious world and allow them to gaze narcissistically from their thrones on the raised dais at their own apotheosis. Among the more spectacular effects was a flying serpent which expanded to fill the stage and shrank to the size of the actress on its back, and a peacock which walked about, opened its tail and flew away. The performance finished with a short piece that was an abridged version of Molière's *Le Bourgeois Gentilhomme*, *El labrador gentil-hombre* – a reflection of increasing French influence at court (some of the musicians were French) but sadly symptomatic, too, of a sense of the decline of native talent. The fact that Caudi and the stage and theatre painters seem to have received far, far more for their work than did Calderón himself is an eloquent pointer to the court's priorities in these matters – spectacle was all; but at least a coach was sent to transport the aged playwright to the Retiro.[27]

The death of Calderón on Pentecost Sunday of 1681 brings our period to its end. The court theatre continued, of course, but very much along existing lines, apart from refinements, both practical and artistic: in 1684 the Coliseo was provided with fifty leather buckets for water in case of fire, and towards the end of the century functional scenery, with usable doors and windows, began to replace purely descriptive background scenery. The search for novelty continued – in the course of Bances Candamo's *La restauración de Breda* (*The Restoration of Breda*, 1686) exploding mines blew bodies to bits – but so did the search for economies. Major court performances were limited to Madrid apart from the sumptuous revival of Calderón's *La fiera, el rayo y la piedra* in Valencia in 1690, existing scenery and properties were re-used or cannibalized, and revivals outnumbered contemporary plays. The Coliseo was used now for plays from the acting companies' existing repertoires as well as for special new productions, and effectively came to constitute Madrid's third public theatre in the full sense of the term, with royalty and public watching together. This seems to have been part of a concerted attempt on the part of the Palace to turn the Coliseo into a profit-making venture; in 1685 even the royal servants and guards were required to pay for admission to the play that had been performed in the Coliseo for the Queen's birthday when it was opened up to the public under the administration of the lessees of the *corrales*. The rapid deterioration in the sickly and impotent Charles II's health in the late 1690s had no visible effects on the theatre of the court, which continued as before honouring and entertaining the powerful, scheming Queens who, first mother, then wives, effectively reigned in his place.

When he finally died on 1 November 1700, bringing Spain's remarkable Hapsburg era to its close, the court theatre naturally closed with it, for a time at least. To all intents and purposes, however, the court drama and indeed the seventeenth-century Spanish theatre as a whole, had expired twenty years before – a transition brought about not by the death of a king but by the passing of a dramatist. In the partnership between theatre and court it was after all the hired hand, the commissioned producer of performable texts, who really counted.

It has been forcefully and persuasively argued that the Spanish court plays of the period cannot and must not be seen as literary texts independent of the circumstances of their performance, on the grounds that those circumstances are an integral part of the play's dramatic identity.[28] The admonition is a necessary one; *Celos aun del aire matan (Jealousy Even of the Air Kills)*, which is actually not the most impressive of the plays, was regarded at the time as the summit of Calderón's operatic achievement. The court plays, like the plays written for the *corrales*, were indeed in one sense a commodity determined by the consumers for whom they were produced and the identity of this commodity must be acknowledged. Like the *corral* comedias, however, they were also the expression of an individual vision and this identity, too, needs to be recognized. Their identity as festival plays cannot be properly understood outside their immediate historical context as an integral part of an elaborate entertainment where not only *loa*, play, *entremés* and dancing, but performances, stage decoration and audience were bound together into a significant, single spectacle. On the other hand these plays were subsequently performed before the public in the *corrales* in very different circumstances which focused attention much more closely on them as plays in their own right. Furthermore, they were written in the knowledge that they would be read. They are not superior libretti, but fully elaborated plays in their own right constructed with all the artistic skill of which Calderón was capable. Like the *comedias* written specially for the *corrales*, therefore, the court plays, certainly in the hands of Calderón, have a multiple not a single identity – the perfect compromise between art and a specific consumer audience – and as literature they necessarily transcend the circumstances of their initial performance. Not to venture beyond their festive identity is tantamount to maintaining that *Hamlet* must not be interpreted outside the circumstances of *its* initial performance or that a Rembrandt portrait is no more than a likeness painted to order to please a wealthy client. That the court theatre had a political role in the reigns of Philip III and especially Philip IV is unquestionable. It was used as an instrument of the Crown to create a charismatic court ambience, an impression of wealth and power; it was an attempt to achieve the sublime in the service of the state. It is probably fair to see it as an instrument of the royal favourites in particular, used to massage the ego of the sovereigns for their own purposes, distracting them with a pomp and ceremony which left ministers freer to govern themselves. But it is necessary to emphasize here that it was as spectacle that the plays directly served the purposes of government. As literary texts they functioned as propaganda only in the widest sense that they endorse the generally accepted values of their time, and even so their recommendations are directed as much at the monarchy itself as at its faithful subjects. The court drama saw its role *vis-à-vis* the Crown as that of educator as well as celebrant, pointing out in suitably discreet fashion the dangers that beset the leader, the strain between private inclination and public duty, the need for self-knowledge and self-control. The very nature of the material – the mythological and chivalresque – in this respect acted as a sort of safety device by ostensibly removing the plays from contemporary reality, though, as we saw, the feeling is now growing that the plays contain more in the way of contemporary social and political relevance than meets the eye.[29] The writer of a court play had a brief of sorts to work to but it was not a brief that inevitably constrained him. The lofty mythological world that was alone deemed suitably sublime for an august royal audience on public display offered a dramatist like Calderón, with a strong taste for allegory, great human as well as poetic potential, and allowed him to continue exploring his permanent preoccupations undistracted by the exigencies of 'contemporary' plots. The ethos of contemporary Spain, or perhaps more accurately of contemporary Spain as depicted in the theatre, is still detectable, as we saw, in some of the values and assumptions that energize the action in these plays, but their broad concerns represent a significant process of interiorization, a turning away from the world of seventeenth-century man to concentrate on the unchanging aspects of the nature of Man, on the eternal verities of human existence. This is not to deny, of course, that their mythological formulation makes the plays less accessible and congenial to a modern audience or reader: it does, and it is in this respect above all that the plays are prisoners of their time, for all the myths' supposedly universal nature. But they were certainly not prisoners of their courtly provenance, for they were greatly enjoyed by the ordinary theatre-going public of the day. The *comedia*, even in its courtly manifestation, was able to the end to be all things to all men.

9

Theatre in the street: the
auto sacramental

No picture of the Spanish stage in the sixteenth and seventeenth centuries would be complete without that most highly developed form of religious theatre, the *auto sacramental*.[1] We have seen how plays on religious and even doctrinal themes formed part, often a spectacular part, of the staple diet of the *corrales* – not just the *comedias de santos* (saints' plays) which dramatize the conversion and/or martyrdom of famous names in the Church's calendar of saints, but ostensibly secular or quasi-secular plots which nonetheless turn thematically on some issue of faith or doctrine. The play that makes great human drama out of the religious preoccupations of the time was Spain's most distinctive contribution to the European theatre. A special group of these plays, however, were not performed in the *corrales* at all, but in the streets as part of the ritual of what had become the greatest festival in the Church calendar – the Feast of Corpus Christi, celebrated on the Thursday after Trinity Sunday (the first Sunday after Whitsun).

Confirmed as a general Church festival in 1311 by Pope Clement V, with a liturgy specially written by St Thomas Aquinas, Corpus Christi day was by the end of the century being celebrated in the east of Spain with processions which contained a substantial if rudimentary representational element, probably in the form of numerous colourful tableaux with costumed and often masked figures. What little we know of the beginnings of Corpus Christi drama in central Spain is discussed in chapter 1. It is now clear that Corpus festivities were not nearly as slow to develop in Castile as was hitherto thought. Certainly by the beginning of the sixteenth century, drama in Castile, as in eastern Spain, had become a central element of the Corpus festivities financed by the guilds. Short plays were performed by amateurs (priests and lay persons) on floats carrying decorative scenery, as an integral part of the civic and religious pageantry along with tableaux, musicians, mummers, St George and the dragon, the traditional two wild men and ecclesiastical and municipal processions; indeed the Church's own ambivalence towards performances in places of worship – many ecclesiastics were strongly opposed – may well have encouraged the growth of pageant drama in the streets and marketplaces. The Corpus drama from its earliest days, therefore, played a much more prominent and spectacular role in public life than the church-bound Christmas and Easter plays.

At this stage the Corpus plays used biblical events (including the Nativity) and the lives of the saints, rather than symbolism and allegory, to commemorate the feast's abstract and rather difficult *raison d'être* – Christ's atonement for the sins of mankind celebrated in the presence of Christ in the Eucharist. They were, in other words, versions of the mystery and miracle plays which flourished in Europe during the later Middle Ages – in Spain no distinction was made between the two groups. In Castile the Corpus plays were still, in dramatic and production terms, relatively simple affairs. In the east, however, as we saw, there is evidence of a much more sophisticated and elaborate dramatic tradition akin to the French mystery plays and probably influenced by them, involving in some cases the use of a multiple stage[2] (several simultaneously visible scenes) and in due course machinery. Some of these eastern mystery plays continued to be performed at Corpus Christi – alongside the *autos sacramentales* in the sixteenth and seventeenth centuries – right down to the beginning of the twentieth century. The longest surviving mystery play of eastern Spain is *The Mystery of Elche*, which is still performed over two days every year in the church of Santa María in Elche by a cast of local men and boys; they use a text which belongs to the sixteenth century but is probably a version of an earlier text. This extraordinary theatrical dinosaur, which celebrates not Corpus but that other great Catholic Feast, the Assumption, is a slow-moving, charmingly naive enactment of the events leading up to the Virgin's ascent to Heaven, with huge, lumbering platforms (*araceli*) which are winched up to and down from the church dome, guitar-playing, yellow-curled angels and at the end a rain of golden tinsel. It offers a unique surviving taste of the theatrical devotion of the medieval mysteries. With the procession of penitents, the fireworks and other secular revelry that accompany it, *The Mystery of Elche* recreates exactly that potent mix of public fiesta and religious piety which characterized the great Church feasts of the later Middle Ages and which in Spain survived the Renaissance and the Counter-Reformation to endure even today.[3]

Although probably influenced in some respects by the eastern mystery play tradition, indoor and open air, the *auto sacramental* of the sixteenth and seventeenth centuries, the play that dealt directly or indirectly with the redemption of Man through the Body and Blood of Christ, seems to have been essentially a product of central Spain, an indigenous development of the simple Corpus plays of Castile which in due course Castile exported to the rest of Spain. Relatively little is known with any precision about the performance of Corpus plays (or other religious plays for that matter) in the sixteenth century, although there is no doubt that from early on the representations, or *autos* as they came to be called, were performed both on floats (*carretas*, later *carros*) during the procession and on stages (*tablados*) inside or at the door of the church or cathedral from which the procession started and to which it returned. It seems clear, however, that the major development in *auto* performances came towards the middle years of the century; and it is, of course, no coincidence that these years saw the rise of the professional actor and the emergence of a public secular theatre. The process was one of mutual influence. The existence of acting companies encouraged the composition of more sophisticated and therefore more demanding religious representations, but the companies themselves came into being largely to meet the need created by the growing role being played in Spanish life by religious drama and consequently drama in general.

By this time two *carros*[4] carrying scenery or scenic structures were regularly being used for each *auto*, in conjunction with a linking, bare, multi-purpose stage which was supplied either by a third movable cart or by a platform set up inside or outside the church or at some designated place along the processional route. This eminently practical adaptation of the tableaux floats of earlier processions allowed the carts to contribute to the moving spectacle of the procession yet at the same time permitted more ambitious and flexible staging. It was to become the standard *auto sacramental* arrangement and its patent resemblance to the multiple stage of the mysteries suggests the natural influence of the more elaborate drama of eastern Spain. The scenery of the *carros* incorporated curtains or doors to be used for discoveries and, in many cases, an upper stage level to depict, for example, Heaven; before long machinery was introduced to allow special effects. In other words, the staging of the religious drama of the streets and that of the secular plays in the *corrales*, although essentially different, did have some features in common, which is hardly surprising in view of the fact that they were performed by the same companies of actors; amongst them, as we saw, were Lope de Rueda in the 1540s, 1550s and early 1560s and the Italian Ganassa in the 1570s.

As a result of this increase in professionalism and sophistication, the expense of financing the representations began to weigh heavily on the guilds, which had formerly vied with one another to supply carts for the pageant, and the responsibility for providing them was accordingly transferred to the town councils (in 1544 in Seville, where events at this time are better documented than elsewhere). As a result fewer representations were given – the normal number in Madrid and Seville appears to have become first three, later four – but these became correspondingly more important. The acting companies competed for selection, submitting *autos* either written to order or from their existing repertoires for consideration, along with models of their proposed carts. A prize, *la joya* (jewel), as it was called, which was at first a length of cloth then later a sum of money, came to be awarded for the best *carro*: in 1575 in Seville Ganassa and his *commedia dell'arte* company received it for the most successful performance. The Corpus *autos* had become, and would remain, a highly organized part of municipal life and the most prestigious and sumptuous event in the public theatre's calendar – their status being reflected in the requirement that the players should wear rich costumes of silk, satin and taffeta, the cost of which was normally subsidized by the authorities. Since the festivities included secular plays and comic interludes, dances, singing and even conjuring tricks, and since the pageantry included the traditional tableaux, the *tarasca* (a dragon with the mechanical figure of a woman on top) which knocked off onlookers' hats, and from 1580 on giant figures to frighten small children, it is little wonder that the Feast of Corpus Christi was one of the great highlights of the Spanish year. Indeed it has been suggested that the specifically sacramental *auto* was first introduced into the Corpus festivities in Spain in the middle of the sixteenth century as an instrument of reform, in an attempt to re-inject into the celebrations something of their original spiritual meaning and intention.[5]

The ingredients of the Corpus celebrations varied according to local tradition and financial resources, but by the end of the sixteenth century a substantial dramatic element seems to have been standard everywhere. It was in the cities and large towns, naturally, that it was most fully developed and here nothing was left to chance. Previews were held to make sure that the actors, scenery and costumes came up to scratch and if they did not, then specific instructions were issued for their improvement: better-quality breeches to be provided for Delight, sleeves, stockings and garters to match, gold and silver swords to be worn instead of steel, long kid gloves to be found for Death, players to know their lines better, painted scenery to be improved, and so on.[6] In some towns *autos* continued to be performed inside church or cathedral before moving outside with the procession, but generally speaking they now constituted a theatre of the open-air. In the case of the larger towns more than one troupe would be engaged to perform, with a company perhaps putting on two or even three *autos* in addition to several interludes; collaborative efforts were not uncommon.

The first performance was usually given before municipal and ecclesiastical dignitaries outside the church which was the focal point of the celebrations, after or sometimes before Mass. In the capital the privileged spectators, seated on specially constructed and designated platforms, included members of the Councils of State and the King himself. The carts were provided by the Church in some cases, by the municipality in others and were usually decorated in advance to the acting companies' requirements. Other *autos* by different companies were often performed during the eight days of the Octave of Corpus when this became an established observance, while those players who had acted for the festival itself performed subsequently to different audiences or took their plays, new and old, on tour around the surrounding towns and villages – an arrangement satisfactory to towns and players alike, for it at once maximized available resources and increased the companies' profits. Repeat performances in secondary towns presumably often had to be less elaborate, though contracts sometimes stipulated the same costumes and staging; most towns, however, would have possessed pageant carts and many would have organized representations of their own for the Feast Day itself.

The better-known acting companies were in great demand – in 1577 the Madrid Council tried, unsuccessfully it seems, to persuade Alonso de Cisneros to contract to perform the Corpus *autos* for the rest of his life – and the standard of performance must have varied considerably. In 1579 the Madrid Council was so dissatisfied by the preview given by the company it had hired that it prohibited them from acting and tried to get Ganassa to put on something instead; pressure of time, however, forced it to rescind this decision and use the original company after all. Licences to perform in the *corrales* of Madrid in the late spring were granted with an eye to securing the services of the most talented companies for the Corpus. Indeed the authorities forbade players to leave the capital at the end of the theatrical year before Lent until the companies for the Corpus *autos* had been selected, sometimes confiscating their goods as surety. Similarly no other companies could be formed until the Corpus companies had been constituted – the Madrid Council brooked no competition and throughout the seventeenth century went to considerable trouble to secure the services of the foremost players of the day. It became standard practice for the best actors and actresses to be brought if necessary from other parts of Spain at the city's expense to swell the ranks of the selected companies; players who refused ran the risk of ending up in prison. These arrangements, of course, had enormous advantages for the Madrid theatres. Exclusive use of the *corrales* between Easter and Corpus and, before work-day performances of plays became standard practice, permission to perform on certain weekdays, were part of the deal negotiated by *autores* for their companies.

From the end of the sixteenth century to 1645 four *autos* with their accompanying interludes were performed in Madrid each year by two companies. These performances no longer took place in front of the church of Santa María as had formerly been the case. Typically performances of all four *autos* were given first before the King at the Palace and again before the Council of Castile in the Plazuela de la Villa (Plaza de San Salvador). Another performance was given in the square the following day for the benefit of municipal dignitaries, and further performances were on occasion given to honour specific individuals. Later on in the seventeenth century the Council of Castile and the City Council would watch together in the Plaza Mayor or the Plazuela de la Villa after the King had seen the first performance the previous afternoon, but the arrangement was not popular and at the end of the seventeenth century separate performances were reintroduced. The various other Councils of State were for some years allowed performances of two out of four of the *autos* in front of the houses of their Presidents; they had to pay if they wished to see all four. Attempts were made in 1635 and 1637 to streamline the organization by bringing all the Councils together in the Plazuela de la Villa for one grand performance, but these ran into space problems and were discontinued. Two-storey roofed stands were built for the spectators on all these occasions, the wives sitting at stage level and their husbands above. The public were allowed to watch as much of all the performances as they could catch a glimpse of but there were two official public performances as well, one in the Plaza Mayor and one at the Puerta de Guadalajara (now the Plaza de San Miguel). It also became the custom for the companies to perform the *autos* in the *corrales* before touring the surrounding towns and villages, and again when they returned, in order to recoup the money they had paid the playwrights for the *autos*.

By this time the *autos*, particularly in Madrid, had come a long way from the simple processional performances of earlier days. The wheels that had been used to carry the devotional tableaux from cathedral or church and back again were now used to ensure that the plays were seen by everyone of consequence in proper order of precedence. The Corpus plays had become an instrument of national and municipal protocol and pride, as much as a shared expression of faith. We must not for all this underestimate their ritual identity – candles burned throughout the performances even in broad daylight – nor their role as a means of instruction and public witness; Calderón defined them as 'sermons in verse', as theology translated into actable ideas.[7] It is no coincidence that the Corpus plays began really to flourish in Spain at the start of the Counter-Reformation, the period when Catholic Europe, particularly Spain, sought an answer to the wave of reform that was sweeping Europe in a concerted, militant reassertion of its own beliefs. The *auto* was both a lesson in which the tenets of Catholic belief were explained and reaffirmed in an effort to deepen public understanding of them, and an act of faith and devotion in which the enemies of God – Protestant and Moslem – and their ways were symbolically confounded.[8] Biblical stories were enacted and historical events as well as points of doctrine were allegorized on the Corpus stage as part of a general campaign against the anti-Christ in which national and religious interests were one.[9] The Corpus festivities are the supreme example of that complete fusion of religious and secular life that characterizes late sixteenth- and particularly seventeenth-century Spain.

The organization required by these elaborate arrangements, which were modified from time to time for diplomatic as well as practical reasons, was entrusted to various committees of municipal officers under the general supervision of a Protector who was a member (in time the senior member) of the Council of Castile. Later on, in 1676, a series of financial crises would lead to the substitution of these bodies by one central organizing committee, still under the supervision of the Protector, in an attempt to cut costs and increase efficiency.[10] The carts were constructed, painted, repaired and housed in the municipal workshop (*Obrería*). The original prize for the best cart and performance became an honorarium divided equally between the two Corpus companies and if the number of performances required by the authorities in any one year made it impossible for the troupes to fulfil contracts elsewhere, then compensation had to be paid as well. In order to comply with the demands made on them the companies might have to give up to three performances in succession in different locations, with the last starting if necessary quite late at night. In 1663, for example, the King's performance started at four o'clock, this was followed by the Council of Castile's performance and then at ten o'clock by one before the Council of Aragon. We know that night-time performances were not uncommon from contemporary eye-witness accounts[11] and from the records of the huge amounts paid out on that precious commodity, wax. By the second half of the seventeenth century the Corpus plays were taking up to a month of the

Plate 12 Drawing for *auto* cart (end on), 1646

two major companies' time, first in Madrid and then on tour in the surrounding region.

The *carros* themselves were what distinguished the *auto* performances from those of other plays. They were essentially wheeled platforms which carried towering structures of scenery, at once decorative and functional, made of vividly painted canvas over a wooden frame, with a painted balustrade in front (see Plate 12). They were pulled through the streets by bullocks with gilded horns and manoeuvred into position by hired labourers. *Carrillos*, little carts, also with a painted balustrade, provided the central stage for performances in places where no fixed stage was specially erected. The two *carros* were drawn up one on either side of the stage with their long side facing the audience, although in 1635 and 1637, when the Plazuela de la Villa was filled with an extra large audience of the combined

Councils of State, the carts had to be placed end on behind the stage. The main action normally took place on the bare stage between them, which was the same height as the *carro* platforms. The players usually entered from the lower storey of the carts, which served as a dressing room (*vestuario*) as well as a discovery space.

The *carros* were effectively spectacular boxes of tricks – impressive anyway in height, form and decoration, they housed not only players and musicians but the wherewithal for sound effects, and mechanisms, consisting mainly of a series of winches and pulleys, to produce a variety of ingenious pictorial effects. There might be machines for articulating serpents and dragons, for opening clouds and rocks and moving hills, for making characters suddenly appear (the *bofetón*), for allowing them to make vertical and diagonal ascents and descents, for revealing discoveries, for turning sets to reveal other scenes and other discoveries (the *desvanadera*), for allowing concealed scenery to rise from the top of existing scenery (the *elevación*), for towers and triumphal cars to grow and worlds to collapse. Upper facades folded down to produce ramps and ladders, and discoveries hid other discoveries like a Russian doll; space was at a premium and the inventiveness and skill of the *carros'* designers were tested to the utmost.

Scenically the *carros* might represent allegorical pairings such as the House of Doubt and the House of Faith, the Paths to Virtue and Hell, the cradle and the grave, the stage of the world and the glory of heaven. Or they might depict separate scenes, allegorical or representational, such as a hill, a desert, a globe, a garden or a cave, Vanity, the Church or Justice. The two storeys, the inner discovery spaces and the use of both decorative and functional scenery allowed maximum versatility; thus a cart could represent a house or palace below and the throne of God above; or, by means of a discovery, reveal Hell or Heaven within the Theatre of the World. The carts could be used either one at a time at different junctures in the action, in close sequence for a rapid succession of discoveries, or all together for maximum theatrical effect, for example for simultaneous discoveries or scene turning. Sometimes an *auto* made very specific and elaborate demands upon the designers. For example, for *El adulterio de la esposa* (*The Wife's Adultery*, 1608), assumed to be Lope's *La adúltera perdonada* (*The Pardoned Adulteress*), the cart of Divine Justice, which was painted with scales, swords and hell-fire, had to carry at the upper level a blue star-strewn cloud or globe which divided into four to reveal three people; while the other, representing the Church, had to carry a throne in the form of a chapel or church and a dragon with seven heads spewing flames and surmounted by a woman. The instructions to the designer conceded that this could be painted, if a 'real' dragon proved too difficult to construct. On the other hand, *La iglesia sitiada* (*The Besieged Church*), attributed to Calderón, was comparatively simple, demanding an upper level with a throne with a descent to the stage and some straightforward discoveries, although it is admittedly difficult to tell from the text itself what the performance might have involved in practice. In some *autos* the carts came into use only towards the end of the performance; in others the square where the *auto* was being performed was itself used as an extension of the stage. As was only to be expected given the immense prestige of the Corpus plays, in the second half of the seventeenth century court scenographers such as Baccio del Bianco and José Caudi were hired to apply their expertise and ingenuity to the Corpus carts.

The carts' exact dimensions during most of the seventeenth century are not known, but clearly they had to be both large and robust enough to accommodate machinery and players. The instructions for the 1641 Valencia production of Calderón's *El gran teatro del mundo* (*The Great Theatre of the World*) stipulate that the cart representing the stage of the world had to be large enough to accommodate the entire cast (the *auto* has ten characters in all). By the end of the seventeenth century, in 1692, the carts, we know, were sixteen feet long and anything up to thirty-two feet high. The size of the central stage varied but even in the first half of the seventeenth century could be anything up to fifty feet wide by about sixteen feet deep; it was probably as high as six feet. It was sometimes provided with a curtain, as it was for example for *El gran teatro del mundo* where the curtain was used to symbolize primeval chaos. The carts were repainted and re-used whenever possible but wear and tear on the Madrid carts was such that the municipality normally required that two of the complement of eight carts (two for each of four *autos*) were completely reconstructed each year. Very occasionally an *auto* might in special circumstances be performed without carts; for example, in 1613 the Madrid *autos* were taken without their carts to the Escorial for the Royal Family. Calderón's *El socorro general* (*Succour for All*) was actually written for a stage (of the new type with curtain and backcloth) without carts for performance at Corpus in Toledo in 1644.[12] On the other hand, occasionally a three-act *comedia*-type play might be performed *with* carts. The first version of Calderón's *El mágico prodigioso*, for example, which was written for performance at Corpus in Yepes in 1637,[13] opens with the Devil arriving in the square at Yepes to the sound of a trumpet call, on a cart painted with hell-flames and drawn by two dragons, and then leaping on to the stage; the second cart depicted a black ship which was also meant to cross the square, while on this occasion yet a third cart carried a mountain that opened. The use of carts presumably depended on practical considerations such as whether the play was to be performed in only one place and whether the carts were to play a processional role. The Corpus carts were essentially a practical way of supplying scenery, effects and an off-stage area for open-air productions which were to be given in one place after another. They were accordingly borrowed on occasion to act as triumphal cars for processions and perform-ances of plays held to celebrate other special religious occasions such as canonizations and beatifications, inaugurations of new churches and victor-ies of the faith. In seventeenth-century Spain both the drama and the triumphal car were an indispensable part of all public festivities, secular and religious.

The entertainment provided by the carts and their accompanying stages was similar in its general shape to that of the *corrales* and the court theatre. The *auto* was preceded by a *loa* which was often on the same theme as the *auto* and employed the same symbolism, though it was not necessarily written by the same author, and it was accompanied by a comic interlude, colourful dances or dance-narratives (*bailes*), music and singing. The *autos* themselves up to the middle of the seventeenth century were not all strictly speaking *sacramentales*, although they were normally given this name because they were performed in honour of the Eucharist. In other words, they were not all allegorical plays directly concerned, whatever their plot, with illuminating some aspect of the Eucharist and its meaning, but dealt with other, related religious themes as well, though in Madrid the City Council normally stipulated that at least one of the four *autos* should be specifically sacramental. It was with the ascendency of Calderón that the *auto sacramental* proper came to predominate. From 1648, when Rojas Zorrilla died, until his own death in 1681 Calderón was the exclusive author of the Corpus *autos* in Madrid, receiving a gratuity each year from the municipality (by 1657 this had settled at 4,400 *reales*) as well as a fee of 700 *reales* from each of the companies concerned.

This second stage in the history of the Corpus plays saw some significant changes in their presentation as well. In 1646 a royal order banned the performance of both plays and *autos*. In 1647 a plea by Madrid that the theatres be re-opened was refused, but in June last-minute permission was granted for the Corpus plays to go ahead provided 'there was nothing indecent in the *autos*, dances or interludes'.[14] Probably as a result of the shortage of time – the *autos* had to be written, learnt, rehearsed, and performed in less than a fortnight – the number of *autos* to be performed was reduced from four to two, one by Calderón, the other by Rojas Zorrilla. The eight carts were accordingly shared between them, four to each *auto*. The new arrangement was obviously a success for thereafter it became standard practice, though whether Calderón's monopoly of the *autos* after this was the outcome partly of the new two-*auto* pattern is not clear. It may well have been the decision to make the *autos* entirely his responsibility which transformed a one-off practical necessity into a new tradition.

Since under the new arrangement all four carts could not stand at the sides, two were henceforth positioned at the back. This in turn meant that the *carrillos*, or wheeled stages, were no longer big enough and although they continued to be used from time to time when a fixed stage was not possible, to all intents and purposes they disappear at this point. The new positioning of the carts was occasionally altered for practical reasons. In 1665, when all the Councils of State were again brought together for one performance, pressure of space meant that all four carts had to be drawn up end on behind a stage large enough (seventy-two feet by thirty feet) to accommodate them. A similar arrangement appears to have been adopted at the Palace from 1677 on, when the building of stone arches in the Palace square reduced the space available for the Corpus performances before the King.

All the *autos* written by Calderón after 1647, therefore, were designed for four-cart staging with its four separate entrances. Calderón himself provided the cart designers with descriptions of the scenery and effects he wanted – descriptions which reveal a strong sense of the pictorial, on occasion clearly influenced by the artists of his time. Fortunately his signed memoranda for the designers from 1659 on have survived.[15] His instructions, while leaving the technical details to the experts, are explicit and reveal that, as in the case of his court plays, text and performance were conceived as parts of a united whole. Since the *autos* are entirely allegorical and operate at no realistic level, the fusion in them of theme, symbolism and staging is much more complete than in the mythological court plays, with everything on stage – scenery, effects, action, patterns of movement, characters and their costumes and the identifying objects they often carried – becoming an integral part of the imagery and symbolism. The *autos* are, of course, intellectually and theologically self-contained, and work perfectly as literary texts, but whereas it is possible to envisage an effective performance of one of the mythological plays without all the pyrotechnics of a court presentation, the *autos* arguably can have no true *theatrical* existence other than in a performance which has some capacity at least to inspire awe and wonder, to move the faithful to devotion. The seventeenth century's pursuit of the marvellous and the sublime finds its ultimate expression in this art form at the very heart of which lie belief in the miraculous, faith in the unknowable, and awe before the power and mystery of God. The admiration and suspended disbelief experienced by the audience as the carts performed their magic to the accompaniment of impressive music was a paradigm of the religious wonder and faith which the *auto*'s text set out to provoke. Calderón himself stressed the importance of the technical effects and the music to the *auto*'s message in the preface he wrote to the twelve *autos* he published in 1677. The magic does not have to be the magic of the Baroque carts, but magic of some sort there has to be. The finest *autos* are stunning theatre,[16] the consummate example of religious propaganda, of art in the service of religion. Even the most abstract of them work on their audience emotionally rather than intellectually in spite of their theological rigour, and that emotion, for all the artistry of Calderón's text, depends on a performance which does theatrical justice to those two linchpins of drama which Calderón exploits so effectively in his exploration of the Fall and Redemption of Man – conflict and metamorphosis. The *carro* system with its possibilities for variable pairings of carts was perfectly suited to the dualities and contrasts that Calderón saw at the heart of man's nature and predicament, and the productions could be so powerfully visual as to render words scarcely necessary to an understanding of the play for a contemporary audience.

The best way to give the modern reader some idea of what an *auto sacramental* was like is probably to describe one of the texts in conjunction with Calderón's memorandum on its staging. *La vida es sueño* (not to be confused with the play of the same name), which belongs to the best period of Calderón's purely dogmatic *autos*, will serve admirably; not only is it a very abstract work and therefore illustrative of the *auto* at its most sophisticated, but it combines conceptual and structural complexity with an elegant simplicity of staging which makes it easy to visualize.

Like various of Calderón's *autos La vida es sueño* traces in skilfully compressed allegorical form the spiritual history of Man from his creation, through his fall from grace, to his redemption. The characters, apart from Man himself, are all abstractions symbolizing the cosmos, the Divinity, the forces of good and evil and the nature of Man: they are the four elements Earth, Water, Air and Fire; Power, Wisdom and Love, representing the three persons of the Trinity; Shade (Chaos) and Light (Grace); the Prince of Darkness (Sin); Understanding and Will. The upper storeys of the four carts were to take the form of four huge globes, painted to represent, respectively, the earth, sea, air and heaven, corresponding to the four elements. The globe of the earth on the left was to divide into two halves, one remaining fixed, the other opening down onto scenery representing two supporting trees, in order to allow a woman mounted on a lion to emerge. The globe of the sea at the back opened onto two supports painted with marine life to reveal a woman seated on a dolphin. The globe of the air, also at the back, opened onto creatures with birds' heads to produce a woman seated on an eagle. The globe of Heaven on the right opened down onto two columns representing pyramids of fire to allow a woman seated on a salamander to come forward. In addition the terrestrial cart was to have in its lower storey a rocky grotto which would part to reveal a man asleep on a rock.[17]

The play begins when the four as yet undifferentiated elements of primeval chaos emerge, presumably from the lower level of their respective carts, and struggle in a circle for possession of the crown of primacy. They cease to squabble when the concerted voices of Power, Wisdom and Love, echoed by musicians, proclaim off-stage the elements' unity in diversity. The three divine attributes enter – Power dressed as a venerable old man, Wisdom and Love as young gallants – and in the course of the dialogue identify themselves. The three then proceed to conjure up between them a majestic vision of the creation of universal order, to which Fire responds by leading the elements and concealed musicians in a hymn and dance of benediction which echoes the rhythmic ordering of the act of creation. To complete the ordering of the universe Fire, as spokesman for the cosmos, asks Power to designate a leader. Power reveals to them his original intention to make Human Nature, his wife, and their son, Man, heirs to the Universe, but admits his reluctance now, in view of the rebellion and fall of Lucifer, to risk another disappointment. Wisdom predicts that Man, if released from the prison of non-being, will introduce disharmony and death into the world, and is about to prophesy his own incarnation and death as Christ when Love interrupts to plead for Man to be created nonetheless. Man, he argues, will have Understanding as well as reason and judgement to enable him to distinguish between good and evil, along with Will to help him to choose. Power yields to Love and resolves to translate Man from the prison of non-being to a green paradise, giving him Grace as his companion and guide. He makes the elements swear allegiance to Man as long as he proves worthy of his role, and as the musicians off-stage once again sing the elements' hymn of praise they depart (presumably into the cart of Heaven) to help Power with Man's creation. The scene is set, therefore, for Man's entry into the world and the conditions of his inheritance have been made clear.

At this point Shade (light and shade constitute the *auto*'s symbolic and poetic leitmotif) enters from the opposite side of the stage (this would be the terrestrial cart), bitterly echoing the elements' song, and her enraged complaints at her exclusion from the newly-ordered universe succeed in conjuring up the villain of the piece, the Prince of Darkness. She repeats her grievances, bewailing the fact that light has been allocated the role of Grace and she, Shade, that of Shame. The heir to the universe, she complains, will no longer be Shade (the principle of chaos and non-being) but Man – an Idea hidden until now in the belly of the Earth – who is about to be created as a little world in his own right. As the Prince of Darkness contemplates the grotto where Man is hidden and bewails his imminent birth, it opens to discover a rock with Man, dressed in skins, asleep upon it, and Grace carrying an illuminated torch alongside. Man wakes up in bewilderment, knowing only that he does not know what he is, will be or was. He is about to follow the light of Grace along the path of self-knowledge and the proper exercise of free will, when he is distracted by the Prince of Darkness, who questions the very existence of Man's freedom. Beset by doubt Man is led off to assume his inheritance, leaving the Devil to plot Man's downfall with Shade by means of a poison which will induce a dream-like state and render him incapable of fulfilling his appointed role. Shade's speech, interweaving dream with death, death with sin and sin with darkness, legitimizes her own role in the conspiracy and seems to guarantee its success.

In the next scene, the elements, accompanied by music and singing, dress Man in the robes of his inheritance while he makes the acquaintance of Understanding and Will. He shows a decided disrespect for Understanding and begins already to display the wilfulness that will prove his downfall. Shade and the Prince of Darkness enter, the first disguised as a shepherdess, the second as a gardener, reiterate in speech and song their determination to bring about Man's destruction, and hide to await their opportunity. An altercation between Man, Understanding and Will follows, in which Understanding warns Man that unless he takes care the prison that was his cradle will be his grave; but Man, prompted by Will, exhibits only vanity and presumption. The argument between them moves into a deftly handled symbolic scene, full of suspense, in which Will inadvertently gives Shade and the Prince of Darkness four opportunities to poison Man. First, Will bids Water offer Man a mirror in which to admire himself; Shade tries to put poison on the mirror, only to catch in it a glimpse of immaculacy (alluding to the Immaculate Conception) which renders her impotent.[18] When Will bids Fire bring the sword of the four theological virtues of justice, fortitude, temperance and prudence to gird on Man, Shade goes to poison its tip but recoils before the symbol of the cross that forms its handle. When Will then orders Air to bring Man's hat and Shade tries to poison its plumes (vanity again), she glimpses the ascent to heaven of the Virgin.Mary and is again rendered impotent. Even when Will bids Earth offer its flowers to regale Man, Shade sees in the lily and the rosé a vision of virginal beauty and suffering that stays her hand. It is the exasperated Prince of Darkness who finally hits on the right stratagem. He presses a poisoned apple on Shade who then uses her shepherdess's wiles to seduce Man. Infuriated by Understanding's desperate attempts to restrain him, Man with Will's help throws Understanding over and bites into the apple.

An earthquake shatters the newly-created harmony of the universe, the elements are thrown into confusion and Grace's lighted torch goes out, plunging the world back into darkness. In vain Man appeals for help, first to Will then to the elements, and after piteously expressing his total disorientation and alienation from himself he falls into the sleep of sin that mimics death. Power, Wisdom and Love reappear, Power laments Man's fall and the elements join in the chorus of condemnation. Love, however, pleads his case and when Power argues that Man alone is impotent to redeem himself, Wisdom intervenes to point out that if Power, Wisdom and Love combine to save Man, then there is one who can make up for Man's inadequacies – Wisdom in human form is sufficient to atone for infinite sin.

The mood of the *auto* now changes to one of hope. Man is brought back on by the elements, dressed once more in his animal skins and in chains. Dreaming that he is still heir to the universe, he wakes to the bitter reality of sin and the confusion and torment of the memory of his 'dream' of greatness. Discovering from Shade that the dream was not a dream, he battles with the apparent paradox that Man's greatness has nonetheless the precariousness of a dream, and, yearning for his lost kingdom, bewails the loss of his understanding. Understanding answers his call and when Shade denounces him as useless without Will, Understanding with Man's consent drags Will to Man's feet. Shade is still confident that Man's sin is too great for redemption and although Understanding assures her that Man's contrition will enable him to be saved and although the ringing of heavenly voices seems to confirm this, she goes off to consult the Prince of Darkness about the voices, confident that Man is safely captive.

As Shade retreats, Man proclaims a new dawn and asks Understanding and Will to free him. Their inability to do so (the bond of love being broken) initiates more recriminations – Understanding accuses Will of inclining Man to evil whereupon Will reminds him that he can only incline and not compel. Heavenly voices intervene to herald the arrival of Wisdom, dressed as a pilgrim, and at Man's behest Will and Understanding together call him to them. Man beseeches Wisdom to try to free him so that he can go in search of his lost kingdom whose vanished greatness 'although it passed like a dream torments like the Truth'.[19] Wisdom frees Man from his chains and while Man flees the return of Shade, Wisdom assumes Man's wretchedness by putting on his chain and taking his place in the grotto. Shade reappears with the Prince of Darkness, resolved to destroy Man before he can be saved. The Prince equips Shade with the branch of a tree but as he beats the recumbent figure of Wisdom, Wisdom's voice announces the redemption of Man and the death of death, and a second great earthquake (echoing that after the Crucifixion) brings Shade and the Prince to the ground. Man, Understanding and Will enter to find the pilgrim clinging to the branch in the form of a cross, with Shade and the Prince of Darkness at his feet.

Wisdom reassures bewildered Man that the scene is both tragic and victorious, since although Shade and the Prince of Darkness have killed him, he has destroyed them and made infinite retribution for infinite sin. Shade (in a typical point of clarification for the sake of the audience which breaches the *auto*'s self-contained world) explains that the three-day period of the resurrection has been compressed into one 'representable scene'; and Wisdom at the Prince of Darkness's insistence explains Christ's sacrifice and the workings of Grace. Water now enters with a shell containing water to wash away the sins of Man. When Power has proclaimed the permanent restoration of harmony and love in the Holy Sacrament, Earth arrives carrying the corn and vines (bread and wine) of eternal nourishment. Air promises the words that will convert bread and wine into Body and Blood, and Fire offers the love necessary to the miracle. At this juncture Love himself enters and offers the Eucharist as an eternal pledge. The *auto* ends with the confusion of Shade and the Prince of Darkness, with Power marrying Man to Grace and warning him that since life is but a dream he must pay heed not to wake to the ultimate sleep of death – Man remains free to accept or reject a perfection now made eternally possible – and with Man, Understanding and Will promising to play their parts. The elements sing a hymn of exaltation and praise that reiterates the *auto*'s message of love, mercy and redemption, the musicians sing a benediction, trumpets sound, the carts close. The *auto* is over.

Neither the text nor Calderón's memorandum give any indication of when the globes opened but this probably took place, as often happened, towards the end, in order to dramatize the moment when the elements re-emerge one by one with their contributions to Man's salvation, and to provide a suitably imposing and triumphant finale. The elements would have entered each time from their own carts, and different carts would have been used for the entrances and exits of the other characters (with Power, Wisdom and Love using the heavenly cart, and Shade and the Prince of Darkness the terrestrial, as the lowest of the four) in order to reinforce the play's symbolism. The iconography of the globes themselves, the costumes, Grace's torch and the tree in the form of a cross would all have helped the audience grasp the implications of the action.

Such a bare summary can obviously not convey the rhetorical power and subtle patterning of Calderón's verse nor his impressive control of the play's Augustinian theology.[20] Obviously the intricacies of this would have escaped most contemporary spectators, though since they were by and large familiar with the *autos'* themes they would have been able to understand the allegory (even if only, many of them, at a basic level) with the help of the explanations of procedural points that Calderón often builds into the dialogue, as we saw.[21] I hope it gives some impression, however, of the way in which Calderón set about transforming a set of theological abstractions into drama which not only explained their relevance to man but projected that relevance with a force and an immediacy which commands the imagination and the emotions as well as the intellect. Here is no simple enactment of the struggle between good and evil but a skilful fusion of theological, psychological, poetic, structural, dramatic and narrative elements into a beautifully orchestrated whole that combines the formal elegance of a Mozart with the visionary majesty of a Bach. Man's pathetic wavering between bewilderment and presumption is finely judged; so are the tragic frustrations and grievances of Shade and her Prince. Both allegory and verse carry their burden of complex ideas without strain. The vision of Man's relationship with the universe, the profound sense of the compelling duality of his nature and the sheer plausibility of those forces without and within him which militate against his well-being, make of the play, furthermore, a work which has philosophical reverberations that go beyond Catholicism. Its most impressive feature, however, is the equilibrium it maintains between intellectual brilliance and dramatic and human appeal – no dramatist has ever combined these qualities in greater measure.

The years from 1648 to 1681 represent the full flowering of the *auto sacramental* – a genre which Calderón made so completely his own that the very name is now associated with his. We saw in chapter I that religion in Spain in the sixteenth century had had at its disposal some major dramatic talents, above all Lucas Fernández and Diego Sánchez de Badajoz. In their hands religious drama had become richer, more imaginative and more forceful, with symbolic and allegorical elements gradually assuming a significant role in creating the necessary balance between instruction and entertainment. The Corpus plays were from the first different because they drew on such a wide range of source material – eventually everything from the Bible and the lives of the saints to medieval ballads, legend, classical mythology, everyday life and contemporary history. The justification was that the Eucharist lay at the very heart of Catholicism's theological and ethical system; everything that had gone before found its culmination and resolution in Christ's atonement, everything since derived meaning from it. However, the festivity only produced its own distinctive dramatic form when the particular appropriateness of symbolism and allegory to the feast's doctrinal *raison d'être* was realized and plays began to be written specifically with the intention of explaining and illustrating the significance of Corpus Christi. The essentially imitative Valencian poet Juan de Timoneda had in the second half of the sixteenth century performed the invaluable task of giving some shape and direction to the hitherto very tentative sacramental play, but not until Calderón was the difficult task of combining theology with theatre perfected. The dramatists who immediately preceded him tackled the exacting demands and restrictions of the *auto sacramental* with varying degrees of success. Lope, predictably, was the most prolific and his *autos* with their lyricism and their simple allegories are amongst the most effective. The finest of Calderón's predecessors, however, is now acknowledged to have been José de Valdivielso, a priest and exclusively religious dramatist who was highly regarded by his contemporaries and who has now been rescued from critical neglect and revealed to be a writer of skill and originality second only to Calderón.[22] He alone seems to have shared Calderón's clear conception of what the nature and purpose of an *auto sacramental* really were.

It was only Calderón, however, who possessed the precise theological knowledge, the intellectual control and the imaginative range necessary to harness poetic drama tightly to the purposes of Christian doctrine, to make of theology something inseparable from verse, allegory and dramatic structure, rather than something grafted on to them. In his *autos* the theology and moral teaching (which is an eclectic mixture of Augustinian, Franciscan and Thomist ideas, though his approach can be independent when dramatically necessary[23]) are woven into the very fabric of the plays, creating a mutually illuminating partnership between poetry and theology which the admiring censor of Calderón's 1677 edition of twelve of his *autos* aptly described as 'celestial architecture'. He also responded more keenly than other writers to the sheer drama inherent in the story of Man's fall and redemption, and translated this to the stage by portraying with far greater force the element of conflict, struggle and change in Man's painful journey towards salvation.

His is an astonishing record – two plays illustrating different aspects of the same set of ideas nearly every year for a period of thirty-three years[24] in an age when ingenuity and variety were prized almost above all else. Writing year after year for an audience which stayed essentially the same but which, like all Spanish theatre audiences, represented the whole spectrum from King through professional theologian to labourer, Calderón produced a remarkable range of variations on his single subject. He sometimes rewrote early *autos* and frequently returned to schemes, patterns and ideas he had already used, in *comedias* as well as in *autos*, but always in pursuit of a more complete fusion of action and allegory. The inevitable repetitions of later years were more than compensated for by the gain in subtlety and by his developing mastery of plot, poetry and symbolism in combination. The reason for his sustained success lay largely in the nature of the undertaking. The *auto* was the theatrical form which within a single unit allowed all his distinctive interests and qualities full play: not only his profound grasp of theology, his leaning towards the intellectual and the abstract, his interest in the transcendental and his powerful absorption with the nature of man and his place in the cosmos, but also his love of symbolic patterning and symmetrical structures, his gift for allegory, his responsiveness to both sides of man's nature, his preoccupation with filial revolt and generational conflict and his intense sense of drama and theatre: the *auto sacramental*, after all, dramatized a story of revolt and dissension which gambles with the highest prize of all – eternity.

Not all Calderón's *autos* by any means are as impressive as *La vida es sueño* – the balance between ingenuity and rhetoric on the one hand and depth of meaning on the other was not an easy one to maintain. Some pieces, less ambitious than *La vida es sueño*, are, probably for that reason, arguably finer in terms of their humanity and forcefulness. A few, including *La viña del Señor* (*The Lord's Vineyard*, 1647) and *El día mayor de los días* (*The Day of Days*, 1678), are considered more effective in bringing home the relevance of the Redemption to man's experience of life; *La vida es sueño* focuses rather on the need for redemption. Neither are the *autos* all alike in approach, technique or effect. Like previous Corpus *autos* they utilize a wide range of sources – biblical or evangelical stories, medieval topoi, pagan myths, popular legends, even contemporary events and the plots of existing *comedias*. They vary in their complexity, their degree of realism or abstraction, their thematic emphasis, the subtlety of their thinking, their poetic quality and in the conviction they carry, as well as in their scenic effects. Some are vigorously dramatic, some intensely moving, others are more detached and contemplative. They have been divided into five main groups, according to their purpose rather than their plot: the ethical, the dogmatic, the scriptural, the apologetical and the hagiological or devotional. The ethical *autos* have proved to be amongst those with the greatest surviving appeal perhaps because they are the most readily understood. This type presented relatively few problems and accordingly Calderón mastered it fairly early on, writing none after 1658. The first great *auto sacramental, La cena del rey Baltasar* (*King Belshazzar's Feast*, 1634?) is one of the best known of these and justly so, for the confrontation in the person of Baltasar between human vanity and mortality has a tragic force that still translates magnificently to the stage today.[25] Another is the beautifully crafted *El gran teatro del mundo* (1645?) which dramatizes the implications of the Senecan analogy between living and acting (a favourite theme of Baroque drama) in a very moving way that presents man as a social as well as a spiritual being. The *autos* that dramatize the mystery of the Redemption itself, which form the largest group, understandably presented the greatest difficulties to a dramatist intent on creating a highly complex and intricately-wrought allegory without loss of dramatic impact, and these Calderón continued to experiment with throughout his career. His first real success is regarded as being *El pintor de su deshonra* (*The Painter of His Dishonour*, between 1653 and 1659), with complete mastery of the translation of dogma into fully actable and convincing drama coming only in the last seven years of his life, with *La nave del mercader* (*The Merchant Ship*), *La viña del Señor, El nuevo hospicio de pobres* (*The New Hospital for the Poor*), *El Pastor Fido* (*The Faithful Shepherd*) and *El día mayor de los días*.[26] This last play is a splendid illustration of an original device used by Calderón in a number of *autos* whereby the whole action is conceived and created in the mind of one of its characters, in this case *Ingenio* (Ingenuity). In most of them the imaginative impulse comes from man's arch-enemy, the Devil himself, forever plotting man's downfall; *No hay más fortuna que Dios* (No Fortune But God) is a notable example.[27]

A. A. Parker, whose sympathy for and understanding of the *autos* are profound but whose critical scrutiny of them is nonetheless severe, has proposed an exacting criterion for the perfect *auto* – that the theology, by the demonstration of its relevance to experience, should be rendered so effective as drama that even an unbeliever should be convinced that the dogmas expressed are viable. This requirement, thus formulated, seems to ask too much. All we should legitimately demand of a fine *auto*, surely, is that it convince the unbelieving spectator or reader poetically and dramatically, compelling his admiration artistically and conceptually and commanding his intellectual and emotional assent *for the duration of the play*. The lasting measure of Calderón's achievement as a religious dramatist is the substantial number of his *autos* which do just that. And while a knowledge of the *autos'* scholastic background is certainly necessary to a full understanding and appreciation of this difficult genre which time and the changes it brings with it have rendered apparently remote and esoteric, many of them by way of bonus work convincingly at a psychological, ethical or philosophical level as well, carrying a charge of human interest that transcends their immediate religious context.

After his death in 1681 Calderón's *autos* continued to be performed, since the manuscripts all belonged to the City of Madrid and had naturally been preserved. One new *auto* by the King's chaplain was chosen in 1683 in a commendable attempt to encourage new talent but it was not until 1687 that both the Corpus plays were chosen from new submissions. Even so, Calderón's pre-eminence went unchallenged, for no real successor and no major innovations were forthcoming. The master's imprint was too powerful to allow subsequent writers to do anything but continue the tradition he had established, and Calderón's *autos* were performed regularly in Spain until 1765.

Scenically there were some late changes. The court scenographer José Caudi persuaded the City of Madrid to invest in a new set of improved carts, more solidly built and adorned with statues. They were christened in 1688 with two *autos* by Calderón, *Mística y real Babilonia* (*Mystic and Royal Babylon*) and *A María el corazón* (*To Mary the Heart*) but not used the following year because the *autos* were cancelled owing to the death of the queen. The new carts were much heavier and less manoeuvrable; one actually toppled over in 1691 injuring two actresses and the *autor* himself, and there had been previous accidents. It was decided, therefore, to avoid the usual cumbersome changeover between the first *auto* and the second by placing all eight carts in position round the stage before the start of the performances at the Palace and in the Plazuela de la Villa. To accommodate two carts on either side as well as the four at the back, the stages constructed on these sites had to be considerably deepened; the one at the Palace in 1692 was to measure fifty feet wide by thirty-six feet deep, with carts sixteen feet long and not more than thirty-two feet high. The new carts, as well as being less practical, do not seem to have been as versatile in their effects as the old ones – the statues must have taken up space – and one imagines that having them all drawn up at once must have been scenically much less satisfactory, not to say confusing. This may have partly accounted for the King's decision in 1697 that after the first *auto* was over its four carts should be removed to the Plazuela de la Villa in readiness for the performances there the following day. It is not at all unlikely that these considerations contributed to the decision after 1705 not to perform the *autos* on carts in the streets in the traditional way any longer, although the major reasons for the change were external – the War of the Spanish Succession and the lack of interest shown in the Corpus theatricals by the new Bourbon dynasty.

From this time on the *autos* were performed instead in the playhouses, where they survived for another sixty years. They retained much of their popular appeal, though, deprived now of their ritual role and reduced to the status of playhouse entertainment, they could not for the most part compete with the *corrales'* more seductive secular blandishments.[28] Eventually they fell inevitable victim to the changed ethos of a different age. Whereas Spain's earlier classicizing theorists seem tacitly to have recognized them as a special case, eighteenth-century neo-classical aesthetics disapproved of them on account of their lack of verisimilitude and their historical anachronisms. More importantly, they provoked the indignation of Enlightenment reformers: the mixing of the sacred and the profane by putting religion on the stage – the very act indeed of using earthly symbolism for sacred truths – was deemed to be an offence against reverence and good taste; the place for religion was tucked away in church.[29] Accordingly after 1765 the *autos* were prohibited. Now, in the way these things have of coming full circle, it is not the *autos* but the mocking objections of their literal-minded eighteenth-century critics which strike us as jejune: 'Is it possible for Spring to talk? Have you ever in your life heard Appetite utter a single word?'[30] Happily, the unfettered activity of the imagination in an exploration outside time and space of the nature and condition of man is something that we can now better understand, even in our radically different, secularized world.

Postscript

This book has concentrated on the Spanish drama as theatre, as a national institution. Talking about the plays themselves, however, acknowledges their identity as literary texts and it is as literature rather than as performed theatre that they have for the most part come down to us. Their full identity as literature, as a product aimed at a different sort of consumer, and therefore as an object of textual study, came into being at the moment of their publication. However, the nature of the entire process whereby texts were produced for performance and subsequently printed has created severe problems for the study of the Spanish drama of the period. Since the playwright normally sold his play to the *autor* and thereby lost all control over it, few autograph manuscripts of Golden-Age plays survive and the relationship of the original 'ideal' text to the play as we know it is to say the least uncertain. The success of the theatre meant that printings of plays proliferated – published both singly (*sueltas*) and in single-author or miscellaneous collections of twelve plays each which sometimes then became parts of series (*partes*). In many cases the earliest known printed edition is no more than one of several versions produced from an original which was first cut about, altered and probably on occasion added to by acting companies,[1] then reproduced by often careless copyists, and finally mutilated by editors and printers, either deliberately as they sought to improve on an adulterated text or make sense of a foul copy, or unwittingly as an illegible script was misread or mechanical printing errors crept in. Subsequent seventeenth-century editions based on or reproducing these versions might then introduce modifications and errors of their own – used type was not kept so reprinting always meant resetting – creating an editorial nightmare for textual scholars attempting to establish the relationship between all the various versions in the hope of producing a definitive text. Juan de Vera Tassis, for example, a close friend of Calderón's, made a large number of seemingly arbitrary 'improvements' as well as corrections when he edited Calderón's plays in nine volumes in the 1680s and early 1690s, in a well-intentioned attempt to rid them of what he knew or took to be corruptions; until comparatively recently the vulgate version of Calderón derived ultimately from these doctored texts, and it is still possible that in a few instances Vera Tassis's texts are the most reliable – that some were based on recasts made by Calderón himself for later court performances.[2] In the case of many plays, therefore, a number of different seventeenth-century versions survive which are often significantly different in detail and sometimes in substance; and because so many sources have disappeared, their relative reliability does not necessarily correspond to their nearness in time to the date of the play's composition. Pirate performances and pirate printings increased the spread of corrupt texts and, to make matters worse, in the latter dates were often faked. As we saw, by 1617 Lope de Vega had become so incensed by the state in which his plays were appearing in print and by the attribution to him of plays which he had never written and to other playwrights of plays which he had, that he insisted on supervising the printing of his plays himself from then on, retaining for himself the *privilegio* (the royal permit to print which prohibited unauthorized printings or the import of other editions for a determined number of years). This did not prevent pirate printings but it did at least ensure that an authorized edition of the plays was available. For the same reason, in 1636 and 1637 Calderón's brother José gathered together and published in two *partes* as many of the dramatist's plays as he could get his hands on; it is not clear, however, whether he had access to the originals or whether he even took any part in the preparation of the texts. Two more *partes* were published with what appears to have been Calderón's permission during his lifetime but even these cannot be regarded as reliable. It is interesting in this respect that in the prologue to *Parte XI* of his plays Lope talks of producing printed texts from 'my originals'. This suggests that he had kept the manuscripts, or copies of them, of some of his plays or had been able to recover them from the *autores* – perhaps a combination of both. No playwright, however, seems to have made a systematic effort to preserve his originals.

One of the problems where piracy was concerned was that the licensing process operated separately in the different historical kingdoms of Spain, and although in theory no book could be sold in Castile until it had first obtained a Castilian licence and no Castilian work could be printed elsewhere until it had such a licence, these rules were often flouted. Books were often produced illegally outside Castile and then imported, or printed by Castilian presses and passed off as editions licensed elsewhere. These measures were frequently resorted to during the period 1625–34 when the Council of Castile, implementing the recommendations of the Committee for Reform it had set up in 1621, banned the publication of all plays and novels.[3] The printings of corrupt pirate editions of plays inevitably increased as a result and Lope's attempts to control the publication of his plays received a severe setback, though he himself did some illegal publishing outside Castile during this time. In 1635 Lope obtained a *privilegio* to print again but died that year before the next *parte* of his plays appeared.

Another aspect of the publication process also had an impact on the texts of plays – censorship. The degree and effect of self-censorship are of course imponderable. Obviously playwrights did not waste their time writing plays they knew would be banned, and there is no reason to believe that they would have wanted to do so, though occasionally, as in the case of Lope's *El divino africano*, they misjudged the outcome.[4] On the evidence of the texts, however, and of those censorial cuts we know about, they do not seem to have felt unduly constrained by the thought of censorship in the detail of their writing. The impression they give is of having gone as far as they dared – on occasion just beyond – leaving the *censor* and the *fiscal* to worry about fine distinctions regarding what was or was not objectionable. One imagines that seeing what they could get away with became something of a sport for some dramatists. Inquisitorial intervention was obviously a more serious matter. Lope, who was by then a familiar of the Inquisition himself, was very upset by the confiscation of his St Augustine play in 1608, claiming in his unsuccessful appeal against the Inquisition's decision that his honour and reputation had been impugned as a result of the widespread speculation that the ban had provoked.[5] Routine stage censorship, as we saw, was variable in its strictness but was seriousminded nonetheless. There can be no way of knowing what was lost to censorial objection on religious, moral or other grounds and it is impossible to say how much was added to a text or how much of what had been cut found its way back into performance and text once the licence had been granted.[6] In theory the Protector had to see the play performed before it was vetted and the censor and fiscal were supposed to be present at the first public performance to make sure their stipulations had been carried out, but it seems unlikely in view of the turn-over of plays that these rules were always adhered to in practice.

Before the text of a play became available to the reading public, a further censorial hurdle had to be overcome. A printing permit (*privilegio*) for any book could be obtained from the Crown only after a licence (*licencia*) attesting to the suitability of the work for publication had been issued by the Council of Castile. Each work was therefore examined by a censor who had to sign every page, along with any alterations he had made, and his statement of approval (*aprobación*) and the licence issued on the basis of it had then to be printed at the beginning of the work along with the official price. All subsequent reprintings went through the same procedure. Sometimes material cut from the performance text of a play found its way back into the published text with official blessing, for the simple reason that censors considered performances to be more influential than texts and theatre audiences to be more vulnerable and impressionable than the better-educated reading public. On the other hand, material passed for performance was occasionally objected to at the time of publication on account of excessive censorial zeal or even over-literal interpretations of metaphorical passages.[7] The stage censor and fiscal served on a regular basis, often for years at a stretch, and must have had their work cut out at times to keep up with the demands made upon their services, whereas the task of vetting books for publication seems to have been divided out between a wider range of competent people – clerics, scholars and men of letters. Calderón was acting as censor for plays and other works by the mid-1630s and went on doing so at the same time that other censors were scrutinizing his own plays. Not surprisingly most of these writers and censors knew one another and friends often took the opportunity of being asked to provide an *aprobación* to puff the author and his work in general.

Inevitably the censorship process was therefore a little hit and miss, depending as it did on the judgement of a variety of people, laymen and ecclesiastics, disinterested or not as the case might be. Gillet's view of the expurgated version of Torres Naharro's *Propalladia* published in 1573 was that the expurgation (by a cosmographer and grammarian from Burgos, Juan López de Velasco) had been done with 'good-natured indifference', leaving what Gillet called the play's 'lusty naturalism' unchanged.[8] Some plays were passed almost without a second glance on the basis of the censor's recollection of a performance he had seen years before or, in the case of Calderón later on in life, on the strength of the author's reputation. Censors' views were sometimes challenged by other authorities and over-ruled. The total effect on a text of the different censorial processes, before each new performance and each new printing, however, could not have been negligible in some cases. On the other hand, the greatest damage to the play as conceived by its author is far more likely to have been caused by the combined interference of players and printers; there can be no doubt that many a play that has come down to us is a closer reflection of the play in

performance than of the play as it was originally written. The possibility
that the dramatists themselves modified the texts in the light of performances in the *corrales*, as Shakespeare is thought to have done, is not a very
real one, though it does seem more feasible in the context of the court
drama or even perhaps the *autos*. Court plays were modified for the *corrales*
and *corral* plays were sometimes rejigged for performance at court;
Calderón, as we saw, adapted his Corpus play *El mágico prodigioso* for
performance in the public playhouses. But these alterations were occa-
sioned by a radical change of venue and occasion, not by any conviction that
the text of a play was a fluid and provisional thing until it had been tested in
performance. The Spanish playwrights were not intimately connected with
performances in the *corrales* and the nature and rate of theatrical production
and consumption made textual refinement of this sort unlikely. Authors
wrote with the needs of *corrales* and acting-companies in mind, but even so
circumstances might necessitate the subsequent suppression or modi-
fication of lines, characters or even whole scenes. Measures could be taken
by a few, as we saw, to try to ensure that printed plays at least conformed as
closely as possible to the playwrights' originals, but the majority of
playwrights seem to have commanded neither the authority nor the will to
preserve their original texts for posterity.

The loss of Golden-Age plays, by accident or inadvertency, is therefore
another of the drama's problematic aspects. At a conservative estimate only
half of Lope's plays have survived, only a quarter if we believe the larger
claims made by and for him. In the case of every major dramatist, and many
others, we have the titles but not the texts of plays they are known or
thought to have written, and it is clear that hundreds of other plays have
disappeared without trace. Some very prolific dramatists with high reputations in their own day – Miguel Sánchez and Alonso Remón amongst
them – have virtually fallen from sight, leaving behind a scant handful of
texts. The deliberate or accidental attribution of plays to the wrong authors
confuses the situation still further; editions of plays, including plays
written by Lope, Tirso and Calderón, were published under the names of
two or even three different dramatists, often with different titles, with the
result that Calderón earlier on this century was accused of having plagia-
rized works by Lope when in fact what he had done was rewrite plays of his
own.[9] The problem was a function not only of the sheer size of the drama
but of its commercial identity – plays were products rapidly consumed and
often as rapidly forgotten. Printers published plays not to preserve them
but to turn a small profit for themselves (and in the process, of course, for
the *autores* who sold them the texts and therefore the hospitals themselves),

and paid scant heed either to accuracy or the law. But for all their
shortcomings they at least ensured the survival of a substantial part of the
drama of the period and in the process enabled subsequent playwrights to
rewrite old plays and subsequent *autores* to perform them – a further aid to
survival. The problem of size is a continuing one, for all that so many of the
works that were written are gone. Many surviving plays languish in rare or
antiquated editions in specialist libraries from which there is neither the
money nor the scholarly manpower to rescue them; more readily available
editions are often unreliable and although there has been an increase of late
in the serious-minded editing of Golden-Age plays, the works in question
tend to be those which are already well known rather than those that need
rescuing from undeserved (or for that matter deserved) neglect.

There is also a related problem of dispersal, a problem that was largely
the outcome of the *comedia*'s success. Spain was a major European power
with far-reaching connections in the Old World and the New. Spanish
plays were performed from time to time in princely courts in Vienna and
other cities with Hapsburg connections, and the texts of plays and versions
of plays printed singly and in collections were widely scattered outside
Spain – some possibly still lie undiscovered or unidentified in European
and American libraries. No fewer than 900 *suelta* editions of *comedias* have
ended up in the Library of Cambridge University alone. Such was the
renown of the Spanish drama in seventeenth-century Europe that presses in
Venice, Milan, Antwerp, Brussels, Paris and Lyons constantly published
plays by Spaniards, both in Spanish and adapted in translation. In 1636,
Fabio Franchi from Perugia, who claimed to have lived in Madrid from
1630 to 1632 solely for the pleasure of seeing Lope's plays performed,
observed, 'In Italy and France theatrical players, in order to increase their
takings, have only to announce on the posters that they are going to put on a
play by Lope de Vega to find that they have not a theatre large enough for
the audience or a money-box big enough for the receipts.'[10] In the middle
of the century the occasional Spanish acting troupe even found its way to
France and England.

Spanish plays were not only widely read but widely imitated, particularly
in France. In the seventeenth century French dramatists from Corneille
and Molière, through Scarron and Le Sage, to a large number of lesser
writers such as Rotrou, Boisrobert, D'Ouville and Hauteroche borrowed
plots, situations and characters, on occasion whole acts, not only from
Lope, Tirso and Calderón but from Castro, Rojas Zorrilla, Mendoza,
Alarcón, Moreto and others – sometimes from more than one at a time for a
single play. The three famous borrowings are Corneille's *Le Cid*, based on

Castro's *Las mocedades de Rodrigo*, his *Le Menteur*, based on *La verdad sospechosa* (not by Lope de Vega as Corneille thought, but by Alarcón), and Molière's *Don Juan*, taken from Tirso's *El burlador de Sevilla*, probably via an Italian adaptation. Otherwise what the French playwrights took from the inexhaustible mine of Spanish plays were principally romantic and comic intrigues with a sprinkling of serious honour plots and historical themes. The borrowings were in almost every case superficial, giving no indication that the French dramatists understood or cared what the Spaniards were about; only Corneille and Molière succeeded in producing plays comparable to – in the case of *Le Cid* superior to – the originals. Interestingly, *El burlador* and *La vida es sueño* apart, none of the serious Spanish dramas that are now so highly regarded seem to have found their way onto the French stage.[11]

In Italy and the Netherlands Spanish plots – again for the most part comedies – were reworked and plundered by seventeenth-century playwrights, and the authority of Lope's *Arte nuevo* was occasionally invoked by Italian playwrights eager to break the neo-classical rules. In Germany, too, in the late seventeenth and eighteenth centuries the popular theatrical repertoire owed a lot to the *comedia*, particularly to Calderón. The range of Spanish plays known and adapted in Germany seems to have been wider than elsewhere and to have included some of Calderón's finest serious dramas, but reworkings and productions were often based on Italian and French versions of the Spanish plays rather than on the originals themselves.

In England the situation was rather different. Spanish literature, particularly Spanish prose fiction, was well-known in translation there as it was elsewhere and it was extensively used by English dramatists. Although fond of including the word 'Spanish' in play-titles as a promise of exoticism, however (sixteen or seventeen such titles survive), they were much less profligate, certainly than the French, in their use of plays from Spain. They had far less access to translations of Spanish plays than other European playwrights, and some English plays of the time which hitherto were assumed to have been based on Spanish originals are now thought to have drawn instead on common sources. Knowledge of the Spanish drama in England appears in fact to have been patchy and to have depended to a large extent on intermediary French versions. As in France few of the best Spanish plays were known in England; Aphra Behn's *The Young King* is one of the only examples of a borrowing from one of the great serious plays (*La vida es sueño*). In the early part of the century the *comedia* seems not to have been known to English playwrights at all, though of course it is possible that borrowings have been lost to sight. However from the 1630s on English dramatists did sporadically borrow from and adapt specific Spanish plays – the first was Henry Shirley who used Lope's *Don Lope de Cardona* for his *The Young Admiral* (1633) and Tirso's *El castigo del penséque* (*The Penalty for Jumping to Conclusions*) for *The Opportunity* (1634).[12] Sir John Suckling in *The Goblins* (1637–41) mentions Mendoza's *Querer por sólo querer*, so clearly more Spanish plays were known than were actually plundered. Then in the 1660s the 'Spanish plot' as it was known came very much into fashion as the Cavalier playwrights closely imitated the cape and sword plays, particularly those of Calderón. Wildblood in Dryden's *An Evening's Love* says, 'I hate your Spanish honour ever since it spoyl'd our English plays', but nonetheless both Dryden and Wycherley in their different ways experimented with ingredients from Spanish drama,[13] and Dryden's *The Indian Emperour* would seem to owe a great deal to Calderón's *El príncipe constante*.[14] On the face of it indirect borrowings from the *comedia* seem to have been fairly frequent but the lines of influence are extremely difficult to trace. As with that of other countries, the English debt to the *comedia* was one that in most cases scarcely penetrated below the surface of the plot, basically because the cultural differences were considerable and because the Spaniards' conception of what was acceptable to good drama was too liberal by now even for the English.

Since the seventeenth century the Spanish drama has suffered like most literature of the past from changing fashions in taste and critical theory, inside and outside Spain. In the eighteenth century the decline of the theatre after the death of Calderón and the general sense of inferiority *vis-à-vis* the outside world felt by reformers and intellectuals in Bourbon Spain led to a revival of belief in neo-classical principles amongst theorists who despised the inferior *comedia* imitations being written by contemporary hacks, for all their popularity with the public. Although respectful on the whole towards the great dramatists of the past, they regarded them essentially as popular playwrights and ascribed the degeneration of the drama in Spain to their lack of discipline and neglect of the rules. With the advent of Romanticism at the end of the eighteenth century there was an influential revival of interest in and admiration for the Golden-Age theatre on the part of German writers, led by A. W. Schlegel, who admired the exuberance, the stagecraft and what they considered the sublime idealism of the Spaniards. In particular they lavished ecstatic praise on Calderón, ranking him as the equal of Shakespeare. Goethe, who produced several of his plays and read others, considered Calderón a theatrical genius and an inspired poet, claiming of *El príncipe constante*, 'I would even venture to say, if poetry vanished entirely from this world, it would be possible to reconstruct it on the basis of this play.'[15] The influence of Calderón's *El mágico prodigioso* on Goethe's *Faust* is now generally acknowledged. As a result of the esteem in which he was held, a broad selection of Calderón's works were translated – faithfully, not in approximate versions as before – acted and also published in Spanish in Germany in the early decades of the nineteenth century.

The nineteenth century witnessed renewed respect in Spain, too, for its theatrical past. Spanish scholars began to devote themselves to the task of publishing the enormous legacy of plays that the sixteenth and seventeenth centuries had bequeathed to posterity, and serious *comedia* scholarship got underway. Whereas Calderón had been the great favourite of the German Romantics, however, in Spain and elsewhere the move away from Romanticism towards Realism led to the downgrading of Calderón's refined, symbolic style in favour of what was seen as the spontaneous naturalism of Lope de Vega. At the end of the century, Spanish liberals and reformers with only a very superficial knowledge of his work turned against Calderón for reminding them too vividly, as they thought, of a Catholic and imperial past they preferred to forget, taking their authority from the great Spanish scholar Marcelino Menéndez y Pelayo who in his early twenties, in a series of lectures given in 1880 to commemorate the death of Calderón, destroyed the dramatist's reputation with a youthful impetuosity and arrogance he lived to regret. In Spain Calderón's reputation even today has still not completely recovered from this deeply misguided attack. Outside Spain, however, the twentieth-century rehabilitation of the complex, metaphorical style of the Baroque brought with it a revaluation of Calderón and an intensity of critical interest in his plays which survives to the present day.

Value judgements are rarely any longer made between the two theatrical giants of Spain's Golden Age, in many ways so different, but it is Calderón who still inspires the livelier debate and the greater volume of critical work, particularly in book form. There are a number of reasons for this, modern interests, preferences and even needs amongst them, but not unimportant is the practical consideration that the sheer size of Lope's *oeuvre* makes generalization difficult and critics understandably wary. In the second half of the twentieth century, *comedia* studies in general have flourished as never before. In recent decades theatre studies have already brought rich rewards where the Spanish drama is concerned and new developments in critical theory are inevitably and properly finding their way into *comedia* criticism. However, there are still large areas of the Spanish Golden-Age drama which need radical revaluation and others which have hardly been studied in any depth at all. Few national literatures can offer students such a fertile field not merely for new readings but for primary investigation as well. At the same time few national dramas can offer theatre directors and audiences such a rich store of virtually unknown or unacted plays. In Spain, in spite of there being no classical acting tradition, serious and often very successful efforts have been made of late to rescue Spain's great theatrical heritage from oblivion for modern theatre audiences, but elsewhere the dramatic genius of sixteenth- and seventeenth-century Spain is virtually unrecognized outside the circle of Hispanic studies. In the mid-1980s, when two of Calderón's plays, *Life is a Dream* and *The Mayor of Zalamea*, were put on in London at the Barbican and the National Theatre respectively, British theatre critics hailed the discovery of a remarkable 'new' dramatist. More recently the National Theatre's production of Lope de Vega's *Fuenteovejuna* elicited a similar response. The fact is that not just two remarkable playwrights but a remarkable theatre to all intents and purposes still awaits rediscovery.

Notes

1 The birth of the drama

1 For the medieval drama see K. Young, *The Drama of the Medieval Church* (Oxford, 1933), 2 vols; A. M. Kinghorn, *Medieval Drama* (London, 1968); R. Axton, *European Drama of the Early Middle Ages* (London, 1974); Glynne Wickham, *The Medieval Theatre* (London, 1974); W. Tydeman, *The Theatre in the Middle Ages* (Cambridge, 1978).

2 For a detailed account of these dramatic tropes in eastern Spain and the often elaborate performances with costumes, wigs, painted figures, properties, scenery and mechanical effects, see N. D. Shergold, *A History of the Spanish Stage* (Oxford, 1967), 1–25.

3 R. Lapesa, 'Sobre el *Auto de los Reyes Magos*: sus rimas anómalas y el posible origen de su autor', *Homenaje a Fritz Krüger*, II (Mendoza, 1954), 591–9.

4 *The Liturgical Drama of Medieval Spain* (Toronto, 1958).

5 *Tradición y creación en los orígenes del teatro castellano* (Madrid, 1968).

6 F. Lázaro Carreter cautiously allowed the possibility of a primitive church drama in the thirteenth and fourteenth centuries in his *Teatro medieval*, 3rd edn (Madrid, 1970), 86–90, while largely discounting its influence on the later drama. But F. Ruiz Ramón, *Historia del teatro español*, 4th edn (Madrid, 1981), 21–31, and J. L. Alborg, *Historia de la literatura española, Tomo I. Edad Media y Renacimiento*, 2nd edn (Madrid, 1972), 177–221 and 485–515, argue firmly for the existence of a medieval drama in Castile.

7 It is possible that he may just have been repeating the strictures of his canon-law sources and of papal decretals.

8 Carmen Torroja Menéndez and María Rivas Palá, *Teatro en Toledo en el siglo XV. 'Auto de la Pasión' de Alonso del Campo* (Madrid, 1977).

9 Martínez's most famous work is that known as *El corbacho*, a treatise against the sin of lust that contains *exempla* that reveal him as an impressive satirist and a very gifted stylist.

10 The contemporary poem in question is Diego de San Pedro's *La pasión trobada*. Torroja Menéndez and Rivas Palá ascribe the *Auto de la Pasión* to Alonso del

Campo, cathedral chaplain in charge of Corpus festivities in Toledo from 1481 to 1499.

11 The current view is that the author was the Franciscan Íñigo de Mendoza; see J. Rodríguez-Puértolas, 'Sobre el autor de las *Coplas de Mingo Revulgo*', *Homenaje a A. Rodríguez-Moñino*, 2 vols. (Madrid, 1966), II, 131–42. For a fascinating account of the connection between the *Coplas* and the constitutional dramatic ritual of the day, see A. Mackay, 'Ritual and Propaganda in Fifteenth-Century Castile', *Past and Present*, 107 (1985), 1–43.

12 For an introduction to Encina and his work, see Henry W. Sullivan, *Juan del Encina* (Boston, 1976).

13 R. B. Williams, *The Staging of Plays in the Spanish Peninsula Prior to 1555* (Iowa, 1935), uses the evidence of the texts themselves to establish the use of fixed or unlocalized scenes, properties, costumes, etc. in the early drama.

14 Sullivan, *Juan del Encina*, 79–81.

15 B. W. Wardropper, 'Metamorphosis in the Theater of Juan del Encina', *SPhil*, 59 (1962), 41–51.

16 For an introduction to Fernández, see John Lihani, *Lucas Fernández* (New York, 1973) and *El lenguaje de Lucas Fernández. Estudio del dialecto sayagués* (Bogotá, 1973).

17 The proximity of its date of composition to 1492, the year in which Spanish Jewry was given the choice between compulsory conversion to Christianity or banishment, probably goes a long way towards explaining the play's vehement anti-Semitism.

18 The *Celestina*'s original title was *Comedia de Calisto y Melibea*, changed ten years later to *Tragicomedia de Calisto y Melibea*. Later in the sixteenth century the work became known by the name of the bawd/witch Celestina who helps Calisto to seduce Melibea – a reflection of how the emphasis in reader interest in the book had changed.

19 John Brotherton, *The 'Pastor-Bobo' in the Spanish Theatre Before the Time of Lope de Vega* (London, 1975), 153–4. This work studies the changing role of the figure of the comic rustic.

20 All but five of his works were published by his son in 1562 in mutilated form after Inquisition censorship in 1536; the other five (three of which are now lost) had been banned. By 1747 fourteen of his plays had been suppressed. See Stephen Reckert, *Gil Vicente: Espíritu y Letra. I Estudios* (Madrid, 1977).

21 Laurence Keates, *The Court Theatre of Gil Vicente* (Lisbon, 1962), 88.

22 On this play see Thomas R. Hart Jr., 'Gil Vicente's "Auto de la Sibila Casandra"', *HR*, 26 (1958), 35–51; I. S. Révah, '"L'Auto de la Sibylle Cassandre" de Gil Vicente', *HR*, 27 (1959), 167–93; Leo Spitzer, 'The Artistic Unity of Gil Vicente's "Auto de la Sibila Casandra"', *HR*, 27 (1959), 56–77.

23 See Melveena McKendrick, *Woman and Society in the Spanish Drama of the Golden Age* (Cambridge, 1974), 45–51.

24 See Thomas R. Hart's introduction to his edition of the plays, *Gil Vicente. Obras dramáticas castellanas* (Madrid, 1962), xxv–xxxvi.

25 For a discussion of the role of the garden see Dámaso Alonso's introduction to his edition of the play (Madrid, 1942).

26 Reckert, *Gil Vicente*, 41–5, points out that tourneys were often preceded by processions of mummers who announced the coming festivities.

27 See T. P. Waldron's introduction to his edition of the play (Manchester, 1959) and also Hart's introduction to his edition of the Castilian plays.

28 Courtly love and the chivalric ethic exerted enormous power over the European imagination but were by no means invariably taken seriously. Cf. Leonard Forster, *The Icy Fire: Five Studies in European Petrarchism* (Cambridge, 1969): 'what for Petrarch himself was deadly serious became for his successors a game, which like all games can be serious or not as circumstances require ... It was surely this flexibility which accounted for its enormous popularity for so long' (66–7).

29 Waldron, *Amadís de Gaula*, 11.

30 For an introduction, with bibliography, to Torres Naharro, see John Lihani, *Bartolomé de Torres Naharro* (Boston, 1979).

31 See J. E. Gillet's magisterial edition of Torres Naharro's plays, *Propalladia and Other Works of Bartolomé Torres Naharro*, 4 vols. (Bryn Mawr, 1943–61), vol. III, 22–7 and vol. IV, 426–7.

32 Literally 'stage' (of a journey), 'span' or 'shift'. Gillet (IV, 36) thinks the term was Torres Naharro's own invention. Torres Naharro justifies it by saying that the acts seem to him to be like resting places (he presumably means the pauses between the acts) which allow the players to perform better and aid the audience's concentration.

33 The Spanish humanist Juan de Valdés, in his *Diálogo de la lengua*, 1535, criticized Torres for not himself adhering to the rule of decorum, probably because the language of some of Torres's gentlemen, even gentlewomen, is rather more robust than Valdés would have deemed fitting.

34 See John Lihani, 'Play–Audience Relationships in Bartolomé de Torres Naharro', *BCom*, 31 (1979), 95–102.

35 The device of using the adjectival form of the subject or, more commonly, the chief character's name, for his title was Torres Naharro's invention.

36 The conjectural chronology is that of Gillet, IV, 47a.

37 J. V. Falconieri suggests that Torres Naharro might have derived the idea of the point of honour from Boccaccio's *Decameron*, no. 6; see 'La situación de Torres Naharro en la historia literaria', *Hispanófila*, 21 (957), 32–40. But the Spaniard's concern for his honour is amply documented in the Middle Ages.

38 Gillet, II, 285, lines 253–4.

39 This play and Torres's last, the *Comedia Aquilana*, were written after the Naples *Propalladia* of 1517, but *Calamita* appeared in the Seville edition of 1520 and *Aquilana* in the Seville edition of 1526.

40 For a detailed examination of possible mutual debts see Gillet, 'Torres Naharro and the Spanish Drama of the Sixteenth Century', *Homenaje a A. Bonilla y San Martín*, vol. II (Madrid, 1930), 437–68; and Falconieri, 'La situación de Torres Naharro en la historia literaria'.

41 Carolina Michaëlis de Vasconcellos believes Vicente's *Exortacão da guerra* was inspired by the *Comedia soldadesca*, *Notas Vicentinas*, IV (Lisbon, 1949), 360.

42 For example, Jaime de Güete, Agustín Ortiz, Francisco de las Natas, Bartolomé Palau, Cristóbal Castillejo; for a full list of plays and authors see A. Bonilla y San Martín, *Los Bacantes* (Madrid, 1921), 127; and Falconieri, 'La situación de Torres Naharro en la historia literaria', 38. The dramatist Juan de la Cueva would later mention in his *Ejemplar poético* six learned Sevillian dramatists of the first half of the sixteenth century of whose plays nothing at all is known.

43 See Bonilla y San Martín, *Los Bacantes*, 108, for a list. Amongst the most notable of the plays modelled on *La Celestina* was the anonymous *Comedia Thebaida* published in 1521; see the edition by G. D. Trotter and Keith Whinnom (London, 1969). The poet Garcilaso de la Vega must probably count as the most distinguished pastoral dramatist, since his three eclogues are all declaimable, even actable, and the second was almost certainly intended for performance of a sort (see R. Lapesa, *La trayectoria poética de Garcilaso*, 2nd edn (Madrid, 1968), 110–13).

44 For the 1548 play, see p. 46.

45 Ed. J. E. Gillet (Princeton, 1932).

46 Critics cannot agree whether any direct influence is detectable or even feasible; see, for example, F. Weber de Kurlat, 'Gil Vicente y Diego Sánchez de Badajoz. A propósito del *Auto da Sibila Casandra* y de la *Farsa del juego de cañas*', *Filología*, 9 (1963), 127; and 'Relaciones literarias; *La Celestina*, Diego Sánchez de Badajoz y Gil Vicente', *Philological Quarterly*, 51 (1972), 105–22.

47 Ed. F. Weber de Kurlat (Buenos Aires, 1968).

48 See J.-M. Díez Borque's introduction to his edition of the *Farsas* (Madrid, 1978).

49 B. W. Wardropper, *Introducción al teatro religioso del Siglo de Oro: la evolución del 'auto sacramental' 1500–1648* (Madrid, 1953), 185–6.

50 *Introducción al teatro religioso*, 202.

51 *Colección de autos, farsas y coloquios del siglo XVI*, ed. L. Rouanet (Madrid, 1901), 4 vols.

52 See J. López Prudencio, *Diego Sánchez de Badajoz. Estudio crítico, biográfico y bibliográfico* (Madrid, 1951), 235ff.

53 For his *Historia de la gloriosa Santa Orosta* Palau even had recourse to a subject from Spanish history, possibly the first playwright ever to do so.

54 Described in Juan Cristóbal Calvete de Estrella's *El felicissimo viaje del muy alto y muy poderoso Principe don Philippe* (Antwerp, 1552). See also p. 46.

55 See, for example, J. Jacquot (ed.), *Les Fêtes de la Renaissance*, 2 vols (Paris, 1956–60); and Roy Strong, *Splendour at Court: Renaissance Spectacle and Illusion* (London, 1973).

56 J. Sánchez Arjona, *Noticias referentes a los anales del teatro en Sevilla desde Lope de Rueda hasta fines del siglo XVII* (Seville, 1898), 47.

57 See W. H. Shoemaker, *The Multiple Stage in Spain during the Fifteenth and Sixteenth Centuries* (Princeton, 1935).

2 From drama to theatre

1 See J. García Soriano, *El teatro universitario y humanístico en España* (Toledo, 1945), 13.

2 In his dedication of his play *Virtud, pobreza y mujer* (*Virtue, Poverty and Woman*).

3 Agustín de Rojas's reference in the *Loa de la comedia* in his *Viaje entretenido* (1603) to Encina's 'three eclogues' clearly indicates that we now have access to much early drama that had been lost to sight by the second half of the sixteenth century.

4 See Cervantes's prologue to his *Ocho comedias y ocho entremeses* (1615) and Rufo's 'Alabanza de la comedia' in *Las seiscientas apotegmas* (1596).

5 Andrés Muñoz gives a brief description of the performances in *Viaje de Felipe II a Inglaterra* (Zaragoza, 1554).

6 See F. González Ollé's introductions to his editions of Rueda's plays: *Eufemia; Armelina* (Salamanca, 1967); *Los engañados; Medora* (Madrid, 1973); *Pasos* (Madrid, 1983).

7 Two religious *autos* he is known to have produced, *El hijo pródigo* (*The Prodigal Son* – Corpus, Seville, 1559) and *Naval y Abigail* (Corpus, Toledo, 1561) are sometimes attributed to him.

8 For the debt owed by Rueda and his contemporaries to Italian sources, see Othón Arróniz, *La influencia italiana en el nacimiento de la comedia española* (Madrid, 1969).

9 In his prologue to the *Ocho comedias* (1615).

10 See N. D. Shergold, 'Ganassa and the "Commedia dell'Arte" in Sixteenth-Century Spain', *MLR*, 51 (1956), p. 359.

11 Arróniz, *La influencia italiana*, 238–9 and Narciso Alonso Cortés, *El teatro en Valladolid* (Madrid, 1935).

12 H. A. Rennert's *The Spanish Stage in the Time of Lope de Vega* (New York, 1909), 141, cites two agreements of 1584 by actors and their wives with actor-managers which suggest that women were involved in some way in performances.

13 Cervantes says of Navarro: 'He increased the stage furnishings somewhat ... he brought the musicians, who hitherto used to sing behind the curtain at the back, out into the theatre; he removed the players' beards, for until then no one acted without a false beard and ... he invented stage machinery, clouds, thunder and lightning, fights and battles, though these did not reach the sublime heights they are now at.' Prologue to the *Ocho comedias* (1615).

14 This practice later on became illegal, but it still seems to have continued; see chapter 7 and Postscript.

15 For example in some of Lope's earlier wife-murder plays. See Melveena McKendrick, 'La victoria de la honra and La locura por la honra: Towards a Reassessment of Lope's Treatment of Conjugal Honour', *Studies in Golden-Age Drama, BHS*, 64 (1987), 1–14.

16 See García Soriano, *El teatro universitario y humanístico*, 13.

17 See Esperabé Arteaga, *Historia de la Universidad de Salamanca* (Salamanca, 1914), I, 203.

18 For the Jesuit drama in Spain see García Soriano, *El teatro universitario y humanístico*; and 'El teatro de colegio en España', *BRAE*, 14 (1927), 243–77, 374–411, 535–65, 620–50; 15 (1928), 62–93, 145–87, 396–446, 651–69; 16 (1929), 80–106, 223–43; 19 (1932), 485–98, 608–24. For the Jesuit drama in Europe see *Dramaturge et Société: rapports entre l'oeuvre théâtrale, son interprétation et son public au XVIe et XVIIe siècles*, ed. J. Jacquot, 2 vols. (Paris, 1968), vol. II; particularly, for Spain, L. E. Roux, 'Cent ans d'expérience théâtrale dans les collèges de la Compagnie de Jésus en Espagne', 479–523.

19 See Shergold, *A History of the Spanish Stage*, 173.

20 The other best-known sixteenth-century Jesuit dramatist was P. Juan Bonifacio. The best-known play, however, was the five-act, anonymous *Tragedia de San Hermenegildo*, presented at the college in Seville.

21 So successful was the Jesuit drama throughout Europe that in 1599 the decree *Ratio studiorum* attempted to regularize theatrical activities in Jesuit schools and halt the tendency towards secularization.

22 See José Pellicer y Tobar, *Avisos históricos*, ed. A. Valladares de Sotomayor, *Semanario erudito* (Madrid, 1788), XXXI, newsletter of 2 October 1640, 218–19, quoted by García Soriano, *El teatro universitario y humanístico*, 397. For more details see José Simón Díaz, *Historia del Colegio Imperial de Madrid* (Madrid, 1952), 2 vols.

23 See N. D. Shergold, 'Juan de la Cueva and the Early Theatres of Seville', *BHS*, 32 (1955), 1–7; and J. Sánchez Arjona, *El teatro en Sevilla en los siglos XVI y XVII* (Madrid, 1887).

24 For the literary, social and political life of Seville at the time see A. Coster, *Fernando de Herrera (el Divino) 1534–1597* (Paris, 1908); for Mal Lara himself see F. Sánchez Escribano, *Juan de Mal Lara, su vida y sus obras* (New York, 1941).

25 *Ejemplar poético*, III, 697–702 and 532–7.

26 Richard F. Glenn, *Juan de la Cueva* (Boston, 1973), points out that Cueva's plays were in demand even in the New World.

27 The dramatist Virués earned more praise from Cervantes and Lope de Vega over many years than any other early dramatist, yet it is not at all clear that Lope even knew his works. See John G. Weiger, *Cristóbal de Virués* (Boston, 1978), 27–31.

28 Marcel Bataillon's contention (reprinted in translation in *Varia lección de clásicos españoles* (Madrid, 1964), 206–13) that Lope's failure to mention Cueva suggests that he was a totally insignificant playwright, was an overreaction to the traditional view of Cueva as initiator of the national drama. Cueva was certainly praised in other contemporary reminiscences about the theatre, for example by Cervantes in *La Galatea* and by A. de Rojas in the 'Comedia de la loa' in *El viaje entretenido* (1604). It is hard to believe that all Cueva's innovations were made by other playwrights whose works just happen not to have survived. Chance is not that selective. Even if Cueva in some instances followed the trends rather than

set them, he is the only representative we know of a stage crucial to the formation of the national theatre. For two opposed views of Cueva's relations to Lope and the *comedia nueva* see R. Froldi, *Lope de Vega y la formación de la comedia* (Salamanca, 1968) and H. López Morales, *Tradición y creación*, 24n.

29 S. G. Morley, 'Strophes in the Spanish Drama before Lope de Vega', *Homenaje ofrecido a Menéndez Pidal*, 3 vols. (Madrid, 1925), I, 505–31. Interestingly, Cueva, unlike Lope, did not use the ballad metre, presumably because he considered this popular form too humble for the art of drama.

30 E. S. Morby, 'The Influence of Senecan Tragedy in the Plays of Juan de la Cueva', *SPhil*, 34 (1937), 383–91.

31 If A. I. Watson's thesis is correct: see *Juan de la Cueva and the Portuguese Succession* (London, 1971).

32 Plot summaries were added subsequently for publication.

33 But no more a prototype for Don Juan Tenorio than the play itself is a forerunner of the *capa y espada* plays – both claims have been made – though in each case there are superficial resemblances.

34 See B. W. Wardropper, 'Humanismo y teatro nacional en Juan de la Cueva', *Historia y crítica de la literatura española*, ed. F. Rico, II, *Siglos de Oro: Renacimiento*, ed. F. López de Estrada (Barcelona, 1980).

35 This is not to say that there are not occasional examples of these in the *comedia*.

36 For their controversial relationship to similar plays by the Portuguese dramatist Antonio Ferreira, see A. Hermenegildo, *La tragedia en el Renacimiento español* (Barcelona, 1973), 169–75.

37 J. P. Wickersham Crawford, *Spanish Drama Before Lope de Vega* (revised edn, Philadelphia, 1967), 161–4.

38 See Cristóbal de Virués's prologue to his plays published in 1609, in *Poetas dramáticos valencianos*, ed E. J. Martínez, 2 vols. (Madrid, 1929), I, l-lii, n. 1. Also Rey de Artieda's prologue to *Los amantes*, p. xxvi.

39 *La tragedia en el Renacimiento español*, 403–17.

40 R. Froldi, *Lope de Vega y la formación de la comedia*, 94–5, objects to the grouping of playwrights whose plays are in many ways very diverse. It remains the case, however, that the group did all produce tragedies, whereas the popular tradition did not, that they were all self-conscious aspiring writers who believed in the controls of art, and that they shared a sense subsequently of having been rejected for this reason by the commercial theatre.

41 See H. Mérimée, *Spectacles et Comédiens à Valencia (1580–1630)* (Toulouse and Paris, 1913), and Shergold, *A History of the Spanish Stage*, 195.

42 See for example the prologue to Virués's *La infelice Marcela*, *Poetas dramáticos valencianos*, I, 118.

43 Along with some other critics Hermenegildo (200) thinks that Rey de Artieda's reference in his prologue to the play to his having recently read Bermúdez's *Nises* (published 1577) indicates that *Los amantes* was written as early as 1578. However, this presupposes that the prologue was written at the same time as the text of *Los amantes*, rather than for publication, which is more likely. Further-

more, Rey de Artieda gives no indication as to how long after the publication of Bermúdez's plays he read them.

44 The more famous play of this period on this subject is Tirso de Molina's *Los amantes de Teruel*; see Carmen I. de Ebersole, 'Andrés Rey de Artieda y *Los amantes de Teruel*', *Hispanófila*, 41 (1971), 13–21 for a comparison. The best known dramatization in Spanish, however, is Juan Eugenio Hartzenbusch's nineteenth-century *Los amantes de Teruel*.

45 For example, Rinaldo Froldi, *Lope de Vega y la formación de la comedia*, Hermenegildo, *La tragedia en el Renacimiento español*, and John G. Weiger, *Cristóbal de Virués* (Boston, 1978).

46 This is the consensus of opinion; the outside dates suggested are 1575 and 1590. It seems unlikely to me that the play which we are fairly certain was his last, *La infelice Marcela*, was written as late as 1590. Since it is both different from and yet very similar to Lope's new style, and since it found little favour with the public, it is probable that it coincided with the period when Lope was exerting a powerful influence but had not quite swept all before him (1584–6). Even if we allow for a time delay in case Virués was not directly in touch with the theatre in Madrid, a date later than 1587 or 1588 is not very convincing.

47 Weiger has argued that Formio and Felina are only apparently low-born and are in fact of noble descent, but he does not offer any explanation for such a curious complication. See *Cristóbal de Virués*, and *Hacia la comedia: de los valencianos a Lope* (Madrid, 1978), 92–7.

48 Cueva had exploited the ballads, as we saw, but used a different technique, inserting lines from them into his *redondillas* – eight-syllabled lines rhyming abba.

49 Hermenegildo (211–12) thinks the plays ought to be read against the background of contemporary court life, particularly the Escobedo scandal.

50 By Othón Arróniz, *Teatros y escenarios del Siglo de Oro* (Madrid, 1977), 173–83.

51 In his *Arte nuevo de hacer comedias*. Although it is generally accepted that Virués and Lope did become personally acquainted, Lope was probably going on hearsay, for he was not exiled to Valencia until 1588 and Virués's plays were published *after* the *Arte nuevo de hacer comedias*. A three-act play had been written as early as 1551, Avendaño's *Comedia Florisea*.

52 Seen by Hermenegildo (211–12) as a reflection, perhaps, of the manipulations and power-politicking at Philip II's court of the Princess of Eboli. For Virués's women see also Cecilia Vennard Sargent, *A Study of the Dramatic Works of Cristóbal de Virués* (New York, 1930); and Melveena McKendrick, *Woman and Society*, 61–72.

53 By J. P. Wickersham Crawford, 'Notes on the Tragedies of Lupercio Leonardo de Argensola', *RR*, 5 (1914), 31–44.

54 O. H. Green, *Vida y obras de Lupercio Leonardo de Argensola* (Zaragoza, 1945), 25, 103.

55 In his prologue to his *Ocho comedias y ocho entremeses* (1615).

56 See F. Ruiz Ramón, *Historia del teatro español*, 116.

57 Edward H. Friedman, *The Unifying Concept: Approaches to the Structure of Cervantes's Comedias* (York, South Carolina, 1981) sees the unifying principle in Cervantes's plays as being a 'mental unity', that is a thematic or conceptual connection.

58 See Melveena McKendrick, *Cervantes* (Boston, 1980), 60–89.

59 *Adjunta al Parnaso (Postscript to Parnassus)*, 1614. The play in question was *La confusa (Comedy of Confusion)* which he contracted on 5 March to supply, along with another play, to the theatre company manager Gaspar de Porras in Madrid.

60 *Historia del teatro español*, 108.

61 See J. Sánchez Arjona, *Noticias*, 50.

62 Prologue to *La infelice Marcela*.

63 See the discussion on the theatre between the Canon and the Priest in *Don Quixote*, chap. xlviii.

64 'Epístola a don Antonio Hurtado de Mendoza', *Colección escogida de obras no dramáticas*, Biblioteca de Autores Españoles, XXXVIII, 401.

65 From 'Al libro', in *Coro febeo de romances historiales*, quoted by Margarete Newels, *Los géneros dramáticos en las Poéticas del Siglo de Oro* (London, 1974), 137, no. 31.

66 In spite of some recent objections (e.g. Froldi, *Lope de Vega ya la formación de la comedia*, 43), I feel there is a useful distinction to be made between the largely unself-conscious drama produced for entertainment (Rueda et al., the *commedia dell'arte*) and that with self-confessed literary aspirations (Cueva, Virués and the other tragedians). It was a distinction which writers at the time were conscious of and the second group shared in due course a common sense of rejection.

67 E. Juliá Martínez in his introduction to *Poetas dramáticos valencianos* was one of the first to suggest that the Valencians were a significant group worthy of study in their own right. More recently the cudgels have been taken up by Froldi, *Lope de Vega y la formación de la comedia*; and, in more restrained fashion, by F. Lázaro Carreter, *Lope de Vega: Introducción a su vida y obra* (Salamanca, 1966), 169–78 and by John G. Weiger, *The Valencian Dramatists of Spain's Golden Age* (Boston, 1976) and *Hacia la comedia*.

68 See the testimony of the actor-manager Gaspar de Porras quoted in H. A. Rennert and A. Castro, *Vida de Lope de Vega* (Madrid, 1919), 56.

69 S. Griswold Morley and C. Bruerton, *The Chronology of Lope de Vega's 'Comedias'* (New York, 1940).

70 Froldi's blunt assertion (*Lope de Vega y la formación de la comedia*, 125) that Tárrega was the real initiator of the *comedia* is just not substantiated.

71 Froldi points out that Baltasar Gracián in his *Agudeza y arte de ingenio* (1648, Discurso XLV) refers to Tárrega in a way that suggests he preceded Lope and mentions his inventiveness and metrical skill. But this is hardly the same as crediting him with the invention of the new genre. Gracián's random observations suggest a very hazy knowledge of the early theatre. Other writers of the period, including Cervantes, lumped Tárrega indiscriminately with the other Lopistas.

72 C. López Martínez, *Teatros y comediantes sevillanos del siglo XVI* (Seville, 1940), 31.

73 Cervantes in his *Ocho comedias* praised his discrimination and inventiveness, Gracián his inventiveness and metrical flair (n. 71). Most of the other eulogies are unspecific, as was the general custom.

3   The *comedia*; some definitions and problems

1 See Oscar M. Villarejo, 'Lista II de *El Peregrino*: la lista maestra del año 1604 de los 448 títulos de las comedias de Lope de Vega', *Segismundo*, 3 (1966), 57–89.

2 See S. G. Morley and C. Bruerton, 'How many *comedias* did Lope de Vega write?', *Hisp*, 19 (1936), 217–34.

3 C. V. Aubrun, *La comédie espagnole (1600–1680)* (Paris, 1966), p. v.

4 Arróniz, *La influencia italiana*, 305–7; Carmen Bravo-Villasante, *La mujer vestida de hombre en el teatro español* (Madrid, 1955). See also Juana de José Prades, *Teoría sobre los personajes de la comedia nueva en cinco dramaturgos* (Madrid, 1971).

5 Donald Larson, *The Honor Plays of Lope de Vega* (Cambridge, Mass, 1977); Melveena McKendrick, 'Honour/Vengeance in the Spanish *comedia*: A Case of Mimetic Transference?', *MLR*, 79 (1984), 313–35.

6 R. Schevill, *The Dramatic Art of Lope de Vega* (Berkeley, California, 1918), 19.

7 It is clear from the *Genealogía, origen y noticias de los comediantes de España*, ed. N. D. Shergold and J. E. Varey (London, 1985), that the theatre companies did occasionally hire middle-aged women to play minor roles, but since the roles do not normally call for an older woman it was presumably a question either of a shortage of younger actresses or of special circumstances – favours, relations, etc.

8 Thornton Wilder, 'Lope, Pinedo, Some Child Actors and a Lion', *RPhil*, 7 (1953), 19–26; S. E. Leavitt, 'Lions in Early Spanish Literature and on the Spanish Stage', *Hisp*, 44 (1961), 272–6.

9 A. A. Parker's seminal essay *The Approach to the Spanish Drama of the Golden Age*, first published in 1957 (Diamante, VI) but revised as 'The Spanish Drama of the Golden Age: A Method of Analysis and Interpretation', *The Great Playwrights*, ed. Eric Bentley (New York, 1970), vol. 1, insists on the primacy of theme over plot in the Spanish *comedia*. The relationship between theme and plot is governed for Parker by the principles of causality and poetic justice. The second of these remains a bone of contention, unlike the rest of his analysis which has met with general acceptance, particularly with regard to Calderón. The inner cohesion of the *comedia* has been described in different ways. The term 'thematic structure' was used by R. Pring-Mill to describe the critical emphasis of Parker and other British *calderonistas* in 'Los calderonistas de habla inglesa y *La vida es sueño*: métodos del análisis temático-estructural', *Litterae Hispanae et Lusitanae*, ed. H. Flasche (Munich, 1968), 369–413. B. W. Wardropper, 'The Implicit Craft of the Spanish "Comedia"', *Studies in Spanish Literature*

of the Golden Age Presented to Edward M. Wilson, ed. R. O. Jones (London, 1973), 339–56, stresses what he calls 'poetic coherence', by which he means the dramatic elaboration of a poetic idea. H. W. Sullivan has recently maintained that the neo-Aristotelian unities of time, action and place were replaced in Spain by unities of theme, structure and imagery, 'Vélez de Guevara's *Reinar después de morir* as a Model of Classical Spanish Tragedy' in *Antigüedad y Actualidad en Luis Vélez de Guevara: Estudios críticos*, ed. C. George Peale (Philadelphia, 1983), 144.

10 *Arte nuevo de hacer comedias*, 323–6.

11 The study of the implications of the *corrales'* dependence on the auditory is still fairly new. J. E. Varey's various studies of the texts in performance have blazed the trail; Weiger's recent study of the Valencian dramatists, *Hacia la comedia*, emphasizes this aspect too.

12 The failure to do this has generated much sterile controversy in recent decades about the nature of the *comedia*. Explicitly involved in the controversy have been A. G. Reichenberger, 'The Uniqueness of the *Comedia*', *HR*, 27 (1959), 303–16; Eric Bentley with his answer to this, 'The Universality of the *Comedia*', *HR*, 38 (1970), 147–62; and Reichenberger again with his reply, 'The Uniqueness of the *Comedia*', *HR*, 38 (1970), 163–73. But much recent commentary implicitly engages with the debate, which in the last analysis concerns the universal value and status of the *comedia*, specifically with regard to its attitude to tragedy and its relationship to establishment values. Both issues will be considered in due course.

13 F. Sánchez Escribano y A. Porqueras Mayo, *Preceptiva dramática española del Renacimiento y el Barroco*, 2nd edn (Madrid, 1972), 170.

14 E. S. Morby, 'Some Observations on *Tragedia* and *Tragicomedia* in Lope', *HR*, 40 (1943), 185–209. With regard to the inconsistent use of the label *tragicomedia*, there is no very obvious reason, for example, for calling *Peribáñez y el comendador de Ocaña* one but denying the label to the two other plays on peasant honour, *Fuenteovejuna* and *El mejor alcalde el rey*.

15 Michael J. Ruggiero, 'The term *Comedia* in Spanish Dramaturgy', *RPhil*, 84 (1972), 277–96, maintains that Spaniards were clearly fully aware of the traditional division between tragedy and comedy from the fifteenth century onwards.

16 The term was jokingly coined by Plautus himself when criticized for calling his *Amphitryon* a 'comoedia', in spite of the fact that it had gods in it.

17 Ruggiero, 'The term *Comedia* in Spanish Dramaturgy', points out that the Spanish dramatist Ricardo de Turia in plagiarizing Guarini's treatise for his defense of the *comedia* (*Apologético de las comedias españolas*, 1616), left out all reference to endings.

18 The terms are Lionel Abel's in *Metatheatre: A New View of Dramatic Form* (New York, 1963), 58.

19 *Cymbeline* was reckoned among the tragedies of Shakespeare in the folio of 1623 and *Richard III* was called a tragedy at the time. *Romeo and Juliet* has always

been considered a tragedy in spite of the fact that its agonists are not lofty figures.

20 For example by Abel, *Metatheatre*, who believes *Macbeth* to be the only true tragedy because Macbeth and Macduff are the only true daemons in Shakespeare, that is, individuals propelled beyond the ordinarily human by suffering.

21 Walter Kerr's words in his plea for a more encompassing approach to tragedy in *Tragedy and Comedy* (London, 1967), 7–8.

22 *Principles of Tragedy. A Rational Examination of the Tragic Concept of Life and Literature* (Coral Gables, Florida, 1968).

23 Northrop Frye's paraphrase of Aristotle in *Anatomy of Criticism* (Princeton, NJ, 1957).

24 Tragedies which ended 'in prosperity' were regarded at the time as a 'sell-out' to popular taste. See Francisco Cascales, *Tablas poéticas* (pub. 1617), ed. B. Brancaforte (Madrid, 1975), 192.

25 See E. S. Morby, 'Some Observations on *Tragedia* and *Tragicomedia* in Lope de Vega'. Reichenberger, 'The Uniqueness of the *Comedia*', denies true tragic status even to *El castigo sin venganza*, declared by Donald Larson, *The Honor Plays of Lope de Vega* (131), to project a tragic vision comparable to that of Sophocles, Euripedes or Shakespeare.

26 *Religion and Literature* (London, 1971).

27 Clifford Leech, *Tragedy* (London, 1969) goes as far as to say that 'the concept of tragedy, as it is now generally understood, is a creation of the last two centuries' (p. 23).

28 Leicester Bradner, 'From Petrarch to Shakespeare' in *The Renaissance* (New York: Harper and Row, 1962), 97–119, points out that this propensity for the hero to prepare his own suffering is a distinctive feature of modern (as opposed to classical) tragedy, including Marlowe and Shakespeare.

29 Interestingly enough, Abel, *Metatheatre*, believes that Shakespeare's intended tragedies, *Macbeth* apart, fail because they are too naturalisic and their protagonists too normally human.

30 See Parker's 'Towards a Definition of Calderonian tragedy', *BHS*, 39 (1962), 222–37, and *'El médico de su honra* as Tragedy', *Hispanófila Especial*, num. 2 (1975), 1–23. Gwynne Edwards, *The Prison and the Labyrinth: Studies in Calderonian Tragedy* (Cardiff, 1978), opposes Parker's view of the causal nature of Calderonian tragedy with an interpretation which sees chance or Fate, rather than responsibility, as the major determinant in Calderón's tragedies. Other studies of general import on Golden-Age tragedy have been: G. Bradbury, 'Tragedy and Tragicomedy in the Theatre of Lope de Vega', *BHS*, 58 (1981), 103–11; Gwynne Edwards, 'Calderón's *La hija del aire* and the Classical Type of Tragedy', *BHS*, 44 (1967), 161–94; C. A. Jones, 'Brecht y el drama del Siglo de Oro en España', *Segismundo*, 3 (1965), 41–54, and 'Tragedy in the Golden Age' in *The Drama of the Renaissance: Essays for Leicester Bradner*, ed. Elmer M. Blistein (Providence, RI, 1970), 100–7; R. R. MacCurdy, 'The "Problem" of Spanish Golden-Age Tragedy', in *The Tragic Fall: Don Álvaro de Luna and other*

Favourites in Spanish Golden-Age Drama (Chapel Hill, 1978), 17–37; A. G. Reichenberger, 'Thoughts about Tragedy in the Spanish Theatre of the Golden Age', *Hispanófila Especial*, 1 (1974), 39–45, J. M. Ruano de la Haza, 'Hacia una nueva definición de la tragedia calderoniana', *BCom*, 35 (1983), no. 2, 165–80; F. Ruiz Ramón, *Calderón y la tragedia* (Madrid, 1984).

31 Robert Ter Horst's 'From Comedy to Tragedy: Calderón and the New Tragedy', *MLN*, 92 (1977), 181–201, is the most interesting contribution to the subject of Spanish tragedy to have appeared for some years.

4 Lope de Vega

1 For Lope's life see H. A. Rennert and A. Castro, *Vida de Lope de Vega*. His correspondence is published in *Epistolario de Lope de Vega*, ed. A. G. de Amezúa (Madrid, 1935–43). See also F. Lázaro Carreter, *Lope de Vega. Introducción a su vida y obra*.

2 See, for example, J. F. Montesinos, *Estudios sobre Lope de Vega* (Mexico, 1951); J. F. Gatti (ed.), *El teatro de Lope de Vega y su tiempo* (Buenos Aires, 1962); Donald R. Larson, *The Honor Plays of Lope de Vega*; Manuel Criado de Val (ed.), *Lope de Vega y los orígenes del teatro español*, *Actas del primer congreso internacional sobre Lope de Vega* (Madrid, 1981).

3 See, for example, N. Salomon, *Recherches sur le thème paysan dans la 'comedia' de Lope de Vega* (Bordeaux, 1965); V. A. Dixon, 'The Symbolism of *Peribáñez*', *BHS*, 43 (1966), 11–24, and his introduction to his edition of the play in Tamesis Texts (London, 1980); J. M. Ruano de la Haza, 'Malicia campesina y la ambigüedad esencial de *Peribáñez y el Comendador de Ocaña* de Lope', *Hispanófila*, 84 (1985), 21–30; J. E. Varey, 'The Essential Ambiguity in Lope de Vega's *Peribáñez*: Theme and Staging', *Theatre Research International*, 1 (1976), 157–78; and E. M. Wilson, 'Images et structures dans *Peribáñez*', *BHisp*, 51 (1949), 125–59.

4 Amongst the many interesting studies on the play are: A. Almasov, 'Fuenteovejuna y el honor villanesco en el teatro de Lope de Vega', *Cuadernos hispanoamericanos*, 161–2 (1963); E. Forastieri Braschi, 'Fuenteovejuna y la justificación', *Revista de Estudios Hispánicos, Puerto Rico*, 2 (1972), 89–99; J. B. Hall, 'Theme and Structure in Lope's *Fuenteovejuna*', *FMLS*, 10 (1974), 57–66; William C. McCrary, '*Fuenteovejuna*: Its Platonic Vision and Execution', *SPhil*, 58 (1961), 179–92; J. A. Madrigal, 'Fuenteovejuna y los conceptos de metateatro y psicodrama: un ensayo sobre la formación de la conciencia en el protagonista', *BCom*, 31 (1979), 15–23; G. W. Ribbans, 'The Meaning and Structure of Lope's *Fuenteovejuna*', *BHS*, 31 (1954), 150–70.

5 See Javier Herrero's 'The New Monarchy: A Structural Interpretation of *Fuenteovejuna*', *Revista Hispánica Moderna*, 36 (1970–1), 173–85, which gives a useful résumé of other interpretations.

6 See E. M. W. Tillyard, *The Elizabethan World Picture* (London, 1943).

7 See J.-M. Díez Borque, 'Estructura social de la comedia de Lope: a propósito de

"El mejor alcalde, el rey'", *Arbor*, 85 (1973), 121–34; and J. E. Varey, 'Kings and Judges: Lope de Vega's *El mejor alcalde, el rey*', *Themes in Drama*, ed. James Redmond (London, 1979), 37–58.

8 The label is used by Francisco Bances Candamo in his late seventeenth-century treatise *Theatro de los theatros de los passados y presentes siglos*, ed. Duncan W. Moir (London, 1970). Bances's overall division of the Spanish drama into two – love plays and historical plays – is far too crude.

9 For a different interpretation of the play as an affirmation of harmony, see J. E. Varey, 'Towards an interpretation of Lope de Vega's *El villano en su rincón*', *Studies in Spanish Literature of the Golden Age Presented to E. M. Wilson*, ed. R. O. Jones (London, 1973), 315–37. M. Bataillon, 'El villano en su rincón', reprinted in *Varia lección de clásicos españoles* (Madrid, 1964), 329–72, and P. Halkhoree, 'Lope de Vega's *El villano en su rincón*: An Emblematic Play', *Romance Notes*, 14 (1972), 1–5, discuss the play's possible emblematic significance in the context of contemporary politics. See also E. W. Hesse's 'The Sense of Lope de Vega's *El villano en su rincón*', *SPhil*, 57 (1960), 165–77, reprinted in *Análisis e interpretación de la comedia* (Madrid, 1970), 30–42, for a discussion of the role of love in the play.

10 For Lope's preoccupation with the effect of self-interest on love see A. Trueblood, *Experience and Artistic Expression in Lope de Vega* (Cambridge, Mass., 1974), especially 520–8.

11 See Lawrence Stone, *The Family, Sex and Marriage in England, 1500–1800* (London, 1977).

12 See, for example, Donald R. Larson, '*La dama boba* and the comic sense of life', *RF*, 85 (1973), 41–62; and B. W. Wardropper, 'Lope's *La dama boba* and Baroque Comedy', *BCom*, 13 (1961), 1–3.

13 See Melveena McKendrick, *Woman and Society*, 281–8.

14 This early play is generally accepted as being by Lope in spite of some formal oddities and the treatment of the *mujer esquiva* theme certainly suggests Lope.

15 Louis C. Pérez, '*La moza de cántaro*, obra perfecta' in *Lope de Vega y los orígenes del teatro español*, *Actas del primer congreso internacional sobre Lope de Vega* (Madrid, 1981), 441–8.

16 For a still useful discussion of the play in the context of the theme of conjugal honour, see W. I. Fichter's introduction to his edition of the play (New York, 1925).

17 See Javier Herrero, 'Lope de Vega y el Barroco: la degradación por el honor', *Sistema*, 6 (1974), 49–71, p. 55.

18 J. W. Sage's 'The context of comedy: Lope de Vega's *El perro del hortelano* and related plays', *Studies in Spanish Literature of the Golden Age Presented to Edward M. Wilson*, ed. R. O. Jones (London, 1973), 247–66, gives a summary of various critical views of the play. See also V. A. Dixon's introduction and bibliography to his edition (London, 1981), and Margaret Wilson's 'Lope as a satirist: two themes in *El perro del hortelano*', *HR*, 40 (1972), 271–82.

19 Though *Las dos bandoleras* is generally accepted as Lope's, authorship is not certain.

20 See R. O. Jones, '*El perro del hortelano* y la visión de Lope', *Filología*, 10 (1964), 135–42.

21 For Lope's skill in adapting the Italian novelle for the stage, as well as his debt to *commedia dell'arte* techniques, see Nancy L. D'Antuono, *Boccaccio's Novelle in the Theatre of Lope de Vega* (Potomac, Maryland, 1983).

.22 See J. W. Sage's discussion of the play in the Critical Guides to Spanish Texts series (London, 1972). *El caballero de Olmedo* has provoked a wide variety of critical interpretations for which Sage's bibliography is very useful; see more recently Peter Evans, 'Alonso's Cowardice: Ambiguities of Perspective in *El caballero de Olmedo*', *MLR*, 78 (1983), 68–78 and L. Fothergill-Payne, '*El caballero de Olmedo* y la razón de diferencia', *BCom*, 36 (1984), 111–24.

23 It is also called a tragedy in the fourth line from the end of the text.

24 The first to argue cogently for the Duke as tragic protagonist was A. A. Parker in his seminal *The Approach to the Spanish Drama of the Golden Age*. The critical literature on the play is very large. Apart from the commentaries mentioned in these notes, English readers might consult C. A. Jones's introduction to his edition (Oxford, 1966); T. E. May, 'Lope de Vega's *El castigo sin venganza*. The Idolatry of the Duke of Ferrara', *BHS*, 37 (1960), 154–82; V. A. Dixon, '*El castigo sin venganza*: The Artistry of Lope de Vega', *Studies in Spanish Literature of the Golden Age Presented to E. M. Wilson*, ed. R. O. Jones (London, 1973), 63–81; Peter Evans, 'Character and Context in *El castigo sin venganza*', *MLR*, 74 (1979), 321–34.

25 See R. Pring-Mill's introduction to *Lope de Vega. Five Plays* (New York, 1961), translated by Jill Booty, xxxiii–xxxvi.

26 See E. W. Hesse, 'The Art of Concealment in Lope's *El castigo sin venganza*', *Oelschläger Festschrift, Estudios de Hispanófila*, 36 (Chapel Hill, 1976).

27 The Spanish is 'Pagó la maldad que hizo/por heredarme' where 'por heredarme' can mean either 'in order to be my heir' or 'on account of/through being my heir'.

28 For a fuller examination of the role of language in the play, see Melveena McKendrick, 'Language and Silence in *El castigo sin venganza*', *BCom*, 35 (1983), 79–95.

29 See Gregorio Marañón, *El Conde-Duque de Olivares. La pasión de mandar*, 3rd edn (Madrid, 1952), 38, and Jonathan Brown and J. H. Elliott, *A Palace for a King* (New Haven and London, 1980), 32. This may be one of the reasons why *El castigo sin venganza*, according to Lope's own testimony, was performed only once when it first appeared. It is not improbable that Olivares had it stopped.

30 Clifford Leech, *Shakespeare's Tragedies and Other Studies in Seventeenth-Century Drama* (London, 1950), 18–19.

31 See H. J. Muller, *The Spirit of Tragedy* (New York, 1956), 149.

32 *The Civilization of the Renaissance in Italy* (New York, 1954): 'It was the

Inquisitors and Spaniards who cowed the Italian spirit and rendered impossible representation of the greatest and most sublime themes' (235).

33 See Juana de José Prades, '*El arte nuevo de hacer comedias en este tiempo*' (Madrid, 1971).

34 As he says in *El remedio en la desdicha* (*Help in Misfortune*), 'El versos hacer y amar/naturalmente ha de ser' – 'making love and writing poetry must come naturally'.

35 Guarini was a natural authority for Spaniards seeking to justify the *comedia*. The Valencian dramatist Ricardo de Turia borrowed heavily from him for his defence of the Spanish drama, *Apologético de las comedias españolas*, 1616.

36 The prologue to *Parte XVI de las comedias de Lope de Vega*.

37 In the dedication to *Virtud, pobreza y mujer* (*Virtue, poverty and woman*) (Parte xx, Madrid, 1625). For a comprehensive account of Lope's pronouncements on the drama, see L. C. Pérez and F. Sánchez Escribano, *Afirmaciones de Lope de Vega sobre preceptiva dramática* (Madrid, 1961).

38 Ed. Alfredo Carballo Picazo, 3 vols. (Madrid, 1953 and 1973).

39 Ed. B. Brancaforte (Madrid, 1975).

40 See M. Menéndez y Pelayo, *Historia de las ideas estéticas en España*, vol. 3 (Madrid, 1920), 449.

41 'Al Apolo de España', *Cartas filológicas*, ed. J. García Soriano, 3 vols (Madrid, 1930–41), II, 37–8.

42 *Cigarral primero*. Quoted in Sánchez Escribano and Porqueras Mayo's *Preceptiva dramática española*, 208. The analogy between poetry and painting was not of course original to Tirso. Lope likened himself to both art and nature as a painter (in the double sense of imitator and creator) of reality. See Pérez and Sánchez Escribano, *Afirmaciones de Lope de Vega sobre preceptiva dramática*, 137–74.

5 Tirso de Molina and the other Lopistas

1 See David H. Darst, *The Comic Art of Tirso de Molina* (Chapel Hill, 1974); I. T. Agheana, *The Situational Drama of Tirso de Molina* (New York, 1972); Ruth L. Kennedy, *Studies in Tirso de Molina, I: The Dramatist and his Competitors, 1620–26* (Chapel Hill, 1974); I. L. McClelland, *Tirso de Molina: Studies in Dramatic Realism* (Liverpool, 1948); S. Maurel, *L'univers dramatique de Tirso de Molina* (Poitiers, 1971); Henry W. Sullivan, *Tirso de Molina and the Drama of the Counter Reformation* (Amsterdam, 1976); and Margaret Wilson, *Tirso de Molina* (Boston, 1977).

2 In his *Los cigarrales de Toledo* and in a scene interpolated for the purpose in his play *Antona García*.

3 See Ruth L. Kennedy, '*La prudencia en la mujer* and the Ambient that Brought it Forth', *Publications of the Modern Languages Association*, 63 (1948), 1131–90.

4 J. C. J. Metford, 'Tirso de Molina and the Conde-Duque de Olivares', *BHS*, 36

(1959), 15–27; and Ruth L. Kennedy, 'La perspectiva política de Tirso en *Privar contra su gusto*, y la de sus comedias posteriores', *Homenaje a Tirso de Molina* (Revista Estudios, Madrid, 1981), 199–238.

5 Marie Gleeson Ó Tuathaigh, 'Tirso's Pizarro Trilogy: A Case of Sycophancy or Lèse-Majesty?', *BCom*, 38 (1986), 63–82.

6 See A. K. G. Paterson (ed.), *La venganza de Tamar* (Cambridge, 1969), 28.

7 In an essay first published in Spain in 1949, republished as 'Bandits and Saints in the Spanish Drama of the Golden Age', *Critical Studies of Calderón's Comedias*, ed. J. E. Varey, vol. 19 of *The Comedias of Calderón*, ed. D. W. Cruickshank and J. E. Varey (London, 1973), 151–68. See also Melveena McKendrick, 'The *bandolera* of Golden-Age drama: a symbol of feminist revolt', *Critical Studies of Calderón's Comedias*, 169–90.

8 Authorship has been disputed but the play is now generally accepted as Tirso's. For the background to the play, see Daniel Rogers' introduction to his edition (Oxford, 1974).

9 Tirso anticipates the audience's surprise, referring them at the end to two theological sources for the events he describes.

10 Paulo consistently holds that what the 'angel' said was that if Enrico were damned he would also be damned, whereas if Enrico were saved then that would be his fate too. This is in fact his own reading of the Devil's words, born, like the Devil's appearance itself, of his own obsession.

11 In addition to Parker's article, among the many studies of the play are I. L. McClelland, *Tirso de Molina: Studies in Dramatic Realism*; C. V. Aubrun, 'La comédie doctrinale et ses histoires de brigands. *El condenado por desconfiado*', *BHisp*, 59 (1957), 137–51; T. E. May, *El condenado por desconfiado*. 1 .The enigmas. II. Anareto', *BHS*, 35 (1958), 138–56; C. A. Pérez, 'Verosimilitud psicológica de *El condenado por desconfiado*', *Hispanófila*, 27 (1969), 1–21.

12 The play has a complicated textual history and may not in fact be Tirso's although it is generally accepted as his. For a discussion of the play and bibliography see Daniel Rogers, *Tirso de Molina: El burlador de Sevilla*, Critical Guides to Spanish Texts (London, 1977).

13 See Dorothy McKay, *The Double Invitation and the Legend of Don Juan* (Stanford and London, 1943).

14 For a general account of Castro's drama see E. Juliá Martínez's introduction to his edition of Castro's plays (Madrid, 1925–7); William E. Wilson, *Guillén de Castro* (New York, 1973); L. García Lorenzo, *El teatro de Guillén de Castro* (Barcelona, 1976). See also John G. Weiger, *The Valencian Dramatists of Spain's Golden Age* and James Crapotta, *Kingship and Tyranny in the Theater of Guillén de Castro* (London, 1983).

15 For a general account of Mira's drama see James A. Castañeda, *Mira de Amescua* (Boston, 1977). See also, R. Dietz, *Antonio Mira de Amescua, Studien zum Werke eines spanischen Dichters des 'Siglo de Oro'* (Frankfurt, 1974).

16 See Raymond R. MacCurdy, 'Tragic Hamartia in *La próspera y adversa fortuna*

de don Álvaro de Luna', *Hispania*, 47 (1964), 82–90; Margaret Wilson, '*La próspera fortuna de don Álvaro de Luna*: An Outstanding Work by Mira de Amescua', *BHS*, 33 (1956), 25–36.

17 See James A. Castañeda's introduction to his edition of the play (Madrid, 1980).

18 See F. E. Spencer and R. Schevill, *The Dramatic Works of Luis Vélez de Guevara, Their Plots, Sources and Bibliography* (Berkeley, CA, 1937); C. George Peale (ed.), *Antigüedad y actualidad en Luis Vélez de Guevara: estudios críticos* (Amsterdam and Philadelphia, 1983; this volume is largely in English in spite of its title); also Edward Nagy, *Villanos, hampones y soldados en tres comedias de Luis Vélez de Guevara* (Valladolid, 1979).

19 See Michael D. McGaha, '*La luna de la sierra*: a Nonviolent Honour Play', *Antigüedad y actualidad*, 58–64; and Charlotte Stern, 'Convention and Innovation in *La luna de la sierra*', *Antigüedad y actualidad*, 65–88.

20 Melveena McKendrick, *Woman and Society*, 115–18.

21 See Antonio Castro Leal, *Juan Ruiz de Alarcón, su vida y su obra* (Mexico, 1943); Walter Poesse, *Juan Ruiz de Alarcón* (New York, 1972).

22 *Algunas hazañas de las muchas de don García Hurtado de Mendoza, Marqués de Cañete* was written by nine collaborators including Mira, Castro, Vélez and Alarcón. *La luna africana* was the work of eight, including Moreto. In such cases collaboration was obviously a sort of courtly game.

23 See J. Canavàggio, *Cervantès dramaturge: un théâtre à naître* (Paris, 1977); J. Casalduero, *Sentido y forma del teatro de Cervantes* (Madrid, 1951); R. Marras, *Miguel de Cervantès dramaturge*, Paris, 1957).

24 See Melveena McKendrick, *Cervantes*.

25 See Melveena McKendrick, *Woman and Society*, 75–82.

26 The *sainete* and *mojiganga* of the later seventeenth century were also farcical interludes.

27 *Arte nuevo de hacer comedias*, lines 69–76.

28 See Eugenio Asensio, *Itinerario del entremés desde Lope de Rueda a Quiñones de Benavente* (Madrid, 1965); Hannah E. Bergman, *Luis Quiñones de Benavente y sus entremeses* (Madrid, 1965), and *Luis Quiñones de Benavente* (New York, 1972).

29 In the prologue to a collection of his pieces, *Jocosería*, quoted by Eugenio Asensio, *Itinerario del entremés*, 15.

30 See Jean-Louis Flecniakoska, *La loa* (Madrid, 1975), no. IX, lines 125–60. This *loa* seems to have been one of Lope's. *Loa* XI grumbles about the behaviour of women spectators, while *Loa* XIII, by Quiñones de Benavente, describes the constitution and activities of a theatrical troupe.

6 The reign of Calderón

1 The theatre of Calderón has in the last fifty years generated more critical and scholarly studies than that of any other Golden-Age dramatist. The following are only a selection: A. E. Sloman, *The Dramatic Craftsmanship of Calderón* (Oxford,

1958); B. W. Wardropper (ed.), *Critical Essays on the Theater of Calderón* (New York, 1965); E. W. Hesse, *Calderón de la Barca* (New York, 1967); A. A. Parker, 'The Spanish Drama of the Golden Age: A Method of Analysis and Interpretation'; Edwin Honig, *Calderón and the Seizures of Honor* (Cambridge, Mass., 1972); J. E. Varey, *Critical Studies of Calderón's Comedias* (ed.), vol. XIX of D. W. Cruickshank and J. E. Varey (eds.), *The Comedias of Calderón*, 19 vols. (London, 1973); A. Valbuena Briones, *Calderón y la comedia nueva* (Madrid, 1977); John V. Bryans, *Calderón de la Barca: Imagery, Rhetoric and Drama* (London, 1977); James A. Maraniss, *On Calderón* (Columbia, Mo., 1978); F. A. Armas, D. M. Gitlitz, J. A. Madrigal (eds.), *Critical Perspectives on Calderón de la Barca* (Lincoln, Nebraska, 1981); Robert Ter Horst, *Calderón: The Secular Plays* (Lexington, Kentucky, 1982); W. R. Blue, *The Development of Imagery in Calderón's Comedias* (York, S. Carolina, 1983); D. J. Hildner, *Reason and the Passions in the Comedias of Calderón* (Philadelphia, 1982); A. J. Cascardi, *The Limits of Illusion: A Critical Study of Calderón* (London, 1984); Michael D. McGaha (ed.), *Approaches to the Theater of Calderón* (Lanham, 1982).

2 For the mythological plays and the *autos* see also chapters 8 and 9.

3 See A. A. Parker, 'Metáfora y símbolo en la interpretación de Calderón', *Actas del Primer Congreso Internacional de Hispanistas*, ed. F. Pierce and C. A. Jones (Oxford, 1964), 141–60. Also E. M. Wilson, 'The Four Elements in the Imagery of Calderón', *MLR*, 31 (1936), 34–47; and 'La poesía dramática de don Pedro Calderón de la Barca', *Litterae Hispanae et Lusitanae*, ed. H. Flasche (Munich, 1968), 487–500.

4 It was A. E. Sloman's study of some of Calderón's adaptations of his source plays which first fully revealed the extent and nature of his craftsmanship; see *The Dramatic Craftsmanship of Calderón*.

5 See for example: Dámaso Alonso's 'La correlación en estructura del teatro calderoniano', *Seis calas en la expresión literaria española* (Madrid, 1951), 115–86; A. A. Parker, 'La estructura dramática de *El alcalde de Zalamea*', *Homenaje a J. Casalduero*, ed. R. P. Sigeler and G. Sobejano (Madrid, 1972), 411–18; P. R. K. Halkhoree, 'The Four Days of *El alcalde de Zalamea*', *RJ*, 22 (1971), 284–96; and *El alcalde de Zalamea*, Critical Guides to Spanish Texts Series (London, 1972); P. N. Dunn's edition of the play (Oxford, 1966), 16–24; Melveena McKendrick, 'Pedro Crespo: Soul of Discretion', *BHS*, 57 (1980), 103–12.

6 Of the many interesting studies of this play see: A. I. Watson, 'Peter the Cruel or Peter the Just? A Reappraisal of the Role played by King Peter in Calderón's *El médico de su honra*', *RJ*, 14 (1963), 322–46; F. P. Casa, 'Crime and Responsibility in *El médico de su honra*', *Homenaje a William L. Fichter*, ed. A. David Kossoff and J. Amor y Vázquez (Madrid, 1971); D. W. Cruickshank, '"Pongo mi mano en sangre bañada a la puerta": Adultery in *El médico de su honra*', *Studies in Spanish Literature of the Golden Age Presented to Edward M. Wilson*, ed. R. O. Jones (London, 1973), 45–62; Daniel Rogers, '"Tienen los

celos pasos de ladrones": Silence in Calderón's *El médico de su honra'*, *Critical Studies of Calderón's Comedias*, ed. J. E. Varey; E. W. Hesse, 'A Psychological Approach to *El médico de su honra'*, *RJ*, 28 (1977), 326–40.

7 See, for example, T. E. May, 'The Folly and the Wit of Secret Vengeance: Calderón's *A secreto agravio, secreta venganza'*, *FMLS*, 2 (1966), 114–22; Edwin Honig, 'Calderón's Secret Vengeance: Dehumanizing Honor', *Homenaje a William L. Fichter*; Walter Holzinger, 'Ideology, imagery and the literalization of metaphor in *A secreto agravio secreta venganza'*, *BHS*, 54 (1977), 203–14.

8 Pinavel in *El castigo del discreto*: 'El matar una mujer / puesto que al honor deleite / es hacer la sangre aceite / y la deshonra extender' ('To kill one's wife may delight one's honour but it turns blood into oil and the dishonour spreads').

9 See A. I. Watson, *'El pintor de su deshonra* and the Neo-Aristotelian Theory of Tragedy', *BHS*, 40 (1963), 17–34; A. K. G. Paterson, 'The Tragic and Comic Melancholy of Juan Roca: A Study of Calderón's *El pintor de su deshonra'*, *FMLS*, 5 (1969), 244–61; and 'Juan Roca's Northern Ancestry: A Study of Art Theory in Calderón's *El pintor de su deshonra'*, *FMLS*, 7 (1971), 195–210.

10 For an analysis of this collective responsibility see A. A. Parker, 'Towards a definition of Calderonian Tragedy'.

11 'Hacia una interpretación de *El pintor de su deshonra'*, *Ábaco*, 3 (1970), 49–85; reprinted in *Spanish and English Literature of the Sixteenth and Seventeenth Centuries: Studies in Discretion, Illusion and Mutability* (Cambridge, 1980), 65–89, where Professor Wilson unfortunately translated his original phrase 'crean su propia impotencia' with the less striking 'They have themselves brought about their own powerlessness'.

12 See Gwynne Edwards, 'Calderón's *La hija del aire* in the Light of His Sources', *BHS*, 43 (1966), 177–96; Daniel Rogers, '"¡Cielos! ¿Quién en Ninias habla?" The Mother–Son Impersonation in *La hija del aire'*, *BCom*, 20 (1968), 1–4.

13 For example, in addition to *La hija del aire* and *La vida es sueño*, in *Los tres afectos de amor*, *El mayor monstruo los celos*, *Los cabellos de Absalón*, *Eco y Narciso*, *Apolo y Climene*, *Hado y divisa de Leonido y Marfisa*, *El monstruo de los jardines*.

14 A. A. Parker pertinently draws attention to the way in which Calderón's in fact very diversified treatment of the theme of free will has been subsumed by his working out of the theme in *La vida es sueño*, in 'Prediction and its Dramatic Function in *El mayor monstruo los celos'*, *Studies in Spanish Literature of the Golden Age Presented to Edward M. Wilson*, ed. R. O. Jones (London, 1973), 173–92. See also *'El monstruo de los jardines* y el concepto calderoniano del destino' in *Hacia Calderón. Cuarto Coloquio Anglogermano, Wolfenbüttel 1975*, ed. H. Flasche, K.-H. Körner and H. Mattauch (Berlin and New York, 1979), 92–101.

15 See, for example: P. N. Dunn, 'The Horoscope Motif in *La vida es sueño'*, and Margaret S. Maurin, 'The Monster, the Sepulchre and the Dark: Related Patterns of Imagery in *La vida es sueño'*, published in 1953 and 1967 respectively but both reprinted in *Critical Studies of Calderón's Comedias*, ed. J. E. Varey; R. D. F. Pring-Mill, 'Los calderonistas de habla inglesa y *La vida es sueño*:

métodos del análisis temático-estructural', *Litterae Hispanae et Lusitanae*, ed. H. Flasche (Madrid, 1968), 369–413; Daniel L. Heiple, 'The Tradition Behind the Punishment of the Rebel Soldier in *La vida es sueño*', *BHS*, 50 (1973), 1–17 (one of several studies of this aspect of the play).

16 See for example: E. M. Wilson and W. J. Entwhistle, '*El príncipe constante*: Two Interpretations', *MLR*, 24 (1939), 207–22; B. W. Wardropper, 'Christian and Moor in Calderón's *El príncipe constante*', *MLR*, 53 (1958), 512–20; R. W. Truman, 'The Theme of Justice in Calderón's *El príncipe constante*', *MLR*, 59 (1964), 43–52; P. N. Dunn, '*El príncipe constante*: a Theatre of the World', *Studies in Spanish Literature of the Golden Age Presented to Edward M. Wilson*, ed. R. O. Jones, 83–101; P. R. K. Halkhoree and J. E. Varey, 'Sobre el tema de la cárcel en *El príncipe constante*', *Hacia Calderón, Cuarto Coloquio Anglogermano, Wolfenbüttel 1975*, ed. H. Flasche, K.-H. Körner and H. Mattauch, 30–40.

17 See B. W. Wardropper's edition of the play (Madrid and Potomac, Md., 1982) and the forthcoming edition by Melveena McKendrick and A. A. Parker; also, for example, W. J. Entwhistle, 'Justina's Temptation: An Approach to the Understanding of Calderón', *MLR*, 40 (1945), 180–9; T. E. May, 'The Symbolism of *El mágico prodigioso*', *RR*, 54 (1963), 95–112.

18 For a discussion of the Devil in Calderón see A. A. Parker, 'The Theology of the Devil in the Drama of Calderón', reprinted in *Critical Essays on the Theater of Calderón*, ed. B. W. Wardropper, New York, 1965.

19 See A. A. Parker, 'Bandits and Saints in the Spanish Drama of the Golden Age', 'The Spanish Drama of the Golden Age: A Method of Analysis and Interpretation', 'Towards a Definition of Calderonian Tragedy' and 'The Father–Son Conflict in the Drama of Calderón', *FMLS*, 2 (1966), 99–113; also J. E. Varey, 'Imágenes, símbolos y escenografía en *La devoción de la cruz*', *Hacia Calderón. Segundo Coloquio Anglogermano, Hamburgo 1970*, ed. H. Flasche (Berlin and New York, 1973), 155–70.

20 See A. A. Parker, 'The Spanish Drama of the Golden Age: A Method of Analysis and Interpretation' and 'Towards a Definition of Golden-Age Tragedy'.

21 See McKendrick, *Woman and Society*, chapter on the *bandolera*.

22 See Jean Seznec, *La survivance des dieux antiques* (London, 1940), trans. as *The Survival of the Pagan Gods* by Barbara F. Sessions (New York, 1953), 91–121.

23 For the mythological plays of Calderón see: W. G. Chapman, 'Las comedias mitológicas de Calderón', *Revista de Literatura*, 5 (1954), 35–67; N. E. Haverbeck Ojeda, 'La comedia mitológica calderoniana: soberbia y castigo', *RFE*, 56 (1973), 69–94; C. V. Aubrun, 'Estructura y significación de las comedias mitológicas de Calderón', *Hacia Calderón. Tercer Congreso Anglogermano*, ed. H. Flasche (Berlin, 1976); T. A. O'Connon, 'On Love and the Human Condition: A Prolegomenon to Calderón's Mythological Plays', *Calderón de la Barca at the Tercentenary: Proceedings of the Comparative Literature Symposium*, vol. 14 (Lubbock, 1981), 119–34; S. Neumeister, *Mythos und Repräsentation. Die*

Mythologischen Festspiele Calderóns (Munich, 1978). For the staging of the plays see chapter 8.

24 E. M. Wilson suggested, for example, that *Fieras afemina amor* may have been a political allegory of the court of Charles II during the regency of Queen Mariana; see his edition of the play (with C. Bainton and D. W. Cruickshank, Kassel: Edition Reichenberger, 1984), 46. Michael McGaha in his recent edition of Lope's mythological play *La fábula de Perseo* (Kassel, 1985) argues that the play, performed before Philip III and his ministers, was intended as a warning about the abuse of power, though my own suspicion is that if Lope was slyly subverting anything in this play it was the moral solemnity with which myth itself was approached during the Renaissance.

25 See D. W. Cruickshank's edition of the play (London, 1971).

26 For example, to see a wife-murder play as a sequel to a *comedia de capa y espada*: B. W. Wardropper, 'El problema de la responsabilidad en la comedia de capa y espada de Calderón', *Actas del Segundo Congreso Internacional de Hispanistas*, ed. Jaime Sánchez Romeralo y Norbert Poulussen (Nijmegen, 1967), 693.

27 See, for example, Robert Ter Horst, 'The ruling temper of Calderón's *La dama duende*', *BCom*, 27 (1975), 68–72; B. W. Wardropper, 'Calderón's comedy and his serious sense of life', *Hispanic Studies in Honor of Nicholas B. Adams* (Chapel Hill, 1966), 179–93; Wardropper, 'El problema de la responsabilidad'; J. E. Varey, '*Casa con dos puertas*: Towards a Definition of Calderón's View of Comedy', *MLR*, 67 (1972), 83–94; C. A. Jones, 'Some Ways of Looking at Spanish Golden-Age Comedy', *Homenaje a William L. Fichter* (Madrid, 1971), 329–39; E. M. Wilson, 'The Cloak and Sword Plays', in *Spanish and English Literature of the Sixteenth and Seventeenth Centuries*, 90–104; C. I. Lewis, unpublished Cambridge University doctoral thesis, 'A Study of the Relationship Between the Themes of Love, Honour and Jealousy in Calderón's *comedias de capa y espada*', 1982.

28 See, for example, Elder Olson, *The Theory of Comedy* (Bloomington, Indiana, 1968); A. B. Cook, *The Dark Voyage and the Golden Mean* (Cambridge, Mass., 1949); Northrop Frye, *Anatomy of Criticism*; Susanne Langer, *Feeling and Form* (New York, 1953); Moelwyn Merchant, *Comedy*, The Critical Idiom Series, 21 (London, 1972).

29 For a detailed analysis of the structure of one of the plays, see J. M. Ruano de la Haza's edition of *Cada uno para sí* (Kassel, 1982), 108–38.

30 E. M. Wilson and D. W. Moir, *A Literary History of Spain*, ed. R. O. Jones, *The Golden Age: Drama 1492–1700* (London, 1971), 105–6.

31 See Raymond R. MacCurdy, *Francisco de Rojas Zorrilla and the Tragedy* (Albuquerque, 1956), and *Francisco de Rojas Zorrilla* (New York, 1968).

32 The date of the performance is unknown. The first reference to it occurs in 1661: see Américo Castro's introduction to his edition of the play, Teatro Antiguo Español, II (Madrid, 1917), 172. Since Rojas died in 1648 the play's unfavourable reception clearly caused enough of a stir to be remembered years later.

33 There are too many independent-minded women, particularly honour-conscious women who embark on some sort of revenge, in Rojas's plays for me to agree with Raymond MacCurdy, *Francisco de Rojas Zorrilla and the Tragedy*: 'He was writing revenge tragedies in which the revengers happened to be women' (p. 36).

34 See also F. Ruiz Ramón, *Historia del teatro español*, 258–66.

35 See James A. Castañeda, *Agustín Moreto* (New York, 1974); Ruth Lee Kennedy, *The Dramatic Art of Moreto* (Philadelphia, 1932); E. Caldera, *Il teatro di Moreto* (Pisa, 1960); Frank P. Casa, *The Dramatic Craftsmanship of Moreto* (Cambridge, Mass., 1966).

7 The *corrales* and their audience

1 I am indebted, for the factual information regarding the *corrales*, to N. D. Shergold's indispensable *A History of the Spanish Stage* and to John J. Allen, *The Reconstruction of a Spanish Golden-Age Playhouse: El Corral del Príncipe 1583–1744* (Gainesville, 1983).

2 The curtained discovery space was also probably used to enable acts to end without characters leaving the stage; for example the scene at the end of Act II of Tirso's *La venganza de Tamar*, where Amón is about to rape Tamar, was played on the inner stage.

3 See pp. 47–8.

4 For the organization and operation of the theatrical world, see: Casiano Pellicer, *Tratado histórico sobre el origen y progresos de la comedia y del histrionismo en España* (Madrid, 1804), 80; H. A. Rennert, *The Spanish Stage in the Time of Lope de Vega*; J.-M. Díez Borque, *Sociedad y teatro en la España de Lope de Vega* (Barcelona, 1978); and, most importantly, J. E. Varey and N. D. Shergold, *Teatros y comedias en Madrid: 1600–1650. Estudios y documentos* (London, 1971).

5 A study of the Casa de Comedias, as it was called, in Córdoba, by Angel García Gómez, is to appear soon. The lay-out of the Córdoba theatre was, in spite of its apron stage, in some ways strikingly different.

6 See A. Rodríguez, *Almagro y su corral de comedias* (Ciudad Real, 1971).

7 Américo Castro, 'Una comedia de Lope de Vega, condenada por la Inquisición (*El divino africano*)', *RFE*, 9 (1922), 311–14. Castro suggested that the cause of the trouble was Augustine's pre-conversion scepticism in the play about the validity of the Christian faith.

8 E. M. Wilson, 'Fray Hortensio Paravicino's Protest against *El príncipe constante*', *Ibérida-Revista Filológica*, no. 6 (December, 1961), 245–66, reprinted in London 1966. See also his 'Calderón and the Stage-Censor in the Seventeenth Century. A Provisional Study', *Symposium*, 15 (1961), 165–84. A full study of stage censorship in Spain at the time is yet to be undertaken.

9 See p. 205–6.

10 This is mentioned by J. de Pellicer y Tobar, *Avisos históricos*. A full account of the legislation and of the controversy about the theatre's legitimacy is given in

E. Cotarelo y Mori, *Bibliografía de las controversias sobre la licitud del teatro en España* (Madrid, 1904).

11 See N. D. Shergold, '*La vida es sueño*: ses acteurs, son théâtre et son public', *Dramaturge et Société. Rapports entre l'oeuvre théâtrale, son interprétation et son public au XVI et XVII siècles*, ed. J. Jacquot, 1 (Paris, 1968), 93–109.

12 See J. Subirá, *El gremio de representantes españoles y la cofradía de Nuestra Señora de la Novena* (Madrid, 1960).

13 For a detailed discussion of the social status of the actor see Díez Borque, *Sociedad y teatro*, 61–90.

14 In *El Licenciado Vidriera* (*The Licenciate of Glass*).

15 Edited by N. D. Shergold and J. E. Varey (London, 1985).

16 The crucial role of the *autor* has been emphasized by C. A. Aubrun, *La comédie espagnole*, 37–8, and by Díez Borque, *Sociedad y teatro*, 44–61.

17 Two months in any one year was the statutory limit for each company but contracts for up to four months seem to have been signed, see Varey and Shergold, *Teatros y comedias*, 57. Long contracts, of course, reduced travelling expenses.

18 Estimates vary. A. Domínguez Ortiz's estimate is a population of 130,000 in 1621 with a floating population bringing the figure up to nearer 180,000. The population of Madrid thereafter seems to have remained fairly stable for much of the century; see *La sociedad española en el siglo XVII* (Madrid, 1963), 129–34.

19 Díez Borque goes into the question of equivalent value in some detail in an attempt to establish whether Lope could have been as hard-pressed financially as he always claimed: *Sociedad y teatro*, 93–117.

20 Printing profits were in any case negligible. In 1616 two batches of twelve of Lope's plays (twenty-four in all) were sold by *autores* to a printer for not much more than a leading player might earn in a week: Díez Borque, *Sociedad y teatro*, 99.

21 See J.-L. Flecniakoska, *La loa*, loa XI, 179–82.

22 Rennert, *The Spanish Stage*, 244, n. 2. and Shergold, *A History of the Spanish Stage*, 314.

23 Sánchez Arjona, *El teatro en Sevilla*, 124–5.

24 Varey and Shergold, 'Datos históricos sobre los primeros teatros de Madrid: contratos de arriendo, 1615–41', *BHisp*, 62 (1960), 182.

25 *Arte nuevo de hacer comedias*, 181–7 and 231–45.

26 Very occasionally (in Valencia on 12 September, 1623, for example) a morning performance might be held to avoid a clash with some other festivity; see H. Mérimée, *Spectacles et comédiens à Valencia (1580–1630)*, 48.

27 Lope de Vega in his *Arte nuevo* (lines 36–9) claims that it was the popularity amongst 'the common herd and women' ('el vulgo y las mujeres') of plays which were 'monsters full of mechanical devices' ('monstruos de apariencias llenos' – monsters, presumably, because of their hybrid, undisciplined nature) that forced him to abandon the rules and keep returning to 'that barbarous habit' ('aquel hábito bárbaro'). In fact Lope used such effects rather sparingly and it

was probably the feeling that they were being used by some playwrights as a substitute for inventiveness which made him ambivalent about them.

28 Lope mentions the popularity of masculine disguise for actresses in his *Arte nuevo*, lines 280–3.

29 See Shergold and Varey, *Genealogía*, 422.

30 Aubrun, *La comédie espagnole*, 37, and Díez Borque, *Sociedad y teatro*, 207.

31 *Psychoanalytic Exploration in Art* (New York, 1952), 42.

32 *Arte nuevo*, lines 272–7: 'describa los amantes con afectos / que muevan con extremo a quien escucha; / los soliloquios pinte de manera / que se transforme todo el recitante y, con mudarse a sí, mude al oyente'.

33 Edited by A. Carballo Picazo (Madrid, 1953), III, 285: 'el actor, con el movimiento de su persona, debe declarar y manifestar y dar fuerza a la palabra del poeta'.

34 III, pp. 288–90.

35 *Philosophia Poetica Antigua*, III, 285–8.

36 Noël Salomon stresses the Spanish theatre-going public's role as listeners rather than spectators in 'Sur quelques problèmes de sociologie théâtrale posés par *La humildad y la soberbia*, "comedia" de Lope de Vega', *Dramaturge et Société*, ed. J. Jacquot, vol. I, 13–30, p. 13, n. (1).

37 J. M. Ruano de la Haza, 'An early rehash of Lope's *Peribáñez*', *BCom*, 35 (1983), 6–29.

38 Lope de Vega explicitly mentions the problems posed by the multi-layered audience in his *Prólogo dialogístico* to *Parte XVI* of his *comedias*.

39 Above all J. A. Maravall, *Teatro y literatura en la sociedad barroca* (Madrid, 1972), also *Estado moderno y mentalidad social* (Madrid, 1972). For a discussion of the problem, see Sebastian Neumeister, 'Las clases del público en el teatro del Siglo de Oro', *Ibero-Romania*, 7 (1978), 106–19.

40 See E. M. Wilson, 'Nuevos documentos sobre las controversias teatrales 1650–1681', *Actas del Segundo Congreso Internacional de Hispanistas*, ed. Jaime Sánchez Romeralo y Norbert Poulussen (Nijmegen, 1967), 155–70, 164.

41 See Jonathan Brown and J. H. Elliott, *A Palace for a King*, 50.

42 J. H. Elliott in his review of J. A. Maravall's *The Culture of the Baroque*, *New York Review of Books*, 9 April, 1987, p. 28.

43 Lope actively supervised the publication of his plays for the first time in 1617 (*Parte IX* of his *comedias*), no longer willing to tolerate the mangled texts that had been appearing under his name. He somewhat anxiously protested in the prologue that he had never intended his plays to be read, to be transferred from 'the ears of the theatre to armchair criticism' ('de los oídos del teatro ... a la censura de los aposentos'), but even in his earlier plays the text often has a depth that belies any impression his statement might give that he had been writing plays that were merely superficial 'stories'. He was really only making the entirely valid point that a play, to be fully appreciated, must be seen performed. Shergold makes the point that José de Valdivielso's second *aprobación* to Calderón's *Primera parte* of 1636 indicates a clear awareness of an audience of

readers as well as spectators: '*La vida es sueño*: ses acteurs, son théâtre et son public', 108–9.

44 For the view that some of Lope's honour–vengeance plays have been completely misread in this respect, see Melveena McKendrick, 'Celebration or Subversion? *Los comendadores de Córdoba* Reconsidered', *Golden-Age Studies in Honour of A. A. Parker*, *BHS*, 61 (1984), 352–60; and '*La victoria de la honra* and *La locura por la honra*: Towards a Reassessment of Lope's Treatment of Conjugal Honour'.

45 There is no historical evidence whatsoever to support the old view that wife-murder was commoner in seventeenth-century Spain than in any society at any time in history; see Melveena McKendrick, 'Honour/Vengeance in the Spanish *comedia*: A Case of Mimetic Transference?'.

46 *Diálogo de las comedias*, anon. 1620, in Cotarelo, *Controversias*, 210. Cotarelo's work is still indispensable for the morals controversy but for further documentation see Wilson, 'Nuevos documentos', 155–70. Sensitivity to this sort of inappropriateness is not entirely a thing of the past: when Lew Grade filmed the life of Christ in the 1970s he asked Robert Powell, who was to play Christ, to marry his girlfriend before he took her with him on location.

47 L. Cabrera de Córdoba, *Relaciones de las cosas sucedidas en la corte de España desde 1599 hasta 1614* (Madrid, 1857), 59–60.

48 See p. 49.

49 Sir Richard Wynn, *Account of the Journey of Prince Charles's Servants into Spain in the Year 1623*, quoted by Shergold, *A History of the Spanish Stage*, 266.

50 See *The Comedias of Calderón*, a facsimile edition prepared by D. W. Cruickshank and J. E. Varey (London, 1973), vol. XIV. See also Wilson, 'Nuevos documentos'.

51 See the text of the *chacona* given by Rennert, *Spanish Stage*, 73, n. 1, and Tirso de Molina's *La venganza de Tamar*, Act II, lines 85–124.

52 *Arte nuevo*, line 329.

53 Such as the garrotted captain in Calderón's *El alcalde de Zalamea* or the body of Amón slumped over a table with a dagger in his throat in Tirso's *La venganza de Tamar*.

54 Cotarelo, *Controversias*, 164.

55 'lobo carnicero de las almas', anonymous, 1620; quoted by Wilson, 'Nuevos documentos', 160.

56 'Lope de Vega había hecho más daño con sus comedias en España que Martín Lutero en Alemania', Fray Pedro de Tapia, 1649, quoted by Wilson, 'Nuevos documentos', 161.

8   Theatre at court

1 See pp. 39, 46 and 42. The major sources of factual information on the court theatre are Shergold's *A History of the Spanish Stage* and Shergold and Varey, *Representaciones palaciegas 1603–1699; estudio y documentos* (London,

1982), to which I refer the reader for more detailed accounts of court performances.

2 A contemporary account of the occasion is given by the Portuguese Tomé
Pinheiro da Veiga in his *Fastiginia*, trans. Narciso Alonso Cortés (Valladolid,
1916), 65–6.

3 Varey and Shergold, *Teatros y comedias*, 57.

4 See Rennert, *The Spanish Stage*, 232–3.

5 Curiously Lope omitted from the revised text the clutch of marriages which
marked the ending of the Lerma performance; see Shergold, *A History of the
Spanish Stage*, 255. It is conceivable, of course, if unlikely, that he revised the
play for publication in 1621.

6 Professor Varey tells me that he has found no evidence of any author being paid
again when a court play was performed in the *corrales* or even of his being paid a
rewriting fee.

7 Shergold, *A History of the Spanish Stage*, 266.

8 See Gareth A. Davies, *A Poet at Court: Antonio Hurtado de Mendoza* (Oxford,
1974).

9 See Shergold, *A History of the Spanish Stage*, 273–4. The embroidered version of
the story, spread abroad by seventeenth-century travellers to Spain, is the one
given by Rennert, *The Spanish Stage*, 238–9, taken from Martin Hume, *The
Court of Philip IV* (London, 1907).

10 Rennert, *The Spanish Stage*, 234–6, provides a list.

11 For the date of the opera, which was previously assigned to 1629, see Shirley B.
Whitaker, 'Florentine Opera Comes to Spain. Lope de Vega's *La selva sin amor*',
JHP, 9, 1 (1984), 43–66.

12 *Obras de Lope de Vega*, Real Academia Española XIII, Biblioteca de Autores
Españoles, vol. 188, p. 188.

13 'Donde el agua y el fuego / se han hecho amigos'.

14 'la traza de ella no es representable por mirar mas a la ynbencion de las tramoyas
que al gusto de la representacion'; Shergold, *A History of the Spanish Stage*,
280.

15 For example, on Shrove Tuesday, 1638, the Count-Duke of Olivares and
Velázquez were amongst the courtiers who took part, dressed as women, in a
mojiganga (farce) on the theme of 'the world upside down'; see Hannah E.
Bergman, 'A Court Entertainment of 1638', *HR*, 42 (1974), 67–81.

16 See J. E. Varey, 'Calderón, Cosme Lotti, Velázquez and the Madrid festivities
of 1636–7', *Renaissance Drama*, 1 (1968), 253–82.

17 Compare the 800 *reales* that was the standard payment for a *corral* play in 1647;
see p. 191.

18 See J. E. Varey, 'L'Auditoire du Salón Dorado de l'Alcázar de Madrid au XVIIᵉ
Siècle', *Dramaturge et Société*, ed. J. Jacquot (Paris, 1968), 77–91.

19 See J. E. Varey, 'The Audience and the Play at Court Spectacles: The Role of
the King', *Golden-Age Studies in Honour of Alexander A. Parker*, ed. Melveena
McKendrick, *BHS*, 61 (1984), 399–406.

20 J. E. Varey, 'Dos telones para el Coliseo del Buen Retiro', *Villa de Madrid*, 19, 71 (1981), 15–18.
21 See Varey, 'The Audience and the Play', 404.
22 They were first published by Phyllis Dearborn Massar in 'Scenes from a Calderón Play by Baccio del Bianco', *Master Drawings*, 15 (1977), 365–75. Ten of them are reproduced in Brown and Elliott, *A Palace for a King*, 208–12.
23 See E. Cotarelo y Mori, *Ensayo histórico sobre la zarzuela* (Madrid, 1933), and J. Subirá, *Historia de la música teatral en España* (Barcelona and Madrid, 1945). It ought to be said, however, that the history of the opera and the *zarzuela* in the second half of the seventeenth century is in the process of revision; see, for example, J. Sage, 'Nouvelles lumières sur la genèse de l'opéra et la zarzuela en Espagne', *Baroque*, 5 (1972), 107–14, which contains musical extracts from *Celos aun del aire matan*; also 'Texto y realización de *La estatua de Prometeo* y otros dramas musicales de Calderón', *Hacia Calderón, Segundo Congreso Anglogermano, Exeter 1969*, ed. H. Flasche (Berlin, 1970), 37–52.
24 *Memoirs of Lady Fanshawe* (London, 1905), 166–70 and 194.
25 Published together in *Juan Vélez de Guevara, Los celos hacen estrellas*, ed. J. E. Varey and N. D. Shergold, with an edition and study of the music by J. Sage (London, 1970).
26 Along with *Ni amor se libra de amor* Calderón's plays included *El hijo del sol, Faetón* and *La púrpura de la rosa*. Rojas Zorrilla's *Entre bobos anda el juego* and Coello's *El celoso extremeño* (*The Jealous Extremaduran*) and the unidentified *El manchego* (*The Man from La Mancha*) were also performed.
27 The sums quoted by Shergold (346) are: 11,000 *reales* for Caudi, 22,000 *reales* to one painter and his assistants; 10,200 *reales* to a second painter and no fewer than 20,500 *reales* to a third for painting the set of the Royal Hall of Fame, a garden set and the curtain. It is not clear, admittedly, what proportion of some of these payments constituted profit.
28 See S. Neumeister, 'La fiesta mitológica de Calderón en su contexto histórico (*Fieras afemina amor*)', *Hacia Calderón. Tercer coloquio Anglogermano, 1973*, ed. Hans Flasche (Berlin, 1976), 156–70; and *Mythos und Repräsentation. Die mythologischen Festspiele Calderóns*. See also Varey, 'The Audience and the Play'.
29 See p. 164.

9   Theatre in the street: the *auto sacramental*

1 For a description of the Corpus see F. G. Very, *The Spanish Corpus Christi Procession: A Literary and Folkloric Study* (Valencia, 1962). For a detailed account of the development and context of the religious *auto* in Spain before Calderón, see J.-L. Flecniakoska, *La Formation de l'"Auto" religieux en Espagne avant Calderón, 1550–1635* (Montpellier, 1961); and for a survey of the development of the *auto sacramental* up to 1648 see B. W. Wardropper, *Introducción al teatro religioso*. For the *autos* of Calderón, see A. A. Parker's authoritative *The Allegorical Drama of Calderón. An Introduction to the 'Autos*

Sacramentales' (Oxford, 1947) which concentrates on three of the *autos* but also discusses the theology and the dramatic nature of the *autos* in general. See also his 'Notes on the Religious Drama in Medieval Spain and the Origins of the *Auto Sacramental*', *MLR*, 30 (1935), 170–82, and 'The Chronology of Calderón's *Autos Sacramentales* from 1647', *HR*, 37 (1969), 164–88.

For the *autos* in performance, see N. D. Shergold and J. E. Varey, *Los autos sacramentales en Madrid en la época de Calderón, 1637–1681. Estudios y documentos* (Madrid, 1961); Shergold, *A History of the Spanish Stage*, chs. 15–17, and articles by Shergold and Varey cited in the Shergold bibliography; C. Pérez Pastor, *Nuevos datos acerca del histrionismo español en los siglos XVI y XVII. Primera serie* (Madrid, 1901) and *Segunda serie* (Barcelona, 1914).

2 See Shergold, *A History of the Spanish Stage*, 52–84: on the multiple stage see Shoemaker, *The Multiple Stage in Spain*. Shergold's view (70) is that Shoemaker overestimates the influence of the French multiple-stage technique on the Spanish plays and indeed the concern in Spain for located scenes in general. The use of an unlocated stage in princely and royal halls in Spain and later on on the *corrales* suggests that he is right.

3 In 1979 the mystery was filmed in its entirety and shown on BBC television.

4 Strictly speaking, each cart was regarded as a half-cart (*medio carro*), the two together making up the *carro*. The reason for this is not known, but the most likely explanation is that the original, larger pageant floats were constructed in two sections for ease of storage and manoeuvring and that this subsequently inspired the two-cart performance.

5 Marcel Bataillon, 'Essai d'explication de l'*Auto Sacramental*', *BHisp*, 42 (1940), 193–212.

6 Shergold and Varey, *Los autos sacramentales*, 31.

7 In the *loa* to *La segunda esposa* (*The Second Wife*): 'Sermones / puestos en verso, en idea / representable cuestiones / de la Sacra Teología'.

8 Bataillon was almost certainly right, however, in maintaining that the *auto sacramental* was not intended as a specifically anti-heretical weapon; see his 'Essai d'explication'. On this aspect of the *autos* see also, G. P. Andrachuk, 'The *Autos Sacramentales* and the Reformation', *JHP*, 10 (1985), 1, pp. 7–38.

9 Calderón's *La protestación de la fe* (*The Protestation of Faith*, 1656), for example, deals with the conversion to Catholicism of Queen Christina of Sweden.

10 The Corpus finances are described in Shergold and Varey, *Los autos sacramentales*.

11 See Antoine de Brunel, *Voyage d'Espagne, curieux, historique et politique. Fait en l'année 1655* (Paris, 1665), ed. C. Claverie, 'Voyage d'Antoine de Brunel en Espagne (1655)', *RHisp*, 30 (1914), 118–375, pp. 200–5.

12 Calderón's instructions are reproduced by A. Valbuena Prat in *Pedro Calderón de la Barca. Obras Completas* III: *Autos Sacramentales* (Madrid, 1952), 316.

13 The Yepes manuscript was published by A. Morel Fatio (Paris and Madrid, 1877). A forthcoming composite edition of the play by Melveena McKendrick and A. A. Parker will contain the original text and its stage instructions. It is not

known why Calderón used this hybrid formula for Yepes; it seems to have been an experiment. There is in fact no record of the play's having been performed there, and it was subsequently adapted for performance in the *corrales*.

14 N. D. Shergold and J. E. Varey, 'A Problem in the Staging of *Autos Sacramentales* in Madrid 1647–1648', *HR*, 32 (1964), 12–35, 16.

15 They are published in Shergold and Varey, *Los autos sacramentales*.

16 The breathtaking performance (without carts) of *La cena del rey Baltasar* given in 1981 before the High Altar in the Basilica of San Fernando in Madrid in honour of the third centenary of Calderón's death was a brilliant example.

17 Shergold and Varey, *Los autos sacramentales*, 256.

18 There is a pronounced Marianic strand in Calderón's theology and he wrote two *autos* specifically on the Immaculate Conception, *La hidalga del valle* (*The Gentlewoman from the Valley*) and *Las órdenes militares* (*The Military Orders*).

19 'aunque pasó como sueño, como verdad atormenta', ed. A. Valbuena Prat, Clásicos castellanos (Madrid, 1951), lines 1652–3.

20 For this see A. A. Parker's still unsurpassed *The Allegorical Drama of Calderón*.

21 For example, explanations of what allegory is, why it need not obey strictures of time, place, etc.

22 For a discussion of the strengths and weaknesses of Calderón's predecessors see Wardropper, *Introducción al teatro religioso*. Wardropper thinks that in some ways Valdivielso was the equal of Calderón.

23 See Parker, *The Allegorical Drama of Calderón*, 69–70.

24 No *autos* were performed from 1666–9 inclusive for reasons of economy.

25 See n. 16.

26 See Parker, *The Allegorical Drama of Calderón*, 58–105.

27 See A. A. Parker's edition (Manchester, 1949). In *El mágico prodigioso* the Devil also instigates the plot.

28 See René Andioc, *Teatro y sociedad en el Madrid del siglo XVIII* (Madrid, 1976), 345–80.

29 Even in the seventeenth century visitors to Spain, including Catholics, had regarded the *autos* as bizarre, even amusing evidence of Spain's exotic backwardness. The rest of Europe had long outgrown the medieval tradition of religious drama, which reached its full flowering in Spain only in the seventeenth century.

30 Nicolás Moratín, *Desengaño del teatro español*, 1763.

Postscript

1 A. Salas Barbadillo in 'Los cómicos andantes' in *La casa del placer honesto* mentions actors who made their own contributions to plays, though how much of this, if any, found its way into printed texts it is, of course, impossible to say. See Shergold, 'Ganassa and the Commedia dell'arte', 367.

2 See N. D. Shergold, 'Calderón and Vera Tassis', *HR*, 23 (1955), 212–18.

3 See Jaime Moll, 'Diez años sin licencias para imprimir comedias y novelas en los reinos de Castilla: 1625–1634', *BRAE*, 54 (1974), 97–103.

4 See p. 185.

5 See p. 185 and n. 7.

6 See p. 185 and n. 8.

7 See E. M. Wilson, 'Calderón and the Stage Censor in the Seventeenth Century. A Provisional Study'.

8 J. E. Gillet, *Propalladia*, vol. 1, 70.

9 See for example A. E. Sloman, '*La selva confusa* restored to Calderón', *HR*, 20 (1952), 134–48; and more recently Melveena McKendrick, '*La cruz en la sepultura* y *La devoción de la cruz:* el joven Calderón en busca de su estilo', *El mundo del teatro en el siglo de oro: ensayos dedicados a John E. Varey*, ed. J. M. Ruano de la Haza, *Cuadernos Hispánicos de Ottowa*, 1988.

10 Quoted by R. Menéndez Pidal, 'Lope de Vega. El arte nuevo y la nueva biografía', *RFE*, 22 (1935), 337–98, p. 374.

11 See Alexandre Cioranescu, *Bibliografía francoespañola 1600–1715* (Madrid, 1977).

12 See G. E. Bentley, *The Jacobean and Caroline Stage*, 7 vols. (Oxford, 1941).

13 John Loftis, *The Spanish Plays of Neoclassical England* (New Haven and London, 1973).

14 N. D. Shergold and P. Ure, 'Dryden and Calderón: A New Spanish Source for *The Indian Emperour*', *MLR*, 61 (1966), 369–83; and Loftis, *The Spanish Plays*, 178–208.

15 See Henry W. Sullivan, *Calderón in the German Lands and the Low Countries: His Reception and Influence 1654–1980* (Cambridge, 1983).

Bibliography

Texts of plays

References for the pre-Lope theatre are given in end notes. The plays of Lope de Vega were published by the Real Academia Española in fifteen volumes in 1890–1913, with a new edition in thirteen volumes in 1916–30. Plays by Lope, Tirso de Molina, Calderón and other *comedia* writers are to be found in the collected editions published in Biblioteca de Autores Españoles, Clásicos castellanos and Aguilar, and many exist in good modern editions published, for example, by Tamesis, Pergamon and Cátedra.

Translations

In recent years a limited number of Golden-Age plays have been translated into English. Five of Lope de Vega's plays have been translated by Jill Booty, with an introduction by Robert Pring-Mill (New York, 1961). Six of Calderón's comedies have been translated, with an introduction, by Ann L. Mackenzie and Kenneth Muir, published by the Kentucky University Press, 1980 and 1985. There is also a translation of *El mágico prodigioso* by B. W. Wardropper, published by Studia humanitatis, Madrid, 1982. Very recently Aris and Phillips have begun to publish parallel translations of Spanish classical plays with notes and introductions; available so far are – Lope de Vega: *Peribáñez, Fuente Ovejuna* and *Justice Without Revenge*; Tirso de Molina: *Damned for Despair, Tamar's Revenge* and *The Trickster of Seville and the Stone Guest*; Calderón: *Love is No Laughing Matter, The Great Theatre of the World, Jealousy, the Greatest Monster, The Painter of His Dishonour* and *The Schism of England*.

Abel, Lionel. *Metatheatre: A New View of Dramatic Form.* New York, 1963.

Agheana, I. T. *The Situational Drama of Tirso de Molina.* New York, 1972.

Alborg, J. L. *Historia de la literatura española, Tomo I. Edad Media y Renacimiento,* 2nd edn. Madrid, 1972.

Allen, John J. *The Reconstruction of a Spanish Golden-Age Playhouse: El Corral del Príncipe 1583–1744.* Gainesville, 1983.

Almasov, A. '*Fuenteovejuna* y el honor villanesco en el teatro de Lope de Vega', *Cuadernos hispanoamericanos,* 161–2 (1963), 701–55.

Alonso, D. 'La correlación en estructura del teatro calderoniano', *Seis calas en la expresión literaria española* (Madrid, 1951), 115–86.

(ed.) *Tragicomedia de Don Duardos*. Madrid, 1942.

Amezúa, A. G. de (ed.) *Epistolario de Lope de Vega*. Madrid, 1935–43.

Andioc, R. *Teatro y sociedad en el Madrid del siglo XVIII*. Madrid, 1976.

Andrachuk, G. P. 'The *Autos Sacramentales* and the Reformation', *JHP*, 10 (1985), 1, 7–38.

Armas, F. A., D. M. Gitlitz and J. A. Madrigal (eds.) *Critical Perspectives on Calderón de la Barca*. Lincoln, Nebraska, 1981.

Arróniz, Othón, *La influencia italiana en el nacimiento de la comedia española*. Madrid, 1969.

Teatros y escenarios del Siglo de Oro. Madrid, 1977.

Arteaga, Esperabé, *Historia de la Universidad de Salamanca*. Salamanca, 1914.

Asensio, Eugenio. *Itinerario del entremés desde Lope de Rueda a Quiñones de Benavente*. Madrid, 1965.

Aubrun, C. V. 'Estructura y significación de las comedias mitológicas de Calderón', *Hacia Calderón. Tercer Congreso Anglogermano*, ed. H. Flasche (Berlin, 1976), 148–55.

'La comédie doctrinale et ses histoires de brigands. *El condenado por desconfiado*', *BHisp*, 59 (1957), 137–51.

La comédie espagnole (1600–1680). Paris, 1966.

Axton, R. *European Drama of the Early Middle Ages*. London, 1974.

Bataillon, M. 'El villano en su rincón', *Varia lección de clásicos españoles* (Madrid, 1964), 329–72.

'Essai d'explication de l'*Auto Sacramental*', *BHisp*, 42 (1940), 193–212.

'Simples réflexions sur Juan de la Cueva', *BHisp*, 37 (1935), 329–36; reprinted in translation in *Varia lección de clásicos españoles*. Madrid, 1964.

Bentley, Eric, 'The Universality of the *Comedia*', *HR*, 38 (1970), 147–62.

Bentley, G. E. *The Jacobean and Caroline Stage*, 7 vols. Oxford, 1941.

Bergman, Hannah, E. 'A Court Entertainment of 1638', *HR*, 42 (1974), 67–81.

Luis Quiñones de Benavente. New York, 1972.

Luis Quiñones de Benavente y sus entremeses. Madrid, 1965.

Blue, W. R. *The Development of Imagery in Calderón's Comedias*. York, South Carolina, 1983.

Bonilla y San Martín, A. *Los Bacantes*. Madrid, 1921.

Bradbury, G. 'Tragedy and Tragicomedy in the Theatre of Lope de Vega', *BHS*, 58 (1981), 103–11.

Bradner, Leicester. 'From Petrarch to Shakespeare', *The Renaissance*. (New York, Harper and Row, 1962), 97–119.

Brancaforte, B. (ed.) *Francisco Cascales. Tablas poéticas*. Madrid, 1975.

Bravo-Villasante, C. *La mujer vestida de hombre en el teatro español*. Madrid, 1955.

Brereton, Geoffrey. *Principles of Tragedy. A Rational Examination of the Tragic Concept of Life and Literature*. Coral Gables, Florida, 1968.

Brotherton, John. *The 'Pastor-Bobo' in the Spanish Theatre Before the Time of Lope de Vega*. London, 1975.
Brown, Jonathan, and J. H. Elliott. *A Palace for a King*. New Haven and London, 1980.
Bruerton, C. *See under* Morley, S. G. and C. Bruerton.
Brunel, Antoine de. *Voyage d'Espagne, curieux, historique et politique. Fait en l'année 1655* (Paris, 1665), ed. C. Claverie, 'Voyage d'Antoine de Brunel en Espagne (1655)', *RHisp*, 30 (1914), 118–375.
Bryans, John V. *Calderón de la Barca: Imagery, Rhetoric and Drama*. London, 1977.
Burckhardt, Jacob. *The Civilization of the Renaissance in Italy*. New York, 1954.
Cabrera de Córdoba, L. *Relaciones de las cosas sucedidas en la corte de España desde 1599 hasta 1614*. Madrid, 1857.
Caldera, E. *Il teatro di Moreto*. Pisa, 1960.
Calvete de Estrella, Juan Cristóbal. *El felicissimo viaje del muy alto y muy poderoso Principe don Philippe*. Antwerp, 1552.
Canavaggio, J. *Cervantès dramaturge: un théâtre à naître*. Paris, 1977.
Carballo Picazo, A. (ed.) *Alonso López Pinciano. Philosophia Antigua Poetica*, 3 vols. Madrid, 1953.
Carreres y de Calatayud, F. 'Lope de Rueda y Valencia', *Anales del Centro de la Cultura Valenciana*, 7 (1946), 128–38.
Casa, F. P. 'Crime and Responsibility in *El médico de su honra*', *Homenaje a William L. Fichter*, ed. A. David Kossoff and J. Amor y Vázquez (Madrid, 1971), 127–37.
    The Dramatic Craftsmanship of Moreto. Cambridge, Mass., 1966.
Casalduero, J. *Sentido y forma del teatro de Cervantes*. Madrid, 1951.
Cascardi, A. J. *The Limits of Illusion: A Critical Study of Calderón*. London, 1984.
Castañada, James A. *Agustín Moreto*. New York, 1974.
    Mira de Amescua. Boston, 1977.
    (ed.) *Mira de Amescua. El esclavo del demonio*. Madrid, 1980.
Castro, Américo (ed.) *Cada cual lo que le toca*. Teatro Antiguo Español, II, Madrid, 1917.
    'Una comedia de Lope de Vega, condenada por la Inquisición (*El divino africano*)', *RFE*, 9 (1922), 311–14.
    See also Rennert, H. A. and A. Castro.
Castro Leal, Antonio, *Juan Ruiz de Alarcón, su vida y su obra*. Mexico, 1943.
Chapman, W. G. 'Las comedias mitológicas de Calderón', *Revista de Literatura*, 5 (1954), 35–67.
Cioranescu, Alexandre. *Bibliografía francoespañola 1600–1715*. Madrid, 1977.
Cook, A. B. *The Dark Voyage and the Golden Mean*. Cambridge, Mass., 1949.
Cortés, Narciso Alonso. *El teatro en Valladolid*. Madrid, 1935.
Coster, A. *Fernando de Herrera (el Divino) 1534–1597*. Paris, 1908.
Cotarelo y Mori, E. *Bibliografía de las controversias sobre la licitud del teatro en España*. Madrid, 1904.
    Ensayo histórico sobre la zarzuela. Madrid, 1933.

(ed.) *Obras de Lope de Rueda*, 1. Madrid, 1908.

Crapotta, James, *Kingship and Tyranny in the Theater of Guillén de Castro*. London, 1983.

Crawford, J. P. Wickersham, 'Notes on the Tragedies of Lupercio Leonardo de Argensola', *RR*, 5 (1914), 31–44.

Spanish Drama Before Lope de Vega, Revised edn, Philadelphia, 1967.

The Spanish Pastoral Drama. Philadelphia, 1915.

Criado de Val, Manuel (ed.) *Lope de Vega y los orígenes del teatro español, Actas del primer congreso internacional sobre Lope de Vega*. Madrid, 1981.

Cruickshank, D. W. (ed.) *En la vida todo es verdad y todo mentira*. London, 1971.

'"Pongo mi mano en sangre bañada a la puerta": Adultery in *El médico de su honra*', *Studies in Spanish Literature of the Golden Age Presented to Edward M. Wilson*, ed. R. O. Jones (London, 1973), 45–62.

Cruickshank, D. W. and J. E. Varey (eds.) *The Comedias of Calderón*, 19 vols. London, 1973.

D'Antuono, Nancy L. *Boccaccio's Novelle in the Theatre of Lope de Vega*. Potomac, Maryland, 1983.

Darst, David H. *The Comic Art of Tirso de Molina*. Chapel Hill, 1974.

Davies, Gareth, A. *A Poet at Court: Antonio Hurtado de Mendoza*. Oxford, 1974.

Dietz, R. *Antonio Mira de Amescua, Studien zum Werke eines deutschen Dichters des 'Siglo de Oro'*. Frankfurt, 1974.

Díez Borque, J.-M. *Diego Sánchez de Badajoz, Farsas*. Madrid, 1978.

'Estructura social de la comedia de Lope: a propósito de *El mejor alcalde el rey*', *Arbor*, 85 (1973), 121–34.

Sociedad y teatro en la España de Lope de Vega. Barcelona, 1978.

Dixon V. A. '*El castigo sin venganza*: The Artistry of Lope de Vega', *Studies in Spanish Literature of the Golden Age Presented to Edward M. Wilson*, ed. R. O. Jones (London, 1973), 63–81.

'The Symbolism of *Peribáñez*', *BHS*, 43 (1966), 11–24.

(ed.) *El perro del hortelano*. London, 1981.

(ed.) *Peribáñez y el comendador de Ocaña*. London, 1980.

Domínguez Ortiz, A. *La sociedad española en el siglo XVII*. Madrid, 1963.

Donovan, R. B. *The Liturgical Drama of Medieval Spain*. Toronto, 1958.

Dunn, P. N. (ed.) *El alcalde de Zalamea*. Oxford, 1966.

'*El príncipe constante*: A Theatre of the World', *Studies in Spanish Literature of the Golden Age Presented to Edward M. Wilson*, ed. R. O. Jones, 83–101.

'The Horoscope Motif in *La vida es sueño*', *Critical Studies of Calderón's Comedias*, ed. J. E. Varey, vol. 19 of *The Comedias of Calderón*, ed. D. W. Cruickshank and J. E. Varey (London, 1973), 117–31.

Ebersole, Carmen I. de. 'Andrés Rey de Artieda y *Los amantes de Teruel*', *Hispanófila*, 41 (1971), 13–21.

Edwards, Gwynne. 'Calderón's *La hija del aire* and the Classical Type of Tragedy', *BHS*, 44 (1967), 161–94.

'Calderón's *La hija del aire* in the Light of His Sources', *BHS*, 43 (1966), 177–96.

The Prison and the Labyrinth: Studies in Calderonian Tragedy. Cardiff, 1978.

Elliott, J. H. Review of J. A. Maravall's *The Culture of the Baroque*, *New York Review of Books*, 9 April, 1987.

See also Brown, Jonathan, and J. H. Elliott.

Entwistle, W. J. 'Justina's Temptation: An Approach to the Understanding of Calderón', *MLR*, 40 (1945), 180–9.

See also under Wilson, E. M.

Evans, Peter. 'Alonso's Cowardice: Ambiguities of Perspective in *El caballero de Olmedo*', *MLR*, 78 (1983), 68–78.

'Character and Context in *El castigo sin venganza*', *MLR*, 74 (1979), 321–34.

Falconieri, J. V. 'La situación de Torres Naharro en la historia literaria', *Hispanófila*, 21 (1957), 32–40.

Fanshawe, Lady. *Memoirs*. London, 1905.

Fichter, W. I. (ed.) *El castigo del discreto*. New York, 1925.

Flecniakoska, J.-L. *La Formation de l'"Auto" religieux en Espagne avant Calderón, 1550–1635*. Montpellier, 1961.

La loa. Madrid, 1975.

Forastieri Braschi, E. '*Fuenteovejuna* y la justificación', *Revista de Estudios Hispánicos, Puerto Rico*, 2 (1972), 89–99.

Forster, Leonard. *The Icy Fire: Five Studies in European Petrarchism*. Cambridge, 1969.

Fothergill-Payne, L. '*El caballero de Olmedo* y la razón de diferencia', *BCom*, 36 (1984), 111–24.

Friedman, Edward H. *The Unifying Concept: Approaches to the Structure of Cervantes's Comedias*. York, South Carolina, 1981.

Froldi, R. *Lope de Vega y la formación de la comedia*. Salamanca, 1968.

Frye, Northrop. *Anatomy of Criticism*. Princeton, NJ, 1957.

García Lorenzo, L. *El teatro de Guillén de Castro*. Barcelona, 1976.

García Soriano, J. (ed.) *Cartas filológicas*, 3 vols. Madrid, 1930–41.

'El teatro de colegio en España', *BRAE*, 14 (1927), 243–77, 374–411, 535–65, 620–50; 15 (1928), 62–93, 145–87, 396–446, 651–69; 16 (1929), 80–106, 223–43; 19 (1932), 485–98, 608–24.

El teatro universitario y humanístico en España, Toledo, 1945.

Gardner, Helen, *Religion and Literature*. London, 1971.

Gatti, J. F. (ed.) *El teatro de Lope de Vega y su tiempo*. Buenos Aires, 1962.

Gillet, J. E. *Propalladia and Other Works of Bartolomé Torres Naharro*, 4 vols. Bryn Mawr, 1943–61.

'Torres Naharro and the Spanish Drama of the Sixteenth Century', *Homenaje a A. Bonilla y San Martín*, vol. II. Madrid, 1930.

(ed.) *Micael de Carvajal. Tragedia llamada Josefina*. Princeton, 1932.

Glenn, Richard F. *Juan de la Cueva*. Boston, 1973.

González Ollé, F. (ed.) *Lope de Rueda. Eufemia; Armelina*. Salamanca, 1967; *Los engañados; Medora*. Madrid, 1973; *Pasos*. Madrid, 1983.

Green, Otis H. *Vida y obras de Lupercio Leonardo de Argensola*. Zaragoza, 1945.

Halkhoree, P. R. K. *El alcalde de Zalamea*. Critical Guides to Spanish Texts. London, 1972.

'Lope de Vega's *El villano en su rincón*: An Emblematic Play', *Romance Notes*, 14 (1972), 1–5.

'The Four Days of *El alcalde de Zalamea*', *RJ*, 22 (1971), 284–96.

Halkhoree, P. R. K. and J. E. Varey. 'Sobre el tema de la cárcel en *El príncipe constante*', *Hacia Calderón. Cuarto Coloquio Anglogermano, Wolfenbüttel 1975*, ed. H. Flasche, K.-H. Körner and H. Mattauch (Berlin and New York, 1979), 30–40.

Hall, J. B. 'Theme and Structure in Lope's *Fuenteovejuna*', *FMLS*, 10 (1974), 57–66.

Hart, Thomas R. 'Gil Vicente's "Auto de la Sibila Casandra"', *HR*, 26 (1958), 35–51.

(ed.) *Gil Vicente. Obras dramáticas castellanas*. Madrid, 1962.

Haverbeck Ojeda, N. E. 'La comedia mitológica calderoniana: soberbia y castigo', *RFE*, 56 (1973), 69–94.

Heiple, Daniel L. 'The Tradition Behind the Punishment of the Rebel Soldier in *La vida es sueño*', *BHS*, 50 (1973), 1–17.

Hermenegildo, A. *La tragedia en el Renacimiento español*. Barcelona, 1973.

Herrero, Javier. 'Lope de Vega y el Barroco: la degradación por el honor', *Sistema*, 6 (1974), 49–71.

'The New Monarchy: A Structural Interpretation of *Fuenteovejuna*', *Revista Hispánica Moderna*, 36 (1970–1), 173–85.

Hesse, E. W. 'A Psychological Approach to *El médico de su honra*', *RJ*, 28 (1977), 326–40.

Calderón de la Barca. New York, 1967.

'The Art of Concealment in Lope's *El castigo sin venganza*', *Oelschläger Festschrift*, *Estudios de Hispanófila*, 36 (Chapel Hill, 1976).

'The Sense of Lope de Vega's *El villano en su rincón*', *SPhil*, 57 (1960), 165–77, reprinted in *Análisis e interpretación de la comedia* (Madrid, 1970), 30–42.

Hildner, D. J. *Reason and the Passions in the 'Comedias' of Calderón*. Philadelphia, 1982.

Holzinger, Walter. 'Ideology, Imagery and the Literalization of Metaphor in *A secreto agravio, secreta venganza*', *BHS*, 54 (1977), 203–14.

Honig, Edwin. *Calderón and the Seizures of Honor*. Cambridge, Mass., 1972.

'Calderón's Secret Vengeance: Dehumanizing Honor', *Homenaje a William L. Fichter*, ed. A. David Kossoff and J. Amor y Vázquez (Madrid, 1971), 295–306.

Hume, Martin. *The Court of Philip IV*. London, 1907.

Jacquot, J. (ed.) *Dramaturge et Société: rapports entre l'oeuvre théâtrale, son interprétation et son public au XVIe et XVIIe siècles*, 2 vols. Paris, 1968.

(ed.) *Les Fêtes de la Renaissance*, 2 vols. Paris, 1956–60.

Jones, C. A. 'Brecht y el drama del Siglo de Oro en España', *Segismundo*, 3 (1965), 41–54.

'Some Ways of Looking at Spanish Golden-Age Comedy', *Homenaje a William L. Fichter* (Madrid, 1971), 329–39.

'Tragedy in the Golden Age', *The Drama of the Renaissance: Essays for Leicester Bradner*, ed. Elmer M. Blistein (Providence, RI, 1970), 100–7.

(ed.) *El castigo sin venganza*. Oxford, 1966.

Jones, R. O. '*El perro del hortelano* y la visión de Lope', *Filología*, 10 (1964), 135–42.

José Prades, J. de. *El arte nuevo de hacer comedias en este tiempo*. Madrid, 1971.

Teoría sobre los personajes de la comedia nueva en cinco dramaturgos. Madrid, 1971.

Juliá Martínez, E. (ed.) *Obras de Guillén de Castro y Bellvís*, 3 vols. Madrid, 1925–7.

Keates, Laurence. *The Court Theatre of Gil Vicente*. Lisbon, 1962.

Kennedy, Ruth L. 'La perspectiva política de Tirso en *Privar contra su gusto* y la de sus comedias posteriores', *Homenaje a Tirso de Molina* (Revista Estudios, Madrid, 1981), 199–238.

'*La prudencia en la mujer* and the Ambient that Brought it Forth', *Publications of the Modern Languages Association*, 63 (1948), 1131–90.

Studies in Tirso de Molina, I: The Dramatist and his Competitors, 1620–26. Chapel Hill, 1974.

The Dramatic Art of Moreto. Philadelphia, 1932.

Kerr, Walter. *Tragedy and Comedy*. London, 1967.

Kinghorn, A. M. *Medieval Drama*. London, 1968.

Kris, Ernst. *Psychoanalytic Exploration in Art*. New York, 1952.

Langer, Susanne. *Feeling and Form*. New York, 1953.

Lapesa, R. *La trayectoria poética de Garcilaso*, 2nd edn. Madrid, 1968.

'Sobre el Auto de los Reyes Magos: sus rimas anómalas y el posible origen de su autor', *Homenaje a Fritz Krüger*, 2 (Mendoza, 1954), 591–9.

Larson, Donald R. '*La dama boba* and the comic sense of life', *RF*, 85 (1973), 41–62.

The Honor Plays of Lope de Vega. Cambridge, Mass., 1977.

Lázaro Carreter, F. *Lope de Vega: Introducción a su vida y obra*. Salamanca, 1966.

Teatro medieval, 3rd edn. Madrid, 1970.

Leavitt, S. E. 'Lions in Early Spanish Literature and on the Spanish Stage', *Hisp*, 44 (1961), 272–6.

Leech, Clifford. *Shakespeare's Tragedies and Other Studies in Seventeenth-Century Drama*. London, 1950.

Tragedy. London, 1969.

Lewis, C. I. 'A Study of the Relationship Between the Themes of Love, Honour and Jealousy in Calderón's *comedias de capa y espada*'. Unpublished doctoral thesis. Cambridge University, 1982.

Lihani, John, *Bartolomé de Torres Naharro*. Boston, 1979.

El lenguaje de Lucas Fernández. Estudio del dialecto sayagués. Bogotá, 1973.

Lucas Fernández. New York, 1973.

'Play–Audience Relationships in Bartolomé de Torres Naharro', *BCom*, 31 (1979), 95–102.

Loftis, John. *The Spanish Plays of Neoclassical England*. New Haven and London, 1973.

López Martínez, C. *Teatros y comediantes sevillanos del siglo XVI*. Seville, 1940.

López Morales, H. *Tradición y creación en los orígines del teatro castellano*. Madrid, 1968.

López Prudencio, J. *Diego Sánchez de Badajoz. Estudio crítico, biográfico y bibliográfico*. Madrid, 1951.

McClelland, I. L. *Tirso de Molina: Studies in Dramatic Realism*. Liverpool, 1948.

McCrary, William C. '*Fuenteovejuna*: Its Platonic Vision and Execution', *SPhil*, 58 (1961), 179–92.

MacCurdy, Raymond R. *Francisco de Rojas Zorrilla*. New York, 1968.

Francisco de Rojas Zorrilla and the Tragedy. Albuquerque, 1956.

'The "Problem" of Spanish Golden-Age Tragedy', *The Tragic Fall: Don Álvaro de Luna and Other Favourites in Spanish Golden-Age Drama* (Chapel Hill, 1978), 17–37.

'Tragic Hamartia in *La próspera y adversa fortuna de don Álvaro de Luna*', *Hisp*, 47 (1964), 82–90.

McGaha, Michael D. '*La luna de la sierra*: A Nonviolent Honor Play', *Antigüedad y actualidad en Luis Vélez de Guevara*, ed. C. George Peale. Amsterdam and Philadelphia, 1983.

(ed.) *Approaches to the Theater of Calderón*. Lanham, 1982.

(ed.) *La fábula de Perseo*. Kassel, 1985.

Mackay, A. 'Ritual and Propaganda in Fifteenth-Century Castile', *Past and Present*, 107 (1985), 1–43.

McKay, Dorothy, *The Double Invitation and the Legend of Don Juan*. Stanford and London, 1943.

McKendrick, Melveena. 'Celebration or Subversion? *Los comendadores de Córdoba* Reconsidered', *Golden-Age Studies in Honour of A. A. Parker*, *BHS*, 61 (1984), 352–60.

Cervantes. Boston, 1980.

'Honour/Vengeance in the Spanish *comedia*: A Case of Mimetic Transference?', *MLR*, 79 (1984), 313–35.

'*La cruz en la sepultura* y *La devoción de la cruz*: el joven Calderón en busca de su estilo', *El mundo del teatro en el siglo de oro: ensayos dedicados a John E. Varey*, ed. J. M. Ruano de la Haza, *Cuadernos Hispánicos de Ottowa*, 1988.

'*La victoria de la honra* and *La locura por la honra*: Towards a Reassessment of Lope's Treatment of Conjugal Honour', *Studies in Golden-Age Drama*, *BHS*, 64 (1987), 1–14.

'Language and Silence in *El castigo sin venganza*', *BCom*, 35 (1983), 79–95.

'Pedro Crespo: Soul of Discretion', *BHS*, 57 (1980), 103–12.

'The *bandolera* of Golden-Age drama: a symbol of feminist revolt', *Critical Studies of Calderón's Comedias*, ed. J. E. Varey, vol. 19 of *The Comedias of Calderón*, ed. D. W. Cruickshank and J. E. Varey. London, 1973.

Woman and Society in the Spanish Drama of the Golden Age. Cambridge, 1974.

McKendrick, Melveena and A. A. Parker. *El mágico prodigioso: A Composite Edition.* Forthcoming.

Madrigal, J. A. '*Fuenteovejuna* y los conceptos de metateatro y psicodrama: un ensayo sobre la formación de la conciencia en el protagonista', *BCom*, 31 (1979), 15–23.

Maraniss, James A. *On Calderón.* Columbia, Mo., 1978.

Marañón, Gregorio. *El Conde-Duque de Olivares. La pasión de mandar*, 3rd edn. Madrid, 1952.

Maravall, J. A. *Teatro y literatura en la sociedad barroca.* Madrid, 1972.

Estado moderno y mentalidad social. Madrid, 1972.

Marras, R. *Miguel de Cervantès dramaturge.* Paris, 1957.

Martínez, E. J. (ed.) *Poetas dramáticos valencianos*, 2 vols. Madrid, 1929.

Massar, Phyllis Dearborn. 'Scenes from a Calderón Play by Baccio del Bianco', *Master Drawings*, 15 (1977), 365–75.

Maurel, S. *L'univers dramatique de Tirso de Molina.* Poitiers, 1971.

Maurin, Margaret S. 'The Monster, the Sepulchre and the Dark: Related Patterns of Imagery in *La vida es sueño*', *Critical Studies of Calderón's Comedias*, ed. J. E. Varey, vol. 19 of *The Comedias of Calderón*, ed. D. W. Cruickshank and J. E. Varey (London, 1973), 133–49.

May, T. E. '*El condenado por desconfiado*. I. The enigmas. II. Anareto', *BHS*, 35 (1958), 138–56.

'Lope de Vega's *El castigo sin venganza*. The Idolatry of the Duke of Ferrara', *BHS*, 37 (1960), 154–82.

'The Folly and the Wit of Secret Vengeance: Calderón's *A secreto agravio, secreta venganza*', *FMLS*, 2 (1966), 114–22.

'The Symbolism of *El mágico prodigioso*', *RR*, 54 (1963), 95–112.

Menéndez y Pelayo, M. *Historia de las ideas estéticas en España*, 9 vols. (Madrid, 1920).

Menéndez Pidal, R. 'Lope de Vega. El arte nuevo y la nueva biografía', *RFE*, 22 (1935), 337–98.

Merchant, Moelwyn. *Comedy.* The Critical Idiom Series, 21. London, 1972.

Mérimée, H. *Spectacles et comédiens à Valencia (1580–1630).* Toulouse and Paris, 1913.

Metford, J. C. J. 'Tirso de Molina and the Conde-Duque de Olivares', *BHS*, 36 (1959), 15–27.

Michaëlis de Vasconcellos, Caroline. *Notas Vicentinas*, 4 vols. Lisbon, 1949.

Moir, Duncan W. (ed.) *Francisco Bances Candamo. Theatro de los theatros de los passados y presentes siglos.* London, 1970.

'The Classical Tradition in Spanish Dramatic Theory and Practice in the Seventeenth Century', *Classical Drama and its Influence*, ed. M. J. Anderson (London, 1965), 191–228.

See also Wilson, E. M. and D. W. Moir.

Moll, Jaime. 'Diez años sin licencias para imprimir comedias y novelas en los reinos de Castilla: 1625–1634', *BRAE*, 54 (1974), 97–103.

Montesinos, J. F. *Estudios sobre Lope de Vega*. Mexico, 1951.

Moratín, Nicolás. *Desengaño del teatro español*. 1763.

Morby, E. S. 'Some Observations on *Tragedia* and *Tragicomedia* in Lope', *HR*, 40 (1943), 185–209.

'The Influence of Senecan Tragedy in the Plays of Juan de la Cueva', *SPhil*, 34 (1937), 383–91.

Morel Fatio, A. (ed.) *El mágico prodigioso*. Paris and Madrid, 1877.

Morley, S. G. 'Strophes in the Spanish Drama before Lope de Vega', *Homenaje ofrecido a Menéndez Pidal*, 3 vols. Madrid, 1925.

Morley, S. G. and C. Bruerton. 'How Many *comedias* Did Lope de Vega Write?', *Hisp*, 19 (1936), 217–34.

The Chronology of Lope de Vega's 'Comedias'. New York and London, 1940.

Muller, H. J. *The Spirit of Tragedy*. New York, 1956.

Muñoz, Andrés. *Viaje de Felipe II a Inglaterra*. Zaragoza, 1554.

Nagy, Edward. *Villanos, hampones y soldados en tres comedias de Luis Vélez de Guevara*. Valladolid, 1979.

Neumeister, S. 'La fiesta mitológica de Calderón en su contexto histórico (*Fieras afemina amor*)', *Hacia Calderón. Tercer Coloquio Anglogermano, 1973*, ed. H. Flasche (Berlin, 1976), 156–70.

'Las clases del público en el teatro del Siglo de Oro', *Ibero-Romania*, 7 (1978), 106–19.

Mythos und Repräsentation. Die mythologischen Festspiele Calderóns. Munich, 1978.

Newels, Margarete. *Los géneros dramáticos en las Poéticas del Siglo de Oro*. London, 1974.

O'Connon, T. A. 'On Love and the Human Condition: A Prolegomenon to Calderón's Mythological Plays', *Calderón de la Barca at the Tercentenary: Proceedings of the Comparative Literature Symposium*, vol. 14 (Lubbock, 1981), 119–34.

Ó Tuathaigh, Marie Gleeson. 'Tirso's Pizarro Trilogy: A Case of Sycophancy or Lèse-Majesty?', *BCom*, 38 (1986), 63–82.

Olson, Elder. *The Theory of Comedy*. Bloomington, Indiana, 1968.

Parker, A. A. 'Bandits and Saints in the Spanish Drama of the Golden Age', *Critical Studies of Calderón's Comedias*, ed. J. E. Varey, vol. 19 of *The Comedias of Calderón*, ed. D. W. Cruickshank and J. E. Varey. London, 1973.

'*El médico de su honra* as Tragedy', *Hispanófila Especial*, 2 (1975), 1–23.

'*El monstruo de los jardines* y el concepto calderoniano del destino', *Hacia Calderón. Cuarto Coloquio Anglogermano, Wolfenbüttel 1975*, ed. H. Flasche, K.-H. Körner and H. Mattauch (Berlin and New York, 1979), 92–101.

'La estructura dramática de *El alcalde de Zalamea*', *Homenaje a J. Casalduero*, ed. R. P. Sigeler and G. Sobejano (Madrid, 1972), 411–18.

'Metáfora y símbolo en la interpretación de Calderón', *Actas del Primer Congreso Internacional de Hispanistas*, ed. F. Pierce and C. A. Jones. Oxford, 1964.

'Notes on the Religious Drama in Medieval Spain and the Origins of the *Auto Sacramental*', *MLR*, 30 (1935), 170–82.

'Prediction and its Dramatic Function in *El mayor monstruo los celos*', *Studies in Spanish Literature of the Golden Age Presented to Edward M. Wilson*, ed. R. O. Jones (London, 1973), 173–92.

'Segismundo's Tower: A Calderonian Myth', *BHS*, 59 (1982), 247–56.

The Allegorical Drama of Calderón. An Introduction to the 'Autos Sacramentales'. Oxford, 1947.

The Approach to the Spanish Drama of the Golden Age, Diamante, VI, 1957, revised as 'The Spanish Drama of the Golden Age: A Method of Analysis and Interpretation', *The Great Playwrights*, ed. Eric Bentley, vol. I, New York, 1970.

'The Chronology of Calderón's *Autos Sacramentales* from 1647', *HR*, 37 (1969), 164–88.

'The Father–Son Conflict in the Drama of Calderón', *FMLS*, 2 (1966), 99–113.

'The Theology of the Devil in the Drama of Calderón' reprinted in *Critical Essays on the Theater of Calderón*, ed. B. W. Wardropper. New York, 1965.

'Towards a Definition of Calderonian Tragedy', *BHS*, 39 (1962), 222–37.

(ed.) *No hay más fortuna que Dios*. Manchester, 1949.

See also under McKendrick, Melveena.

Paterson, A. K. G. 'Juan Roca's Northern Ancestry: A Study of Art Theory in *El pintor de su deshonra*', *FMLS*, 7 (1971), 195–210.

'The Tragic and Comic Melancholy of Juan Roca: A Study of Calderón's *El pintor de su deshonra*', *FMLS*, 5 (1969), 244–61.

(ed.) *Tirso de Molina. La venganza de Tamar*. Cambridge, 1969.

Peale, C. George (ed.) *Antigüedad y actualidad en Luis Vélez de Guevara: estudios críticos*. Amsterdam and Philadelphia, 1983.

Pellicer, Casiano. *Tratado histórico sobre el origen y progresos de la comedia y del histrionismo en España*. Madrid, 1804.

Pellicer y Tobar, J. de. *Avisos históricos*, ed. A. Valladares de Sotomayor, *Semanario erudito*. Madrid, 1788.

Pérez, C. A. 'Verosimilitud psicológica de *El condenado por desconfiado*', *Hispanófila*, 27 (1969), 1–21.

Pérez, Louis C. '*La moza de cántaro*, obra perfecta', *Lope de Vega y los orígenes del teatro español, Actas del primer congreso internacional sobre Lope de Vega* (Madrid, 1981), 441–8.

Pérez, Louis C. and F. Sánchez Escribano. *Afirmaciones de Lope de Vega sobre preceptiva dramática*. Madrid, 1961.

Pérez Pastor, C. *Nuevos datos acerca del histrionismo español en los siglos XVI y XVII. Primera serie*. Madrid, 1901. *Segunda serie*, Barcelona, 1914.

Poesse, Walter. *Juan Ruiz de Alarcón*. New York, 1972.

Pring-Mill, R. Introduction to *Lope de Vega. Five Plays*, trans. Jill Booty. New York, 1961.

'Los calderonistas de habla inglesa y *La vida es sueño*: métodos del análisis temático-estructural', *Litterae Hispanae et Lusitanae*, ed. H. Flasche (Munich, 1968), 369–413.

Reckert, Stephen. *Gil Vicente: Espíritu y Letra. I. Estudios*. Madrid, 1977.

Regueiro, José M. Review of Lihani's *Lucas Fernández* in *HR*, 44 (1976), 182.

Reichenberger, A. G. 'The Uniqueness of the *Comedia*', *HR*, 27 (1959), 303–16.

'The Uniqueness of the *Comedia*', *HR*, 38 (1970), 163–73.

'Thoughts about Tragedy in the Spanish Theatre of the Golden Age', *Hispanófila Especial*, 1 (1974), 37–45.

Rennert, H. A. *The Spanish Stage in the Time of Lope de Vega*. New York, 1909.

Rennert, H. A. and A. Castro. *Vida de Lope de Vega*. Madrid, 1919.

Révah, I. S. '"L'Auto de la Sibylle Cassandre" de Gil Vicente', *HR*, 27 (1959), 167–93.

Ribbans, G. W. 'The Meaning and Structure of Lope's *Fuenteovejuna*', *BHS*, 31 (1954), 150–70.

Rico, Francisco (ed.) *Lope de Vega, 'El caballero de Olmedo'*, 2nd edn (Salamanca, 1970).

Rodríguez, A. *Almagro y su corral de comedias*. Ciudad Real, 1971.

Rodríguez-Puértolas, J. 'Sobre el autor de las Coplas de Mingo Revulgo', *Homenaje a A. Rodríguez-Moñino*, 2 vols. (Madrid, 1966), II, 131–42.

Rogers, Daniel. '"¡Cielos! ¿Quién en Ninias habla?": The Mother–Son Impersonation in *La hija del aire*', *BCom*, 20 (1968), 1–4.

'"Tienen los celos pasos de ladrones": Silence in Calderón's *El médico de su honra*', *Critical Studies of Calderón's Comedias*, ed. J. E. Varey, vol. 19 of *The Comedias of Calderón*, ed. D. W. Cruickshank and J. E. Varey. London, 1973.

Tirso de Molina. El burlador de Sevilla. Critical Guides to Spanish Texts. London, 1977.

(ed.) *Tirso de Molina. El condenado por desconfiado*. Oxford, 1974.

Rouanet, L. (ed.) *Colección de autos, farsas y coloquios del siglo XVI*, 4 vols. Madrid, 1901.

Roux, L. E. 'Cent ans d'expérience théâtrale dans les collèges de la Compagnie de Jésus en Espagne', *Dramaturge et Société*, ed. J. Jacquot. Paris, 1968.

Ruano de la Haza, J. M. 'An early rehash of Lope's *Peribáñez*', *BCom*, 35 (1983), 6–29.

'Hacia una nueva definición de la tragedia calderoniana', *BCom*, 35 (1983), no. 2, 165–80.

'Malicia campesina y la ambigüedad esencial de *Peribáñez y el Comendador de Ocaña* de Lope', *Hispanófila*, 84 (1985), 21–30.

'The Staging of Calderón's *La vida es sueño* and *La dama duende*', *BHS*, 64 (1987), 51–63.

(ed.) *Cada uno para sí*. Kassel, 1982.

Ruggiero, Michael J. 'The term *Comedia* in Spanish Dramaturgy', *RPhil*, 84 (1972), 277–96.

Ruiz, Ramón, F. *Historia del teatro español*, 4th edn. Madrid, 1981.

　　Calderón y la tragedia. Madrid, 1984.

　　(ed.) *Calderón: Tragedias*. Madrid, 1969.

Sage, J. W. *El caballero de Olmedo*. Critical Guides to Spanish Texts. London, 1972.

　　'Nouvelles lumières sur la genèse de l'opéra et la zarzuela en Espagne', *Baroque*, 5 (1972), 107–14.

　　'Texto y realización de *La estatua de Prometeo* y otros dramas musicales de Calderón', *Hacia Calderón. Segundo Congreso Anglogermano, Exeter 1969*, ed. H. Flasche (Berlin, 1970), 37–52.

　　'The context of comedy: Lope de Vega's *El perro del hortelano* and related plays', *Studies in Spanish Literature of the Golden Age Presented to Edward M. Wilson*, ed. R. O. Jones (London, 1973), 247–66.

　　See also under Varey, J. E. and N. D. Shergold.

Salomon, N. *Recherches sur le thème paysan dans la 'comedia' de Lope de Vega*. Bordeaux, 1965.

　　'Sur quelques problèmes de sociologie théâtrale posés par *La humildad y la soberbia*, "comedia" de Lope de Vega', *Dramaturge et Société*, ed. J. Jacquot (Paris, 1968), I, 13–30.

Sánchez Arjona, J. *El teatro en Sevilla en los siglos XVI y XVII*. Madrid, 1887.

　　Noticias referentes a los anales del teatro en Sevilla desde Lope de Rueda hasta fines del siglo XVII. Seville, 1898.

Sánchez Escribano, F. *Juan de Mal Lara, su vida y sus obras*. New York, 1941.

Sánchez Escribano, F. and A. Porqueras Mayo. *Preceptiva dramática española del Renacimiento y el Barroco*, 2nd edn. Madrid, 1972.

Sargent, Cecilia Vennard. *A Study of the Dramatic Works of Cristóbal de Virués*. New York, 1930.

Schevill, R. *The Dramatic Art of Lope de Vega*. Berkeley, California, 1918.

　　See also under Spencer, F. E. and R. Schevill.

Seznec, Jean. *La survivance des dieux antiques* (London, 1940), trans. as *The Survival of the Pagan Gods*, by Barbara F. Sessions (New York, 1953), 91–121.

Shergold, N. D. *A History of the Spanish Stage from Medieval Times Until the End of the Seventeenth Century*. Oxford, 1967.

　　'Calderón and Vera Tassis', *HR*, 23 (1955), 212–18.

　　'Ganassa and the "Commedia dell'Arte" in Sixteenth-Century Spain', *MLR*, 51 (1956), 359–68.

　　'Juan de la Cueva and the Early Theatres of Seville', *BHS*, 32 (1955), 1–7.

　　'*La vida es sueño*: ses acteurs, son théâtre et son public', *Dramaturge et Société. Rapports entre l'oeuvre théâtrale, son interprétation et son public au XVIe et XVIIe siècles*, ed. J. Jacquot. Paris, 1968.

Shergold, N. D. and P. Ure. 'Dryden and Calderón: A New Spanish Source for *The Indian Emperour*', *MLR*, 61 (1966), 369–83.

Shergold, N. D. and J. E. Varey. 'A Problem in the Staging of *Autos Sacramentales* in Madrid 1647–1648', *HR*, 32 (1964), 12–35.

Los autos sacramentales en Madrid en la época de Calderón, 1637–1681. Estudio y documentos. Madrid, 1961.

Representaciones palaciegas 1603–1699; estudio y documentos. Colección Tamesis, Serie C. Fuentes para la historia del teatro en España I. London, 1982.

'Some Palace Performances of Seventeenth-Century Plays', *BHS*, 40 (1963), 212–44.

(eds.) *Genealogía, origen y noticias de los comediantes de España.* London, 1985.

See also under Varey, J. E. and N. D. Shergold.

Shoemaker, W. H. *The Multiple Stage in Spain during the Fifteenth and Sixteenth Centuries.* Princeton, 1935.

Simón Díaz, José. *Historia del Colegio Imperial de Madrid.* 2 vols. Madrid, 1952.

Sloman, A. E. '*La selva confusa* restored to Calderón', *HR*, 20 (1952), 134–48.

The Dramatic Craftsmanship of Calderón. Oxford, 1958.

Socrate, Mario. 'El caballero de Olmedo nella seconda epoca di Lope', *Studi di Letteratura Spagnola* (Rome, 1965), 95–173.

Spencer, F. E. and R. Schevill. *The Dramatic Works of Luis Vélez de Guevara, Their Plots, Sources and Bibliography.* Berkeley, California, 1937.

Spitzer Leo. 'The Artistic Unity of Gil Vicente's "Auto de la Sibila Casandra"', *HR*, 27 (1959), 56–77.

Stegman, A. 'Le rôle des Jésuites dans la dramaturgie française', *Dramaturge et Société*, ed. J. Jacquot. Paris, 1968.

Stern, Charlotte. 'Convention and Innovation in *La luna de la sierra*', *Antigüedad y actualidad en Luis Vélez de Guevara*, ed. C. George Peale. Amsterdam and Philadelphia, 1983.

'Sayago and Sayagués in Spanish History and Literature', *HR*, 29 (1961), 217–37.

'The Coplas of Mingo Revulgo and the Early Spanish Drama', *HR*, 44 (1976), 311–32.

Stone, Lawrence. *The Family, Sex and Marriage in England, 1500–1800.* London, 1977.

Strong, Roy. *Splendour at Court: Renaissance Spectacle and Illusion.* London, 1973.

Subirá, J. *El gremio de representantes españoles y la cofradía de Nuestra Señora de la Novena.* Madrid, 1960.

Historia de la música teatral en España. Barcelona and Madrid, 1945.

Sullivan, Henry W. *Calderón in the German Lands and the Low Countries: His Reception and Influence, 1654–1980.* Cambridge, 1983.

Juan del Encina. Boston, 1976.

Tirso de Molina and the Drama of the Counter Reformation. Amsterdam, 1976.

'Vélez de Guevara's *Reinar después de morir* as a Model of Classical Spanish Tragedy', *Antigüedad y actualidad en Luis Vélez de Guevara: Estudios críticos*, ed. C. George Peale (Philadelphia, 1983), 144–64.

Surtz, Ronald E. *The Birth of a Theater. Dramatic Convention in the Spanish Theater from Juan del Encina to Lope de Vega*. Princeton and Madrid, 1979.

Ter Horst, Robert. *Calderón: The Secular Plays*. Lexington, Kentucky, 1982.

'From Comedy to Tragedy: Calderón and the New Tragedy', *MLN*, 92 (1977), 181–201.

'The ruling temper of Calderón's *La dama duende*', *BCom*, 27 (1975), 68–77.

Teyssier, P. *La langue de Gil Vicente*. Paris, 1959.

Tillyard, E. M. *The Elizabethan World Picture*. London, 1943.

Torroja Menéndez, C. and María Rivas Palá. *Teatro en Toledo en el siglo XV*. *'Auto de la Pasión' de Alonso del Campo*. Madrid, 1977.

Trotter, G. D. and Keith Whinnom (eds.) *Comedia Thebaida*. London, 1969.

Trueblood, A. *Experience and Artistic Expression in Lope de Vega*. Cambridge, Mass., 1974.

Truman, R. W. 'The Theme of Justice in Calderón's *El príncipe constante*', *MLR*, 59 (1964), 43–52.

Turner, John H. *The Myth of Icarus in Spanish Renaissance Poetry*. London, 1977.

Tydeman, W. *The Theatre in the Middle Ages*. Cambridge, 1978.

Ure, P. *See under* Shergold, N. D. and P. Ure.

Valbuena Briones, A. *Calderón y la comedia nueva*. Madrid, 1977.

Valbuena Prat, A. (ed.) *Pedro Calderón de la Barca. Autos Sacramentales I*. Madrid, 1951.

(ed.) *Pedro Calderón de la Barca. Obras Completas III: Autos Sacramentales*. Madrid, 1952.

Van Beysterveldt, A. A. *La poesía amatoria del siglo XV y el teatro profano de Juan del Encina*. Madrid, 1972.

Varey, J. E. 'Calderón, Cosme Lotti, Velázquez and the Madrid festivities of 1636–7', *Renaissance Drama*, 1 (1968), 253–82.

'*Casa con dos puertas*: Towards a Definition of Calderón's View of Comedy', *MLR*, 67 (1972), 83–94.

'Dos telones para el Coliseo del Buen Retiro', *Villa de Madrid*, 19, 71 (1981), 15–18.

El teatro clásico español: Cosmovisión y escenografía. Madrid, 1987.

'El teatro palaciego y las crisis económicas del siglo XVII', *Homenaje a José Antonio Maravall* (Centro de Investigaciones Sociológicas 1986), 441–6.

'Imágenes, símbolos y escenografía en *La devoción de la cruz*', *Hacia Calderón. Segundo Coloquio Anglogermano, Hamburgo 1970*, ed. H. Flasche (Berlin and New York, 1973), 155–70.

'Kings and Judges: Lope de Vega's *El mejor alcalde el rey*', *Themes in Drama*, ed. James Redmond (London, 1979), 37–58.

'*La dama duende* de Calderón: Símbolos y Escenografía', *Calderón. Actas del Congreso Internacional Sobre Calderón y El Teatro del Siglo de Oro. Segismundo*, Anejo 6, 166–83.

'L'Auditoire du Salón Dorado de l'Alcázar de Madrid au XVIIe Siècle', *Dramaturge et Société*, ed. J. Jacquot (Paris, 1968), 77–91.

'*Reinar después de morir*: Imagery, Themes, and Their Relation to Staging', *Antigüedad y actualidad en Luis Vélez de Guevara*, ed. C. George Peale (Amsterdam and Philadelphia, 1983), 167–81.

'Staging and Stage Directions', *Editing the Comedia*, ed. Frank P. Casa and Michael D. McGaha (Michigan Romance Studies, 1986), 146–61.

'The Audience and the Play at Court Spectacles: The Role of the King', *Golden-Age Studies in Honour of Alexander A. Parker*, ed. Melveena McKendrick, *BHS*, 61 (1984), 399–406.

'The Essential Ambiguity in Lope de Vega's *Peribáñez*: Theme and Staging', *Theatre Research International*, 1 (1976), 157–78.

'The Staging of Night Scenes in the "Comedia"', *The American Hispanist*, 2, 15 (1977), 14–16.

'The Use of Costume in Some Plays of Calderón', *Calderón and The Baroque Tradition*, ed. Kurt Levy, Jesús Ara and Gethin Hughes (Ontario, 1985), 109–18.

'Towards an interpretation of Lope de Vega's *El villano en su rincón*', *Studies in Spanish Literature of the Golden Age Presented to Edward M. Wilson*, ed. R. O. Jones (London, 1973), 315–37.

'Valores visuales de la comedia española en la época de Calderón', *Edad de Oro*, 5 (1986), 271–97.

Varey J. E. and N. D. Shergold. 'Datos históricos sobre los primeros teatros de Madrid: contratos de arriendo, 1615–41', *BHisp*, 62 (1960), 163–89.

(eds.) *Teatros y comedias en Madrid: 1600–1650. Estudios y documentos*. London, 1971.

(eds.) *Juan Vélez de Guevara, Los celos hacen estrellas*, with an edition and study of the music by J. Sage. London, 1970.

See also Cruickshank. D. W. and J. E. Varey; Halkhoree, P. R. K. and J. E. Varey; and Shergold, N. D. and J. E. Varey.

Very, F. G. *The Spanish Corpus Christi Procession: A Literary and Folkloric Study*. Valencia, 1962.

Villarejo, Oscar M. 'Lista II de *El Peregrino*: la lista maestra del año 1604 de los 448 títulos de las comedias de Lope de Vega', *Segismundo*, 3 (1966), 57–89.

Wade, Gerald E. 'The *comedia* as play', *Studies in Honor of Everett W. Hesse* (Lincoln, Nebraska, 1981), 165–77.

'The *comedia* and two theories of the comic: a review article', *BCom*, 36 (1984), 175–90.

Waldron, T. P. (ed.) *Amadís de Gaula*. Manchester, 1959.

Wardropper, B. W. 'Calderón's comedy and his serious sense of life', *Hispanic Studies in Honor of Nicholas B. Adams* (Chapel Hill, 1966), 179–93.

'Christian and Moor in Calderón's *El príncipe constante*', *MLR*, 53 (1958), 512–20.

'El problema de la responsabilidad en la comedia de capa y espada de Calderón', *Actas del Segundo Congreso Internacional de Hispanistas*, ed. Jaime Sánchez Romeralo y Norbert Poulussen (Nijmegen, 1967), 693.

'Humanismo y teatro nacional en Juan de la Cueva', *Historia y crítica de la literatura española*, ed. F. Rico, II, *Siglos de Oro: Renacimiento*, ed. F. López de Estrada. Barcelona, 1980.

Introducción al teatro religioso del Siglo de Oro: la evolución del 'auto sacramental' 1500–1648. Madrid, 1953.

'Lope's *La dama boba* and Baroque Comedy', *BCom*, 13 (1961), 1–3.

'Metamorphosis in the Theater of Juan del Encina', *Studies in Philology*, 59 (1962), 41–51.

'The Implicit Craft of the Spanish "comedia"', *Studies in Spanish Literature of the Golden Age Presented to Edward M. Wilson*, ed. R. O. Jones (London, 1973), 339–56.

'The ruling temper of Calderón's *La dama duende*', *BCom*, 27 (1975), 68–72.

(ed.) *Critical Essays on the Theater of Calderón*. New York, 1965.

(ed.) *El mágico prodigioso*. Madrid and Potomac, Md., 1982.

Watson, A. I. '*El pintor de su deshonra* and the Neo-Aristotelian Theory of Tragedy', *BHS*, 40 (1963), 17–34.

Juan de la Cueva and the Portuguese Succession. London, 1971.

'Peter the Cruel or Peter the Just? A Reappraisal of the Role Played by King Peter in Calderón's *El médico de su honra*', *RJ*, 14 (1963), 322–46.

Weber de Kurlat, F. (ed.) *Diego Sánchez de Badajoz. Recopilación en metro*. Buenos Aires, 1968.

'Gil Vicente y Diego Sánchez de Badajoz. A propósito del *Auto da Sibila Casandra* y de la *Farsa del juego de cañas*', *Filología*, 9 (1963), 127.

'Relaciones literarias: *La Celestina*, Diego Sánchez de Badajoz y Gil Vicente', *Philological Quarterly*, 51 (1972), 105–22.

Weiger, John G. *Cristóbal de Virués*. Boston, 1978.

Hacia la comedia: de los valencianos a Lope. Madrid, 1978.

The Valencian Dramatists of Spain's Golden Age. Boston, 1976.

Whinnom, Keith. *See under* Trotter, G. D. and Keith Whinnom.

Whitaker, Shirley B. 'Florentine Opera Comes to Spain. Lope de Vega's *La selva sin amor*', *JHP*, 9, 1 (1984), 43–66.

Wickham, G. *The Medieval Theatre*. London, 1974.

Wilder, Thornton. 'Lope, Pinedo, Some Child Actors and a Lion', *RPhil*, 7 (1953), 19–26.

Williams, R. B. *The Staging of Plays in the Spanish Peninsula Prior to 1555*. Iowa, 1935.

Wilson, E. M. 'Calderón and the Stage-Censor in the Seventeenth Century. A Provisional Study', *Symposium*, 15 (1961), 165–84.

(ed.) *Fieras afemina amor*, with C. Bainton and D. W. Cruickshank. Kassel, 1984.

'Fray Hortensio Paravicino's Protest Against *El príncipe constante*', *Ibérida-Revista Filológica*, no. 6 (19 December), 245–66, reprinted London 1966.

'Hacia una interpretación de *El pintor de su deshonra*', *Ábaco*, 3 (1970), 49–85.

'Images et structures dans *Peribáñez*', *BHisp*, 51 (1949), 125–59.

'La poesía dramática de don Pedro Calderón de la Barca', *Litterae Hispanae et Lusitanae*, ed. H. Flasche (Munich, 1968), 487–500.

'Nuevos documentos sobre las controversias teatrales 1650–1681', *Actas del Segundo Congreso Internacional de Hispanistas*, ed. Jaime Sánchez Romeralo y Norbert Poulussen (Nijmegen, 1967), 155–70.

Spanish and English Literature of the Sixteenth and Seventeenth Centuries: Studies in Discretion, Illusion and Mutability. Cambridge, 1980.

'The Four Elements in the Imagery of Calderón', *MLR*, 31 (1936), 34–47.

Wilson, E. M. and W. J. Entwistle. '*El príncipe constante*: Two Interpretations', *MLR*, 24 (1939), 207–22.

Wilson, E. M. and D. W. Moir. *A Literary History of Spain*, ed. R. O. Jones, *The Golden Age: Drama 1492–1700*. London, 1971.

Wilson, Margaret. '*La próspera fortuna de don Álvaro de Luna*: An Outstanding Work by Mira de Amescua', *BHS*, 33 (1956), 25–36.

'Lope as a satirist: two themes in *El perro del hortelano*', *HR*, 40 (1972), 271–82.

Spanish Drama of the Golden Age. Oxford and London, 1969.

Tirso de Molina. Boston, 1977.

Wilson, William E. *Guillén de Castro*. New York, 1973.

Wiltrout, Anne E. *A Patron and a Playwright in Renaissance Spain: The House of Feria and Diego Sánchez de Badajoz*. London, 1987.

Young, K. *The Drama of the Medieval Church*. 2 vols. Oxford, 1933.

Index